A COMPANION TO THE HISTORY OF CRIME AND CRIMINAL JUSTICE

Edited by Jo Turner, Paul Taylor, Karen Corteen
and Sharon Morley

First published in Great Britain in 2017 by

Policy Press
University of Bristol
1-9 Old Park Hill
Bristol BS2 8BB
UK
t: +44 (0)117 954 5940
pp-info@bristol.ac.uk
www.policypress.co.uk

North America office:
Policy Press
c/o The University of Chicago Press
1427 East 60th Street
Chicago, IL 60637, USA
t: +1 773 702 7700
f: +1 773 702 9756
www.press.uchicago.edu
sales@press.uchicago.edu

© Policy Press 2017

British Library Cataloguing in Publication Data
A catalogue record for this book is available from the British Library

Library of Congress Cataloging-in-Publication Data
A catalog record for this book has been requested

ISBN 978-1-4473-2587-1 paperback
ISBN 978-1-4473-2586-4 hardcover
ISBN 978-1-4473-2589-5 ePub
ISBN 978-1-4473-2590-1 Mobi
ISBN 978-1-4473-2588-8 ePdf

The right of Jo Turner, Paul Taylor, Karen Corteen and Sharon Morley to be identified as editors of this work has been asserted by them in accordance with the 1988 Copyright, Designs and Patents Act.

The statements and opinions contained within this publication are solely those of the authors and not of the University of Bristol or Policy Press. The University of Bristol and Policy Press disclaim responsibility for any injury to persons or property resulting from any material published in this publication.

Policy Press works to counter discrimination on grounds of gender, race, disability, age and sexuality.

Cover design by Andrew Corbett
Front cover image: www.alamy.com
Printed and bound in Great Britain by TJ International, Padstow
Policy Press uses environmentally responsible print partners

Contents

Contents

Contributors

Zoe Alker is a Lecturer in Criminology in the Department of Sociology, Social Policy and Criminology, University of Liverpool. Zoe's research interests lie in the history of young offenders and youth justice, as well as the application of digital methods to the history of Victorian crime.

Sascha Auerbach is currently a Lecturer in the History Department of the University of Nottingham, where he specialises in the cultural, social and legal history of London and the British Empire in the late 19th and early 20th centuries. In 2011, he served as the inaugural Fulbright-King's College London Scholar on the staff of the School of Law. His first monograph, *Race, law, and 'the Chinese puzzle' in Imperial Britain*, was published in 2009, and his research has appeared in a variety of scholarly journals, including the *Journal of Social History*, *Law and History Review*, the *Journal of British Studies* and *Comparative Studies in Society and History*. He is currently working on a historical reassessment of indentured labour in the 19th-century British Empire.

Steve Banks is a Fellow of the Royal Historical Society and an Associate Professor in Criminal Justice and Legal History at the University of Reading. His research focuses on both popular justice rituals in 18th- and 19th-century English society, and, more broadly, upon the role of violence in the construction of social norms. Prior to becoming an academic, he spent almost 20 years in law enforcement and now teaches in the areas of the interception of communications, surveillance and security, as well as criminal justice policy.

David G. Barrie is Associate Professor of History at the University of Western Australia. His recent publications include (with Susan Broomhall) *Police courts in nineteenth-century Scotland. Volume 1: Magistrates, media and the masses* (Ashgate, 2014) and *Volume 2: Boundaries, behaviours and bodies* (Ashgate, 2014). He is currently working on a project funded by the Australian Research Council entitled 'Prosecution, punishment and the printed word in Enlightenment Scotland, 1747–1815' (DP130104804), which helped to fund his contributions to this collection.

Alana Barton is a Senior Lecturer in Criminology in the Department of Law and Criminology at Edge Hill University, UK. She has published journal articles and book chapters on areas such as critical histories of punishment, popular representations of the prison and the concept of the 'criminological imagination'. Her first book, *Fragile moralities and dangerous sexualities: Two centuries of semi-penal institutionalisation for women*, was published by Ashgate in 2005 and she is co-editor of *Expanding the criminological imagination: Critical readings in criminology* (Willan, 2007). Her current research focuses on the concept of agnotology in relation to the 'criminological imagination', neoliberal shifts in higher education and the representation of the poor in reality TV.

Kate Bates is Senior Lecturer in Criminal Justice at Liverpool John Moores University and holds a PhD in Criminology from Keele University. Prior to her career as an academic, she gained extensive experience of criminal justice, having served as both a police officer and a civilian caseworker investigating police complaints, and has also served as a panel member for Children's Hearings Scotland. Her research interests are primarily focused on the history of crime and criminal justice, the sociology of punishment, and representations of crime in the media. She is currently working on a research monograph based upon her PhD.

Alyson Brown is a History Professor at Edge Hill University and is a crime historian with a specific interest in English prisons and penal policy. More recently, she has directed her attention to the exploration of prison tourism and also the reconstruction and significance of individual recidivist prisoners during the interwar period. She has published two major texts on the prison: *English society and the prison* (Boydell, 2003) and *Inter-war penal policy and crime in England: The Dartmoor convict prison riot, 1932* (Palgrave, 2013).

James Campbell is Senior Lecturer in American History at the University of Leicester. He works on the history of crime and punishment in the US, the Commonwealth Caribbean and British Overseas Territories. His publications include *Slavery on trial: Race, class, and criminal justice in antebellum Richmond, Virginia* (Florida, 2007), *Crime and punishment in African American history* (Palgrave, 2012) and journal articles on topics including lynching, parole and the death penalty.

Wayne Campbell, PhD, is a Researcher in Criminal Justice at the School of Law, Liverpool John Moores University, whose thesis and main academic interests lie in desistance, penal reform and the role of civil society within policy and practice.

Samantha Caslin is a Lecturer in History at the University of Liverpool, where she specialises in Modern British History. Sam is particularly interested in the areas of gender history, prostitution and policy, the history of venereal disease in Liverpool, and local feminist activism. She has published her research in *Women's History Review* and *History and Policy*, and is currently working on a monograph for Liverpool University Press.

Iain Channing is a Lecturer in Criminology and Criminal Justice Studies at Plymouth University. He is an interdisciplinary scholar whose research crosses the fields of Criminology, History and Law. His publications include the monograph *The police and the expansion of public order law in Britain, 1829–2014*, which underlines his focus on police history, public order law and political extremism. These interests were established in his doctoral research on the legal responses to

Sir Oswald Mosley's British Union of Fascists. He has presented his research at various conferences across the UK.

David Churchill is a Lecturer in Criminal Justice at the University of Leeds. He works on policing, security and crime control in Britain since the 18th century. He has written several articles on these themes, and is currently completing a book on policing and civilian crime control in the Victorian city. He also works on historical criminology and is interested in how historical research can be used to speak to present issues and challenges in crime and justice.

Karen Corteen is a Senior Lecturer in Criminal Justice at Liverpool John Moores University. Karen has published in the areas of victimology, critical criminology, hate crime and the harms of the professional wrestling industry. Currently, she is exploring the occupational-related harms of professional wresting in the US through the lens of political economy and corporate crime. She is interested in occupational cultures and post-occupational experiences.

Kelly-Ann Couzens is a PhD candidate in History at the University of Western Australia. In 2016, she was awarded both the Patricia Crawford Research Award in History and the Frank Broeze Post-Graduate Scholarship from the University of Western Australia to further facilitate her PhD research on Scottish criminal justice history. Her thesis is focused on the development, evolution and impact of medical expertise within criminal trials for violent crimes at Edinburgh's High Court of Justiciary from the 1820s to the early 1900s. Kelly-Ann's research interests include histories and studies of forensic medicine, 19th-century criminal justice and the Victorian press.

David J. Cox is a Reader in Criminal Justice History at the University of Wolverhampton. He is the author/co-author of numerous books, with his most recent publications being: *Crime, regulation and control during the Blitz* (with P. Adey and B. Godfrey) (Bloomsbury Academic, 2016); *Victorian convicts: 100 criminal lives* (with H. Johnston and B. Godfrey) (Pen & Sword True Crime, 2016); *Public indecency in England 1857–1960: 'A serious and growing evil'* (with K. Stevenson, J. Rowbotham and C. Harris) (*SOLON explorations in crime and criminal justice histories series*; Routledge, 2015); and *Crime in England, 1688–1815* (Routledge, 2014).

Pamela Cox is a Professor at the University of Essex and teaches and researches across Social History, Sociology and Criminology. She is the author of *Bad girls in Britain* (2003, reprinted 2012) and a member of the teams co-authoring *Young criminal lives: Life courses and life chances from 1850* (forthcoming) and *Criminology: A sociological introduction* (3rd edn) (2014). She is also a co-editor (with Heather Shore) of *Becoming delinquent: European youth, 1650–1950* (2003).

Adam Crymble is a Lecturer of Digital History at the University of Hertfordshire, and an editor of 'The Programming Historian', a suite of open-access peer-reviewed tutorials for scholars seeking to learn digital humanities skills. His research looks at the history of migration and community in 18th- and 19th-century Britain, with a particular focus on conflict and crime between ethnic communities in London.

Nell Darby is a historian, writer and journalist. Her PhD thesis looked at the role of the magistrate in rural communities during the long 18th century, focusing on evidence from summary proceedings. She has presented several papers on aspects of gender and crime, including marital violence in the 18th century, and press perceptions of women and crime in 19th-century Wales. Her latest book, publishing in August 2017, looks at crime and the theatre in Victorian Britain.

Andrew Davies is a Reader in History at the University of Liverpool, where he teaches modern social and cultural history. He has published widely on youth gangs, crime and policing in Britain during the 19th and 20th centuries. His books include *The gangs of Manchester* (2008) and *City of gangs: Glasgow and the rise of the British gangster* (2013). In 2009, he worked with MaD Theatre Company on 'Angels with Manky faces', an original stage play inspired by *The gangs of Manchester*.

Michael Fiddler is a Senior Lecturer in Criminology at the University of Greenwich. His published research explores the ways in which space, architecture and visual arts coalesce to inform understandings of crime and punishment. His current research project draws upon these ideas through the lens of Derrida's notion of hauntology.

Matt Garrett is a Senior Lecturer in Law at the University of Chester, he has undertaken extensive research on the development of the Poor Law over the 19th and early 20th centuries. His MPhil thesis centres on the mid-19th century and his PhD thesis on the late 19th and early 20th centuries, with a focus on two Poor Law Unions in mid-Wales. He has also presented at the British Legal History Conference in July 2015 on issues arising from the Poor Law and is co-director of the Chester Legal History Forum.

Barry Godfrey is Professor of Social Justice and Associate Pro-Vice Chancellor at Liverpool University. Barry has over 20 years of experience in researching comparative criminology, particularly international crime history, desistence studies and longitudinal studies of offending. Over that time, he has led projects on the treatment of dangerous or habitual offenders, private policing, violence in society and sentencing patterns over long periods of time. He is now principal investigator on the Arts and Humanities Research Council-funded project 'The Digital Panopticon'.

Drew Gray is a Principal Lecturer and Head of History at the University of Northampton. He researches, writes and lectures on crime and punishment in the 18th and 19th centuries, and his most recent book, *Crime, policing & punishment in England, 1660–1914*, was published by Bloomsbury in 2016. Drew is currently working on a volume exploring a series of case studies of murder in the late 18th century. He also writes a daily blog on the newspaper coverage of the London police courts in the 1800s called 'The police magistrate'. His fascination with the Ripper murders began 40 years ago.

Kirsty Greenwood is a PhD candidate in Criminology and Graduate Teaching Assistant at Liverpool John Moores University. She is also a Visiting Lecturer in Criminology and Sociology at Chester University. Kirsty's master's thesis investigated the regulation of 'deviant' women within Liverpool Female Penitentiary (1809–1921). Her research focused upon the coerced physical and social mobilisation underpinning admissions into the Penitentiary and the subsequent internal carceral regimes of feminisation, domestication, infantilisation and Christianisation. Kirsty's PhD explores the origin, aims and operationalisation of contemporary women's centres as a form of community intervention in England, drawing upon criminological discourses of gender responsivity and the widening of the penal gaze to analyse implications for female offenders.

Cerian Charlotte Griffiths is currently a PhD student on 'The Digital Panopticon' project within the University of Liverpool, and is writing her thesis on the prosecution of fraud in the metropolis, 1760–1820. Cerian has previously researched and written on the Prisoners' Counsel Act 1836, the treatment of 19th-century company shareholders and the abolition of the Grand Jury in England. Before starting her PhD in April 2014, Cerian was a Lecturer in Law at the University of Warsaw, Poland, and prior to that, at Birkbeck College, University of London. Cerian was called to the Bar in 2007, going on to work for a number of prosecuting agencies, including the Serious Fraud Office, the Financial Services Authority and the Office of Fair Trading before entering academe full-time in 2012.

Amanda Holt, PhD, is a Reader in Criminology at the University of Roehampton, London. She has researched in the fields of children, families and harm for more than a decade, and in recent years, she has researched and published widely on the issue of violence towards parents.

Lesley Hulonce is a Historian and Lecturer of Health Humanities in the College of Human and Health Sciences at Swansea University. Her research interests include the histories of children, disability, poverty, gender and prostitution via state and voluntary action. She is co-director of the Research Group for Health, History and Culture and founder of Academics for a Publishing Revolution (see: https://www.facebook.com/groups/1765167210380167/). She blogs at

Workhouse Tales (see: https://lesleyhulonce.wordpress.com) and Pauper Children and Poor Law Childhoods (see: https://pauperchildrenandpoorlawchildhoods. wordpress.com). She tweets at @LesleyHulonce and @HistHealthCult. She can be contacted via the above sites and at: l.hulonce@swansea.ac.uk

Richard W. Ireland (rwi@aber.ac.uk) is Senior Lecturer in Aberystwyth Law School, where he teaches, among other things, courses on legal and criminological history. He is a Committee Member of the Welsh Legal History Society and of the Centre for Welsh Legal Affairs. His many publications include the monographs *'A want of order and good discipline': Rules, discretion and the Victorian prison* and *Land of white gloves? A history of crime and punishment in Wales.*

Helen Johnston is a Reader in Criminology at the University of Hull. Her research interests lie in the experience and administration of imprisonment in local and convict prisons in the 19th and early 20th centuries and in offenders' lives after release. She has written widely on this field and is the author of *Crime in England, 1815–1880: Experiencing the criminal justice system* (Routledge, 2015) and co-author of *Victorian convicts: 100 criminal lives* (with Godfrey and Cox) (Pen & Sword, 2016). She previously edited *Punishment and control in historical perspective* (Palgrave Macmillan, 2008) and (with Jewkes) *Prison readings* (Willan, 2006).

Christine Kelly is a British Academy Postdoctoral Fellow in the School of Law at the University of Glasgow. She is a qualified solicitor and received her PhD from the University of Glasgow in 2012. Her research interests focus on the history of juvenile justice in Scotland over the course of the 19th and 20th centuries, and include criminalisation, social theory and the histories of criminal law, criminal justice, childhood and philanthropy. Her monograph on *Juvenile justice in Victorian Scotland* is to be published by Edinburgh University Press.

William W. Knox is an Honorary Senior Research Fellow, University of St Andrews. He is the author of a number of books analysing the historical development of modern Scotland, with particular reference to class, gender and political change. His recent published work has dealt with the history of lethal violence, policing and socio-political protest in the 18th and 19th centuries.

John Locker completed his PhD in 2004, which focused on the emerging problem of respectable, white-collar crime in Victorian England. Between 2001 and 2005, he worked as a Lecturer in Criminology at Keele University, and since 2005, he has worked for New Zealand Police in various research and evaluation roles. He has published a number of articles in the area of respectable crime, including '"Quiet thieves, quiet punishment": private responses to the "respectable" offender, c.1850–1930', *Crime, History & Societies* (2005) 9, 1 (winner of the 2004 Herman Diederiks Prize).

Anne Logan is Senior Lecturer in Social Sciences at the University of Kent. She has written several articles and chapters about the first women magistrates in England and Wales, the involvement of women volunteers in the construction of criminal justice policy in the period c.1920–70, and the history of crime and criminology. Her book, *Feminism and criminal justice: A historical perspective*, was published by Palgrave in 2008. She is currently working on a book entitled *The politics of penal reform: Margery Fry and the Howard League*.

Joanne McEwan is a Research Associate for the ARC Discovery Project 'Prosecution, punishment and print in Enlightenment Scotland' (DP130104804), led by David Barrie and Robert Shoemaker, and a Research Assistant with the Australian Research Council Centre of Excellence for the History of Emotions (Europe, 1100–1800), based at the University of Western Australia. Her research focuses on gender, crime, families, households and emotional attachments in Britain from the 17th to the 19th century.

Vivien Miller is Associate Professor of American and Canadian Studies at the University of Nottingham. She is the author of *Hard labor and hard time: Florida's 'Sunshine Prison' and chain gangs* (2012) and *Crime, violence and sexual clemency: Florida's Pardon Board and penal system in the progressive era* (2000), and co-editor of *Transnational penal cultures: New perspectives on discipline, punishment and desistance* (2014) and *Cross-cultural connections in crime fictions* (2012). She has published articles on crimes of passion, kidnapping, jewel thieves, convict leasing and capital punishment. She is currently working on the death penalty in the pre-1972 US.

Jayne Mooney is Associate Professor of Sociology at John Jay College of Criminal Justice and a member of the Sociology, Women Studies and Criminal Justice faculties at the Graduate Center, City University of New York (CUNY). Her focus of scholarship is in the areas of gender and crime, the sociology of violence, social deviance, and the history of crime and punishment. She is currently working on a PSC-CUNY-funded project 'Bringing criminology to life: theory in place, time and context'.

Sharon Morley is Deputy Head of the Department of Social and Political Science and a Senior Lecturer in Criminology at the University of Chester. Sharon's research interests include young women's experiences of violence, gender, space and self-regulation. More recently, her research and publications have spanned the areas of violence in society and the victimisation of health and social care professionals, as well as media representations of mentally disordered offenders. Sharon is a member of a number of sexual violence research networks.

Bronwyn Morrison has a PhD in Criminology from Keele University. She has worked as a government researcher in New Zealand for the last decade. Since 2015, she has worked as a Principal Research Advisor for the Department of

Corrections. She has undertaken research on female inebriates, bias in the criminal justice system, family violence perpetrators, the female prison population and post-release employment outcomes. She is also the main author of the 2009 New Zealand Crime and Safety Survey.

David Nash is Professor in History at Oxford Brookes University, where he specialises in radicalism in Britain, blasphemy, the history of religion and the cultural history of law and crime. David is a fellow of the Royal Historical Society and an officer of the Social History Society of Great Britain. He is a Director of the SOLON project, which links a number of university departments in studying the interdisciplinary dimensions of crime and bad behaviour from both contemporary and historical perspectives. He is also a Director of the Centre for Inquiry (London).

Ian O'Donnell is Professor of Criminology at University College Dublin. He is an Adjunct Fellow of Linacre College Oxford, a Member of the Royal Irish Academy, a Member of the Academia Europaea, a Fellow of the Royal Historical Society and a Fellow of the British Psychological Society. His most recent book is *Prisoners, solitude, and time* (Oxford University Press, 2014). He is currently writing an account of capital punishment and clemency.

Deborah Oxley is Professor of Social Science History at the University of Oxford, and Fellow of All Souls College. She has published widely on convict Australia, including *Convict maids: The forced migration of women to Australia* (Cambridge University Press, 1996), and is presently part of the Arts and Humanities Research Council-funded 'Digital Panopticon' project examining the global impact of London punishments, 1780–1925. Research into the health and welfare of prisoners forms part of a Leverhulme Major Research Fellowship investigating 'Weighty matters: a somatic history of the Industrial Revolution'.

Alana Piper is a Postdoctoral Research Fellow at Griffith University, Brisbane. Her fellowship on the social identity of thieves in 19th- and 20th-century Australia is part of the ARC-Laureate Fellowship project 'The prosecution project'. She has a broad range of interests concerning the social and cultural history of gender, deviance and crime, but is particularly interested in economically motivated crimes such as theft, fraud, prostitution and fortune-telling. Her work has appeared in such publications as *Journal of Social History*, *History Workshop Journal*, *Australian and New Zealand Journal of Criminology*, *Criminal Law Journal*, *Labour History* and *Journal of Australian Studies*.

Jason Powell is Professor of Social Gerontology and Sociology and teaches on the Criminology programme at the University of Chester. He has published extensively, with 500 publications, including 65 books/monographs on issues associated with public policy, ageing, surveillance, populational politics and crime.

He is the Editor-in-Chief of *Illness, Crisis & Loss* for Sage and an Associate Editor of *The Canadian Journal of Sociology*. He is the Springer Series Editor-in-Chief of International Ageing. He currently holds four Honorary Professorships on Ageing in Australia, Russia, the US and China.

Lizzie Seal is Senior Lecturer in Criminology at the University of Sussex. She is the author (with Maggie O'Neill) of *Women, murder and femininity: Gender representations of women who kill* (Palgrave, 2010), *Transgressive imaginations: Crime, deviance and culture* (Palgrave, 2012) and *Capital punishment in twentieth-century Britain: Audience, justice, memory* (Routledge, 2014). She has also published a number of articles in the area of historical criminology.

Heather Shore is a Reader in History at Leeds Beckett University. She is the author of two monographs, *Artful dodgers: Youth and crime in early nineteenth-century London* (Boydell Press, 1999) and *London's criminal underworlds, c. 1720–c. 1930: A social and cultural history* (Palgrave Macmillan, 2015). She has produced numerous articles and chapters in books, as well as two co-edited books, ranging across the history of crime, juvenile justice and penality from the 18th to the 20th century. She is currently co-writing a monograph based on a Leverhulme-Trust-funded project (with B. Godfrey, P. Cox and Z. Alker), *Young criminal lives: Life courses and life chances from 1850* (OUP, 2017).

Haia Shpayer–Makov was educated at the Hebrew University, Jerusalem, and University College, London, and has been teaching at the University of Haifa since 1984. She has published widely on the history of policing, including *The making of a policeman: A social history of a labour force in metropolitan London* (Ashgate, 2002), *The ascent of the detective* (Oxford University Press, 2011) and (co-edited with Professor Clive Emsley) *Police detectives in history, 1750–1950* (Ashgate, 2006).

Esther Snell is a Senior Lecturer in Criminology at Southampton Solent University, where she also works as the Business and Society Research and Innovation Fellow. Her research focuses on mentalities of crime and justice in 18th-century England. In particular, Esther is interested in the construction, dissemination and impact of printed narratives of crime and justice. Her work considers how narratives influenced attitudes towards both offending and the behaviour of, and to, victims.

Rachael Steele is a Senior Lecturer in Criminal Justice at Liverpool John Moores University. Prior to working in higher education, she spent 15 years working in various capacities within the Probation Service, carrying out research and working with offenders. Her research interests include how offenders make decisions, desistance from crime, probation practice and how psychology informs our work within criminal justice.

Kim Stevenson is Professor of Sociolegal History at Plymouth University, specialising in the law relating to sexual offences and child sexual exploitation. She is the Co-Founder and Co-Director of SOLON Interdisciplinary Studies in Law, Crime and History and general editor of its associated journal *Law, Crime and History* and the SOLON Routledge book series *Explorations in crime and criminal justice histories*. Recent publications include *Crime news in modern Britain: Press reporting and responsibility 1820–2010* (Palgrave Macmillan, 2013) and *Public indecency in England 1857–1960* (Routledge SOLON, 2015).

Carolyn Strange is a Senior Fellow in the School of History at the Australian National University. She is a specialist in the history of gender, crime and criminal justice. She has published extensively on the history of punishment and discretion in Canada, Australia, Britain and the US. Her latest book is *Discretionary justice: Pardon and parole in New York, from the Revolution to the Depression*.

Paul Taylor is Deputy Head of the Department of Social and Political Science and a Senior Lecturer in Criminology at the University of Chester. He is the Associate Editor of the journal *Illness, Crisis & Loss* (Sage) and sits on a number of journal editorial boards. Paul has written and researched in the area of the importance of occupational culture in fields such as the military, mental health care and policing. In addition to this, he publishes in the area of ageing, psychiatric care/ control and mental health, and criminal justice discourse and policy convergence.

Maryse Tennant is a Senior Lecturer in Criminology at Canterbury Christ Church University. She completed her doctoral studies at Keele University in 2011. Her research interests include crime history, victimology and sustainability. She has presented at a number of conferences, both nationally and internationally, and has published on criminal justice history and the relationship between sustainability and criminology. She contributes to the undergraduate and postgraduate criminology and policing programmes, teaching a range of subjects, including police history, crime heritage and punishment.

Jo Turner is a Senior Lecturer in Criminology at the University of Chester and holds a PhD in Criminology from Keele University. Her research interests are varied but primarily focused upon the history of crime and criminal justice, spanning the disciplines of criminology, history and gender studies. Essentially, Jo is interested in female offending in the past, women's treatment by the criminal justice system in the past and outcomes for women in the past following their contact with that system – much of which Jo has written and published on.

Maurice Vanstone is Emeritus Professor of Criminology at Swansea University. His work in the Probation Service involved managing one of the experimental day training centres and, later, overseeing research and development (including the introduction of the Straight Thinking on Probation experiment in the early 1990s). In his subsequent academic career, his research and writing has covered: the effectiveness of community sentences; voluntary aftercare of ex-prisoners; community; the resettlement of short-term prisoners; the motivations and strategies of child sexual abusers; black and Asian probationers; the history of probation in England and Wales; the international origins of probation; rehabilitation and cinema; and the skills and practice of probation officers in Jersey.

Richard Ward is a Research Associate in History at the University of Sheffield. He is currently a researcher on a major project funded by the Arts and Humanities Research Council, 'The Digital Panopticon: The global impact of London punishments, 1780–1925'. Between 2011 and 2013, he worked as a Research Associate on a Wellcome Trust-funded project, 'Harnessing the power of the criminal corpse'. Richard's first monograph, *Print culture, crime and justice in eighteenth-century London* (Bloomsbury, 2014), explores the influence of print upon contemporary perceptions of crime and upon the making of the law and its administration in the metropolis.

Emma Deborah Watkins completed her MA (History) at the University of Cardiff, then began an Arts and Humanities Research Council-funded PhD at the University of Liverpool with the 'Digital Panopticon' project. Currently, Emma is using life-course analysis to investigate the criminal careers and lives of 19th-century juvenile convicts who were transported to Van Diemen's Land (Tasmania). This has largely involved digital archives using nominal data linkage, combined with archival work aided by a fellowship with the University of Tasmania.

Lucy Williams specialises in the history of women and crime in the UK and Australia, 1850–1950. Her recent publications include articles on penal outcomes, the historical demography of penal and semi-penal institutions, and intergenerational offending in Victorian England. She received her PhD from the University of Liverpool in 2014 and currently works as a post-doctoral Research Associate on the 'Digital Panopticon' project at the University of Liverpool.

Sarah Wilson is a Senior Lecturer in Law at York Law School, University of York, UK. After qualifying initially in Law at Cardiff Law School, she studied Modern British History, gaining an MA (History) and PhD (History) before taking up posts in a number of UK law schools. Her key research interests lie in Financial Law (financial regulation, including banking, and financial crime), Trust Law and a 'Law and History' combination of Legal History (both traditional and critical) and Modern British History. Sarah has published widely in the sphere of financial crime and wider financial/banking law and regulation, and she is a long-standing contributor to Lloyds Law Reports Financial Crime. Her monograph *The origins of modern financial crime: Historical foundations and current problems in Britain* (Routledge (Criminology), 2014) provided a multidisciplinary analysis of financial crime from c.1830 to the present, and is looking to encourage greater utilisation of history and historical methodology for legal research.

Guy Woolnough completed his doctorate at Keele University after a career in secondary education. He joined the Criminology department at Keele in 2014. Guy's research is focused on police work, exploring the role of the ordinary police officer and the mundane work of policing. The 19th century has been important in this work, analysing the Victorian origins of police cultures and practices. There is a strong cultural interest in Guy's work. He has published on the Victorian fair, cock-fighting, prize-fighting, local newspapers and Victorian Cumbria. Currently, Guy is researching the crimes of the respectable through an investigation into 'gentleman criminals'.

Henry Yeomans is Lecturer in Criminology and Criminal Justice at the University of Leeds. He researches alcohol, behavioural regulation and historical criminology. His recent publications include the monograph *Alcohol and moral regulation* (Policy Press, 2014) and articles in *The International Journal of Drug Policy*, *Sociology*, *The Sociological Review* and *Law, Crime and History*. He was awarded the Socio-Legal Studies Association's Socio-Legal Theory and History Prize in 2015, as well as the Sage Prize for Innovation and Excellence in 2012.

Acknowledgements

The editors would like to sincerely acknowledge and thank Victoria Pittman, Rebecca Tomlinson and all the other staff at Policy Press for their generous support and enthusiasm for this endeavour. Thanks also go to the reviewers who provided encouraging reviews of the original proposal. This *Companion to the history of crime and criminal justice* is the fourth and last in a series that Policy Press originally commissioned in 2012 – it has been a most excellent and professional relationship from the start; long may it continue.

Our sincere and profuse thanks are similarly extended to the 60 contributing authors, who have written 124 entries between them, and without whom this *Companion* would not have been produced. It has been an absolute pleasure to work with colleagues from a range of disciplines, all of whom, despite the ever-increasing calls on an academic's time within the contemporary higher education environment, remained generous with their time, knowledge, thoughts and suggestions throughout the production of this *Companion*. We will be forever grateful.

Preface

A companion to the history of crime and criminal justice is the fourth in a series of companions on different themes commissioned by Policy Press and edited by a team of criminologists at the University of Chester and Liverpool John Moores University. In keeping with its predecessors, in alphabetical order, this *Companion* provides succinct definitions, concise descriptions and critical evaluations of key concepts and issues within the historical framework of crime and criminal justice.

That historical framework is considerable and the size of the *Companion* is limited. Therefore, in compiling this *Companion*, a number of decisions had to be taken regarding its historical and geographical scope. For example, first, it was decided that contributions were needed that had relevance to one another in terms of time and place. Thus, although not easy to delineate where boundaries lie and with some exceptions, this *Companion* is set very much, but not exclusively, in the modern period and with a focus on Britain. Even then, because of the limited size of the *Companion*, sadly, all the topics for entries that have been considered could not have been included. Second, it was decided that contributions not only had to cover topics and issues relevant to that time and place, but also had to reflect new and developing areas of research as well as established work, and be written by scholars selected for their scholarship. Therefore, contributors were approached for their expertise and current or past research, and the *Companion* consequently brings together an array of established and new, burgeoning, areas of research. Even then, the necessary brevity of entries meant that contributors were restricted regarding the length of each entry, which meant that they could not necessarily include all the detail or reflection that they might have wanted to incorporate. To that end, each entry has further reading for those who wish to carry out a more detailed study of the topics covered in the *Companion*. Indeed, many of the contributors have written extensively on their entry's topic. Finally, rather than producing a dictionary, entries for this *Companion* were sought that would be lively, analytical and thought-provoking for a wide range of readers. It is, therefore, an indispensable resource for any interested person, whether within academia or not.

Those decisions were taken in order to produce a robust, timely and fascinating *Companion*. Therefore, it is sincerely trusted and anticipated that this *Companion* will be of interest, and of benefit, to a range of people. It has been compiled in such a way as to make it accessible and useful but always engaging and enlightening. It is expected that historians and criminologists, legal and literature scholars, and students of history, literature, law, sociology, criminology and criminal justice will equally find this *Companion* of interest and of use. It is envisaged that people who work within criminal justice, for example, police officers, prison officers, probation officers, social workers, lawyers and magistrates, will welcome an introductory history of the work that they undertake and the institutions in which they work. Similarly, it is anticipated that those who work in professional settings that deal with the historical aspects of crime and criminal justice, for example, heritage institutions and records offices, and those who visit and make use of the facilities that those settings provide will enjoy and welcome this *Companion*. It is imagined that the people who produce the entertainment that crime and criminal justice provide, such as writers, television programme makers and film-makers, might be interested in being better informed about the history of the topics that they draw on – not least because any attempt to represent crime, offenders and criminal justice without knowledge of the past may be partial. Last, but definitely not least, it is hoped that general readers will find pleasure in this exploration into the dark side of the past – for we believe that the history of crime and criminal justice is firmly part of everyone's heritage.

Jo Turner, Paul Taylor, Karen Corteen and Sharon Morley
(2017)

ADVOCACY IN CRIMINAL TRIALS

A history of legal advocacy in the criminal courts is inextricably linked to the rise of the barrister. A barrister, often referred to as 'counsel', acts as a representative for either the prosecution or the defendant.

While advocates could appear for either the prosecution or the defence from medieval times, it was not until 1836 that the official role of the defence advocate in serious criminal trials was extended beyond the limitation of the questioning of witnesses and ensuring that court process was properly followed (Beattie, 1986). Prior to 1836, if the defendant wanted to put forward a coherent defence statement, they were required to do so themselves. From the 17th to the 19th century, the criminal trial was full of contradictions: counsel was allowed for misdemeanours but not felonies; counsel was not allowed for felony trails, but were for appeals; and counsel could speak to matters of law but not to matters of fact. There were a number of justifications for the limiting of the role of defence counsel, one of which has been identified by John Langbein (2003) as the 'accused speaks' trial, meaning that the prisoner was seen as the most beneficial source of information for ascertaining their own guilt or innocence. It was believed that should the prisoner speak only through a barrister, this valuable source of information would be lost to the court.

Another reason that the role of the advocate was limited within the criminal trial was public and political mistrust of barristers. Such mistrust was related to historically rooted cultural perceptions that barristers would wilfully lie and mislead the court for their own pecuniary advantage (May, 2003). This is particularly apparent from the literature of the age, with lawyers being seen as avaricious and unscrupulous mercenaries, wilfully circumventing justice in the pursuit of their fees. As important to the public perception of barristers was the conduct of advocates in trials. Famous barristers, such as William Garrow, were widely reported in the media of the day. However, these reports were not always favourable as they also reflected the bullying tactics used by advocates when addressing witnesses, as well as widespread sarcasm and quarrelling by members of the Bar. It was not only defence counsel who were disliked by the public, but also prosecuting counsel, who frequently made addresses calling for the execution of prisoners, referred to as 'hanging speeches'.

Regardless of the unpopularity of their profession, barristers continued to expand their role in the criminal trial, pushing the boundaries of witness questioning to the point of providing a full defence statement for the prisoner (Cairns, 1998). However, this expansion of their role was wholly contingent upon the grace of the judge, and it was only following several years of debate and failed legislative initiative that the Prisoners Counsels' Act was finally passed in 1836 (Griffiths, 2014). This Act allowed for all prisoners in felony trials to delegate the presentation of their defence to an advocate. Thus, the barrister's role was officially recognised as not being limited to the questioning of witnesses, but extending to the presentation of a defence narrative to the jury in the form of a closing speech. In 1836, unlike today, defence counsel were not guaranteed the last word in the trial as it was believed that advocates would hold back evidence until the end of the trial in order to sway the jury when the prosecution could not respond.

In summation, while the 1836 Act secured the role of defence advocates in the felony trial, the majority of trials continued without the presence of advocates due to the prohibitive expense of counsel. It was not until the introduction of legal aid in 1903 that advocates became the norm in criminal trials. Regardless of the financial prohibitions limiting the role of the advocate, the Prisoners' Counsel Act 1836 secured the advocate in the criminal trial as the representative of the defendant, thereby silencing the accused in their own trial.

CERIAN CHARLOTTE GRIFFITHS

See also: Assizes; Juries; Legal Representation; Quarter Sessions

Readings
Beattie, J.M. (1986) *Crime and the courts in England 1660–1800.* Oxford: Clarendon Press.

Cairns, D.J.A. (1998) *Advocacy and the making of the adversarial criminal trial 1800–1865*. Oxford: Oxford University Press.

Griffiths, C.C. (2014) 'The Prisoners' Counsel Act 1836: doctrine, advocacy and the criminal trial', *Law, Crime and History*, 2: 28–47.

Langbein, J. (2003) *The origins of the adversary criminal trial*. Oxford: Oxford University Press.

May, A.N. (2003) *The Bar and the Old Bailey 1750–1850*. Chapel Hill, NC: The University of North Carolina Press.

ASSIZES

The courts of assize, or assizes, were periodic courts held in England and Wales between the 14th century and 1971 to deal with countywide civil, criminal and local government business. For more than six centuries, assizes were the country's principal criminal courts for most ordinary purposes (Baker, 1977). Although its roots can be traced back to the 12th century, it was in the early 14th century that the assizes was established as a single and regular system whereby judges of the high courts were assigned to hear pleas and preside over criminal trials within the counties of a defined circuit.

Under the system of assizes, English counties were grouped into six such circuits: Home (ie South East), Midland, Norfolk, Northern, Oxford and Western. London, Middlesex, the county palatines (regions possessing special autonomy within the kingdom, distinct from other counties) of Lancashire, Durham and Cheshire, and a handful of boroughs were not included in the assizes system, having separate jurisdiction to deal with criminal offences. Until 1830, cases in Wales were heard at the Court of Great Sessions of Wales, from which point onwards, Wales was incorporated into the assizes circuit system.

Twice a year (but only once a year on the Northern Circuit), normally in the spring (Lent) and summer (Trinity) vacations, two judges or sergeants were assigned to each of the six assize circuits. At each county within the circuit, they heard pleas and tried indictments, under commissions of assize, oyer and terminer, gaol delivery and *nisi prius*. Assize courts were held in the county town or some other convenient centre of the particular circuit county. By the mid-19th century, it was necessary in some years (particularly on the Home Circuit) to conduct a third, winter, assizes due to the increase in criminal prosecutions.

Criminal cases constituted a large part of the business at assizes, normally occupying at least one of the two judges for the entire duration of the session. The pressures of time meant that criminal trials were extremely short and perfunctory.

In general, the assize court heard the most serious (capital) cases, including murder, robbery, rape and grand larceny, while lesser crimes, such as petty larceny, tended to be dealt with at quarter sessions, though the jurisdiction and practice of the two courts did overlap. Until the Restoration, when the assizes became an almost exclusively judicial tribunal, it also served an important extrajudicial function as a mechanism of executive control in the provinces – a 'mirror of the State', as Sir Francis Bacon called it (cited in Cockburn, 1972, p 154).

Assizes were highly ritualised and ceremonious events that sought to display the majesty of the law and the grandeur of the county gentry. Circuit judges were met by the sheriffs at the county border and rode in cavalcade to the assize town, where they would be welcomed with bells, music and a chaplain's sermon. For those in high society on the right side of the law, the assizes were a focal event in the social calendar, marked by dinners and balls. Some critics abhorred the luxury and intemperance on show, and during moments of disruption from plebeian audiences in the court, the ritual of the assizes could lack the solemnity and dignity that it was supposed to convey.

The assizes never became a distinct 'court' in the same sense as permanent institutions such as King's Bench, its jurisdiction resting instead on the commissions issued ad hoc for each circuit. Nor was any central record system devised for the assizes, and thus a significant proportion of the courts' records (most of which are now held at the National Archives) have been lost.

Yet, for all its oddities, the assizes system remained virtually unchanged for 600 years. A Royal Commission of 1967–69, chaired by Lord Beeching, launched the first serious challenge to the court, recommending that the assizes be replaced by a new system of permanent courts. These recommendations were adopted in the Courts Act 1971 (c 23, s 1), which abolished the courts of assizes and quarter sessions, replacing them with a single, centrally organised Crown Court comprised of a network of some 90 local courts spread across England and Wales.

RICHARD WARD

See also: **Advocacy in Criminal Trials; Juries; Legal Representation; Quarter Sessions**

Readings
Baker, J.H. (1977) 'Criminal courts and procedure at common law, 1550–1800', in J.S. Cockburn (ed) *Crime in England, 1550–1800.* London: Methuen, pp 15–48.
Cockburn, J.S. (1972) *A history of English assizes 1558–1714.* Cambridge: Cambridge University Press.

Cockburn, J.S. (1985) *Calendar of assize records. Home Circuit indictments Elizabeth I and James I: Introduction.* London: HMSO.

AUSTRALIA, CRIME, LAW AND PUNISHMENT

English law was transplanted to the Australian colonies during the late 18th and early 19th centuries, and, in many ways, their experiences of crime, law and punishment would remain similar to England's into the 21st century. In other ways though, the Australian relationship with crime and punishment was unique. The first British settlement, New South Wales, was colonised specifically as a place of punishment, and subsequently Van Diemen's Land (Tasmania), Moreton Bay (Queensland), Swan River Colony (Western Australia) and even briefly Port Phillip district (Victoria) would all receive convict transportees. Australia's penal history shaped long-lasting outlooks on crime, as well as having an immediate effect on the administration of local justice. The law of felony attaint, for instance, was initially relaxed in the penal colonies to allow convicts and emancipists to appear as witnesses, initiate law suits and even practise as lawyers themselves. Continuing prejudice against according the New South Wales populace the right to trial by jury, however, meant that during the 1820s and 1830s, agitation to replace military courts with civilian juries became one of the most significant colonial political struggles of the early 19th century (Castles, 1982). Even after transportation ended, consciousness of Australia's convict roots continued to exert an influence on the authorities' concerns about the local so-called criminal class, and on late 19th- and early 20th-century interest in hereditary explanations of crime and eugenic policies. Conversely, the presence of many with convict forebears and the gradual inclusion of the convict in national myth-making led commentators from the 19th century onwards to conclude that the Australian public generally showed more than usual sympathy for the outlaw (Finnane, 1997).

The administration of justice in colonial jurisdictions also necessarily differed from English experiences in that the act of colonisation brought British settlers and law into contact, and conflict, with indigenous inhabitants and law. This led to considerable debate over whether various outrages perpetrated against Aborigines constituted criminal acts, as well as uncertainty as to what extent Aborigines themselves were subject to British justice. Massacres of Aboriginal groups, often at the hands or with the knowledge of the authorities, occurred from the 18th to the 20th century. Yet, Aborigines were also intermittently protected under the law, with the first colonists convicted of murder of Aborigines in 1799. By the 1830s, it had nominally been determined that cases where Aborigines committed crimes against colonists, and where colonists committed crimes against Aborigines, were subject to British law.

The issue of whether crimes among Aborigines themselves were amenable to colonial justice remained a more vexed question until an 1836 case in which Jack Congo Murrell was charged with the murder of another Aborigine. Murrell's barrister argued that his client was not bound by English law as he was not protected by it, and because the Aboriginal people had never become British subjects either by conquer or by treaty. While the rejection of these arguments by the New South Wales Supreme Court established in principle that Aborigines were subject to British law, in practice, the law was applied haphazardly and dissimilarly across different jurisdictions, particularly in more remote areas. Aborigines were more likely to be prosecuted than protected by British law. This was partly because Aborigines were initially prevented from testifying in court on the grounds that they were unable to make a Christian oath; even after their testimony was admitted, it was held to carry less legal weight, having to be corroborated by other evidence. Nevertheless, in cases involving Aborigines committing violence against other Aborigines, juries well into the 20th century continued to indicate their belief that such occurrences should not be subject to external interference by either acquitting defendants or recommending them to mercy on the grounds that their actions had been in keeping with local customs. Since the 1980s, there has been some return to legal plurality, with recognition of Aboriginal customary laws under some circumstances (Douglas and Finnane, 2012).

There were other unique aspects to Australian experiences of crime as a result of colonial conditions. A special challenge to the maintenance of law and order in colonial Australia was the danger posed by bushranging, which involved escaped convicts and later other outlaws living in the bush and conducting periodic robberies on travellers, homesteads and other targets. The fears inspired by such activities caused colonists to extend the list of capital offences just as England was reducing it (Kercher, 1995). Local justice systems were also adapted to suit a different range of circumstances than those found in England. The use of grand juries, made more difficult by smaller populations and potential jury pools, was either never introduced or was quickly abandoned by the various colonial jurisdictions. By the 1860s, all the jurisdictions were operating on a more streamlined and modern court system than that which prevailed in England, with ultimate jurisdiction in criminal, ecclesiastical and equity matters resting with the Supreme Court of each colony (Castles, 1982). While the possibility of England adopting a uniform criminal code based on its varied mix of case law and statutes had been occasionally debated since 1818, in 1899, Queensland actually adopted one, with Western Australia and Tasmania thereafter following suit (Kercher, 1995). The Australian colonies led England in other developments as well: while the prohibition against defendants providing sworn testimony was not removed in England until 1898, it was lifted in South Australia in 1882, as well as in Victoria and New South Wales in 1891. Queensland likewise became the first jurisdiction in the British Commonwealth to abolish capital punishment in 1922 (Finnane et al, 2016). While there were many similarities between the English and Australian systems of justice, there were thus many important differences as well.

ALANA PIPER

See also: **British Empire, The; Imperialism; Juries; Transportation**

Readings
Castles, A.C. (1982) *An Australian legal history.* Sydney: The Law Book Company Limited.
Douglas, H. and Finnane, M. (2012) *Indigenous crime and settler law: White sovereignty after Empire.* Houndmills, Basingstoke: Palgrave Macmillan.
Finnane, M. (1997) *Punishment in Australian society.* Melbourne: Oxford University Press.
Finnane, M., Kaladelfos, A., Piper, A., Blewer, R., Durnian, L. and Smaal, Y. (2016) 'The Prosecution Project', version 1, 17 July. Available at: https://prosecutionproject.griffith.edu.au
Kercher, B. (1995) *An unruly child: A history of law in Australia.* St Leonards: Allen & Unwin.

B

BENEFIT OF CLERGY

In English law, benefit of clergy was a provision by which clergymen could claim that they were outside the jurisdiction of secular, royal courts and should be tried instead in an ecclesiastical court under cannon law. Through this mechanism, many defendants found guilty of certain felonies were spared the death penalty and given a lesser punishment (Briggs et al, 1996; Sharpe, 1999).

Benefit of clergy arose from medieval disagreements on many issues between the Church and the monarchy (Sharpe, 1999). As part of and during these disagreements, the Church claimed that its own courts had jurisdiction over the clergy. One significant difference between the two was that unlike the lay courts, Church courts did not have the power to impose the death penalty. The term 'clergy' included practically every minor (male) official associated with the Church, as well as priests and bishops. To claim that one was part of the 'clergy' and thus able to claim benefit of clergy, all a man had to do was read a passage from the Bible, normally the opening verse of psalm 51. This verse became known as the 'neck verse' since many people evaded the death penalty through being able to read it (Emsley et al, 2016).

Over time, it was assumed that every literate adult male could claim benefit of clergy for a first offence (Briggs et al, 1996). Those granted benefit of clergy, instead of being sentenced to death, would have the letter 'M' (for murderer) or 'T' (for thief) branded on the palm of his left hand or his thumb to prevent recidivism. Additionally, by being punished by the ecclesiastical courts, the offender claiming benefit of clergy was effectively 'defrocked' – that is, they would be instantly removed from the clergy as part of the punishment (Briggs et al, 1996). Consequently, if the man was accused a second time of murder or grand larceny – theft of items valued at 12 pence (or one shilling) or more, for example – he would be tried in the secular courts and would be executed if found guilty.

A number of modifications were made to the practice of benefit of clergy in the early modern period. Some made access to benefit of clergy more difficult. During the 16th century, for example, a group of offences were removed from those eligible for benefit of clergy, such as: robbery, burglary, sodomy, bestiality, rape, murder, witchcraft, horse stealing and theft from churches (Sharpe, 1999). In the 18th century, other offences were added to that list: sheep stealing, theft from a ship of goods valued at 30 shillings or more and stealing mail (Briggs et al, 1996). Further changes made it easier to claim benefit of clergy, such as the two statutes of 1623 and 1692 that extended benefit of clergy to women; a change that Sharpe (1999, p 96) claims showed the practice of benefit of clergy to be 'a nonsense, a proposition best supported by legislation of 1624 which extended the right to claim benefit of clergy to women in an age when the ordination of women as priests would have been unthinkable'. A later statue of 1706 widened the access even further when it removed the literacy test, probably because increasing lay literacy made such a test meaningless (Emsley et al, 2016).

The most significant change came when the Transportation Act of 1718 made it possible for the courts to sentence non-capital felons (those who could claim benefit of clergy) to seven years' transportation. It also established a term of 14 years' transportation for capital felons (people not eligible for benefit of clergy) who had received a royal pardon. This Act significantly reduced the number of people claiming benefit of clergy – it became the exception rather than the norm. Benefit of clergy was eventually abolished in 1823 with the Judgement of Death Act, which, for the first time, gave judges the discretion to pass lesser sentences for first offenders.

JO TURNER

See also: 'Bloody Code' , The; Corporal Punishment; Pleading the Belly; Transportation

Readings
Baker, J.H. (2002) *An introduction to English legal history* (4th edn). Oxford: Oxford University Press.
Briggs, J., Harrison, C., McInnes, A. and Vincent, D. (1996) *Crime and punishment in England: An introductory history.* New York, NY: St. Martin's Press.

Emsley, C., Hitchcock, T. and Shoemaker, R. (2016) 'Crime and justice – punishments at the Old Bailey', Old Bailey Proceedings Online. Available at: http://www.londonlives.org

Gatrell, V.A.C. (1994) *The hanging tree: Execution and the English people 1770–1868*. Oxford: Oxford University Press.

Sharpe, J.A. (1999) *Crime in early modern England 1550–1750*. London: Longman.

BIGAMY

Before the Bigamy Act 1603 (1 Jac 1 c 11), the offence of bigamy was regarded as a spiritual rather than secular offence and, as such, was heard before Church courts (Ingram, 1987). However, the Bigamy Act declared:

> If any person or persons within his Majesty's Dominions of England and Wales, being married, or which hereafter shall marry, do at any time after the end of the session of this present Parliament, marry any person or persons, the former husband or wife being alive ... then every such offence shall be felony.... Provided always, that neither this Act, nor anything therein contained, shall extend to any person or persons whose husband or wife shall be continually remaining beyond the seas by the space of seven years together, or whose husband or wife shall absent him or herself the one from the other by the space of seven years together, in any parts within his Majesty's Dominions, the one of them not knowing the other to be living within that time.
> (1 Jac 1 c 11, ss 1 & 2)

The offence theoretically carried the death penalty, but this was rarely enforced; many bigamists invoked the legal fiction of 'benefit of clergy', by which an offender could claim to be a member of the clergy by reciting a passage from the Bible (normally psalm 51, known colloquially as the 'neck verse'). By claiming the status of a cleric, offenders could continue to be sentenced under spiritual rather than temporal law; thereby avoiding the ultimate sanction. Although 'benefit of clergy' was not formally abolished until 1827, offenders were rarely able to utilise it after 1718, when the death penalty for bigamy was usually reduced to a period of transportation. In turn, transportation was replaced by a maximum sentence of seven years' penal servitude by the Offences Against the Person Act 1861.

Bigamy has never been a prevalent criminal offence; between 1850 and 1950, just over 22,000 cases were heard in England and Wales, and the number of annual prosecutions in the period 2005–14 averaged under 70 (Cox, 2011; Office of National Statistics, 2015). The reasons behind bigamous relationships were varied; many undoubtedly involved an element of fraud, whereby an unwitting and naive bride-to-be and her family were duped out of money (there are several cases where a serial male bigamist married half-a-dozen or so women before being caught). However, the majority of bigamous offences resulted from a failed marriage, leaving one (or both) partners unable to remarry due to their inability to obtain a divorce. Until 1858, anyone who wished to divorce had to apply for a private Act of Parliament in order to obtain legal consent. This was an extremely costly undertaking (and also carried a considerable social stigma). Following the Matrimonial Causes Act 1857, men and women could divorce slightly more easily (though not on equal terms – men only had to prove adultery on behalf of their wives, whereas women had to prove an additional charge, such as cruelty or desertion by their husbands). This remained the case until 1923, when men and women were both allowed to divorce on grounds of adultery. It was not until 1949 that Legal Aid could be used for divorce proceedings.

As a result, many marriages simply ended in separation and the subsequent illegal remarriage(s) of one or both partners. Statistics suggest that while bigamy remained a predominantly male offence, the proportion of female bigamists was higher than the proportion of female offenders as a whole during the period 1850–1950 (Cox, 2011). This is perhaps understandable as separated women often found it hard to support themselves after their spouses had deserted them. Bigamy could also occasionally be perpetrated following a misunderstanding as to the fate of a spouse; several cases resulted from women remarrying after their husbands had left them for a long period, leading them to suppose that they had subsequently died.

DAVID J. COX

See also: **Benefit of Clergy; Capital Punishment (England and Wales)**

Readings

Cox, D.J. (2011) '"Trying to get a good one": bigamy offences in England and Wales 1850–1950', *Plymouth Law & Criminal Justice Review*, 4: 1–32.

Frost, G. (1997) 'Bigamy and cohabitation in Victorian England', *Journal of Family History*, 22(3): 286–306.

Ingram, M. (1987) *Church courts, sex and marriage in England, 1570–1640*. Cambridge: Cambridge University Press.

Office of National Statistics (2015) 'Crime in England and Wales – year ending December 2014, Table A4: Police recorded crime by offence, 2002/03 to year ending December 2014 and percentage change between year to December 2013 and year to December 2014'. Available at: http://www.ons.gov.uk/ons/rel/crime-stats/crime-statistics/index.html

BLASPHEMY

In the UK, blasphemy has been considered to be scoffing and ribald attacks upon the nature of religion established by law. Initially, these were religious doctrines, but in modern times have become religious feelings. England has, at various times, had both statute law and a common law crime of blasphemous libel, which was by far the most readily used method of proceeding against the offence. Scotland has a separate law that developed differently to that in England, and while the latter has removed this law, it is still in existence in the former (Nash, 1999).

While the origins of legal protection for religion lie in older heresy laws, the genesis of modern law dates from the very end of the 17th century, which also witnessed the only execution of an individual convicted of the offence – that of Thomas Aikenhead in 1697. The statute of most importance in modern times is the 1698 statute (9 & 10 William c 32), which established various progressive and graduated punishments for subsequent offences. This statute stood alongside other security messages aimed at preserving the peace of the kingdom (Nash, 1999).

Later, in England, fears of Jacobin French Revolutionary ideas led to a number of significant figures in this milieu suffering prosecution for blasphemy. Thomas Paine's works were pursued and Thomas Williams was prosecuted in 1897 for selling his *Age of reason* (Roberts, 1992). In the 1820s, Paine's disciple Richard Carlile was again prosecuted for selling the *Age of reason* and his agitation in favour of the freedom of the press led to a number of subsequent prosecutions of his friends, relatives and colleagues all prepared to sell his publications and defend their message. The groundbreaking case of the 19th century involved the prosecution of G.W. Foote's *Freethinker*, which resulted in the landmark judgement whereby religion was no longer 'part and parcel of the law of the land', with the test of offence becoming the manner in which it was expressed, not the opinion itself.

After such a long hiatus, in which blasphemy was considered a 'dead letter' (the Statute of 1698 was quietly repealed in 1967 in the context of the Criminal Justice Act) (Levy, 1993), it was thus a surprise when the common law of blasphemous libel re-emerged as part of one of Mary Whitehouse's crusades against unacceptable content appearing in numerous published and broadcast media. In 1977, the so-called 'Gay News Case' indicted the paper's editor, Denis Lemon, for publishing James Kirkup's poem 'The Love that Dares Not Speak its Name', which depicted a Roman Soldier's involvement in sex acts with the body of the crucified Christ. Despite expert testimony defending the poem's intellectual and artistic merits, the verdict went against the defendant and he was given a 12-month suspended sentence. A crucial outcome of the case was the restoration of the law to its condition before the Foote case – thereby returning emphasis to the fact of publication, not the manner of the expressions within this.

Blasphemy made a sudden and startling reappearance at the end of the 1980s with the publication of Salman Rushdie's *The Satanic verses*, which was widely seen as blasphemous throughout the Islamic world (Ruthven, 1990). In England, attempts to utilise the law of blasphemous libel against this work were prevented by John Patten, the then Home Secretary, arguing that the law only protected the Church of England as the country's established Church.

Nonetheless, the glaring anomaly that this represented also highlighted the UK's wider accountability to the requirements of pan-European jurisdictions. This became even clearer after the film-maker Nigel Wingrove appealed to the European Court of Human Rights over the banning of his film *Visions of ecstasy*, which portrayed the erotic visions of St Theresa of Avila (Nash, 1999). Eventually, the ban was upheld, with the UK allowed to maintain its blasphemy law under the 'Margin of Appreciation', which enabled countries to retain laws that were of particular cultural significance.

Eventually, equalising legal protection for all religions became the impetus behind the House of Lords Select Committee on Religious Offences, which reported in June 2003. This signalled that the issue had become associated with agendas surrounding hate crime, though the Committee was unable to recommend any particular course of action (House of Lords Select Committee on Religious Offences, 2003). Although laws against incitement to religious hatred appeared before the law against blasphemy was repealed, it eventually passed into history in 2008 as a result of the MP Evan Harris's successful proposal of an amendment to the Criminal Justice and Immigration Bill.

DAVID NASH

Readings

House of Lords Select Committee on Religious Offences (2003). Available at: http://www.publications.parliament.uk/pa/ld200203/ldselect/ldrelof/95/95.pdf

Levy, L. (1993) *Blasphemy: Verbal offense against the sacred from Moses to Salman Rushdie*. New York, NY: Knopf.

Nash, D. (1999) *Blasphemy in modern Britain 1789 to the present*. Aldershot: Ashgate.

Roberts, M.J.D. (1992) 'Blasphemy, obscenity and the courts: contours of tolerance in the nineteenth century', in P. Hyland and N. Sammells (eds) *Writing and censorship in Britain*. London: Routledge, pp 141–53.

Ruthven, M. (1990) *A Satanic affair: Salman Rushdie and the wrath of Islam*. London: Chatto and Windus.

'BLOODY CODE', THE

The 'Bloody Code' refers to the body of laws that was established by a substantial increase in the number of capital statutes passed between 1688 and 1815, which together prescribed the death penalty for over 200 separate offences. The precise origin of the term 'Bloody Code' in this sense is unclear. It was in currency among law reformers by the beginning of the 19th century at the latest. However, it was in the 20th century that the term came to prominence through a raft of historical work on the capital code in the long 18th century.

In 1688, about 50 offences carried the death penalty. By 1815, this had increased to over 200. The vast majority, though not all, of these new capital statutes involved property offences. Some targeted types of crime that were on the rise, such as shoplifting, theft by servants and forgery. Others criminalised customary practices of the poor, such as workplace 'perks' and gleaning, and yet others sought to shore up political authority by attacking riotous, treasonable or seditious practices.

Yet, the making of the Bloody Code was not the result of a coherent plan, and the significance of the numerical increase should not be overestimated. Many of the new statutes were narrowly defined, such as the Act mandating the death penalty for the embezzling of banknotes by employees of the Bank of England (35 Geo III, c 66). Several added specific offences to types of crime already made capital in the 16th century. In addition, the opportunities for legislating itself were greatly enhanced by more regular and lengthy meetings of Parliament after 1688.

Aside from those relating to forgery, shoplifting and theft by servants, most of the capital laws passed in the long 18th century were rarely used. The majority of capital convictions continued to be based on common law or statutes enacted in the 16th century. However, despite the rapid increase in the number of offences punishable by death, far fewer lives were, in fact, taken on the gallows in the 18th century than in the 16th. Through the use of mechanisms such as 'benefit of clergy', mitigated verdicts and pardons, the Bloody Code was never fully implemented; its theoretical severity was tempered by a reluctance to hang more than a small number of 'examples'. This was particularly the case on the far northern and western peripheries of Britain, where per capita execution rates for property offences were extremely low. It had a greater impact in London, where levels of execution were much higher, particularly in the 1780s and 1820s.

By the early 19th century, the muddled patchwork of capital statutes that constituted the Bloody Code was widely criticised as an ineffective and inhumane system of law. From the 1830s, it was rare for anyone to be executed for anything other than murder, and a rationalisation of the criminal laws between the 1820s and 1840s – culminating with the Criminal Law Consolidation Acts of 1861

(24 & 25 Vict, cc 94–100), which abolished the death penalty for all crimes except murder, high treason, piracy with violence and arson in the royal dockyards – effectively dismantled the Bloody Code.

The broader significance of the Bloody Code has been the subject of much historical debate. For Douglas Hay (1975), the Bloody Code was as much an attempt by the ruling class to protect its authority as its property. Through selective enforcement of this draconian body of laws, Hay suggests, Hanoverian England's ruling elite were able to fortify the bonds of patronage and deference that formed the basis of aristocratic authority. However, recent findings – particularly those relating to the creation and administration of capital legislation in the long 18th century – have challenged this thesis to some extent, suggesting instead that (although undoubtedly harsh) the Bloody Code might not have been such a powerful tool for the reinforcement of hegemony.

RICHARD WARD

See also: **Benefit of Clergy; Capital Punishment (England and Wales)**

Readings
Devereaux, S. (2013) 'England's "Bloody Code" in crisis and transition: executions at the Old Bailey, 1760–1837', *Journal of the Canadian Historical Association*, 24(2): 71–113.
Gatrell, V.A.C. (1994) *The hanging tree: Execution and the English people, 1770–1868*. Oxford: Oxford University Press.
Hay, D. (1975) 'Property, authority and the criminal law', in D. Hay, P. Linebaugh, J.G. Rule, E.P. Thompson and C. Winslow (eds) *Albion's fatal tree: Crime and society in eighteenth-century England*. London: Allen Lane, pp 17–63.
McGowen, R. (2002) 'Making the "Bloody Code"? Forgery legislation in eighteenth-century England', in N. Landau (ed) *Law, crime and English society, 1660–1830*. Cambridge: Cambridge University Press, pp 117–38.
Radzinowicz, L. (1948) *A history of English criminal law and its administration from 1750. Vol. 1. The movement for reform*. London: Stevens.

BORSTALS

Borstals operated in Britain from 1908 to 1982. They were institutions for young adults aged between 16 and 21 and were originally intended to offer a constructive alternative to prison. They were first introduced as a national system by the Prevention of Crime Act 1908 and were based around a strict routine, discipline and instruction in marketable skills. They were named after an experimental institution set up in 1902 by Sir Evelyn Ruggles-Brise (1857–1935), a prison commissioner. This institution was connected to an adult prison located in the Kent village of Borstal and had, in turn, been inspired by the 1895 Gladstone Committee's call for more institutions that were 'educational rather than punitive'. As Godfrey and Lawrence (2014) have noted, the borstal system was welcomed both by more progressive reformers and more traditional disciplinarians.

There was only ever one borstal for girls, located in Aylesbury in Buckinghamshire and governed for many years by Dame Lilian Barker, who would go on to become Britain's first female assistant prison commissioner. The borstal model and name was exported across many Commonwealth countries, notably, to India, where they still exist. In Britain, the institutions were renamed and reorganised as youth custody centres by the Criminal Justice Act 1982.

The development of the borstal system was part of a broader reform of youth justice. The Children Act 1908 had established juvenile courts (for those aged up to 16) and had ruled that no child younger than this could be sent to prison. Those aged over 16 could still be sent to prison in exceptional circumstances but the majority of young offenders who were given a custodial sentence served this in a borstal. These institutions were thus part of wider efforts stretching back to the earlier 19th century to keep young people out of prison. They were inspired by the same philosophy supporting the establishment of industrial and reformatory schools in the 1850s: that young offenders required early and constructive intervention rather than punishment for its own sake.

Early research on the impact of the borstal system includes a 1934 study (on young men) by Barman and a 1951 study (on young women) by Epps. The 2000 film *Borstal boy* presents elements of Brendan Behan's (1958) autobiographical novel of the same name. Behan was sent to a borstal in England after having been apprehended as a 16-year-old volunteer for the Irish Republican Army (IRA). The film includes sequences depicting borstal life for young men in the 1950s. An overview of the system is offered by Menis (2012).

PAMELA COX

See also: **Industrial Schools; Juvenile Crime in Britain; Reformatory Schools**

Readings
Bailey, V. (1987) *Delinquency and citizenship: Reclaiming the young offender, 1914–48.* Oxford: Clarendon Press.

Barman, S. (1934) *The English borstal system: A study in the treatment of young offenders*. London: P.S. King and Son Ltd.

Behan, B. (1958) *Borstal boy*. London: Hutchinson.

Epps, P. (1951) 'A preliminary survey of 300 female delinquents in Borstal institutions', *British Journal of Delinquency*, 1: 187–97.

Godfrey, B. and Lawrence, P. (2014) *Crime and justice since 1750* (2nd edn). London: Routledge.

Gore, E. (1965) *The better fight: The story of Dame Lilian Barker*. London: Geoffrey Bles.

Menis, S. (2012) 'More insights on the English borstal: "shaping" or just "shaking" the young-offender?', *International Journal of Criminology and Sociological Theory*, 5(3): 985–98.

BOW STREET RUNNERS, THE

The Bow Street Runners were created in 1749 by Henry Fielding (1707–54), who had been appointed as Chief Magistrate of Bow Street Public Office in the previous year. Bow Street Public Office (also known as Bow Street Police Office) was a magistrates' court located near Covent Garden in Westminster, London (Beattie, 2012). Until the creation of the Runners, there was nothing approaching a professional police force in Britain; instead, parishes relied on unpaid parish constables (who were elected from each parish to serve as a law-enforcement officer for a year on a voluntary basis), while many towns and cities employed untrained and poorly paid nightwatchmen to patrol their streets during the hours of darkness. Fielding (now better known as the author of picaresque novels such as *Tom Jones*) was determined to improve upon this situation and employed half-a-dozen former trusted and experienced Westminster parish constables to form the basis of a unique force. With the subsequent involvement of his half-brother Sir John Fielding (1721–80), the Bow Street Runners became the world's first professional plain-clothes detective force.

The original small force of detectives was later supplemented by a hierarchical system of uniformed mounted and foot patrols, which operated in a preventive capacity in both the immediate vicinity of Westminster and the major turnpike approach roads surrounding the capital. However, these various patrols and their officers remained subordinate to the small group of plain-clothes detectives known as the 'Runners'. The men who formed this cadre (never more than a dozen in total at any point in time during their existence) rarely, if ever, referred to themselves as 'Runners', considering the term somewhat derogatory and demeaning; they almost always called themselves either 'Principal' or 'Senior' Officers.

They never wore a uniform, their only badge of office being a small 'tipstaff' (a hollow wooden baton surmounted by a regal crown). Originally sworn in as constables for Westminster, they had few rights beyond those of private citizens in other areas until 1821, when they were attested as constables in the four counties surrounding the metropolis. Despite such restrictions, from the moment of their inception, the Runners were envisaged as operating throughout the nation as a whole, being involved in cases that originated in the provinces of Great Britain (Cox, 2012). They also occasionally operated on the Continent, with at least two of their number being fluent in French. Their services were utilised by wealthy private individuals (it cost a considerable amount to employ a Runner), institutions such as banks or insurance companies, and provincial magistrates when a particularly serious or complex criminal matter required investigation.

They were not, however, free to choose which cases they investigated; they had to first obtain the permission of the Bow Street magistrates, and they operated on a fixed financial scale. They were paid a weekly retaining fee, together with travel expenses and various other amounts for what they euphemistically called their 'trouble', that is, effort in tracking down offenders. These fees could reach a considerable amount – the equivalent to several thousands of pounds in today's prices – and, consequently, they were never employed by poorer members of society. Despite contemporary criticism of individual officers (often linked with suspected or implied corruption or complicity), the Bow Street Runners were, on the whole, a remarkable group of highly intelligent, motivated, diligent and capable men. In 1813, for example, two of them, Harry Adkins and Samuel Taunton, carried out what was probably the first ballistic forensics in the world by matching a bullet retrieved from a murder victim with a bullet mould that they had subsequently discovered (Cox, 2012, p 182).

In 1792, seven other Public Offices were opened in London, each with their own contingent of Runners, but due to their seniority, the Bow Street Runners were regarded as *primus inter pares*, and joining their ranks from another of the Public Offices was undoubtedly viewed as a promotion. They continued as a force until 1839 (10 years after the creation of the preventive Metropolitan Police), when they were disbanded. As professional and effective investigators of serious crimes throughout Britain, they pre-dated the creation of the Metropolitan Police's Detective Department (formed in 1842) by almost a 100 years, and, while now largely forgotten, undoubtedly played an important role in fashioning modern detective policing.

DAVID J. COX

See also: **'New' Police, The; Nightwatchmen; Parish Constables**

Readings

Beattie, J.M. (2012) *'The first English detectives': The Bow Street Runners and the policing of London, 1750–1840*. Oxford: Oxford University Press.

Cox, D.J. (2012) *'A certain share of low cunning': A history of the Bow Street Runners 1792–1839*. London: Routledge.

BREACH OF THE PEACE

The breach-of-the-peace doctrine provides both a power and a duty on the police to make an arrest without warrant when such a breach is committed in their presence, or is reasonably anticipated. However, breach of the peace is not a substantive criminal offence in England and Wales (although it is in Scotland). In the use of this power as a preventive measure, the police must demonstrate to the court that their actions were justified by the facts as well as in theory. However, as the nature of the breach-of-the-peace doctrine is broad and largely subjective, the discretion of the police officer and the interpretation of the judge do not necessarily harmonise. Judicial interpretations have helped shape this common law power and several high court judgements have contributed to its definition and scope.

In *Humphries v Connor* (1864), the power of the police officer to prevent a breach of the peace was set remarkably wide. In this case, Justice Hayes ruled that Sub-Inspector Connor was 'bound' by his duty to prevent a breach of the peace by removing an orange lily from the protestant Ann Humphries as it was provoking the Catholic crowd. Although not dissenting, Justice Fitzgerald recognised that this ruling provided the police with the power to interfere with the 'rights of the Queen's subjects' and was surrendering to mob law (Williams, 1967). In *Beatty v Gillbanks* (1881–82), the police sergeant used his powers under the breach-of-the-peace doctrine to prevent a Salvation Army procession that was expected to provoke disorder from another group who were antagonistic to them. Despite the principle of preventive action being similar to *Humphries*, Justice Field held that there was no authority for the proposition that 'a man may be convicted for doing a lawful act if he knows that his doing it may cause another to do an unlawful act'. While this more libertarian approach appeared to help limit the influence of the police in public order scenarios, subsequent cases again widened their discretionary powers. For instance, *Thomas v Sawkins* (1935) and *Duncan v Jones* (1936) provided the police with the power to close public meetings both on private premises and in public spaces, respectively, where they suspected that a breach of the peace may occur.

More recently, in *R v Howell* (1982), the Divisional Court has since provided the standard definition of a breach of the peace. Lord Justice Watkins stated that a constable, or anyone else, may arrest an offender whenever:

> harm is actually done or is likely to be done to a person or in his presence to his property or a person is in fear of being so harmed through an assault, an affray, a riot, unlawful assembly or other disturbance. ([1982] QB 416: at p 427)

In the same year, Lord Denning MR offered a broader definition of breach of the peace in *R v Chief Constable of the Devon and Cornwall Constabulary, ex parte Central Electricity Generating Board* (1982), stating: 'There is a breach of the peace whenever a person who is lawfully carrying out his work is unlawfully and physically prevented by another from doing it' ([1982] QB 458: at p 471).

Richard Stone and Helen Fenwick have led academic criticism of the breach-of-the-peace doctrine. Stone argues for the desirability of certainty within the law, the retaining of proportionality when infringements of individual rights and freedoms are created, and the undesirability of duplicated legal powers. He contends that the vagueness of the breach-of-the-peace doctrine is not consistent with the European Convention on Human Rights, which stipulates that certain Convention rights can only be restricted where the constraint is 'prescribed by law' (Stone, 2001). Fenwick (2009, p 738) also criticises that, despite the wide use of powers available for policing public protest under the Public Order Act 1986, the police still utilised the 'immensely broad and bewilderingly imprecise powers under the breach of the peace doctrine'.

IAIN CHANNING

See also: Public Order Law; Unlawful Assembly

Readings
Channing, I. (2015) *The police and the expansion of public order law in Britain, 1829–2014*. Abingdon: Routledge.
Fenwick, H. (2009) 'Marginalising human rights: breach of the peace, "kittling", the Human Rights Act and public protest', *Public Law*, 4: 737–65.
Stone, R. (2001) 'Breach of the peace: the case for abolition', 2 *Web JCLI*. Available at: http://webjcli.ncl.ac.uk/2001/issue2/stone2.html
Williams, D. (1967) *Keeping the peace: The police and public order*. London: Hutchinson & Co Ltd.

BRITISH EMPIRE, THE

The administration of justice, both criminal and civil, was a crucial structuring element in the British Empire. It was, in many ways, at the heart of Britain's moral justification for its rule over territories in the Americas, Africa and Asia (Cohn, 1996). Local magistrates played key roles in anchoring imperial rule, particularly in the colonies seized during the Napoleonic wars and the new acquisitions that accompanied the rapid expansion of empire during the period of 'New Imperialism' in the decades between the 1884 Berlin Conference and the outbreak of the First World War in 1914. Initially, the magistracy in these regions consisted of British immigrants, though succeeding generations saw local men who had travelled abroad (usually to England) for their legal education returning to hold these positions (Lambert and Lester, 2010). In a limited capacity, Indian subjects were also incorporated into the local magistracy (Porter, 1999). Although colonial legislative bodies were empowered to pass region-specific regulations, they could not enact legislature in contravention to British law, making concordance a general practice across the system.

Imperial territories played a key role in the criminal justice system of Britain as well. In the 18th and 19th centuries, the punishment of transportation to penal colonies, Australia in particular, was commonly employed. With Britain's courtrooms and prison system overwhelmed by a rising tide of petty offenders, the population of cities rising rapidly due to the economic and demographic transformations of the agricultural and industrial revolutions, and vast expanses of territory being claimed by the British crown, the punishment of criminals was transformed into a colonisation project. With the concept of prisoner rehabilitation yet to gain traction in British penal discourse, removing criminals entirely from society seemed a sensible and practical solution. Penal labour had played a key role in the early colonisation of the Americas, particularly the southern American states, where heat, disease and poor farming made voluntary colonisation less attractive. However, the most notorious destination in the modern era was Australia, which would receive over 160,000 prisoners between the mid-18th and mid-19th centuries (Hughes, 1988). Van Dieman's Land (Tasmania) and Botany Bay (New South Wales), the latter being the first such colony (established in 1788), would become especially famous for their harsh environments, brutal physical punishment and high mortality rate among prisoners.

Criminal law, judges and police, and legal institutions were also central to the economic operation of the British Empire, and to the control of labour in particular. Whether it was slave labour, penal labour, indentured labour or free labour, the authority, principles, mechanisms and personnel of colonial law played crucial roles in the organisation of labour relations, and in the disciplining of labourers more specifically. Slave emancipation and the transition to free labour brought the role of law into sharp focus. Agricultural employers, fearful of production disruptions and loss of revenue, revived and strengthened the 'Master and Servant' laws to maintain control over emancipated workers of African origin (Craven and Hay, 2014). Long-term periods of forced 'apprenticeship' gave what was, in effect, a coercive system the trappings of legality. Such uses of law have encouraged historians to examine the ways in which race was powerfully encoded into legal structures and practice in the Empire. Some scholars have gone so far as to argue that the British, through systematic colonial violence and the destruction of traditional forms of social order in favour of British law and governance, were sources of lawlessness and disorder rather than their opposite (Kolsky, 2010). Legal knowledge, however, could prove a double-edged sword in imperial affairs. Many of the most effective colonial reformers, anti-colonial nationalists and critics of imperialism were trained in British legal institutions and employed the language of law in framing their arguments.

SASCHA AUERBACH

See also: **Australia, Crime, Law and Punishment; Imperialism; Indentured Labour; Slave Trade, The; Transportation**

Readings

Cohn, B. (1996) *Colonialism and its forms of knowledge: The British in India.* Princeton, NJ: Princeton University Press.

Craven, P. and Hay, D. (eds) (2014) *Masters, servants, and magistrates in Britain and the Empire, 1562–1955.* Chapel Hill, NC: UNC Press.

Hughes, R. (1988) *The fatal shore: The epic of Australia's founding.* New York, NY: Vintage Books.

Kolsky, E. (2010) *Colonial justice in British India: White violence and the rule of law.* Cambridge and New York, NY: Cambridge University Press.

Lambert, D. and Lester, A. (eds) (2010) *Colonial lives across the British Empire: Imperial careering in the long nineteenth century.* Cambridge and New York, NY: Cambridge University Press.

Porter, A. (ed) (1999) *The Oxford history of the British Empire: The nineteenth century, volume 3.* Oxford and New York, NY: Oxford University Press.

Price, R. (2008) *Making Empire: Colonial encounters and the creation of imperial rule in nineteenth-century South Africa.* Cambridge and New York, NY: Cambridge University Press.

BROADSIDES

Broadsides were a form of street literature, and for almost 300 years until the mid-19th century, they were a forerunner to our modern tabloid newspapers. Printed and sold all over the country, broadsides were published on a wide range of topics, from politics to royal scandals, but the most popular subjects covered by broadsides were undoubtedly related to crime and punishment, especially murders and executions. These accounts could run to several editions of a series of broadsides and would cover all aspects of the criminal justice process, from details of the crime scene, to the trial and verbatim transcriptions of murderers' last words as they faced the hangman. The publication of this genre of broadside reached a peak in the first half of the 19th century and its popular appeal was greatest among the labouring poor. This has led several scholars to propose two prominent, yet contrasting, arguments, namely, that this 'gallows literature' should be read as either a form of state propaganda or mere sensationalistic entertainment. However, more detailed research of broadside content proposes that broadsides actually reveal ordinary people's thoughts and feelings about crime and criminal justice, and, as such, reflect common moralities and mentalities (Bates, 2014).

The origin of the broadside genre pre-dates that of even print itself, with the written broadside deriving from the traditional oral ballad of the 15th century. However, it was the coming of print that was to transform the broadside into a crucial element of popular culture and literature, which it was to remain throughout the 16th and 17th centuries. This was the first great era of the broadside ballad, but in the 18th century, the genre momentarily lost its appeal. Curiously, though, the broadside did not die out completely, but merely retreated before gathering momentum for its final heyday (Shepard, 1962). An important point to note when considering the *longue durée* of the broadside is that they appear to have flourished at certain periods of history. They ebbed and flowed throughout four centuries, emerging in the 16th, thriving in the 17th, declining in the 18th and finally resurging in the earlier 19th century. From this evolutionary chart, it is noticeable that broadsides were most virulent during periods of social change and urban growth, meaning that broadsides were to become an important source of news and information for their readers, and this was never more true than in the first half of the 19th century when the broadside genre adapted itself to the needs of a more industrialised populace. It was then that the broadside changed in character, becoming more realistic than romantic and concerned with the everyday affairs and anxieties of ordinary people (James, 1976). The early 19th-century street broadside, then, can be distinguished from its predecessors, in that the former focused on topical news and events, whereas the latter was more immersed in the older tradition of folklore.

Broadsides were produced with the intention of being both accessible and affordable, costing the price of only one penny, and thus enabled a wide public consumption. As such, they clearly represent an early example of mass culture and reflect the general public's apparently enduring fascination with crime and punishment. Their popularity in the early 19th century can certainly not be denied as it is documented by contemporaries that they were produced in vast numbers. For example, Henry Mayhew (1861), the famed social investigator, was to note that one particular broadside, reporting the execution and confession of a notorious criminal, sold over 2.5 million copies. Indeed, such was the voracious demand for every detail of the latest serious crime that by the early 19th century, each provincial town had its own organised network of broadside printers, pedlars and eager public. The era of the broadside was not to last, however, since two major developments ensured their demise: first, the emergence of cheap illustrated newspapers in the 1840s and 1850s, which began to focus more on crime and punishment and poached working-class readers from the broadside trade; and, second, the introduction in 1868 of the Capital Punishment Amendment Act, which abolished public executions and finally pronounced the death knell of the broadside's famed 'last dying speeches' of condemned criminals. So ended centuries of a socially and historically significant form of print culture, but the broadside's impact and influence has been far-reaching since its style and content gave birth to many aspects of modern-day journalism, especially with regards to the reporting of crime news.

KATE BATES

See also: **Crime Fiction; Crime Pamphlets; Newspapers and Crime**

Readings

Bates, K. (2014) 'Empathy or entertainment? The form and function of violent crime in early-nineteenth-century broadsides', *Law, Crime & History*, 4(2): 1–27.

Collinson, R. (1973) *The story of street literature: Forerunner of the popular press.* London: J.M. Dent & Sons.

James, L. (1976) *Print and the people 1819–1851.* London: Allen Lane.

Mayhew, H. (1861) *London labour and the London poor; a cyclopaedia of the condition and earnings of those that will work, those that cannot work, and those that will not work. Vol. 1: The London street-folk.* London: Griffin, Bohn, and Company.

Shepard, L. (1962) *The broadside ballad: A study in origins and meaning.* London: Herbert Jenkins.

BURKE AND HARE

Burke and Hare are arguably Scotland's most notorious criminals and yet they are still surrounded by myth, mystery and fanciful folklore. The greatest falsehood regarding their crimes is that they were 'body-snatchers' or 'Resurrection Men', exhuming freshly buried corpses from graveyards and selling them for profit. In fact, Burke and Hare murdered all but one of their 16 victims, making them calculating and predatory serial killers.

William Burke and William Hare were both born and bred in Ireland but moved separately to Scotland in the early 1800s to find work as navvies on the Union Canal. They met while living in Edinburgh's Old Town and soon formed their fateful friendship, with Burke and his common-law wife, Helen McDougal, moving into Hare's lodging house at 10 Tanner's Close, West Port, which he owned with his wife Margaret Laird. Their murderous spree began in February 1828 when a lodger of Hare's, an old pensioner named Donald, died of natural causes, but owing rent money, so Burke and Hare decided to remove his body from the coffin before it was buried by the parish in order to sell it. Ignorant of how to do this, they carried his body to an apothecary's shop, where they met a medical student who told them to take the corpse to the medical college in Surgeons Square. There, they were met by Dr Knox, who, after examining the body, paid them L7, 10s, and in getting so much money when they were in a state of poverty, Burke and Hare were thus encouraged to carry on the trade (Anon, 1829a).

After this, the two men often talked about the subject of murder and decided that the best way to kill their victims was suffocation since it would leave the corpse relatively unmarked. Their subsequent crimes were entirely premeditated, with Burke generally enticing a victim into Hare's lodging house, where they would get them drunk on whisky until they fell asleep, and then one would hold their hands over the victim's nose and mouth, while the other pressed down on the body until dead. They would then hide the corpse in straw under the bed before transferring it, often in a tea chest or herring barrel, to Dr Knox, who would pay between L8 and L10 for each one. Burke would later confess that he chose his victims wisely, preferring older women as they would provide the least physical resistance. In total, it is believed that Burke and Hare murdered 12 women, two men and two young boys, though they themselves claimed to be unsure of this since they paid their victims very little attention (Anon, 1829b).

Burke and Hare were finally arrested, with their respective wives, on 1 November 1828 due to their neighbours' increasing suspicions of foul play. However, it would be only Burke and his wife, Helen McDougal, who would face trial, since the Hares were admitted King's Evidence, making them immune from prosecution. The trial was held on 24 December 1828 before the High Court of Justiciary and lasted 24 hours. Both Burke and McDougal were accused of three murders, those of Mary Paterson, James Wilson and Marjory Docherty, but, ironically, due to the lack of bodies, only that of Docherty, the final victim, was upheld. Burke was unanimously found guilty but the libel against McDougal was found not proven. Burke was sentenced to death by hanging and his body to be given over for dissection. He was executed at the head of Libberton's Wynd, Lawnmarket on Wednesday 28 January 1829 before an immense and tumultuous crowd (Anon, 1829a).

The others involved in the crimes, although escaping judicial sentence, were to fare little better than Burke in the end. Although liberated, Hare, his wife Margaret and Helen McDougal were fated to lives of misery and poverty, being hounded from place to place by vengeful mobs and ultimately dying in obscurity (Anon, 1829c). Dr Knox, who was publically assumed culpable for encouraging the murders, was investigated by a medical committee for his involvement. Cleared on all but having a lax system of receiving corpses, Knox still fell from grace as an eminent anatomist and left for London in 1842, where he worked at the Brompton Hospital for Consumption and Diseases of the Chest (Knight, 2007). In direct consequence of the murders of Burke and Hare, the Anatomy Act was enacted in 1832, which implemented new legislation permitting surgeons to receive bodies donated by the public for the advancement of medical science.

KATE BATES

See also: Criminal Corpse, The; Whitechapel Murders of 1888, The

Readings

Anon (1829a) *West Port murders; or an authentic account of the atrocious murders committed by Burke and his associates; containing a full account of all the extraordinary circumstances connected with them. Also, a report of the trial of Burke and McDougal. With a description of the execution of Burke, his confessions, and memoirs of his accomplices, including the proceedings against Hare, &c.* Edinburgh: Thomas Ireland, Junior.

Anon (1829b) *Execution, confession, and a list of all the horrid murders committed by Burke, also the decision of Hare's case.* Edinburgh: Glass. Edinburgh, National Library of Scotland, The Word on the Street Collection: Murder (Shelfmark: Ry.III.a.6(028)). Available at: http://digital.nls.uk/broadsides (accessed 9 July 2012).

Anon (1829c) 'An account of the last moments and execution of William Burke at Edinburgh for the West Port murders', Edinburgh, National Library of Scotland, The Word on the Street Collection: Murder (Shelfmark: L.C.Fol.74(093)). Available at: http://digital.nls.uk/broadsides (accessed 9 July 2012).

Knight, A. (2007) *The Burke and Hare crime archive*. Kew: The National Archives.

C

CAPITAL PUNISHMENT (ENGLAND AND WALES)

Hanging was the normal form of capital punishment in England from the Anglo-Saxon era onwards. It was used irregularly in the late Middle Ages but more frequently by the Tudor period, when it became a means to attempt to consolidate authority and exert ideological control (Sharpe, 1985). However, it was an enduring feature of the English death penalty that it was never applied as extensively as indicated by its enshrinement in statute. Ways of evading execution included, for certain crimes, being literate and, for women, pregnancy. Mercy was also an important constituent of justice, especially for property crimes and condemned deemed to be 'respectable'.

In the early 18th century, transportation to the American colonies offered an alternative to hanging and this was instrumental in bringing about a decline in death sentences. During this century, there was a huge increase in crimes that were punishable with death but the number of executions was much lower than in the 16th and 17th centuries. This paradox can be explained by the specificity of many of the capital crimes, which meant that it was possible to convict people of similar, non-capital offences instead, and also the use of mercy. From the late 18th century and until the mid-19th century, transportation was to Australian penal colonies. Once transportation had ended, imprisonment was the alternative to death (Gatrell, 1996).

A significant aspect of capital punishment was its pedagogic role, which refers to the values and moral lessons that its use conveyed to the audience (Sharpe,

1985). Until the late 19th century, execution was a public spectacle. This was epitomised by the Tyburn procession in London, when condemned prisoners were driven through the streets in an open cart from Newgate Prison to the gallows at Tyburn. The procession was heavily ritualised, stopping at particular places along the way. Huge crowds turned out to see it and the prisoner, wearing their best clothes, displayed variously courage, cheerfulness or defiance. Once on the scaffold, he or she addressed the crowd and communicated messages that ranged from penitence to sedition (McKenzie, 2007). The procession ended in 1783, after which, those condemned were hanged outside Newgate. Nevertheless, execution continued to draw large crowds. The pedagogic role of the scaffold was varied, incorporating the shoring up of authority, the promotion of order and the cementing of community bonds through shared values. It was also open to subversion if the crowd was sympathetic towards the condemned or if the prisoner used the occasion to challenge authority.

The purpose of hanging had evolved by the mid-19th century. It became more closely oriented towards crime control rather than operating as a spectacle of state power (Garland, 2011). Following a campaign supported by prominent figures such as Charles Dickens, public execution ended in 1868, after which, hangings took place behind prison walls. This shift can be understood as a desire to make capital punishment seem more humane and civilised. Arguably, this imperative reflected an increased squeamishness among elites and the declining acceptability of witnessing bodily pain in public more than it did concern for the condemned. The prisoner still faced the gallows but without the presence or inclusion of the wider community (Gatrell, 1996).

Execution as a private ceremony persisted for another century. Privacy did not mean, however, that capital punishment disappeared from the collective imagination. Newspapers took a close interest in capital cases, and the popular press, in particular, interviewed the friends and relatives of high-profile condemned, capturing the 'human' side of the story. The campaign for abolition was reinvigorated in the 1920s, and after the Second World War, political attempts to abolish the death penalty gathered steam. Several cases widely perceived as miscarriages of justice caught the public imagination and illustrated how capital punishment had, in the modern era, become an increasingly anxious and ambivalent practice (Seal, 2014). The final hangings in England took place in August 1964, and the Murder (Abolition of Death Penalty) Act was passed in 1965 and made permanent in 1969. In 1998, the death penalty was fully removed from the books when it was abolished for treason and piracy with violence.

LIZZIE SEAL

See also: 'Bloody Code', The; Mercy; Transportation

Readings

Garland, D. (2011) 'Modes of capital punishment', in D. Garland, R. McGowen and M. Meranze (eds) *America's death penalty: Between past and present*. New York, NY: New York University Press, pp 30–71.

Gatrell, V.A.C. (1996) *The hanging tree: Execution and the English people 1770–1868*. Oxford: Oxford University Press.

McKenzie, A. (2007) *Tyburn's martyrs: Execution in England, 1675–1775*. London: Hambledon Continuum.

Seal, L. (2014) *Capital punishment in twentieth-century Britain: Audience, justice, memory*. London: Routledge.

Sharpe, J.A. (1985) '"Last dying speeches": religion, ideology and public execution in seventeenth-century England', *Past & Present*, 107: 144–67.

CAPITAL PUNISHMENT (IRELAND)

When the Irish Free State came into existence in 1922, there was some debate about whether the death penalty should be abolished given its long association with the colonial power and public ambivalence towards the practice. However, it was retained on the basis that the ultimate sanction was an essential part of the state's repertoire when it came to dealing with the threat of subversion.

The rationale behind retention was that the decision-making calculus of the political offender would be more likely influenced by a considered assessment of costs and benefits than the criminal who acted in passion (and often under the influence of alcohol). Yet, of 35 executions carried out after independence, only six involved politically motivated offenders and these were dealt with by military tribunals or the non-jury Special Criminal Court (Doyle and O'Donnell, 2012).

There were other curiosities. While the Irish government was prepared to allow the executions of Irish Republican Army (IRA) members on home soil, it lobbied the British government to dissuade it from taking similar action in England and Northern Ireland for fear of making Republican martyrs of the men concerned. Finally, the state found it impossible to recruit a hangman and so looked to England whenever there was an Irish murderer's neck to be broken. The Pierrepoints were usually happy to oblige, but on one occasion each, William Willis and Robert Baxter did the (dis)honours (O'Donnell and Doyle, 2014).

There was a clandestine attempt in the 1940s to train an Irishman to fulfil the executioner's role and the pseudonymous Thomas Johnston travelled to Strangeways prison in Manchester to 'learn the ropes' from Albert Pierrepoint.

He assisted at a small number of executions but his nerve failed when called upon to take the lead and he returned to obscurity, unlamented and soon forgotten.

All but one of those executed was male and all but five were hanged. The alternative to hanging was death by shooting, and this was carried out after conviction by a military court, from which there was no right of appeal. Not all of those sentenced to death had been convicted of murder. False imprisonment and shooting at police with intent to resist arrest were capital crimes under the emergency powers legislation that established the military courts. The firing parties were made up of Irish soldiers. The wheels of justice moved rapidly, especially for political offenders, who tended to be charged, convicted and executed within a matter of three to four weeks.

The president, acting on the advice of the government, had the power to commute a sentence of death to one of penal servitude for life. (Prior to 1937, this had been a task for the governor general, who was the crown's official representative in the Free State). Women were the primary beneficiaries of the clemency power, and when their sentences were commuted, they spent an average of three-and-a-half years in prison compared with about seven-and-a-half years for men. Many of these women had been convicted of the murder of their newborn babies before the introduction of the Infanticide Act 1949; under such circumstances, the court had no option but to pass a sentence of death but this was generally accompanied by a recommendation of mercy from both judge and jury.

The last man hanged in Ireland was Michael Manning, a 24-year-old carter from Limerick, who killed an elderly nurse after a drunken sex attack. He went to the gallows on 20 April 1954, leaving his heavily pregnant wife in a state of distress. After 1964, capital punishment was reserved for killers of on-duty police or prison officers, and in 1990, it was abolished in its entirety. A referendum in 2001, which was carried by a large majority, removed all references to capital punishment from the Constitution and prohibited its reintroduction.

The final chapters in Ireland's complicated relationship with capital punishment were written in 2015. In April of that year, the government decided to grant a posthumous pardon to Harry Gleeson, a farm labourer from County Tipperary, who had been wrongly convicted of murder and executed in 1941, and in December, the last man sentenced to death was released from prison, having served 30 years of his commuted life sentence.

IAN O'DONNELL

See also: **Capital Punishment (England and Wales); Capital Punishment (United States of America)**

Readings

Doyle, D.M. and O'Donnell, I. (2012) 'The death penalty in post-Independence Ireland', *Journal of Legal History*, 33(1): 65–91.

O'Donnell, I. and Doyle, D.M. (2014) 'A family affair? English hangmen and a Dublin jail, 1923–54', *New Hibernia Review*, 18(4): 101–18.

CAPITAL PUNISHMENT (UNITED STATES OF AMERICA)

The United States of America (USA) is one of the last Western industrial nations to retain capital punishment. As of January 2016, the death penalty was still available in 31 states and the federal criminal justice system (down from 38 in 1995), while 19 states and the District of Columbia had abolished capital punishment. According to the Death Penalty Information Center, there have been 1,429 executions in the USA since 1976, but there are marked regional differences in terms of the geography of capital punishment and numbers of persons receiving death sentences, of persons currently on death rows and of executions. Over 80% of executions take place in the southern region, which also has the highest murder rate (5.5 per 100,000), and the most active execution states are Texas, Oklahoma, Virginia and Florida. In fact, 45% of all executions since 1976 have been carried out in two states: Texas and Oklahoma. By contrast, there have been four executions in the north-eastern region since 1976. There are nearly 3,000 people on death rows at present, with the largest numbers in California, Florida, Texas and Alabama. Approximately 44% of death row inmates are white, 43% are African-American and 10% are Hispanic/Latino. Native Americans, Pacific Islanders and 'others' account for 3%. There are nearly 60 women currently on death rows, and 16 women have been executed since 1976. The annual number of executions has decreased during the past decade, from a high of 98 in 1999 to 28 in 2015 (Death Penalty Information Center, 2016).

In the absence of long-term imprisonment, the death penalty was the major punishment for serious crimes, gradually limited to murder, rape and arson by the mid-19th century. The establishment of penitentiaries from the Early Republic period provided alternative punishments for lesser degrees of murder for example, and some northern and mid-western states did abolish or restrict capital punishment before the Civil War. There was little prospect of abolition in the slave states in the southern region however (Banner, 2002).

Until the late 19th century, hanging was the main method of execution, though hanging in chains could be used for slaves and Native Americans where death was not punishment enough, and burning was used in the colonial period for rebellious slaves and women who killed their husbands. Hangings were public, communal events that could draw thousands of spectators, but rising elite and middle-class concerns over the decorum of lower-class execution crowds spurred the relocation of executions behind prison walls from the early 19th century, though public hangings were still taking place in the South until the early 20th century. The last public hangings took place in Kentucky in 1936 and Missouri in 1937 (Banner, 2002).

Social and cultural changes and technological advances also led to new 'progressive' methods of execution. The electric chair was first used in New York in August 1890 and was quickly adopted by other states: 19 by the late 1920s, and a total of 25 plus the District of Columbia by mid-century. An early motion picture, *Execution of Czolgosz* (1901), re-enacted in detail the electrocution of the man who assassinated President McKinley. Lethal gas was first used in Nevada in 1924, followed by Colorado and Arizona in 1933; by the mid-1950s, 11 states had built gas chambers (Banner, 2002; Christianson, 2011). Texas was the first state to use lethal injection in 1982, and most retentionist states currently use a three-drug cocktail of a barbiturate, pancuronium bromide and potassium chloride that is injected directly into the veins of the condemned person (Sarat, 2001). Recent problems obtaining these drugs have led some states to experiment, controversially, with other combinations.

Legal and political challenges to the death penalty itself and its discriminatory application were met with limited success until the 1960s and 1970s. Executions actually stopped in 1967 for a 10-year period. In *Furman v Georgia* (1972), the US Supreme Court ruled five to four that capital punishment was administered in a capricious and discriminatory manner and was therefore unconstitutional. States quickly rewrote their death penalty statutes to address the concerns of the court, introducing, for example, bifurcated trials in which the guilt and sentencing phases were separated, and automatic appellate review of capital sentences. In *Gregg v Georgia* (1976), the US Supreme Court approved these revised capital statutes, and executions resumed, first in Utah in 1977. Since reinstatement, the Court has ruled against capital punishment for rape, and banned the execution of mentally ill and mentally disabled persons, and of juveniles, who were under the age of 18 years when their crime was committed (Banner, 2002; Garland, 2010).

Support for capital punishment has decreased in recent decades for different reasons. Since 1973, more than 150 people have been released from death rows because of clear evidence of wrongful conviction. Support also drops when alternatives, such as 'life without the possibility of parole' plus restitution, are available (Death Penalty Information Center, 2016).

VIVIEN MILLER

See also: **Capital Punishment (England and Wales); Capital Punishment (Ireland)**

Readings

Banner, S. (2002) *The death penalty: An American history*. Cambridge, MA: Harvard University Press.

Christianson, S. (2011) *The last gasp: The rise and fall of the American gas chamber*. Berkeley and Los Angeles, CA: University of California Press.

Death Penalty Information Center (2016) 'Facts about the death penalty', August. Available at: http://www.deathpenaltyinfo.org/

Garland, D. (2010) *Peculiar institution: America's death penalty in an age of abolition*. New York, NY: Oxford University Press.

Sarat, A. (2001) *When the state kills: Capital punishment and the American condition*. Princeton, NJ: Princeton University Press.

CHAIN GANGS

Chain gangs were synonymous with the southern region of the US in the early 20th century, and were found in states such as Florida, Georgia and North Carolina, as convict labour was integral to regional economic development, especially the construction of farm-to-market routes, tourist roads and highways. Following the end of convict leasing in 1909, Georgia's 5,000 felony and misdemeanour convicts, over 90% of whom were African-American, were available for road work. Black female misdemeanants helped build thousands of miles of new roads also, while confronting the ever-present threat of physical and sexual violence. There were over 2,400 prisoners working on county chain gangs in North Carolina by the mid-1920s (Lichtenstein, 1996; Miller, 2012; LeFlouria, 2015).

African-Americans arrested on charges of vagrancy, larceny and 'stealing a ride' on a train, as well as more serious offences, provided a steady stream of labourers to build roads for white planters, industrialists and politicians. Convict labour was an integral part of maintaining racial segregation, black subordination and white supremacy during the years of Jim Crow segregation. Many historians view chain gangs as another form of bonded labour in a region defined earlier by racial slavery (LeFlouria, 2015).

Initially, convicts were housed in mobile steel-barred wagons that followed work crews as they completed grading or construction projects. They slept on tiered iron bunks, washed in a bucket and sewage was collected in a zinc pan underneath the wagon. Convicts wore ankle shackles day and night, and were often chained together and to their bunks at night. Food was monotonous and generally of poor quality. Corporal punishment was frequent; those who failed to 'keep the lick', or keep pace, were flogged, as were those deemed to have committed a range of petty offences, as well as attempted escape, work strikes, assaults on other inmates and guards, and riots. Inmates endured other forms of punishment that included iron collars that were chained to the floor, pickshacks or steel bars padlocked to the ankles, or the jack, a form of stocks where inmates were suspended by their wrists and ankles (Burns, 1997 [1932]; Spivak and Davis, 2012).

Road work was arduous and unrelenting. Striped-suited inmates worked 12–15 hours per day, and in the early years, they literally hand-carved roads and bridges with pickaxes, shovels and very little mechanical assistance. Disease, sickness, injury and mortality rates remained high. Famous exposés of the brutality of southern chain gang life and labour include Robert Burns's 1932 book *I am a fugitive from a Georgia chain gang!* and the similarly titled movie (Burns, 1997 [1932]).

By the late 1930s and 1940s, most states had constructed permanent road prisons, with proper bunkhouses and better sanitary and medical provision. Corporal punishment was slowly replaced by the sweatbox, a form of solitary confinement on reduced rations, but many abuses continued. After the Second World War, leg irons, striped suits and chains gradually disappeared, the working day decreased, and greater vocational and educational provision followed. These modifications were introduced in a period when the numbers of white inmates were increasing (Miller, 2012).

The awarding of construction contracts by southern Democrat state legislators and governors ensured that chain-gang labour remained wedded to political patronage, thus prolonging its use. Many of the lower-class white shotgun guards or walking bosses who watched inmates out on the roads or patrolled the road camps, as well as the wardens and commissary men, owed their appointments to patronage and party loyalty (Lichtenstein, 1996). Professionalism was conspicuously absent until later in the century.

Convict road labour continued into the 1960s and early 1970s in states like Florida, which utilised 'honor squads' of low-risk prisoners for road and highway maintenance into the early 21st century. Several states, including Alabama, Florida and Arizona, revived chain gangs in the 1990s to demonstrate their 'get tough' crime policies as inmate numbers began to rise dramatically, and as the percentage of non-white inmates also began to rise again. As illustrated in Xackery Irving's (1999) documentary *American chain gang*, male inmates wearing ankle shackles and often clad in conspicuous uniforms were set to work clearing roads and highways of litter and weeds, as well as breaking rocks.

VIVIEN MILLER

See also: **Corporal Punishment; Indentured Labour; Slavery in the Americas**

Readings

Burns, R. (1997 [1932]) *I am a fugitive from a Georgia chain gang!* Athens, GA: University of Georgia Press.

LeFlouria, T. (2015) *Chained in silence: Black women and convict labor in the New South.* Chapel Hill, NC: University of North Carolina Press.

Lichtenstein, A. (1996) *Twice the work of free labor: The political economy of convict labor in the New South.* New York, NY: Verso.

Miller, V. (2012) *Hard labor and hard time: Florida's 'sunshine prison' and chain gangs.* Gainesville, FL: University Press of Florida.

Spivak, J. and Davis, D. (2012) *Hard times on a Southern chain gang: Originally published as the novel Georgia nigger (1932).* Columbia, SC: University of South Carolina Press.

COERCIVE CONFINEMENT

'Coercive confinement' is a phrase coined by Eoin O'Sullivan and Ian O'Donnell (2007) to capture the range of institutions in which men, women and children can be involuntarily detained. Using the Republic of Ireland as a case study, O'Sullivan and O'Donnell show how any attempt to use the rate of imprisonment as a proxy for a country's level of punitiveness is fraught with difficulty.

In 1958, there were fewer than 400 prisoners in Ireland, suggesting a harmonious society that was untroubled by serious crime. However, more than 31,000 citizens were coercively confined in psychiatric hospitals, reformatory and industrial schools, mother and baby homes, and Magdalen asylums. The conditions in these institutions were austere, and while some of them were ostensibly directed at the welfare of their inhabitants, they were experienced as degrading, stigmatising and punitive places. Those incarcerated in non-criminal justice institutions, especially unmarried mothers and the mentally ill, tended to spend longer in detention than prisoners (for a range of contemporaneous inmate accounts, see O'Sullivan and O'Donnell, 2012).

The rate of coercive confinement in Ireland during the middle of the 20th century was over 1,000 per 100,000 population. This is significantly higher than the rate of imprisonment in the US in the early 21st century. While the USA's situation has generated considerable interest internationally among scholars, legislators and policymakers, the trend in Ireland is little known. The fact that more than 1% of the country's population was coercively confined during the 1950s is all the more remarkable when one considers that this was a time of huge outward migration.

O'Sullivan and O'Donnell (2007, 2012) suggest that there is much to be gained from rethinking contemporary arrangements in light of a broader understanding of coercive confinement. To make sense of the present, they argue, it is necessary to understand the past. Adopting a wider frame of reference shows that the rising level of imprisonment in the closing decades of the 20th century does not unambiguously suggest a punitive turn, and must be viewed against a background of deinstitutionalisation – particularly of women and children – that has gone largely unremarked.

The level of coercive confinement was stable during the first four decades of independence (the Irish Free State was established in 1922). Why did it remain so high for so long? The explanation, according to O'Sullivan and O'Donnell (2007, 2012), lies in the new state's commitment to a form of rural life that valorised the family farm as the basic unit of agricultural production and social organisation.

The psychiatric hospital provided not only a source of employment to the rural dweller for whom the land was insufficient to yield a living, but also functioned as a repository for supernumerary bachelors and spinsters. The institutions that held mothers who gave birth out of wedlock and arranged the adoption of their children, sometimes by couples on the other side of the Atlantic, meant that the system of inheritance could be maintained. The Roman Catholic Church offered employment opportunities to younger siblings who were unlikely to inherit and unable, or unwilling, to emigrate. This ensured a plentiful supply of staff for many of the institutions that were integral to the apparatus of social control.

The decline in rural Ireland drove the decline in coercive confinement. Economic development created employment opportunities off the land. The religious life became less attractive and vocations declined. Modern treatments were introduced for the mentally ill. The stigma associated with 'illegitimacy' faded and the state introduced allowances that enabled unmarried mothers to survive financially.

Reformatory and industrial schools, or their functional equivalents, were common across Europe, Australia and the US. So, too, were Magdalen asylums and varieties of mother and baby home. The involuntary detention of the mentally ill was commonplace. Given the international reach of these institutional forms, the rubric offered by O'Sullivan and O'Donnell (2007, 2012) might prove useful to researchers outside Ireland. At the very least, it highlights the limitations of any analysis of penal change that limits itself to short-term trends and equates punitiveness with imprisonment.

There is a general acknowledgement – more honoured in the breach than the observance – that to make sense of changing trajectories of social control requires the adoption of a framework of analysis that is historically informed, interdisciplinary and not exclusively focused on the criminal justice system. While the texture of coercive confinement will no doubt vary according to the context in which it is observed, it would be fruitful to apply this concept to other jurisdictions with a view to testing its robustness.

IAN O'DONNELL

See also: **Industrial Schools; Inebriate Institutions; Reformatory Schools; Semi-penal Institutions for Women**

Readings

O'Sullivan, E. and O'Donnell, I. (2007) 'Coercive confinement in Ireland: the waning of a culture of control', *Punishment and Society*, 9(1): 27–48.
O'Sullivan, E. and O'Donnell, I. (2012) *Coercive confinement in Ireland: Patients, prisoners and penitents*. Manchester: Manchester University Press.

CONTAGIOUS DISEASES ACTS, THE

The Contagious Diseases Acts of 1864, 1866 and 1869 concerned the sanitary inspection of prostitute women in a bid to control the spread of venereal disease. All three Acts constructed prostitution not so much as a criminal problem, but as a sexual health problem, associating it with sexually transmitted disease and the risk of infecting healthy male members of society. While it could be argued that the Contagious Diseases Acts were protective Acts designed to secure a reduced absence of women from certain areas of work, they unquestionably constituted the most important vehicles of legislation aimed at women in the 19th century. It was thought that if individual prostitutes were removed and erased from society, then men, or what philanthropists classed as the 'sons of society', would be 'saved from moral danger' (Bartley, 2000, p 31). The administration of the three Acts was not only extraordinarily complex, but reflected an endorsed view that the social underclass was simultaneously degraded and powerless and potentially threatening to the social order (Walkowitz, 1980).

Prostitutes were thus perceived to be symbolic offenders by the middle and upper classes (Faith, 1987), and, according to Heyl (1979, cited in Faith, 1987, p 182), prostitution was recognised as 'an extreme case of sex stratification', whereby female sexuality was commodified and subsequently contributed to the women's devaluation and objectification. Women suspected of prostitution were faced with a spectrum of penalties – none of which were within their power to decide. Rather, it depended upon local practices and a large degree of police and magistrate discretion. The Contagious Diseases Acts gave special police the authority to identify so-called 'common prostitutes' and subject them to an enforced internal examination every fortnight. Women could then be contained within special lock hospitals for up to three months in order to cure their sexually transmitted disease(s) (Bartley, 2000). A diseased illustration of the prostitute had become prevalent due to advocates of the Contagious Diseases Acts. It is also argued that medical rhetoric entrenched in the Contagious Diseases legislation made visible the perceived threat of the prostitute 'by focusing on her sexuality and isolating it as unnatural and deviant' (Mort, 1987, p 77). According to Mort (1987, p 81), medical isolation of female prostitutes in 1860s' England:

> Went hand-in-hand with a range of related social demarcations. These included the respectable/unrespectable divisions made by many philanthropic organisations, distinctions drawn by the newly founded Charity Organisation Society between the deserving and undeserving poor and the healthy/diseased oppositions employed by medical officers of health to identify the carriers of contagion.

The Contagious Diseases Acts embodied a new 'science of sexuality' that was ultimately responsible for identifying sex as a public issue, and that strictly differentiated male from female sexuality (Walkowitz, 1980, p 4). They scrutinised 'extramarital sexuality as the primary area of dangerous sexual activity' and '"incorporated" perversions in individuals who, like the homosexual, were ... accorded an exclusive and distinct sexual identity' (Walkowitz, 1980, p 4):

> Through the control of sexuality, the acts reinforced existing patterns of class and gender domination. They illustrate the obsessive preoccupation with and codification of, sex, that according to Michel Foucault, distinguished Victorian sexuality from the official sexual code of earlier epochs. The modern debate over sex, Foucault argues, was a strategy for exercising power in society. By ferreting out new areas of illicit sexual activity, a new 'technology of power' and 'science of sexuality' were created that facilitated control of an ever-widening circle of human activity. (Walkowitz, 1980, p 4)

Nonetheless, fierce opposition to the Contagious Diseases Acts mounted, with the middle class, Nonconformists, feminists and radical workingmen resisting the acts as 'immoral and unconstitutional' legislation, and calling for their repeal (Walkowitz, 1980, p 4). Organisations such as the National Anti-Contagious Diseases Acts Association and the Ladies National Association also opposed the Acts on the basis that they legalised prostitution. Nevertheless, the highly visible and controversial role assumed by women in these contests revived the debate over women's place in public life, while the Acts and corresponding campaigns to have them repealed placed sex position and sexual identity at the centre of political debate.

KIRSTY GREENWOOD

See also: **Macmillan and Wolfenden Committees, The; Prostitution (19th century); Prostitution (early 20th century)**

Readings
Bartley, P. (2000) *Prostitution: Prevention and reform in England, 1860–1914.* London: Routledge.
Faith, K. (1987) 'Women and the state: changing models of social control', in J. Lowman, R. J. Menzies, and T.S. Palys (eds) *Transcarceration: Essays in the sociology of social control.* Aldershot: Gower, pp 170–87.
Mort, F. (1987) *Dangerous sexualities.* London: Routledge.
Walkowitz, J.R. (1980) *Prostitution and Victorian society: Women, class and the state.* Cambridge: Cambridge University Press.

CONVICT PRISONS

The convict prison system was established from the 1850s, and all the prisons supporting the system that were built or adapted were located in London and the south-east of England. The idea and rationale behind the system was that prisoners would be sentenced to long periods of imprisonment, a sentence known as 'penal servitude'. Penal servitude replaced the sentence of transportation, largely due to the cessation of the transportation of convicts to Australia, and, subsequently, long periods of imprisonment replaced years of banishment overseas (Johnston, 2015). The first Penal Servitude Act 1853 replaced, for example, a sentence of seven years' transportation with one of four to six years' penal servitude. The convict prison system was operated and administered by the government and the system was originally designed by Joshua Jebb, then the Surveyor General and, later, first Chairman of Directors of Convict Prisons. In the early years of the establishment of the system, some offenders were still sent overseas but this ended in 1868, and, subsequently, all offenders (except those sentenced to death) were housed in England in a convict prison (Johnston, 2015).

The convict prisons were either newly built or existing prisons adapted for use. For example, both Millbank and Pentonville prisons were already government-run prisons that had been constructed in earlier decades of the 19th century to hold prisoners before they were transported overseas, and they were adapted to hold convicts under the first stage of penal servitude, separate confinement. Millbank held men and women, Pentonville held only male offenders, and accommodation for women was also provided by Brixton prison (Zedner, 1991; Johnston, 2015). After Millbank was closed in 1886, Wormwood Scrubs prison was used instead. The government also rented cells in other parts of England, for example, at Wakefield and at Perth in Scotland, so convicts could undergo separate confinement at these prisons before being moved down to the south of England to a public works prison.

The second stage of penal servitude was the public works, and these establishments needed further construction to enable convicts to undertake the longest part of the sentence. Public works meant that convicts would be working for the benefit of the public; as such, the prisons needed to be able to facilitate long hours of hard labour (Priestley, 1999; Johnston, 2015). The first purpose-built convict prison was Portland, which opened in 1848, Dartmoor was bought into use in 1850 and Portsmouth opened in 1852. Between 1856 and 1884, a further four public works prisons were newly constructed at Chatham, Chattenden, Fulham (women only) and Borstal (Brodie et al, 2002). Convicts on public works were also held at Woking, Dover, Lewes, Maidstone and Parkhurst during the 19th and into the 20th century. By the end of the 19th century, the female convict population had decreased significantly, and in the 1890s, Aylesbury prison was used to house female convicts; during the 1920s and 1930s, they were also sent to Liverpool prison.

In the interwar years, the total daily average convict prison population was around 1,500 prisoners, women making up around 50 to 60 of this number. The system, therefore, was smaller than the mid- to late 19th-century operation but also more costly. One of the most significant events of this period was a riot at Dartmoor convict prison in 1932, during which 150 prisoners took control of the prison, started fires and caused serious damage to the buildings (Brown, 2013). The convict system was finally dismantled after the Second World War, officially by the Criminal Justice Act 1948, which abolished the sentence of penal servitude. The convict prison population had declined significantly before the outbreak of the war, and despite an increase in the prison population during the war, the proposals that had been put forward over a decade before in the form of the Criminal Justice Bill 1938 were implemented.

HELEN JOHNSTON

See also: **Mark System, The; Penal Servitude; Prison Riots; Transportation**

Readings

Brodie, A., Croom, J. and Davies, J.O. (2002) *English prisons: An architectural history*. Swindon: English Heritage.

Brown, A. (2013) *Inter-war penal policy and crime in England: The Dartmoor convict prison riot, 1932*. Basingstoke: Palgrave Macmillan.

Johnston, H. (2015) *Crime in England, 1815–1880*. Abingdon: Routledge.

Priestley, P. (1999) *Victorian prison lives: English prison biography, 1830–1914*. London: Pimlico.

Zedner, L. (1991) *Women, crime and custody in Victorian England*. Oxford: Oxford University Press.

CORPORAL PUNISHMENT

Corporal punishment can be described as the enactment of physical punishment or sanction amounting to the chastisement of a person by another. In contemporary times, physical punishments against children and young adults by parents and officials within environments such as the home, school and custodial settings have been a subject of controversy for many years (Elliman and Lynch, 2000). The sanctioning of the use of corporal punishment has attracted challenge and opposition, not least on the basis of the infringement of the rights and required protections of a child.

The use of instruments of corporal punishment, such as the belt, cane and tawse, as well as smacking, was a common feature of state and independent schooling in the UK through the 20th century. Justifications for the beating of a child in school or the home have been built up around themes of deterrence, retributive punishments for wrongdoing and a general method of enforcing discipline and gaining control. The infliction of pain and suffering on a child justified on the grounds of it being part of an educative process has had a long tradition within compulsory education and discipline in the home.

The challenge to the legitimacy of corporal punishment has often cited international treaties and declarations as a basis for urgent reform of national legislation (Freeman, 2010). The 1989 United Nations Declaration on the Rights of the Child clearly stipulates the necessity for, and responsibilities of, states and governments to create and maintain various protections for children. These protections should be in place to mitigate against the actuality of violence and harm, maltreatment, neglect, and ill-treatment; not legislating against corporal punishment wagers a risk to adherence to international treaties. Opposition to the use of physical violence by parents or officials in authority as a way to chastise a child has appeared at various times during the 20th century. These challenges to 'justifiable' assaults have played out in different reports, revisions to legislation and legal cases, nationally and in the European Court of Human Rights.

The ability for teachers to use corporal punishment in state schools in the UK was repealed in the 1980s and for all schools (ie private schools) in the 1990s. In contrast, countries such as France had outlawed corporal punishment in education settings from the early part of the 20th century after the First World War. The origins of more public voices of concern can be traced back to the publication of the Plowden Report in 1967, where the author asked for the banning of corporal punishment in primary schools (see Trowler, 2003). With a reduced level of public and professional tolerance towards corporal punishment gaining momentum through the remainder of the century, any justification for sanctioned assaults against a child by a teacher became more and more precarious.

While educational settings have had any sanction on the use of 'corrective' physical punishments curtailed, corporal punishment by a parent illustrates some difference. Charges of wounding, cruelty to a child, causing grievous bodily harm and assault occasioning actual bodily harm can no longer be met with a defence of reasonable chastisement (see the Children Act 2004). However, to date, in Britain, what has remained is the ability of a parent to stage a defence of reasonable chastisement for common assault.

Corporal punishment has not solely been levied against children by adults. Foucault (1977) comments that much of the focus of corporal punishment in earlier industrialising nations focused on the physical demarcation of the adult as well as child human body. For example, branding, whipping and flogging were painful but not fatal punishments. Michel Foucault (1977) illustrates the devastating execution of Damiens in 1757 (after an attempt to assassinate the King of France) as a transported punishment of unbearable sensations. For example, Damiens was horse-drawn and quartered by 'carts', and 'steel pincers' were used on Damiens bodily limbs – all used at the hands of the state. This was a symbolic spectacle to a watching public audience not to attempt any crime against its authority. Foucault compares and contrasts this with a transition of corporal punishment of 'the body', with different devices of pain, to self-surveillance of 'the mind' through the numbing timetabling activities of the rise of imprisonment as a form of punishment. Yet, it could be suggested that Foucault (1977) underestimated the use of corporal punishment through the use of the birch, the cane, the paddle and the strap, which have seen common practice in contemporary prison establishments (eg for internal prison offences) and the military (eg following Court Martial).

This is not to suggest that corporal punishment has declined in its comparative context. For example, judicial-ordered corporal punishment such as flogging, whipping and caning remain in use in some legal territories (eg Saudi Arabia), while in others, such as England and Wales, judicial corporal punishment declined to its absence in the mid-20th century. In the UK, legislating against, and the curtailing of, corporal punishment can largely be attributed to improved recognition of the human rights of children and adults, a decline in the delivery of punishments being a public spectacle, greater insights into and awareness of the permanent harm and hardship that physical punishments exert, and the lack of objective measurement of any type of physical punishment on the grounds of proportionality.

Punishments directed on the body continue to attract critical opposition, be they enacted on the orders of the courts or delivered by a parent, such as in the case of smacking a child. Unevenness in support for its abolition exists (eg parental chastisement defences are retained), suggesting that some may believe that physical punishments may be justifiable in some circumstances. Moreover, while in some jurisdictions, such as the UK, corporal punishment enacted by officials towards adults and children in the care of the state has been banned, onlookers must remain attuned to the fact that corporal punishments may well remain intact. These may present as more discreet, though they remain reasoned as 'sanctionable' and 'justifiable'. Examples such as restraint techniques (including those where pain compliance techniques are incorporated) deployed against children and adults in the care and custody of the state are perhaps illustrative of the continuation of our reliance on disciplining and controlling not through opportunities for learning, but through the administration of force and the infliction of pain and humiliation.

PAUL TAYLOR and JASON POWELL

See also: **Informal Justice**

Readings

Elliman, D. and Lynch, M.A. (2000) 'The physical punishment of children', *Archives of Disease in Childhood*, 83(3): 196–8.

Foucault, M. (1977) *Discipline and punish*. London: Tavistock.

Freeman, M.D. (2010) 'Upholding the dignity and best interests of children: international law and the corporal punishment of children', *Law and Contemporary Problems*, 73(2): 211–51.

Trowler, P. (2003) *Education policy*. London: Routledge.

CRIME FICTION

Crime fiction has a long history. From myth and fairy tale, through to popular literature and modern television drama, society has been fascinated by stories of murder and mayhem, detection and retribution. Indeed, every civilisation since time began has created its own form of crime fiction and this legacy means that this genre of popular culture is truly a deeply rooted criminological and historical phenomenon. Academics from various disciplines have delved into the mystery of its enduring appeal and conflicting theories have emerged. The most simplistic account is that crime fiction is merely a form of cheap, sensational entertainment, which offers its audience the chance to vicariously enjoy titillating violence and voyeuristic villainy (Altick, 1972). This somewhat superficial explanation assumes an inherently debased audience and in no way accounts for crime fiction's widespread popularity and influence. In contrast, others have argued that crime fiction is hegemonic in nature, meaning that beneath the trappings of entertainment lies a monitory message promoting civilising middle-class values and thus producing a covert disciplinary effect on its mass public (Worthington, 2005). This theory is also unsatisfactory since it assumes a level of audience passivity that is not only tenuous, but demeaning.

The majority of studies into the form and function of crime fiction proffer a more insightful interpretation, highlighting the fact that these tales of dramatic deviancy contain a symbolic structure and substance of great social and cultural significance. This is primarily down to the fact that research has shown that various forms of crime fiction have all emerged during periods of immense social strain and historical transformation, and that this specific form of popular culture often reflects the changing cultural attitudes and psychosocial needs of the populace (Cawelti, 1976). For example, the emergence and rise in popularity of classic detective fiction at the end of the 19th century coincided with deep and widespread anxiety regarding the ever-expanding 'society of strangers' that characterised the late-Victorian period. Fictional detectives, such as Conan Doyle's Sherlock Holmes, were to represent the new scientific ideal of policing and began to reassure the public that although society was changing and becoming more complex, so, too, were the legal and social frameworks of control, which were increasingly more than a match for the most cunning of criminals (Moretti, 1988).

In beginning to understand the social, cultural and historical contexts of crime fiction, its forms and features soon take on greater significance. Criminals are social outcasts who violate codes of basic human decency, rejecting moral and behavioural norms, and must therefore be condemned and purged for the safety and sanctity of society. Crime is a symbol of moral disorder and social instability, and represents an insecure public's preoccupation with loss of control in a rapidly changing world (Knight, 1980; Mandel, 1984). Crime fiction is therefore able to examine a society under strain, where mutual trust is lost and personal safety can no longer be guaranteed. The fact that crime fiction almost universally features the crime of murder is also no great feat of authorial choice or chance. The act of murder is the ultimate emblem of depraved inhumanity, and even in a world beyond mortal control, there is general agreement that murder, especially of a young and innocent victim, is reprehensible and to be avenged. Indeed, the repeated use of murder and violence as a narrative framing device in crime fiction is the key to its continuing success and allure, for the more people are shocked and horrified by senseless acts of brutality, the more they respond emotionally and grow ever-more entwined with the playing out of poetic justice (Bates, forthcoming).

Crime fiction, then, although undeniably formulaic and predictable in structure, contains messages of deep meaning for its audience and performs a much-needed social and moral function similar to ancient myths, fables and fairy tales. Drawing upon archetypal figures and forms, crime fiction provides exemplary tales of good versus evil and disorder being brought back into order. It provides comfort and reassurance that, despite living in a world of danger and conflict, heroes will prevail and villains will fall. Crime fiction is thus compellingly cathartic, allowing the dispelling of anxieties and fears, and confirming to the audience that they are not alone. In imaginatively facing the worst of crimes, the audience also experience the best that humanity can offer: sympathy and solidarity with those who suffer and a restored faith in the strength and unity of a civilised and just world.

KATE BATES

See also: **Crime Pamphlets; Newspapers and Crime; Sherlock Holmes**

Readings

Altick, R.D. (1972) *Victorian studies in scarlet: Murders and manners in the age of Victoria.* London: J.M. Dent & Sons.

Bates, K. (forthcoming) *Moralities of the masses: Crime, broadsides and social change.* Basingstoke: Palgrave Macmillan.

Cawelti, J.G. (1976) *Adventure, mystery and romance: Formula stories as art and popular culture.* London: University of Chicago Press.

Knight, S. (1980) *Form and ideology in crime fiction.* London: Macmillan Press.

Mandel, E. (1984) *Delightful murder: A social history of the crime story.* London: Pluto Press.

Moretti, F. (1988) 'Clues', in F. Moretti (ed) *Signs taken for wonders* (rev edn) (trans S. Fischer, D. Forgacs and D. Miller). London: Verso, pp 130–56.

Worthington, H. (2005) *The rise of the detective in early nineteenth-century popular fiction.* Basingstoke: Palgrave Macmillan.

CRIME HERITAGE

Heritage has been defined as 'that part of the past which we select in the present for contemporary purposes' (Graham et al, 2000, p 2) and so refers to the conservation, interpretation and consumption of historical sites and objects. Interest in heritage as an economic and cultural phenomenon developed throughout the 18th and 19th centuries, with an initial focus on preserving great and beautiful monuments. Over time, ideas of heritage broadened to incorporate the darker aspects of the past, though objects from executions and murder scenes were often offered for sale in the 19th century and the sites of crimes, trials and punishment became magnets for visitors. The formal preservation and presentation of objects and sites relating to historical crimes, however, did not really emerge until the 20th century, when there was a growing enthusiasm for the official conservation of crime heritage and the development of museums and other tourist attractions associated with criminality.

Crime heritage exists in a diverse range of forms and the purposes of these vary from sensationalist entertainment to education and even memorialisation. Some examples focus on particular places, such as former court houses, prisons or police stations, all three of which are combined in the Galleries of Justice museum at Nottingham. Another form of crime heritage tied to place involves sites where crimes or atrocities have been committed, for example, the Choeung Ek Genocidal Centre in Cambodia or the 9/11 Memorial Park in New York. The focus in these sites tends to be education and commemoration but there are often contested meanings associated with such events, making interpretation particularly complex. Debates about the limits of what should be preserved and the purposes of preservation are particularly acute in relation to this kind of heritage. At the opposite end of the spectrum lie tourist attractions, which have a primary focus on entertainment, such as the London and York Dungeons or the Chamber of Horrors at Madame Tussaud's wax museum. The emphasis here is on fun through a focus on macabre elements of notable crimes and past punishments in ways that inspire excitement and fear, raising a number of ethical issues about the presentation of past sufferings. Falling between these two extremes are the more traditional crime museums that exhibit collections of artefacts relating to particular, often infamous, crimes and combine both education and entertainment. The most famous of these in the UK is Scotland Yard's Crime Museum but many other police forces have their own historic collections and some also operate museums.

Heritage plays a role in generating and perpetuating particular historical interpretations and meanings, making it not only an economic asset, but also a cultural and political resource. The cultural role of heritage can conflict with its function as an economic commodity, and, as such, tension is inevitably created.

Multiple interpretations can be attributed to the past and the absence of a definite agreement about the meaning of heritage generates dissonance (Graham et al, 2000). This is particularly relevant for crime heritage that involves dissonance in terms of the presentation of the opposing voices of multiple groups (victims and perpetrators) and also requires the communication of troubling and painful narratives. Discussions of 'difficult' heritage highlight the importance of exploring such dissonances and reflecting on the ethical issues involved in preserving and consuming objects associated with pain, harm and shame (Logan and Reeves, 2009). Crime heritage has also been considered to represent an example of dark tourism as it involves the use of death or distress as a tourist experience, and there is a growing literature exploring ways of understanding both the motivations of tourists attending such attractions and the interpretation offered at these sites (Sharpley and Stone, 2009). Godfrey (2014) provides a good recent discussion of the role that historians can play in contributing to this process of interpretation in relation to crime and punishment.

MARYSE TENNANT

See also: **Prison Tourism**

Readings

Godfrey, B. (2014) *Crime in England, 1880–1945*. London: Routledge.

Graham, B., Ashworth, G.A. and Tunbridge, J.E. (2000) *A geography of heritage: Power, culture and economy*. London: Arnold.

Logan, W. and Reeves, K. (2009) *Places of pain and shame: Dealing with 'difficult heritage'*. London: Routledge.

Sharpley, R. and Stone, P.R. (eds) (2009) *The darker side of travel: The theory and practice of dark tourism*. Bristol: Channel View.

CRIME PAMPHLETS

Crime pamphlets constitute an important crime genre. These short, cheap texts emerged in the 1570s and 1580s, and were primarily written by clergymen, in particular, the Ordinaries of Newgate. They were aimed at a popular audience, though members of the higher social ranks also consumed them. The accounts largely featured criminals who were awaiting or had been executed, and so they offered completed narratives. However, they were a stylised genre that presented a stereotypical picture of offenders and offences and do not provide an accurate portrayal of crime during the period.

The pamphlets featured a narrow range of offending, of which murder was most prominent. Peter Lake and James Sharpe have revealed that the pamphlets concentrated on the most spectacular and bloody of crimes, aiming to both shock and titillate with their gratuitous violence. The killings tended to be premeditated homicides, occurring in the home, and most commonly involved the killing of spouses. Lake (1994, pp 263–4) argues that 'perhaps the most common source of disorder, violence and murder was a human, and in particular female, sexuality that had escaped from patriarchal control and was now free to wreak havoc on the social order'. Frances Dolan (1994) suggests that these narratives reveal a fear of the subversive threat of 'familiars' within the household rather than strangers outside of it.

Violent theft was another popular subject. These tales almost always featured highwaymen and were prey to overt fictionalisation as the highwayman became an increasingly romanticised figure of popular myth. Tales of these 'gentlemen of the road' glamorised the lives of these thieves. Sometimes, they were even cast as heroes as they represented, in Peter Linebaugh's (1993, p 189) words, 'personal independence and power', a mentality that accorded with middle-class aspirations of individualism, consumption and self-improvement (Faller, 1967, p 160). Christopher Hibbert (1967, p 119) claims that the highwayman was an 'emblematic figure of liberty and pleasure, rather than … a selfish criminal'. Similarly, their actions might be interpreted as a form of social protest, upholding a type of social justice.

The narratives of highwaymen were, however, largely fictitious. They copied the literary style of the jest-book and picaresque genres. Their narrative content and structure was more varied and loosely defined than those featuring homicide. The thief's life was portrayed as a series of unconnected episodes that proceeded without apparent logic and the tone was often frivolous in their attitude towards the criminal. According to Lincoln Faller, the offender was depersonalised to the extent that he was only a name and the reader was never shown the real man behind the tale. The reasons for this were: to create a vicarious engagement by allowing the reader to place his/her own emotions onto the actions of the offender; to minimise the fear of violent theft by making the thieves appear less threatening; and to reduce societal guilt over the criminal's execution by ensuring the thief was indistinct so that the readers could not remember him.

It has been argued that the pamphlets, especially those featuring murder, expressed overarching Protestant themes (Lake, 1994). The first concerned the connection between crime and sin. The pamphlets provided a biography of the felon from his early life to the gallows, and showed that criminality was different to ordinary moral lapses (such as drinking or missing church) only in scale. The devil, who tempts people to sin, was shown to operate through chains of offending that got progressively worse. It was through cumulative sin that the criminal was led to commit the most serious offences. Such an aetiology sought to regulate the readers' behaviour by encouraging them to identify with the notion of a slippery slope by which they might be led from commonplace sins to outright criminality. It was also a somewhat comforting message because early sins could be nipped in the bud before they developed into something more serious. This was supported by the theme of inevitable retribution: that through divine providence, all crimes would be revealed and the felon would be punished. Therefore, the pamphlets commonly related the (sometimes miraculous) ways in which the felons were brought to justice. Increasingly, the emphasis on providence was replaced with a growing confidence in empirical detection. However, the message was the same: by one means or another, the criminal would be held to account and the chaotic world created by his/her crime would be righted.

The pamphlets performed several functions. They were entertaining but they were also (ostensibly) didactic. Featuring felons who had been arrested and were awaiting or had just been executed, the biography, execution and last dying speech of the condemned provided a warning to the readers of the consequences of sin. In this way, the pamphlets performed a sort of social control in spreading ideas of crime and punishment, though it is unclear just how effective such narratives were.

ESTHER SNELL

See also: **Crime Fiction**

Readings
Dolan, F.A. (1994) *Dangerous familiars: Representations of domestic crime in England 1550–1700*. New York, NY: Cornell University Press.

Faller, L.B. (1967) 'The myth of captain James Hind: a type of primitive fictions before Defoe', *Bulletin of the New York Public Library*, 79: 139–66.

Hibbert, C. (1967) *Highwaymen*. New York, NY: Weidenfeld and Nicolson.

Lake, P. (1994) 'Deeds against nature: cheap print, Protestantism and murder in early seventeenth century England', in K. Sharpe and P. Lake (eds) *Culture and politics in early Stuart England*. London: Macmillan, pp 257–83.

Linebaugh, P. (1993) *The London hanged: Crime and civil society in the eighteenth century*. London and New York, NY: Cambridge University Press.

Sharpe, J.A. (1981) 'Domestic homicide in early modern England', *The Historical Journal*, 24(1): 29–48.

CRIMINAL CLASS, THE

While views and understandings of crime and criminals have changed over time, the concept of the 'criminal class' has long been a convenient way of shifting the blame of crime onto an alien group. In addition to the small number of individuals who were believed to subsist on criminal earnings, the term 'criminal class' implies a homogeneous, separate group, the existence of which historians have debated. Nevertheless, along with growing populations, fears over urbanisation and the anonymity it provided, the increasing visibility of crime brought by criminal statistics, and sensationalist newspaper reporting, the idea of a criminal class rose to become a national issue in the 19th century. Judicial authorities and the general public believed criminals to be a threatening breed apart, fuelling contemporary debate (Emsley, 2010).

With the close of the 18th century and the increasing visibility of crime, there was an increasing concern with the causes of crime. Links were made between social conditions and criminal behaviour. This change was piecemeal, and so crime was accounted for in different ways throughout the 19th century, from some radicals and liberals arguing that poverty caused crime, to those with the moralistic understanding of criminality viewing offending as a conscious, rational decision of individual weakness (Emsley, 2010). Yet, it was these social moralists who drove the notion of a race apart and consequently cemented the idea of a criminal class. For example, journalist Henry Mayhew asserted an 'explicit anti-moralistic sociological perspective on poverty' through stressing environmentalism (cited in Wiener, 1990, pp 31–3). While Mayhew stamped social categories onto individual narratives, Booth (a public health investigator) relied on statistical data to identify generalisations for social administration (Wiener, 1990), all culminating in a perceived threat to the Victorian ideal of social order.

Whig historians, including Tobias, uncritically followed this contemporary rhetoric of the criminal class as a separate group who could be 'distinguished by their clothing and habits and lived wholly or largely on the proceeds of crime' (Tobias, 1967, p 14). Since the 1970s, however, the prevailing 19th-century discourse of the criminal class has been questioned. Along with the move to regional investigation came a more detailed and critical understanding of criminals and crime through a bottom-up exploration of a wider range of sources (see Phillips, 1977; Conley, 1991). Consequently, many historians dismissed the existence of a criminal class. Phillips (1977) found in the Black Country, for example, that only 10% of crimes committed were by 'professional criminals'. Most had normal jobs, stealing only opportunistically or to supplement income (Conley, 1991). No longer over-relying on contemporary middle- and upper-class descriptions, historians revised the uncritical approach and dismissed the concept of the criminal class – but has the historiography gone too far?

The arguments of the revisionists who dismissed the idea of a criminal class in the 1970s have now begun to be questioned. While acknowledging the initial contemporary narrative over-reliance of earlier historians, this second wave of revisionists are putting forward a more nuanced view of crime and criminals, one that allows for a variety of causes, including opportunity, need, desperation, peer pressure, excitement and an occupational strategy. Generally, offenders did not make an active decision to become criminals and most did not spend all their lives committing crimes. However, the fact that few offenders would have described themselves as 'professional' criminals does not necessarily mean that no form of criminal organisation existed. Criminal networks existed in many forms, for example, in the form of fences. Even if this contact was minimal, opportunistic and informal, it does not follow that crime was never committed in response to external demand – a market of goods and offender agency cannot be ignored. Indeed, through the study of juveniles, Heather Shore (1999) was able to demonstrate their ad hoc involvement in such networks. Moreover, through investigating the lives of persistent offenders in Crewe, Godfrey, Cox and Farrall (2007) found that there *was* an interrelationship between offenders. What they termed a 'criminal fraternity' involved offending with and against one another. Yet, ultimately, there were relatively few hardened recidivists; instead, the criminal class perceived by middle- and upper-class society was, in fact, 'a continuing varying cohort of individuals' (Godfrey et al, 2007, pp 72–3).

EMMA DEBORAH WATKINS

See also: **Criminal Statistics; Organised Crime; Underworld, The Criminal**

Readings

Conley, C.A. (1991) *The unwritten law: Criminal justice in Kent.* New York, NY: Oxford University Press.

Emsley, C. (2010) *Crime and society in England, 1750–1900* (4th edn). Harlow: Pearson Longman.

Godfrey, B., Cox, D. and Farrall, S. (2007) *Criminal lives: Family, employment and offending.* Oxford: Oxford University Press.

Phillips, D. (1977) *Crime and authority in Victorian England: The Black Country, 1835–1860.* London: Croom Helm.

Shore, H. (1999) 'Cross coves, buzzers and general sorts of prigs – juvenile crime and the "underworld" in the early nineteenth century', *British Journal of Criminology,* 39(1): 10–24.

Tobias, J.J. (1967) *Crime and industrial society in the nineteenth century.* London: Batsford.

Wiener, M.J. (1990) *Reconstructing the criminal – culture, law, and policy in England 1830–1914.* Cambridge: Cambridge University Press.

CRIMINAL CORPSE, THE

This entry deals specifically with the posthumous treatment of the criminal corpse rather than the various methods of capital punishment utilised within Britain. While capital punishment had existed in Britain since before the limits of legal memory, the treatment of the criminal corpse (together with posthumous sanctions) by the state was not placed on a formal legal footing until the passing of 'An Act for better preventing the horrid crime of murder', widely referred to as the Murder Act 1752 (25 Geo 2 c 37). This Act contained two important developments with regard to criminal corpses. First, it prescribed the anatomical dissection of the bodies of convicted murderers, both male and female, by surgeons as murderers were to be denied burial in consecrated ground (and there was a constant shortage of suitable bodies upon which anatomists could hone their skills). The Act also permitted judges to order the posthumous public hanging in chains (gibbeting) of the bodies of murderers (usually male) in order to act as a visual deterrent to those viewing the caged cadaver.

The systematic physical destruction of the bodies of criminals was not new to the mid-18th century; as Olsen (2007, p 63) has stated, 'grisly images of an executioner dismembering a condemned's limbs from his torso, smashing his chest cavity, gouging his eyes, or piercing his body with hot pokers are the common stuff of scaffold art in the high Middle Ages'. These punishments largely took place upon a living body rather than a lifeless cadaver, though it is accepted that there was also often an element of posthumous punishment involved; many of the offenders who underwent such harrowing and brutal punishment thankfully did not remain alive throughout the entire ordeal. However, from the late Middle Ages onwards, there was a movement from what had been largely considered the purview of personal vengeance against murderers (which could involve physical punishment, both corporal and capital, or financial restitution to the victim's family) to a state-sanctioned and publicly viewable violence against both the living criminal *and* the criminal corpse.

Dissection formed part of this panoply of ritualistic posthumous violence; the corpse ceased to exist as an entity by dint of being formally subdivided into its constituent parts – as shown in Hogarth's cruelly satirical engraving entitled *The reward of cruelty* (Plate IV of his *Four stages of cruelty* series, published in 1751), in which the body of hanged murderer Tom Nero is shown being dispassionately dissected by surgeons in full view of other medical personnel. Body parts, after having served their useful purpose of supplying material for aspiring surgeons and anatomists, were usually disposed of in unmarked mass graves within the grounds of the hospital.

With regard to gibbeting (which was last used as a punishment in Britain in 1832 and was withdrawn from the statute books in 1834), the public spectacle of the condemned criminal swinging in an iron cage was meant to inculcate a feeling of dread and fear among those who viewed it. The gibbet post was usually between 20 and 30 feet high (to ensure maximum visibility of the corpse) and was studded with nails to prevent the friends or family of the criminal cutting it down in order to rescue the body from its posthumous predicament. The gibbet cage was normally made by the local blacksmith and had holes drilled in at strategic points, through which iron rods were screwed into the body of the corpse in order to prevent subsequent disarticulation of the skeleton after the flesh and muscle tissue had decomposed. However, many contemporary accounts of gibbeting stress the almost carnival atmosphere of the crowd; the soon-to-be Poet Laureate, Robert Southey, recorded the following scene at the gibbeting of a murderer near Stourbridge, Worcestershire, in March 1813:

> The day after Mr Robins' murderer was hanged near Stourbridge, a noted party of plunderers assembled under his gibbet, and drank his health! The first Sunday, more than 100,000 persons came to see him hanging in chains; and a kind of wake continued for some weeks for ale and gingerbread etc. (Wood Warter, 1851, p 355)

DAVID J. COX

See also: Burke and Hare; Capital Punishment (England and Wales)

Readings

Leicester University School of Archaeology and Ancient History (2015) 'Harnessing the power of the criminal corpse'. Available at: http://www2.le.ac.uk/departments/archaeology/research/projects/criminal-bodies-1

Mitchell, P. (2012) *Anatomical dissection in Enlightenment England and beyond: Autopsy, pathology and display*. London: Ashgate.

Olsen, T. (2007) 'The medieval blood sanction and the divine beneficence of pain: 1100–1450', *Journal of Law and Religion*, 22(1): 63–129.

Wood Warter, J. (ed) (1851) *Southey's common-place book fourth series original memoranda etc.* London: Longmans.

CRIMINAL LUNATICS

The nexus of criminality and mental disease, illness or disorder, has, for centuries, presented a number of ethical and practical challenges in relation to the nature of legal reasoning in such cases, and what form legal process should take to account for the interests of the parties involved. Nineteenth-century Britain beheld the marriage of terms of the 'criminal' and the 'lunatic', with the 'criminal lunatic' establishing itself as a special category in the legal field.

In advance of legislative introductions in 1800, there was no special category of criminal lunatics (Gordon and Khosla, 2014). The year 1800 marked a watershed moment in the history of legislative developments concerning those who were convicted of crimes and who also endured mental abnormality/ies. Prompted by the case of James Hadfield, parliamentarians, and legal experts rallied to develop and approve new legislation – the Criminal Lunatics Act 1800.

James Hadfield, a former Captain in the 15th Light Dragoons Regiment, attempted to kill King George III by gunshot at the Drury Lane Theatre in May 1800. Hadfield's motivations were that he was acting on the inspiration provided by a higher power; in killing the King, then the world would end for the better. Hadfield was charged with high treason. However, this case brought about seismic changes in the handling of defendants who were undeniably suffering from insanity. Hadfield had sustained battle injuries to the head during the previous decade, and Hadfield's religious delusions had been noted on some occasions before the attempt on the King's life. An immediate change in the law through the introduction of the Criminal Lunatics Act 1800 allowed for Hadfield to be found 'not guilty by reason of insanity', but also authorised the 'safe custody' of criminal lunatics 'at His Majesty's pleasure' (Moran, 1985a).

A Select Committee of the House of Commons in 1807 was ordered to inquire into the state of criminal and pauper lunatics, with their findings reflecting on the need to remove criminal lunatics from county asylums and prisons and into purpose-built accommodation. Little advance was made on these recommendations until the opening of two designated criminal lunatic wards at Bethlem Hospital, London in 1816. The increase in disposals made by the courts under the Criminal Lunatics Act 1800, therefore, required the administrative capacity to deal with it – something which was rapidly becoming critical. Some sixty years since the first Criminal Lunatics Act, the 1860 Act aimed to tackle a large number of cases where a verdict was reached that the accused was 'not guilty by reason of insanity'. The Criminal Lunatics Act 1860 was passed to make 'better provision for the custody and care of criminal lunatics' (see Partridge, 1953; Allderidge, 1974; Hamilton, 1980). Broadmoor Hospital in Berkshire, England, was commissioned to be built and opened its doors in 1863 – with female patients being admitted in the year it opened, and male patients following in 1864. Broadmoor Hospital was the first purpose-built and dedicated asylum for criminal lunatics in Britain. Despite threatened closure in the second decade after opening on the basis of costs incurred, it remained open. Amidst a burgeoning demand for beds, Rampton Hospital in Nottinghamshire, England, the second asylum for criminal lunatics, opened in 1912.

In an attempt to regulate the number of insanity pleas entered at court, and in parallel with the advancements in the various new legislation and facilities for criminal lunatics, the M'Naghten Rules (a legal test for insanity) came into use in 1843 in English courts and elsewhere. Daniel M'Naghten shot dead Prime Minister Robert Peel's Secretary Edward Drummond. M'Naghten had intended the target to be Peel, as he believed that he was being persecuted by the Tory Party. However, M'Naghten discharged his weapon on the wrong person. At his trial, M'Naghten pleaded not guilty, and he was found 'not guilty by reason of insanity'. Amidst outcry and concern from some in the highest echelons of society, the House of Lords were tasked with questioning the British judiciary; their responses were shaped into what is the M'Naghten Rules. They follow that, if a defence is to be upheld, the court must be satisfied that at the time of the alleged offence, the defendant did not know what s/he was doing, or that what s/he was doing was wrong due to a 'defect of reason' arising from a 'disease of the mind' (Moran, 1985b).

The nineteenth century marked a period of discursive, legal and administrative change for those whose offending behaviour was tied to mental aberration. Now redundant in legal parlance, archaic terms such as these have been replaced with descriptions such as 'mentally disordered offender'. However, despite changes in vocabulary, ethical and practical dilemmas exist much the same today as were found in the nineteenth century. Establishing premeditation, blame, fault and responsibility of the accused where mental aberration exists is clearly challenging for the court. For example, defences of insanity are likely to be exploited and under-used in equal measure, victims of crime may feel that the accused has received lenient treatment, or the vulnerable accused may be unfairly disadvantaged in the judicial setting where they have the burden of responsibly to prove the existence of insanity.

The history of the criminal lunatic offers an insight into not only complex legal evolutions and practical outcomes on what to do with a 'special' category of offender, but also the converging authority and influence of psychiatric knowledge. As writers such as Cohen (1985) and Scull (1977) have pointed out, onlookers must continue to critically appraise how, and in what ways a broader and highly developed apparatus of control is functioning. Indeed, the lunatic, the criminal lunatic, and more contemporarily the psychiatric patient and the mentally disordered offender are subject to a number of influences that will dictate their experience, not least the development of psychiatric knowledge and expertise, the extent of psychiatric/medical involvement in the judicial environment, the cultural/political climate of retribution and public protection, and the development of environments of incapacitation beyond the prison.

PAUL TAYLOR

See also: **Advocacy in Criminal Trials; Legal Representation; Medical Testimony in the Judicial Sphere**

Readings

Allderidge, P.H. (1974) 'Criminal insanity: Bethlem to Broadmoor', *Proceedings of the Royal Society of Medicine*, 67(9), 897-904.

Cohen, S. (1985) *Visions of social control: Crime, punishment and classification.* Cambridge: Polity Press.

Gordon, H. and Khosla, V. (2014) 'The interface between general and forensic psychiatry: a historical perspective'. *Advances in Psychiatric Treatment*, 20(5): 350-8.

Hamilton, J.R. (1980) 'The development of Broadmoor 1863–1980', *The Psychiatrist*, 4(9): 130-3.

Moran, R. (1985a) 'The origin of insanity as a special verdict: The trial for treason of James Hadfield (1800)', *Law and Society Review* 487-519.

Moran, R. (1985b) 'The modern foundation for the insanity defense: The cases of James Hadfield (1800) and Daniel McNaughtan (1843)', *The Annals of the American Academy of Political and Social Science*, 31-42.

Partridge, R. (1953) *Broadmoor, a history of criminal lunacy and its problems.* London: Chatto & Windus.

Scull, A.T. (1977) 'Madness and segregative control: The rise of the insane asylum', *Social Problems*, 24(3), 337-51.

CRIMINAL STATISTICS

Crime statistics are often perceived as being the 'hard' facts of crime, and the definitive way in which crime rates can be measured. However, since their inception, there have been problems with exactly what crime statistics do, and do not, include.

Crime statistics were first collected in the UK from the early 1800s, when the courts began recording the numbers of indictable offences committed to trial. The justice system at the time, however, relied on the victim to pay for the investigation, and trial, meaning that only those with the economic power to do so were able to pursue justice (Godfrey et al, 2008). Therefore, many crimes went unresolved due to lack of money, or simply due to the crime being deemed too petty to pursue. These unrecorded crimes are often described as 'hidden crime' or the 'dark figure of crime', an issue that still exists today (Coleman and Moynihan, 1996).

As crime recording became more sophisticated, there was more of a demand for data. From the mid-1800s, the police began to record data on crimes reported, a method that included more incidents than the original court data, but still relied on crime being reported, and thought important enough to be recorded. No national direction existed, so decisions on recording were taken locally, and data from the late 19th century show that changes in crime rates can be correlated with who occupied the role of chief constable at that time (Godfrey et al, 2008).

The nature of the data collected also widened as it was influenced by an understanding of crime at the time, a notable development being the introduction of data collection around offender characteristics, influenced by work being done by criminologists such as Cesare Lombroso on the 'criminal type' in the late 19th century (Godfrey et al, 2008).

Efforts to improve accuracy in recording resulted in an increase in apparent crime rates, enhanced by the introduction of lesser tariffs as an alternative to custody, which meant that more minor offences were brought into the system. Advances in collection techniques and technology mean that crime data has become more sophisticated. However, the issue of 'hidden crime' still remains. One way to try and access this data is to speak to victims of crime, rather than rely on reported crime (see Morris, 2001).

The best-known modern victim survey is the Crime Survey for England and Wales (CSEW). This survey was designed to assess crime levels by asking members of the public directly about their experiences of crime. Unsurprisingly, the CSEW reveals higher volumes of crime than the official statistics, but it is not without problems. The first of these problems is sample size, the CSEW only surveys approximately 1% of the population. It excludes offences of murder, other offences such as fraud and cybercrime, and any victims under the age of 16. Those living in communal settings, such as hostels, are excluded, and the number of crimes that one victim can report is capped, meaning that repeat victims, such as victims of domestic violence, are not able to convey their full experience (Walby et al, 2014).

It is important when interpreting crime statistics from whichever century to understand not only what the statistics include, but also who collected them, and what was left out. Although data are available in some form on the rates and nature of crime within the UK as far back as the early 1800s, it is important to remember that such data can be qualitatively different depending on their purpose, what they include and how they are recorded. Rather than being the facts about crime, they are better understood as being indicative of not only the crime rate, but also the methodology and motivation for data collection at that time.

RACHAEL STEELE

See also: **Criminal Class, The; Life-course Analysis**

Readings

Coleman, C. and Moynihan, J. (1996) *Understanding crime data: Haunted by the dark figure.* Buckingham: Open University Press.

Godfrey, B., Lawrence, P. and Williams, C. (2008) *History and crime.* London: Sage.

Morris, R. (2001) 'Lies, damned lies and criminal statistics: reinterpreting the criminal statistics in England and Wales', *Crime, History & Societies*, 5(1): 111–27.

Walby, S., Towers, J. and Francis, B. (2014) 'Mainstreaming domestic and gender-based violence into sociology and the criminology of violence', *The Sociological Review*, 62(S2): 187–214.

CRIMINOLOGY

The difficulties experienced in outlining the history of criminology (and the following discussion will cover the period up to the beginning of the 20th century) are instructive, for they demand an investigation of exactly what is meant by the term. The word 'criminology' dates back to the late 19th century and was related initially to the school of positivism, which followed Cesare Lombroso's gothic announcement of his radical new insights, coming as he held a skull.

In truth, the question of why people committed crime had been of interest for centuries. Generally, the answer was framed in terms of sin, but sin had a typology and could include worldly elements such as drunkenness as both comprising and explaining vice. In the 18th century, a 'course of life' narrative, proclaimed after executions and ironically parodied in Hogarth's *Industry and idleness* of 1747, became influential: idleness and the neglect of religion led to bad (often female) company, minor wrongdoing and eventually to felony and death. Ultimately, crime was caused by bad choices, influenced by temptation, and this model of rationality underlay the work of influential writers on punishment, notably, Beccaria and Bentham (Rock, 1998; Rafter, 2009). At the same time, however, ancient theories of physiognomy and phrenology (ie the reading of character from the study of the face and the skull, respectively) were being reformulated with an ostensibly empirical basis, by Lavater in the case of the first, and by Gall and Spurzheim in the case of the second. Such ideas may be discounted now, but their influence, manifested in popular fiction as well as more specialist discourse, was considerable (Rafter, 2009). These were general theories of character, which though applicable to criminality, were not exclusively related to it. The claims of criminology to be a 'science' or a 'discipline' (a body of knowledge related to criminality relying upon empirical, inductive reasoning and propounded by a coterie of specialists) were made possible by the incarceration of large numbers of offenders and their bureaucratic management by individuals such as prison surgeons, as well as by the development of statistical methods. So, in Britain, notable early work was done by men such as Wilson, Thomson and Nicolson (Radzinowicz and Hood, 1986; Davie, 2005). Darwin's *Origin of species* of 1859 added a significant element to theoretical models: heredity was clearly important in human development and was a process, a movement, which could presumably go in two directions. Ideas of inheritance and 'degeneration' were the subject of a number of particular formulations in the later part of the 19th century and suggested to some the complementary solution of eugenics (Pick, 1989; Rafter, 2009).

Lombroso's theory of 'atavism', in which some criminals (Lombroso downgraded the proportion in reworkings of his original position) were born into a criminal type, distinguished from other individuals and identifiable by measurable physical characteristics, was first published in *L'Uomo Delinquente* in 1876 and taken up by others. There was considerable interest in, and support for, this 'Positivist School' in continental Europe, though its influence in Britain was much more limited. There, Lomboso's ideas got their first popular airing in Havelock Ellis's *The criminal* of 1890, a translation of Lombroso's own major work into English had to wait until later (Radzinowicz and Hood, 1986; Rock, 1988; Pick, 1989; Rafter, 2009). Its rejection is often attributed to the study published by Goring as *The English convict* in 1913 (Davie, 2005). Even in Continental Europe, however, Lombrosianism was not unchallenged, and international conferences (the very existence of which displays the assumption of an independent specialist scientific knowledge in the field) witnessed considerable debate. In France, the major competing theory came from the sociological theories of Gabriel Tarde, whose work found resonance in Britain, where the influence of social factors in criminality had been evident in earlier writers such Robert Owen and Friedrich Engels. The work of early pioneers of psychology (eg Pinel, Despine, Prichard), whose claims to specialist knowledge also reflected the development of asylum provision in the 19th century, were also significant (Rafter, 2009).

In the 20th century, theories of criminality multiplied and diverged, but the crucial issues of physiological, psychological and sociological factors, of heredity and environment and their interplay, were established in the 19th century. It is perhaps a recognition of the fact that the seductive initial question of 'Why do people commit crime?' is susceptible to no simple answer that has seen the concerns of 'criminology' as a (university) discipline become more wide-ranging and diffuse.

RICHARD W. IRELAND

See also: **Victimology**

Readings

Davie, N. (2005) *Tracing the criminal*. Oxford: Bardwell Press.

Pick, D. (1989) *Faces of degeneration*. Cambridge: Cambridge University Press.

Radzinowicz, L. and Hood, R. (1986) *A history of English criminal law, vol 5*. London: Stevens.

Rafter, N. (2009) *The origins of criminology: A reader*. Abingdon: Routledge.

Rock, P. (ed) (1988) *A history of British criminology*. Oxford: Clarendon Press.

D

DESISTANCE

The concept of desistance is one that is certainly difficult to define as it is a term that is neither self-evident nor straightforward, and it has therefore naturally presented itself historically as difficult to operationalise. The continuing considerable indecisiveness in regards to being able to construct a universally accepted definition of desistance is due to the numerous theoretical interpretations that exist and are in contention with one another. Each of these individual theoretical explanations of desistance has their own distinctive justifications and cohort of supporters. All perspectives claim to accurately assert the reasoning as to why an individual desists from offending, how that individual is able to do so and when that individual can be deemed to have permanently ceased from offending.

The earliest notable theoretical perspective upon desistance to gain prominence was developed by Adolphe Quetelet (1833) in the early 19th century and came to be known as the ontogenetic perspective. The theory proposed that desistance is attributable to a natural process of an individual maturing with age and growing out of crime. It stipulated that an individual's involvement in criminal activity begins in the early teenage years, and then such behaviour will rise rapidly in both frequency and severity during late adolescence until decreasing progressively throughout adulthood (Quetelet, 1833). The reasoning put forth is twofold: first, individuals' health naturally deteriorates with age, reducing the ability to engage in criminal activity; and, second, repeated experiences of the criminal justice process become tiresome and stressful, specifically incarceration.

In opposition to this explanation is the second theoretical standpoint referred to as the sociogenic perspective. This perspective, which gained prominence in the mid-20th century, contends that the establishment and maintenance of social bonds by an individual are essential in both encouraging and supporting their cessation from offending during the life course. It was David Matza (1964) who championed this concept through his notion of 'drift'. Matza claimed that it is by no means the reaching of a precise age that automatically guarantees that an individual will abruptly cease their previous offending, but rather the availability of resources that comes with maturation (Matza, 1964). If positively harnessed, such resources enable a transition from offending to non-offending to become far more seamless (Matza, 1964).

There is a third notable theoretical opinion that has accrued support since the late 20th century to the present day. Entitled the 'liberative perspective', this theoretical explanation of desistance proposes that what distinguishes those who can from those who cannot desist from crime is essentially their narrative script (Maruna, 2001). Whether an individual wishes to alter their previous criminally inclined behaviour is therefore envisioned as decisive. Desistance theorists who advocate this explanation, such as Shadd Maruna, stress the importance of individuals coming to the realisation that such prior involvement in illicit activities was morally and socially wrong (Maruna, 2001). Only upon this realisation can an individual truly begin the process of desistance, harnessing social and human capital so as to impose a committed change from offender to non-offender.

Given that consensus is approximately nil among the theoretical perspectives upon conclusively when, why and how an individual has desisted and ceased from offending, this has consequently naturally resulted in desistance becoming recognised as a process rather than a singular event. Moreover, the belief in an individual 'zigzagging' in and out of crime prior to an eventual cessation of their involvement in illegitimate activity has been one aspect of desistance accepted among all three theoretical interpretations (Glaser, 1964). So, too, do the theoretical perspectives collectively state the necessity to move beyond a concern with primary desistance, and alternatively towards placing theoretical emphasis upon secondary desistance (Maruna and Farrall, 2004).

WAYNE CAMPBELL

See also: Life-course Analysis

Readings
Glaser, D. (1964) *The effectiveness of a prison and parole system.* Indianapolis, IN: Bobbs-Merrill.

Maruna, S. (2001) *Making good: How ex-convicts reform and rebuild their lives.* Washington, DC: American Psychological Association.

Maruna, S. and Farrall, S. (2004) 'Desistance from crime: a theoretical reformulation', *Kolner zeitschrift fur soziologie und sozialpsychologie*, 43: 171–94.

Matza, D. (1964) *Delinquency and drift.* New York, NY: John Wiley & Sons.

Quetelet, A. (1833) *Recherches sur le penchant au crime aux differents ages.* Belgium: Hayez.

DEVIANT WOMEN

Critical studies and research into the punishment of women in 19th-century Britain must be understood within a framework of Victorian morality. In 19th- and early 20th-century Britain, deviant women were perceived by feminists as victims of a social structure that provided limited opportunities and was inhospitable to women who sought to support themselves (Zedner, 1991). Discourses surrounding motherhood, domesticity, respectability and sexuality played a crucial role in the social construction of female deviancy and hence in defining the 'good' woman – 'someone located within the family and who by *nature* is maternal, caring, gentle, modest, unselfish and passive' (Ballinger, 2007, p 67, emphasis in original). The conduct of women within both the public and private domestic sphere was policed, disciplined and controlled to ensure conformity to familial moral standards of behaviour surrounding ideologies of marriage, motherhood, femininity and domesticity (Ballinger, 2007):

> Women's femininity depends upon bodily decorum even in the privacy of family relationships. In public, any indecorum is a sign of lack of respectability which, for women, is always a sexual category associated with promiscuity or prostitution. In transgressing these codes of femininity, the unruly woman demands the right to the satisfaction of her own bodily desires; she eats in excess and has unbridled sexual appetites. (Arthurs, 1999, pp 142–3)

Women who dared stray from expectations of femininity were objectified and associated with danger, temptation, impurity and an uncontrolled sexuality; they were labelled as deviant (Ussher, 1991). They were simultaneously worshipped and defiled, 'evoking horror and desire, temptation and repugnance, fear and fascination': the Madonna–whore dichotomy forcefully palpable throughout Victorian misogynistic society (Ussher, 1991, p 21). The contrived model of the woman as Mary – the purifier and inspirer of the man – was to be invested in the middle-class wife and mother, whose asexual, morally uplifting influence was held as a precaution against the repugnant interference of industrial life. Her role reversal was the 'epitome of female corruption – fallen from innocence, she had plummeted to the depths of degradation and contaminated all who came near her' (Zedner, 1991, p 11).

Deviant behaviour demonstrated an absence of virtue and passivity and, thus, did not concur with male expectations for individual actions. Examples of deviant behaviour are extensive as they encompassed any action, big or small, involved in breaching feminine social rules deemed crucial to cohesion and order within patriarchal society. Breaches of social rules resulted in the increased social control of women. Discussions surrounding sexual immorality and innate wickedness pervade historical archival data from various institutions in Liverpool throughout the 19th century. Examples of moral decency promoted within many institutions, particularly Liverpool Female Penitentiary (1809–1921), a rescue home for deviant women, were believed to provide an idyllic environment to reform and normalise women back to acceptable standards of behaviour. An article within the *Liverpool Mercury* (1894) epitomises the institution's attempts to reform and correct female deviancy:

> Women of various ages, worn with sorrow, care and sin, with the saddest experiences behind them, and with only the faintest gleam of hope before them, seek shelter at its hospitable door, and there receive a kind and loving welcome. They are cheered by the hope and courage of others, taught and trained by patient and untiring perseverance, till they themselves become strong and hopeful, and look forward with God's blessing to a future life of respectability and usefulness. (*Liverpool Mercury*, 1894)

Dominant Victorian morality thus perceived deviant women to be the 'very negation of the feminine ideal', and via the Victorians' fierce imposition of traditional gender roles, the woman who strayed from her elevated moral and familial pedestal was regarded as having fallen a far greater distance than her male counterpart and hence as being far removed from such a feminine ideal (Zedner, 1991, p 15).

KIRSTY GREENWOOD

See also: Drunken Women; Philanthropic Institutions; Prostitution (19th century); Semi-penal Institutions for Women

Readings
Arthurs, J. (1999) 'Revolting women: the body in comic performance', in J. Arthurs and J. Grimshaw (eds) *Women's bodies: Discipline and transgression*. London: Cassell, pp 139–64.

Ballinger, A. (2007) 'The worse of two evils, double murder trials and gender in England and Wales, 1900–1953', in A. Barton, K. Corteen, D. Scott and D. Whyte (eds) *Expanding the criminological imagination: Critical readings in criminology*. Cullompton: Willan, pp 65–93. *Liverpool Mercury* (1894) 'The female penitentiary bazaar', 12 December, p 4.

Ussher, J. (1991) *Women's madness*. Hertfordshire: Harvester Wheatsheaf.

Zedner, L. (1991) *Women, crime and custody in Victorian England*. London: Clarendon Press.

DIGITAL HISTORY

Historians of crime have benefitted enormously in the past decade from the growing number of primary source digital archives, particularly textual archives, but increasingly of image, sound, video and 3D objects. These digital archives include those dedicated to crime history sources, such as court and gaol records, as well as historical legislation, but also those that are tangentially useful. Examples of which can comprise: digitised newspaper collections, whose pages sometimes include supplemental details about crimes; image databases that can provide contemporary depictions of crime; and genealogical databases containing additional information about particular individuals. Some digital archives, such as the Old Bailey Online (OBO), bring together resources held in multiple physical archives, thus making the digital archive more complete for a given source type than any of its physical competitors.

Scholars from around the world have unprecedented access to these digitised sources, many of which are open access. Historians of crime who use these resources save on travel time and costs, while students of all levels around the world now have direct access to primary sources (Davies et al, 2015). This ease of access has led to a surge in studies of the history of crime, with digital resources increasingly driving the research agenda as scholars rely on these surrogates as the basis for their evidence. The OBO, for example, has identified more than 400 peer-reviewed articles and books that, since 2004, have directly cited materials held in their collection. Compared to the pre-digital levels of interest in these records, this is a dramatic increase in use of the underlying records. While this has led to a significant increase in our understanding of the history of crime in early modern London, the ease of use of the collection has drawn scholars to it and thus away from other records that have not been digitised, narrowing scholarly intrigue and leading to a considerable selection bias in source use.

These Web-based archives have also changed the way researchers access and think about the collections. Keyword searching via a search interface has generally replaced the targeted browsing of pages and boxes in the physical archive, or the scrolling of microfilm readers. Scholars used to have to understand how records were ordered so that they could find what they were looking for, whereas there is now a tendency (though not a requirement) to ignore that structure of the collection and instead 'dive in' at item level by seeking a matching keyword. This raises the risk of confirmation bias in the research process, and is particularly troublesome in collections that have been automatically transcribed and that contain considerable but hidden transcription errors. These errors, which are particularly prevalent in newspaper collections, limit the ability of scholars relying on the efficacy of keywords to find relevant sources.

Moving beyond accessibility, the mutable nature of these digital texts also opens up new opportunities for quantitative analyses, data mining, linking and visualisation. Drawing on the social-scientific quantitative turn of the 1960s and 1970s, a number of historians have taken advantage of the digital nature of the texts to measure and look for patterns across large collections of text, which are not feasible to discover through close reading alone (Hitchcock, 2013). These include opportunities to build geospatial models of regional variations in executions over time, or to conduct network analyses of defendants and witnesses in criminal trial accounts to highlight the important players in regional crime and justice networks.

By taking advantage of the computer's vastly larger memory, it becomes possible to link together related records, and to build one's own digital archive to suit the needs of the researcher. This process can provide considerable context to historical arguments, and custom sets of linked data can be shared alongside interpretive texts, taking readers seamlessly between scholarly interpretations and original sources (Hitchcock, 2013). These data sets are slowly being shared openly, allowing others to build directly upon earlier digital work, opening up an environment in which both historical data sets and historical interpretations hold valuable places within the historiography (Howard, 2015).

ADAM CRYMBLE

See also: **Life-course Analysis**

Readings
Davies, A., Peel, M. and Balderstone, L. (2015) 'Digital histories of crime and research-based teaching and learning', *Law, Crime and History*, 5: 93–104.
Hitchcock, T. (2013) 'Big data for dead people: digital readings and the conundrums of positivism', *Historyonics*. Available at: http://historyonics. blogspot.co.uk/2013/12/big-data-for-dead-people-digital.html

Howard, S. (2015) 'Bloody code: reflecting on a decade of the Old Bailey Online and the digital futures of our criminal past', *Law, Crime and History*, 5: 12–24.

DISCHARGED PRISONERS' AID SOCIETIES

Discharged Prisoners' Aid Societies (DPASs) have been the longest-standing and most visible of all voluntary and philanthropic organisations in England that provided local help for people leaving prison. Charitable 'societies' of all forms had their origins in the early 18th century as a philanthropic zeal swept the Western world. Such societies included the Temperance movement to encourage people to abstain from alcohol, missionary movements to 'save' children from poverty and moralising movements to rescue 'fallen women'. DPASs involved themselves specifically in penal affairs, particularly the aftercare of prisoners leaving prison. Their proliferation towards the end of the 18th century coincided with a penal reform inspired by the activities of John Howard. In the absence of any formal help for people released from any type of prison, these DPASs continued to be active in providing voluntary, charitable support for prisoners throughout the 19th century and well into the 20th century. They continued providing voluntary help even after the Probation Service was established with the Probation Act 1907 (Mair and Burke, 2012). Britain was not the only country to have DPASs – France, Austria, Germany, Switzerland, Denmark, Norway, Holland, Russia and the US all had similar endeavours (Carey and Walker, 2002). Due to the disparate and religious nature of their organisation, few records remain of the work of DPASs; hence, with exceptions, for example, Turner and Johnston (2016), research on their activities is scarce.

'Discharged Prisoners' Aid Societies' was an umbrella term for a national but disparate set of different small societies that provided a range of services for people leaving prison. Their chief aim was to find employment and temporary lodgings for a discharged prisoner, or, if he or she had what was considered to be a respectable home, to send the ex-prisoner to his or her home. In cases where there were no relatives and the person concerned consented, the DPASs could organise emigration for the discharged prisoner. Some DPASs worked with prisoners while still incarcerated in planning their life after prison and others literally stood outside the prison gates to help people on release (known as 'prison gate missions'). Occasionally, a DPAS would provide temporary accommodation for people on release, but this was usually for men only. Hence, even rarer was DPAS accommodation for women. The North and South Staffordshire DPASs combined forces in 1878 to set up and run a refuge for women leaving Stafford gaol, entitled the Staffordshire County Industrial Home for Discharged Female

Ex-Prisoners and Friendless Women (Turner, 2012). It is possible that this particular refuge was unique.

The work of the DPASs was recognised in 1862 by the Discharged Prisoners' Aid Act. This Act enabled individual DPASs to be certified by magistrates and be attached to prisons. It also provided small amounts of government money per prisoner to those certified DPASs to help with resettlement (McConville, 1994). Most of these DPASs took the government funding, though some refused all state funding in order to remain independent, for example, the Gloucestershire Society and the York Castle Society. By 1895, the Gladstone Committee reported that each prison had two or three DPASs attached to it (Gladstone Committee, 1895).

Despite their protestations of benevolent purposes, the DPASs were not always well received: other philanthropic organisations working to help prisoners felt their competition overbearing; prisoners baulked at their moralising; and the Prison Commission thought them in need of fundamental reform (McConville, 1994). Such concerns led to the DPASs being scrutinised by the Gladstone Committee in 1895 (Gladstone Committee, 1895). *A report to Her Majesty's Commissioners of Prisons on the operations of Discharged Prisoners Aid Societies*, ordered subsequent to the Gladstone Committee and delivered in 1897, advocated a centralised system of control and for the disparate DPASs to cooperate more with each other (McConville, 1994). Over the following few decades, an unpleasant clash ensued between the Prison Commissioner, Ruggles-Brise (Commissioner between 1895 and 1921), and the DPASs, who fought against reform and centralised control (McConville, 1994; Carey and Walker, 2002).

Finally, reform and centralisation did take place. The Central Discharged Prisoners' Aid Society (Incorporated) was formed in December 1924, and subsequently renamed the National Association of Discharged Prisoners' Aid Societies (NADPAS) in 1935. In 1963, a report on *The organisation of aftercare by the Advisory Council on the Treatment of Offenders* suggested that prison welfare and aftercare should be entrusted to the Probation Service (Carey and Walker, 2002). However, the report also acknowledged that the voluntary sector still had a role to play in service provision, and in 1966, the NADPAS changed its name to the National Association for the Care and Resettlement of Offenders (NACRO). NACRO has since developed into the biggest criminal justice-related charity in England and Wales.

JO TURNER

See also: **Gladstone Report, The; Penal Reform Pressure Groups; Philanthropic Institutions; Police Court Missionaries; Probation; Temperance Movements**

Readings

Carey, M. and Walker, R. (2002) 'The penal voluntary sector', in S. Bryans, C. Martin and R. Walker (eds) *Prisons and the voluntary sector: A bridge into the community*. Winchester: Waterside Press, pp 50–62.

Gladstone Committee (1895) *Report from the Departmental Committee on Prisons (C.7702), Vol. LVI*. London: Home Office.

Mair, G. and Burke, L. (2012) *Redemption, rehabilitation and risk management: A history of probation*. London: Routledge.

McConville, S. (1994) *English local prisons: Next only to death*. Basingstoke: Routledge.

Turner, J. (2012) 'Ordinary female offenders: Stafford borough, 1880–1905', *Crime, Histoire & Sociétiés/Crime, History & Societies*, 16(2): 55–78.

Turner, J. and Johnston, H. (2016) 'Late nineteenth century residential provision for women released from local and convict prisons', *British Journal of Community Justice*, 13(3): 35–50.

DRUNKEN WOMEN

Between 1870 and 1920, women committed the minority of drunkenness offences. They were also significantly less likely to be classified as habitual drunkards compared to their male counterparts (Morrison, 2005). Despite this, in the second half of the 19th century, drunken women became a significant moral and criminal justice concern, and drunkenness became construed as a profoundly gendered problem (Zedner, 1991; Morrison, 2008). Thus, when a new system of inebriate institutions was introduced in the final decades of the 19th century, women became vastly over-represented within it. By 1904, for example, over 90% of those compulsorily sent to inebriate institutions were female (Morrison, 2005, 2008).

While several commentators described why drunkenness became a dominant preoccupation during the Victorian period, few have sought to explain precisely why drunken women became constructed as the principal focus of legal and penal reform. For some, the gendered implementation of the Inebriates Acts was merely an accident of implementation, rather than a deliberately gendered strategy (Wiener, 1994; Johnstone, 1996). However, as other scholars have argued, the focus on female drunkards was undeniably intentional, for it was drunken women, not men, who were consistently defined as 'dangerous' and in need of control within contemporary scientific, medical, statistical, legal and penal discourses (Zedner, 1991; Dobash and McLaughlin, 1992; Morrison, 2008).

There are a number of reasons why the female drunkard, rather than the male drunkard, occupied centre stage in contemporary discourses on drunkenness.

Principally, drunken women were problematic because they transgressed established gender roles. Owing to a number of broader cultural, economic and social shifts occurring during this time, such transgressions took on much greater social and moral significance than had hitherto been the case.

Gendered roles became more entrenched in the Victorian era, against a backdrop of unprecedented social and economic change. The Industrial Revolution had heightened concerns about the devolution of established social hierarchies, including traditional class and gender divisions (Morrison, 2005). Within this context, the institutions of home and family took on new significance: the home was viewed as a moral sanctuary and women were deemed to be a moral linchpin. Women were thus responsible not simply for their own morality, but that of their husbands, children and society more broadly. Women were accordingly expected to be moral exemplars and deemed *naturally* more moral than their male counterparts. To achieve this ideal, women were required to adhere to a range of gender norms, including being a good wife and altruistic mother, being chaste, quiet, passive and in control, and preferably contained within the private context of the domestic (Zedner, 1991). Drunken women were the complete antithesis of this ideal: they were loud, boisterous and out of control (often publicly), and were frequently portrayed as bad mothers and wives. They were therefore doubly deviant, having transgressed the criminal law and gender norms. In a context where women were expected to be moral exemplars, the female drunkard endangered not simply her own moral standing, but that of the nation (Morrison, 2005, 2008).

These concerns were exacerbated by three key interrelated cultural developments. First, the rise of female suffrage over the last few decades of the century heightened anxieties about the erosion of traditional gender norms. Female emancipation, it was alleged, caused women to adopt unnaturally masculine roles, including drunkenness, which their weaker constitution could not withstand. Drunken women thus epitomised what could go wrong when women tried to emulate men's power. Second, growing medical and psychological knowledge played an increasingly prominent role in criminal justice policy at this time. Within such knowledge, women were constructed as 'naturally' more susceptible to drunkenness due to their physiological weaknesses and more nervous disposition. They were also defined as 'naturally' more amenable to treatment. Finally, the increasingly prominent eugenics movement identified women as the main hereditary agent. Within eugenics thinking, drunken women – believed to reproduce at an alarming rate – were defined as a significant threat to future generations, and correspondingly in need of containment and control.

BRONWYN MORRISON

See also: **Deviant Women; Inebriate Institutions; Philanthropic Institutions; Prostitution (19th century); Semi-penal Institutions for Women**

Readings

Dobash, R.P. and McLaughlin, P. (1992) 'The punishment of women in nineteenth-century Scotland: prisons and inebriate institutions', in E. Breitenbach and E. Gordon (eds) *Out of bounds: Women in Scottish society 1800–1945*. Edinburgh: Edinburgh University Press, pp 65–94.

Johnstone, G. (1996) *Medical concepts and penal policy*. London: Cavendish.

Morrison, B. (2005) 'Ordering disorderly women: female drunkenness in England c.1870–1920', unpublished PhD, Keele University, UK.

Morrison, B. (2008) 'Controlling the "hopeless": re-visioning the history of female inebriate institutions c. 1870–1920', in H. Johnston (ed) *Punishment and control in historical perspective*. Basingstoke: Palgrave MacMillan, pp 135–57.

Wiener, M.J. (1994) *Reconstructing the criminal: Cultural, law and policy in England, 1830–1914*. Cambridge: Cambridge University Press.

Zedner, L. (1991) *Women, crime and custody in Victorian England*. Oxford: Oxford University Press.

DUELLING

Although single combats are known throughout history, the origins of what is properly called a 'duel' lie in 16th-century Italy. Closely associated with courtesy literature and, in particular, with Baldassare Castiglione's (1528) *Book of the courtier*, the duel emerged as a method of containing the internecine feuding that characterised Italian city-states. Often set in opposition to Christian doctrine, courtesy literature taught that gentlemen had a reservoir of inner honour that obliged them to treat each other with civility; it also observed that where this was not shown, the proper solution was a single combat (Peltonen, 2003). The innovation was to suggest that all parties should regard the outcome as having decisively resolved the issue in question – thus would the endless family blood feuds, which sometimes ran on long after the original quarrel was forgotten, be eliminated.

Duelling and associated honour culture was probably brought to England by fencing masters such as Rocco Bonetti, who established a fencing school at Blackfriars around 1569. In addition to translations of Italian works such as Girolamo Muzio's (1550) *Il Duello*, an English genre emerged with Simon Robson's (1577) *The court of Ciuill Courtesie* and John Seldon's (1610) *The duello*

—

or single combat. Duelling took root in England under James I, with at least 33 duels between 1610 and 1629.

Early duels, in which the retainers on both sides often joined in with their principals, could scarce be distinguished from the so-called 'chance-medleys', wherein two men or parties met, quarrelled and fought immediately in the heat of passion (Horder, 1992). Where a killing had occurred in hot blood and the party slain had provoked the other, then the offence was mere manslaughter. However, where there was a calculated decision to fight, the killing amounted to murder.

The mere act of issuing a challenge was a misdemeanour. The Court of Star Chamber was particularly active in suppressing challenges, prosecuting more than 200 gentlemen for having issued them between 1602 and 1625 (Banks, 2010). However, James I, and those who followed him, habitually pardoned duellists. For example, no action was taken against Edward Sackville, who killed Edward Bruce, Lord Kinloss, during a scandalous duel in 1613. A Parliamentary committee half-heartedly proposed in 1651 that duellists should lose their right hands. However, by the end of the century, honour culture was firmly ensconced in gentlemanly society, with a particularly celebrated duel between the 4th Baron Mohun and the Duke of Hamilton in 1712.

The later 18th century saw the pistol replace the sword in England around 1770. Around the same time, there emerged independent honour critics, known as Seconds, engaged by parties not to fight, but to independently ensure fair conduct (Banks, 2008). In such a case, there was little prospect of convicting any survivor. Honour culture had penetrated the legal professions. Some barristers duelled and when cases came to trial, judges often directed for acquittal against both evidence and law or else strove to find tenuous suggestions of provocation that would allow a manslaughter conviction to be returned (Banks, 2010). One duellist, Major Campbell, was executed in Dublin in 1808 but he had killed his opponent unfairly: 'His offence was not that he had killed Boyd, but that he had killed him contrary to established rules' (Sabine, 1859, p 72).

Duelling was nonetheless in decline in England. Although there were many duels among military officers during the Napoleonic Wars, duelling failed to recommend itself to the middle classes, who, as the 19th century progressed, were striving to set a new moral tone (Banks, 2010). There was renewed criticism on religious grounds and the elites were themselves increasingly doubtful about the wisdom of so publicly flouting the law when they were striving so hard to persuade the lower orders to obey it. By 1845, the duel was essentially defunct in England, though formal proscription had little to do with it. The last fatal duel, actually between two Frenchmen, occurred at Englefield Green in 1852.

STEVE BANKS

See also: **Informal Justice**

Readings

Banks, S. (2008) 'Very little law in the case: contests of honour and the subversion of the English criminal courts, 1780–1845', *Journal of British Studies*, 47: 528–58.

Banks, S. (2010) *A polite exchange of bullets: The duel and the English gentleman, 1750–1850.* Woodbridge: Boydell and Brewer.

Horder, J. (1992) *Provocation and responsibility.* Oxford: Clarendon Press.

Peltonen, M. (2003) *The duel in early modern England: Civility, politeness and honour.* Cambridge: Cambridge University Press.

Sabine, L. (1859) *Notes on duels and duelling.* Boston, MA: Crosby and Nichols.

ENGLISH DETECTIVES

The detection of crimes began as a private occupation in the course of the 17th century with the rise of the thieftaker – hired by victims chiefly to pursue and apprehend the perpetrator and to recover stolen property. However, in the mid-18th century, official steps were taken by the Bow Street Court in London to engage men who would help the authorities in the investigation and prosecution of crime, as well as in proactive anti-crime measures – an initiative extended to other police courts in the capital towards the close of the century (Beattie, 2012). Half a century later, in the wake of expanding industrialisation and urbanisation, and as part of the current police reform and the strengthening of the public police, fully fledged detective departments, of varying sizes, began to be formed within the newly established police forces in London and in several other large cities (Shpayer-Makov, 2011). From then on, this occupation, with its required skills, accumulated knowledge and norms, was developed in the uniformed police forces, principally in urban areas, where it was easier for offenders to escape the hand of the law. Private detectives continued to offer services to individuals and institutions for pecuniary gain, but it was police detectives, paid by the public purse as full-time employees of central or local government, who were overwhelmingly perceived as the definitive crime fighters in society. So entrenched was the linkage between the police and detection that, with very few exceptions, all police detectives had to have significant experience in uniformed work (Shpayer-Makov, 2011).

Nonetheless, despite mounting recognition by the police of the need for expertise in crime detection, the body of detectives in the English police grew very slowly (never more than a single digit percentage of any police force), with many forces having no distinct detective personnel. This limited expansion took place against the backdrop of widespread unease with plain-clothes officers, who, owing to their involvement with the criminal milieu and the absence of an explicit identity as agents of the law, were viewed as inherently susceptible to wrongdoing and as a threat to liberty (Shpayer-Makov, 2011). Misgivings about covert law enforcement, both within and outside the police, though much diminished in the latter part of the 19th century, had accompanied the development of the occupation of detection in England to a greater extent than in other countries. To appease opposition and attain essentially needed support for plain-clothes policing, police resort to secret methods was, at least compared to the continent, hesitant and restrained, and a relatively overt style of police detection was promoted (Shpayer-Makov, 2011, 2014). This strategy produced the desired effect. With the support of a largely sympathetic press, the 19th century saw a gradual shift in the image of the English detective from a rogue and potentially repressive agent of the state to a dedicated public servant – at times, even achieving a mythic stature – manifested in the growing tendency of the public to appeal to the criminal justice system to attain justice (Shpayer-Makov, 2011, 2014).

Moreover, though mostly coming from a working-class lineage, police detectives figured prominently in all forms of the media, a distinction unmatched by the rival uniformed branch of the police, which was subject to inferior status and conditions of service within the police (Morris, 2006). In fact, few occupations were the object of such insatiable curiosity by the public as detection, whether carried out by police or private agents. Although botched investigations of sensational crimes did reach the headlines, the press generally tended to underplay the extent of corruption, malpractice and heavy-handedness of police detectives and their low level of clearance rates (Shpayer-Makov, 2014). The press, along with the literary world, was also responsible for the intimate association between detectives, on the one hand, and the fight against violent crime, particularly homicide, and the solution of intricate mysteries, on the other, when, in real life, most police detectives dealt with mundane property crime and private detectives were barred from investigating serious offences.

Above all, it was the detective squad at the headquarters of the Metropolitan Police of London, popularly known as Scotland Yard (created in 1842), that acquired the most prestigious reputation and was widely regarded as a model worthy of imitation, even abroad (Shpayer-Makov, 2011). This squad, serving as the nucleus of a network of detective departments in London, as well as a quasi-national body, attracted the bulk of media attention. It handled the more complex crimes not only in London, but also, when called upon, in the country at large, meeting requests by the British and foreign governments, and providing unique services nationwide. Its singular standing was enhanced at the beginning of the 20th century with the adoption of fingerprinting as the most reliable means of identifying criminals – essentially, the end product of the labours of British innovators (Morris, 2006). Notably, until then, English detectives had lagged far behind continental powers in the invention and application of new scientific forensic measures.

During the next 30 years, police authorities continued to prioritise prevention and beat patrols over detection, and detectives remained a small fraction of police manpower in each locality (Home Office, 1939). However, resistance to undercover policing had receded almost completely, especially in the face of the German spy scares before and during the First World War, and further attempts were made to improve the investigative abilities of the police. During Queen Victoria's reign, police detectives received no vocational training, and acquired special skills and insights on the job. At the beginning of the 20th century, however, a specific training programme for detectives was introduced by the Metropolitan Police and later by a number of other forces (Shpayer-Makov, 2011). Greater utilisation was made of technology, such as the telephone, wireless and motor cars, allowing detectives to respond quickly to a crime, and some detectives became specialists in specific types of crime and in the compilation and storage of intelligence for easy retrieval.

Due to the local system of policing, the various criminal investigation departments were never centralised under one authority, but there was growing cooperation between detectives from varied forces, and detective conferences now convened to exchange views on common interests. Record keeping and the circulation of information on crime and criminals in the country became more efficient. Moreover, while women were not employed as police officers, let alone as police detectives, before the First World War, women were thereafter recruited to the police, if in very small numbers – about 100 in the Metropolitan Police in the 1930s – with a handful serving as detectives attached to criminal investigation departments (Home Office, 1939). Apart from clerical duties, their main mission was to take statements from women, girls and children, which may not have been given to men. Nonetheless, police detectives were subject to considerable criticism during the interwar period, particularly in criminal justice circles, but periodically also in the press, though the overall impression in the latter remained complimentary. The criticism was directed at the continued lack of interest in advanced scientific techniques, the poor quality of crime investigations and the limited scope of the few training programmes, reinforced by intermittent allegations of corruption and abuse of detective powers and accusations of failure to stem the rising tide of crime (Home Office, 1939). The measures taken, considered insufficient, were implemented unevenly, with only a few detective departments responsive to the new procedures. While Scotland Yard led the way, this squad, too, was seen as in need of far-reaching reforms.

Consequently, during the 1930s, police detectives experienced noteworthy strides in the professionalisation of their occupational culture. Among other advances: a network of regional forensic laboratories was established in a number of large cities, as well as in the Metropolitan Police of London, to be used by the police; detective training put greater stress on the application of science to detective work; and a national forensic science service was formed by the Home Office. However, only in the latter part of the 20th century did the police system of crime investigation undergo radical change, including the use of computers and the introduction of deoxyribonucleic acid (DNA) analysis, along with other scientific and technical aids, requiring investigators to possess many more specialised skills and broader knowledge than before. Of particular significance in this period is the re-emergence of private solutions in various fields of investigation and the expansion of commercial security services, reflecting a blurring of boundaries between the public and private sectors.

HAIA SHPAYER-MAKOV

See also: **Bow Street Runners, The; 'New' Police, The; Sherlock Holmes**

Readings

Beattie, J. (2012) *The first English detectives*. Oxford: Oxford University Press.

Home Office (1939) *Report of the Departmental Committee on Detective Work and Procedure* (five vols). London: Her Majesty's Stationery Office.

Morris, R.M. (2006) '"Crime does not pay": thinking again about detectives in the first century of the Metropolitan Police', in C. Emsley and H. Shpayer-Makov (eds) *Police detectives in history, 1750–1950*. Aldershot: Ashgate, pp 79–102.

Shpayer-Makov, H. (2011) *The ascent of the detective*. Oxford: Oxford University Press.

Shpayer-Makov, H. (ed and annotator) (2014) *The development of detective policing*. London: Pickering and Chatto.

F

FAR RIGHT, THE

The political ideology of the far right has largely been associated with totalitarianism, anti-communism and ultra-nationalism. Many groups of the far right have also adopted (or tacitly approved of) anti-Semitic, anti-Islamic or racist creeds, which have stimulated the involvement in hate crimes by their supporters. Although far right regimes were established in Italy under Benito Mussolini (1921), Germany under Adolf Hitler (1933) and Spain under Francisco Franco (1939) during the interwar period in Europe, British democracy was never seriously threatened by politically extreme movements. Yet, the growth and activism of some far right movements has caused concerns from a public order perspective and has subsequently helped influence British law.

While early groups such as the British Fascisti and the Imperial Fascist League had harnessed some support, it was not until Sir Oswald Mosley formed the British Union of Fascists (BUF) in 1932 that a government response became necessary. Like the other fascist movements in Britain that were inspired by Mussolini, the BUF also adopted the Blackshirt uniform. By 1934, BUF membership was estimated at 40,000 and their members organised public meetings and uniformed processions across the country (Thurlow, 2009). Although under instruction from Mosley to obey the law, members frequently provoked and engaged in disorder. Furthermore, anti-fascist movements were also formed in some communities and they interrupted far right activism with heckles, singing and stone throwing. Many of the anti-fascist movements had links with the Communist Party of Great Britain.

In response to the disruption of their rallies, the BUF organised and trained stewards to swiftly deal with hecklers. At the BUF meeting at Olympia, London, on 7 June 1934, their stewarding techniques came under the spotlight as members of the audience were brutally ejected. The policing of this meeting was also criticised in Parliament as the police did not intervene inside the hall due to different understandings of their role at meetings held on private premises (Channing, 2015). Later that year, the judgment in *Thomas v Sawkins* (1935) established that the police did have the common law power to be present at a public meeting held on private premises when a breach of the peace was anticipated.

There are also debates on the implementation of police practice in public places. Ewing and Gearty (2004) argue that the police discriminately used their powers to facilitate the fascists and impede both anti-fascists and communists. While there are instances that support this perspective, a more objective view accounts for the inconsistency in police practice across the whole country, highlighting how BUF activism was also restricted by the police (Channing, 2015). Public processions have largely been used by far right groups such as the BUF, the National Front and the English Defence League (EDL) as a 'march and grow' tactic, which also provocatively divides communities. For example, Mosley's planned march through Jewish communities in East London on 4 October 1936 was prohibited following clashes between the police and anti-fascist protestors. The Metropolitan Police Commissioner prohibited the march using his common law powers to prevent further breaches of the peace. What became known as the Battle of Cable Street became 'the straw that broke the camel's back' and the Public Order Act 1936 was rushed through Parliament (Thurlow, 2000). The provisions included the power to prohibit public processions, and this power was later amended by the Public Order Act 1986. These provisions have been used to curtail the provocative activism of several far right movements such as the BUF, the Union Movement, the National Front and, more recently, the EDL.

Current far right groups such as the EDL and Britain First have effectively used the Internet and social media for self-promotion. However, it also helps to demonstrate how many members of far right groups are responsible for hate crimes. For example, two fifths of all anti-Muslim hate crimes reported to TellMama (a public service for measuring anti-Muslim attacks) were known to be related to the far right, including the British National Party and the EDL. Furthermore, nearly half of anti-Muslim online abuse is attributed to supporters of far right movements (Little and Feldman, 2015).

IAIN CHANNING

See also: **Breach of the Peace; Public Order Law**

Readings

Channing, I. (2015) *The police and the expansion of public order law in Britain, 1829–2014.* Abingdon: Routledge.

Ewing, K.D. and Gearty, C.A. (2004) *The struggle for civil liberties: Political freedom and the rule of law in Britain, 1914–1945.* Oxford: Oxford University Press.

Littler, M. and Feldman, M. (2015) *Tell MAMA reporting 2014/2015: Annual monitoring, cumulative extremism, and policy implications.* Middlesbrough: Centre for Fascist, Anti-Fascist and Post-Fascist Studies.

Thurlow, R. (2000) 'The straw that broke the camel's back: public order, civil liberties and the Battle of Cable Street', in T. Kushner and N. Valman (eds) *Remembering Cable Street: Fascism and anti-fascism in British society.* London: Vallentine Mitchell, pp 74–94.

Thurlow, R. (2009) *Fascism in Britain, from Oswald Mosley's Blackshirts to the National Front.* London: I.B. Tauris.

FEMALE MURDERERS

Female murderers are distinguishable by their rarity. While the levels of women's involvement in other crimes have fluctuated historically, they have accounted for a minority of homicides – around 15% in 18th-century London and around 11% in the UK in the 21st century (Brookman, 2005; Durston, 2007). Another historical continuity can be found in the nature of killing by women. Reflecting women's social positioning, it is less likely to take place in public and more likely to be confined to domestic space than men's killing. Related to this, women's victims are typically intimates and very rarely strangers. Contrary to some theories that have predicted otherwise, women's greater entry into the public sphere in the 20th century did not lead to an increase in their perpetration of murder and other types of homicide.

Although comparatively low in terms of occurrence, the threat of fatal violence by women has frequently caused cultural disquiet. In particular, the murder of husbands by wives or employers by female servants raised the prospect that women could unpredictably violate their expected social roles. The female-specific crime of petty treason – killing a husband, employer or clergyman – carried the punishment of being burnt alive until 1787. In the early modern period, popular texts such as pamphlets, ballads and plays frequently depicted husband murder, articulating anxieties about the threat to the divinely mandated social order that such crimes posed (Dolan, 1994).

Female violence contravenes norms of submissiveness, nurturance and gentleness, and subverts the gender order. Ongoing stereotypes of violent women as abnormal, unnatural and unfeminine can be identified. These include the 'masculine' woman, whose use of violence marks her out as manly and deviant, and the dominant woman, who holds sway over others and entices them to commit violence. By way of example, Elizabeth Brownrigg was executed in front of a hostile crowd in 1767 for the murder of a 15-year-old servant girl. Her husband and son were also tried for the crime, but were convicted of lesser charges and escaped execution. Brownrigg was understood to be the dominant one (Durston, 2007).

Furthermore, Swiss-born Maria Manning was hanged with her husband, Frederick, in 1849 for the murder of her lover, Patrick O'Connor. She was seen as dominant over Frederick and was portrayed as masculine. Alongside these portrayals, newspapers and broadsheets depicted her as exotic due to her foreign birth, sexually promiscuous and dangerous (Kay, 2013). This attention to deviant sexuality is another enduring stereotype associated with female murderers.

Recurrent 'stock stories' of women who kill are retold in different places and times. This does not mean that these representations are ahistorical and unchanging; rather, they reflect historically specific anxieties and social change (Seal, 2010). The panic over an 'epidemic' of poisoning in the mid-19th century mobilised long-standing stereotypes of femininity and deception. Associated moves to restrict the sale of poison also reflected the growing professionalisation of pharmacists and doctors, who wished to enhance their control and influence (Nagy, 2015). The conviction of Myra Hindley and Ian Brady in 1966 for the murders of children preceded Hindley's representation as a byword for deviance and evil. The case also resonated with mid-20th-century elite concerns about the democratisation of culture. As working-class young people, Hindley and Brady were perceived as corrupted by exposure to 'intellectual' ideas beyond their comprehension (Seal, 2010).

Whether female murderers receive preferential treatment and lighter punishments than their male equivalents, or whether they are, in fact, subject to exemplary punishment and treated harshly for stepping outside of their expected gender role, is a matter of debate. Historically, proportionately fewer women were executed than men and they were more likely to be reprieved. The picture is complicated, however, by differences in the types of murders that women and men commit, with the domestic context of women's crimes frequently offering potential for mitigation. Some women, such as Myra Hindley, whose sentence was changed to one of 'whole life' in the 1990s and who died in prison in 2002, do seem to have been subjected to exemplary punishment.

LIZZIE SEAL

See also: **Deviant Women; Women and Violent Crime**

—

Readings

Brookman, F. (2005) *Understanding homicide*. London: Sage.

Dolan, F.E. (1994) *Dangerous familiars: Representations of domestic crime in England, 1550–1700*. Ithaca, NY: Cornell University Press.

Durston, G. (2007) *Victims and viragos: Metropolitan women, crime and the eighteenth-century justice system*. Bury St Edmunds: Arima Publishing.

Kay, A. (2013) 'True crime in Bermondsey: representations of Maria Manning', *Clues*, 31(2): 32–45.

Nagy, V.M. (2015) *Nineteenth century female poisoners: Three English women who used arsenic to kill*. Basingstoke: Palgrave.

Seal, L. (2010) *Women, murder and femininity: Gender representations of women who kill*. Basingstoke: Palgrave.

FEMALE THIEVES

While considerable scholarship on the history of gender and crime has been produced since the 1970s, the female thief has attracted far fewer dedicated studies than the murderess, prostitute, abortionist or baby-farmer. Theft, except in specific and limited forms, has never been associated with women in the same way that other offences, such as poisoning or infanticide, have been. Women comprised only a minority of property offenders, usually 10–25%, in various jurisdictions across time. Between the 17th and 20th centuries, the pattern of prosecutions of female thieves was generally one of decline (Emsley, 1996). However, while they may have been the minority of offenders, property crime still constituted the bulk of indictable criminal behaviour by women, accounting for 80–90% of female defendants before the higher courts across the 19th and 20th centuries (D'Cruze and Jackson, 2009). The experiences of female thieves were, moreover, as influenced by gendered contexts as other forms of crime.

Broadly speaking, historically, women committed all the same types of property crimes as men. Yet, gender had a determining influence on the offences most common among female thieves, affecting where their thefts took place and what was stolen. The bulk of women offenders were indicted for simple thefts, often of clothing or household goods. The thefts themselves tended to be opportunistic and unplanned, sometimes involving items stolen or 'borrowed' from neighbours, or clothing 'snow-dropped' from washing-lines. Lynn MacKay (1999) has demonstrated how such stealing in 18th-century England was predicated on women's domestic roles. Occasionally, the goods would be converted to women's personal or familial use; in other cases, they were pawned. As pawning was a common financial management strategy among working-class women, they were less likely to attract attention doing it, which also encouraged high rates of female involvement in the receiving of stolen goods (MacKay, 1999). Other common forms of female theft, such as pickpocketing and shoplifting, were likewise predicated upon gendered opportunities to steal provided, respectively, by prostitution and the growth of shopping as a feminine recreational activity from the late 18th century (Palk, 2006); such contexts also explain why female thieves were more confined to urban areas than their male counterparts (D'Cruze and Jackson, 2009).

Historical explanations for why women stole were also gendered. Despite the overall low number of female thieves, women's greater capacity for deception was said to assist their larcenous schemes, making them especially convincing fraudsters. On the other hand, the limited female involvement in crimes such as burglary or robbery meant that the rare instances of them were attributed to gender deviancy (D'Cruze and Jackson, 2009). Female thieves were frequently described in media and popular culture as having masculine features and attributes; occasional instances of cross-dressing women acting as highwaymen or housebreakers also attracted considerable fascination. If not being accused of appropriating a masculine identity, female thieves were usually said to be acting at men's behest, a construction since challenged by historians. Nineteenth-century discourses concerning the 'criminal classes', though, represented women mainly as accomplices to male thieves, acting as police lookouts during burglaries or luring victims down dark alleys for male companions to rob (Emsley, 1996). Female thieves acting in concert with their husbands were even protected from prosecution under the principle of *coverture*, with the presumption that marital coercion was implicit in such cases not abolished in England until 1925 (Palk, 2006). The construction of female mentality as weaker and more susceptible to influence was also instrumental in the increasing attribution of female thefts to kleptomania in the last decades of the 19th century.

The influence of such gender discourses meant that female thieves were treated differently at various stages of the judicial process. Peter King (2000), in particular, has shown that female thieves fared better throughout pre-trial, trial and sentencing. King (2000) argues that the type of offences that women were most likely to commit discouraged prosecutions against them, sometimes because the offence's petty nature was not worth the effort, and in other instances because the character of the offence made it difficult to prove felonious intent, as with receiving stolen goods. It is also unclear to what degree women were less likely to commit major property crimes, and to what extent they were simply more likely to be charged instead with lesser offences due to prevailing perceptions about women's capacity for more serious criminal undertakings. The trivial nature of female property offences, or at least their construction in this way, meant juries were under less pressure to convict women. That, historically, the majority of female thieves were acquitted while the majority of male ones were convicted was also due to the sympathy engendered by certain types of women, especially those who were young, pregnant or already mothers. Finally, even if convicted, female thieves were sentenced far more lightly, again perhaps due to the perception that female criminals represented less of a danger to society (King, 2000).

ALANA PIPER

See also: **Deviant Women; Women and Violent Crime**

Readings

D'Cruze, S. and Jackson, L.A. (2009) *Women, crime and justice in England since 1660.* Houndmills: Palgrave Macmillan.

Emsley, C. (1996) *Crime and society in England, 1750–1900.* London: Longman.

King, P. (2000) *Crime, justice and discretion in England 1740–1820.* Oxford: Oxford University Press.

MacKay, L. (1999) 'Why they stole: women in the Old Bailey, 1779–1789', *Journal of Social History*, 32(3): 623–39.

Palk, D. (2006) *Gender, crime and judicial discretion 1780–1830.* Martlesham: Boydell Press.

FINANCIAL CRIME

This focus on financial crime originates in Edwin Sutherland's groundbreaking study of unlawfulness among 'the powerful' (eg Croall, 1989), namely, respectable people and their businesses. It arises from Sutherland's identification of two broad types of criminal behaviour found within this sphere, which included 'misrepresentations of asset values' (Sutherland, 1940, p 3). These activities were considered to approximate with 'fraud and swindling' (Sutherland, 1940, p 3), and 'financial crime' as a distinct term is now found in academic study, and also in policy discourse, and even in law itself.

Critical scrutiny of this language also exposes the care required in its use. Criminologists rightly note that financial crimes are committed across the socio-economic spectrum, including within blue-collar communities (Levi, 2002, p 149) and among recipients of state welfare (Law Commission, 1999, para 1.9). Within more elite echelons, ordinary middle-class persons are found engaging in financial impropriety – for example, insurance and mortgage fraud (Karstedt and Farrall, 2007), alongside 'business crime', occurring 'in the commercial sphere' (Law Commission, 1999, para 1.4).

Criminologists do typically analyse financial crime as a 20th-century phenomena, and both historians and criminologists have largely ignored its historical roots. However, in 1969, Harold Perkin observed that the 'railway mania' of 1846–47 exposed Britain to 'a whole new world and vocabulary of ingenious crime', which could only be perpetrated by wealthy (or apparently so) businessmen (Perkin, 1969, p 442).

The field of financial crime study within criminology and history, as well as law, is relatively small, but interesting and varied accounts of 19th-century experiences can be found. These present Britain as a 'haven' for the commission of financial crime (eg Robb, 1992) – and also seek to refute this (Taylor, 2013, pp 5–6) – but also reconstruct determination to ensure that respectable persons were not above the law (Taylor, 2013), notwithstanding the manifest difficulties that this would entail (Wilson, 2014). Narratives tell of a lasting legacy of unintended consequences even for today rooted in how initial responses were directed (Wilson, 2014).

Victorian contemporaries even used the term 'financial crime' and appreciated that such activities were perpetrated across a broad socio-economic continuum, and not only by the very wealthy, with both apparent in contemporary observations of the 'inauguration, development, and rapid progress' of 'High art' crime (Evans, 1859, p 1). This commentary acknowledged that financial dishonesty had been a characteristic of life in Britain since 'time immemorial' (Evans, 1859, p 1), but that through the appearance of activity termed 'commercial crime' and even 'financial crime', the 1850s represented a new era of unlawfulness in business spheres. Alignment of this with Sutherland's classification of 'fraud' and 'swindling' can be seen through the contemporary appreciation of a spectrum of offending, including:

> The apprentice boy, who robs the till of a few shillings [to enjoy himself on a particular evening]; the gigantic forger or swindler who absorbs thousands that he may outshine [others around him] ... the reckless speculator who would risk everything in the hope of sudden gain rather than toil safely and laboriously for a distant reward ... [an otherwise] perfectly honourable man. (Evans, 1859, pp 1–2)

Remarks on the 'honourable' perpetrator also insightfully foresaw the lack of criminal 'self-image' that criminologists observe today among financial offenders (Friedrichs, 1996, p 5). Elsewhere (Wilson, 2014), it is considered how such 19th-century viewpoints also foresaw the trope of 'crime of ambiguity' (Aubert, 1952, p 263) associated with financial crimes today, and even forecast the attacks that have been made on the very terminology of 'financial crime', which has led to the adoption in some quarters of an alternative formulation of 'financial abuse' (International Monetary Fund, 2001, para 7).

SARAH WILSON

See also: **Respectable Criminal, The; White-collar Crime**

Readings

Aubert, V. (1952) 'White-collar crime and social structure', *American Journal of Sociology*, 58: 263–71.

Croall, H. (1989) 'Who is the white-collar criminal?', *British Journal of Criminology*, 29(2): 157–74.

Evans, D.M. (1859/1968) *Facts failures and frauds revelations financial mercantile criminal* (first published 1859: London: Groombridge; reprinted New York: Augustus M. Kelley, 1968).

Friedrichs, D.O. (1996) *Trusted criminals: White collar crime in contemporary society.* California, CA: Belmont Press.

International Monetary Fund (2001) *Financial system abuse, financial crime and money laundering – background paper.* Washington, DC: International Monetary Fund.

Karstedt, S. and Farrall, S. (2007) 'Law-abiding majority? The everyday crimes of the middle classes', *Centre for Crime and Justice Studies Briefing*, 3: 1–8.

Law Commission (1999) *Fraud and deception: A consultation paper*, CP No 155. London: HMSO.

Levi, M. (2002) 'Suite justice or sweet charity?': some explorations of shaming and incapacitating business fraudsters', *Punishment and Society*, 4(2): 147–63.

Perkin, H. (1969) *Origins of modern British society 1780–1880.* London: Routledge and Kegan Paul.

Robb, G. (1992) *White-collar crime in modern England: Financial fraud and business morality, 1845–1929.* Cambridge: Cambridge University Press.

Sutherland, E.H. (1940) 'White collar criminality', *American Sociological Review*, 5: 1–12.

Taylor, J. (2013) *Boardroom scandal: The criminalization of company fraud in nineteenth-century Britain.* Oxford: Oxford University Press.

Wilson, S. (2014) *The origins of modern financial crime: Historical foundations and current problems in Britain.* Abingdon: Routledge.

FIRST-WAVE FEMINISM

The term 'first-wave feminism' was introduced to describe the period of feminist activism that took place between the late 19th and early 20th centuries. First-wave feminism was largely concerned with the granting of equal rights to women and, as such, represented a direct challenge to the application of the principle of formal equality on which modern liberal democracy is founded. Many of the campaigns of first-wave feminism, therefore, centred on the right to vote in political elections, the right to education, property rights and more participation for women in public life. In the UK, first-wave feminism is particularly associated with the suffragette movement. Members of the Women's Social and Political Union (WSPU), founded by Emmeline Pankhurst, chained themselves to railings, set fire to postboxes, broke windows, heckled government ministers, disrupted Parliament and marched for their right to vote. Their militancy often resulted in arrest and imprisonment, and their experiences at the hands of the criminal justice system led the suffragettes to a greater understanding of the plight of other women 'offenders'. Thus, they came to argue for the introduction of women police officers and for the prison system to be reformed to take into account the specific needs of women. They also campaigned on issues related to violence against women and prostitution. The treatment of women in prison and violence against women remain of crucial importance to feminists working within criminology.

While imprisoned, the suffragettes encountered the harshness of prison life and experienced the level of ill-treatment that women inmates were subjected to on a daily basis. As is true today, many of the prisoners they encountered had been convicted of non-violent petty crimes, were poor and had suffered sexual and physical abuse. As Lady Constance Lytton (1914, pp 62–3) wrote, the women that she met were:

> child-burdened women who were left without money, without the means or opportunity or physical power to earn it, who had stolen in order to save their lives and that of their children ... women who from childhood had been trained to physical shame ... women who had been seduced by their employers ... [hardly the] enemies of the state.

Such social injustices were seen by Lytton and other first-wave feminists to have arisen directly from the unequal status of women in society: these women were a symbolic manifestation of the suffragettes' cause. The road for women was not a fair one: 'what was their training, what their choice from the start? Are not the doors of the professions and many trades still barred to them?' (Lytton, 1914, p 63). On a practical level, many of the suffragettes used what voice they had to argue against degrading prison procedures such as the level of searching, restrictions on sanitary provisions and the cutting of women's hair. They also protested at their own treatment; having been labelled 'insane' by the authorities, they fought for the right to be considered political prisoners.

Partly through the very public nature of their activism, the suffragettes often found themselves subjected to male violence. On 18 November 1910, a day that became known as 'Black Friday', many suffragettes were physically and sexually assaulted by both the police and members of the public as they tried to march on Parliament. Such personal experiences led to a greater understanding of the level and impact of male violence. One suffragette, Nina Boyle, was particularly vocal on the subject; after analysing reported cases of violence, she concluded that no crime received such a low level of punishment as that of violence against women. Boyle went on to initiate the campaign for women police officers, which she hoped would result in a more serious attitude towards violence against women and a greater level of fairness in the treatment of women both as victims and offenders.

First-wave feminists did not just focus on violence in public space; for many, the issue of wife beating was of great concern. Frances Power Cobbe's work did much to highlight the extent and severity of the violence inflicted on many wives. In her influential article 'Wife-torture in England', Cobbe (1878) uses the phrase 'wife-torture' to emphasise the cruelty inflicted on many women by their husbands. She also noted the lack of reporting and challenged the image of the battered woman as 'nagging' and 'provocative', which was frequently put forward to the courts. Cobbe was instrumental in campaigning for the introduction of separation orders so that women could be granted an exit from their violent marriages. While this would provide 'some alleviation of their wretched condition' (Cobbe, 1878, p 82), she did not believe, however, that it would resolve the problem. Although Cobbe often cited the orthodox explanations for wife-beating put forward at the time – alcohol, overcrowding and the degradation of working-class life – she believed that the major cause resided in the unequal status of women, in particular, that of wives. Thus, 'the notion that a man's wife is his PROPERTY, in the sense in which a horse is his property, is the fatal root of incalculable evil and misery' (Cobbe, 1878, p 62). There was a strong belief among first-wave feminists in the educational value of being granted formal equality with men, that is, if husbands saw their wives being granted equality by the state, they would be less inclined to regard them as *their* property, which would reduce women's susceptibility to abuse and also encourage women's resistance.

JAYNE MOONEY

Readings

Cobbe, F.P. (1878) 'Wife-torture in England', *Contemporary Review*, April, 55–87 (for information, an extract is also published in: J. Radford and D. Russell [eds] [1992] *Femicide: The politics of women killing*. London: Twayne, pp 46–52).

Lytton, C. (1914) *Prisons and prisoners: Some personal experiences*. London: George H. Doran.

Radford, J. (1989) 'Women and policing: contradictions old and new', in J. Hamner, J. Radford and E.A. Stanko (eds) *Women, policing and male violence: International perspectives*. London: Routledge, pp 13–45.

FORTUNE-TELLING

Fortune-telling was a criminal offence in many jurisdictions throughout the 18th, 19th and 20th centuries. In England, fortune-telling had traditionally been associated with witchcraft; from the Elizabethan period, it was also an offence under vagrancy legislation. While belief in the supernatural had waned by the 18th century, at least among the educated elite, 'pretending' to tell fortunes in exchange for payment remained a crime under the Witchcraft Act 1735, as well as the Vagrancy Act 1824 (Davies, 1999). Under this legislation, fortune-telling was prosecuted not only in England, but also in the Australian, Canadian, Caribbean and African colonies that inherited British laws (Boaz, 2014; Patrick, forthcoming).

The main reason that fortune-telling continued to be outlawed for so long and remains an offence in some jurisdictions even today was its perception as a form of fraud. The object of the 1735 Act was not to stamp out witchcraft, but superstitious belief in its existence; supernatural practitioners were henceforth condemned not for heresy or treason, but for 'pretenses' by which 'ignorant persons' might be 'deluded and defrauded' (Davies, 1999). Under the law, fortune-telling differed from other instances of fraud in that there was no need to prove intent to deceive, which was merely assumed. Into the 20th century, fortune-tellers were prosecuted in British, Australian, Canadian and Caribbean courts despite evidence that they genuinely believed they possessed mystical powers (Patrick, forthcoming). The judiciary in Britain's African colonies eventually did require proof of intent to defraud, but only after convictions began to be overturned on appeal from the early 20th century (Boaz, 2014).

Fortune-telling also had other criminal connotations. It was associated with gypsies or Romani, a people historically vilified for pickpocketing and livestock-stealing, and by the 19th century, it was associated more generally with the criminal classes. This not only bolstered the belief that fortune-telling was a fraudulent enterprise, but also augmented other concerns. The 'cunning-folk' had traditionally both performed divination and offered reproductive advice; this long-standing correlation meant that some fortune-tellers continued to act as intermediaries for women and abortionists into the 20th century. The interest that young women, in particular, showed in having their fortunes told also produced fears that fortune-tellers were acting in collusion with seducers or brothel-keepers to counsel girls to immoral courses, or to funnel them into the white slave trade.

Other fortune-tellers were accused of conveying unfavourable prophecies that drove recipients to suicide or murder (Piper, 2015).

Fortune-telling was furthermore rendered suspect by the class, gender and racial identities of its practitioners and patrons. While in the time of John Dee, astrologer and adviser to Queen Elizabeth I, divination had been popular among an aristocratic clientele, by the 18th century, it was considered the province of the working classes, and, in particular, of an unsophisticated and illiterate rural element (Davies, 1999). The fortune-telling prohibition continued to be justified on the grounds that the lower classes required protection from themselves into the 20th century, when the law was likened to sanitation or compulsory vaccination legislation. Such paternalism was only strengthened by the common observation that the bulk of fortune-telling customers were women, and, in some colonial contexts, that they were usually members of colonised racial groups. That the typical fortune-teller was frequently a working-class woman or person of colour also only increased the scorn that the practice attracted. Yet, given this, its continuing popularity was, if not a threat, then at least an embarrassment to the masculinist Anglo-Saxon culture that authorities were trying to promote in England and its colonies (Piper, 2014).

Despite its suspect status, fortune-telling remained a common diversion for individuals from a range of backgrounds. While it had been assumed in the 18th and early 19th centuries that superstitious activities would die out as educational levels rose, the late 19th and early 20th centuries actually saw a resurgence in the popularity of divination in Western nations, alongside growing interest in spiritualism and alternative religious practices. Prosecutions for fortune-telling remained comparatively infrequent, due, in part, to difficulties that the police encountered in amassing evidence against practitioners. The reluctance of clients to testify meant that the police usually had to conduct undercover operations to confirm that individuals were acting as fortune-tellers. The activity therefore tended to be targeted only in periodic crackdowns that would see an undercover agent visit a number of reputed fortune-tellers within a short space of time. Such crackdowns become especially common during the First World War due to concerns about the defrauding of grieving loved ones (Piper, 2015). By the second half of the 20th century, however, the legislation had largely fallen into disuse and was eventually repealed in many jurisdictions (Davies, 1999).

ALANA PIPER

See also: Criminal Class, The; Female Thieves; White-collar Crime

Readings

Boaz, D. (2014) 'Witchcraft, witchdoctors, and empire: The proscription and prosecution of African spiritual practices in British Atlantic colonies, 1760–1960s', unpublished PhD, University of Miami, USA.

Davies, O. (1999) *Witchcraft, magic and culture 1736–1951*. Manchester: Manchester University Press.

Patrick, J. (forthcoming) *Freedom of religion at the margins: Fortune-telling, witchcraft and the new spirituality*. Vancouver: University of British Columbia Press.

Piper, A. (2014) '"A menace and an evil": fortune-telling in Australia, 1900–1918', *History Australia*, 11(3): 53–73.

Piper, A. (2015) 'Women's work: the professionalisation and policing of fortune-telling in Australia', *Labour History*, 108: 37–52.

GARROTTING PANICS, THE

The 'garrotting panics' describes a discrete period in the 1850s and 1860s in which Victorian London was gripped by fears of violent street crime. Garrotting, now known as 'mugging', connoted a particular style of committing violent robbery; specifically, it involved the use of strangling or, as it was termed in the mid-19th century, 'putting the hug on'.

Crimes of all kinds were reported to be on the increase during the middle decades of the 19th century, but it was violent street crime that generated the most press and state attention. Anxieties about the activities of ticket-of-leave men and habitual criminals following the close of transportation in 1857, and the apparent ineffectiveness of the police and law in controlling crime, created a potent atmosphere in which the establishment drew sharp distinctions between the respectable and unrespectable working poor. The garrotter, as the work-shy savage with a propensity for gratuitous violence, was viewed as the dangerous figurehead of the 'criminal classes' – a criminal underclass that threatened to overthrow society in the middle of the 19th century. Fears over garrotting temporarily subsided in the late 1850s, but were reignited in the summer of 1862.

It was the robbery of Hugh Pilkington MP in the respectable area of Pall Mall that sharpened the focus on garrotting in 1862. Pilkington was returning home from his work at the House of Commons when he was attacked by two 'garrotters' and robbed of his watch. Almost instantly, newspapers, including *The Times*, *Guardian* and *Punch*, published headlines dedicated to the new danger lurking on the streets of respectable London. So prevalent were the fears of garrotting that anti-garrotte materials, including umbrellas and spiked collars, were sold to an anxious public, and famously parodied in a series of *Punch* cartoons.

Historians view the garrotting scares of 1856 and 1862 as a discernible example of a moral panic, that is, an intense overreaction by the press, police and courts to a perceived but unfounded increase in criminal behaviour (Davis, 1980; Sindall, 1987). A moral panic is an episode of misdirected public concern, triggered by alarming media stories and reinforced by a tightening of legal measures, about an issue that appears to threaten the social order (Cohen, 2002). Historians have argued that the mid-Victorian garrotting panics convey little about the reality of violent street crime; rather, the panics were manufactured by the press and resulted in the ill-informed revocation of corporal punishment through the Garrotters Act 1863. Crucially, the effect of intense press reportage encouraged the police to respond with greater vigilance. Public outcry for greater levels of police surveillance resulted in the redirection of police attention towards violent robbery and caused the subsequent inflation in crime statistics, which, in turn, reinforced public fears of garrotting.

The increasing public pressure resulted in Parliament passing a series of hastily designed legislative measures in order to reduce the perceived threat. The passing of the Penal Servitude Act in 1857 abolished transportation and extended prison sentences so that the equivalent sentence to transportation was seven rather than four years' imprisonment. Finally, the panic subsided when the Garrotters Act was passed in 1863. The Act reintroduced flogging for offenders of violent street crime and marked a retreat from the early 19th-century emphasis on reforming and rehabilitating prisoners to the more punitive mid-Victorian regime of 'hard fare, hard bed and hard work'. This legislation was closely followed by the Penal Servitude Act 1864, which made mandatory the police supervision of former convicts released on licence, and increased the minimum sentence of penal servitude to five years for a first offence and seven years for any subsequent offence. The Acts were ad hoc, and while they may have put a stop to the garrotting scares, they marked the increasing severity of 1860s' penal policy. The garrotting panics, then, had little to do with the 'reality' of street crime; rather, the episode demonstrated the ways in which the press, police, courts and law increased the control culture over the 'criminal classes' in the mid-19th century.

ZOE ALKER

See also: **Corporal Punishment; Criminal Class, The; Ticket of Leave; Transportation**

Readings

Cohen, S. (2002) *Folk devils and moral panics: The creation of Mods and Rockers* (3rd edn). London: Routledge.

Davis, J. (1980) 'The London garrotting panic of 1862: a moral panic and the creation of a criminal class in mid-Victorian England', in V.A.C. Gatrell, B. Lenman and G. Parker (eds) *Crime and the law: The social history of crime in Western Europe since 1500.* London: Europa Publications, pp 190–213.

Sindall, R. (1987) 'The London garotting panics of 1856 and 1862', *Journal of Social History*, 12(3): 351–9.

GLADSTONE REPORT, THE

The Gladstone Report, also known as the *Report from the Departmental Committee on Prisons*, presented the findings of a special committee investigating the conditions and effectiveness of prisons in England and Wales. The committee was set up in 1894 and chaired by Under-Secretary of the Home Office Herbert Gladstone.

The Committee and eventual report were borne out of concern in the early 1890s about overcrowding in London prisons and the numbers of habitual criminals living in England. There had also been criticisms levelled at the penal system regarding its capacity to tackle the causes of crime, or lower the rates of actual crime (as opposed to simply lowering the average prison population), and even suggestions that the environment within prisons actively promoted criminal behaviours (Harding, 1988). In part, the report was a reaction to media criticism and public anxiety about incarcerated offenders and the prison system.

The Gladstone Committee attempted to balance a discussion of the administrative and economic reform of the penal estate with the ideological objectives of late 19th-century social reformers. The report was significantly influenced by the rise of criminal anthropology and ongoing debates about the nature and causes of crime. As such, two theories heavily influenced the report. The first was that of hereditism: the idea that crime was a genetic malady and that some were more likely to 'inherit' a propensity for offending than others. The second was environmentalism, which evaluated the social, cultural and environmental causes of criminal behaviour and reform.

The Gladstone Report had six key areas of inquiry: the standard of accommodation and facilities provided for prisoners (particularly in local prisons); the treatment of juvenile and first-time offenders and to what extent they should be treated separately from habitual adult offenders; prison labour and the moral and physical condition of prisoners; regulations governing visits and communication with prisoners; regulations governing prison offences; and arrangements for appointments of warders and deputy governors of prisons. Ultimately, the Gladstone Report raised questions as to whether the current prison system acted as a sufficient deterrent to prisoners and what changes might need to be made for its improvement. Significant questions regarding the experience of inmates – from education and exercise to health, cells and discipline – were raised (Gladstone Committee, 1895). Considerable attention was also given to the administrative practicalities of the prison system.

The Gladstone Report presented several findings and made a number of suggestions for the development of prisons. The report advocated strongly for the better material condition of inmates and for an end to punitive prison labour, which was argued to be more pointless and cruel than it was productive. The Committee attempted to define the meaning of habitual criminality and recommended longer sentences for habitual criminals. It also made the case for the separation of different kinds of prisoners (habituals, drunkards, first-time offenders). It was suggested that deterrence should be the key principle behind penal policy and an emphasis was placed on the ability of prisons to reform offenders rather than just to punish them.

The Gladstone Report was met with both criticism and praise from different factions. While the chairman of the prison commissioners, Sir Edmund Du Cane, resigned his post shortly after the publication of the Gladstone Report, the immediate impact of the Report on the condition of prisons and the penal regime was limited (Harding, 1988). The Gladstone Report is often heralded as the beginning of a shift away from Victorian ideals of imprisonment towards a more modern reform-based system. However, rather than ushering in sweeping change, the Report contributed to a more gradual shift towards more progressive social reforms that developed over the course of the 20th century.

LUCY WILLIAMS

See also: Convict Prisons; Local Prisons; Penal Reform Pressure Groups; Prison Reform

Readings

Harding, C. (1988) '"The inevitable end of a discredited system"? The origins of the Gladstone Committee Report on Prisons, 1895', *The Historical Journal*, 31(3): 591–608.

Gladstone Committee (1895) *Report from the Departmental Committee on Prisons* (C.7702) (c. 7702-1). London: Home Office.

HIGHLAND CLEARANCES, THE

On 16 April 1745 at Culloden Moor above Inverness, about 8,000 of the Duke of Cumberland's soldiers defeated a smaller number of Jacobites in one hour, killing 1,500 of them. Both sides had thought that history was on their side, but it was the Hanoverians who triumphed. The defeat was a turning point in the history of the Highlands as in the next few decades, the Gáidhealtachd (Gaeldom) would be transformed out of all recognition.

The government were determined that what happened in 1745 would never happen again. In the short term, this meant a policy of suppression and intimidation, with the symbols of Highland culture, such as the bagpipes, and Gaelic banned. However, there was also an attempt to incorporate these 'noble savages' into mainstream British culture by forming Scottish military regiments, such as the Seaforth Highlanders. It was estimated that a quarter of Highland men of military age were serving in the armed forces between 1792 and 1815. The drainage of men was part of what came to be known as the Highland Clearances. This was supplemented by outmigration, with around 15,000 Highlanders leaving for North America during the period 1770–1815.

The outward flow of people at this point was voluntary. After the end of the French wars and the onset of economic depression, the Clearances took on a very different hue. Sheep were preferred to people. The forced resettlement of the population on small pieces of land on coastal planes, known as crofts, was achieved on some estates by brutal means, as the following example makes clear. On 13 June 1814, Patrick Sellar, estate manager for the Sutherland family, evicted William Chisholm and his family from their croft by burning down their accommodation while his mother-in-law was still inside. She was rescued by her daughter but died five days later. Sellar was tried for acts of gross inhumanity but was completely exonerated by a jury made up of landowners (Richards, 2008).

The living on uneconomic crofts was a precarious way of life and, as in Ireland, the Highland peasantry were dependent on the potato. When it failed in the mid-1840s, the result was famine, which gave the landowners an opportunity to remove the surplus population from the land. Between 1846 and 1857, over 16,000 people of the poorest type were assisted to emigrate. It was not, however, always a peaceful process. The brutal evictions that took place in North Uist in 1849 and those in Skye in 1853 remain a source of bitterness to this day (Hunter, 1976).

The main phase of the Clearances was over by the end of the 1850s, but there were still unresolved issues that flamed into all-out confrontation and violence in the 1880s – popularly known as the Crofters' Wars. The war began on Skye in April 1882 when crofting families, around 500 strong, obstructed the sheriff's officers, backed by 50 Glasgow policemen, sent in to enforce the collection of rent arrears and carry out evictions, using anything to hand, such as sticks and stones. From Skye, the protest spread through the Scottish islands and land raids were carried out in increasing numbers. On Lewis, a few hundred young men occupied the Park deer forest, which was a part of the Matheson estate, and slaughtered a large number of deer (Devine, 1994). The Liberal government responded: first, by sending in a boatload of marines; and, second, and more positively, by setting up a royal commission to look into the conditions of crofters. The commission gave the crofters the three things they were after: fixity of tenure, free sale and fair rents.

Although more than 2,700 new crofts were created and a further 5,160 were enlarged between 1886 and 1950, it failed to relieve the tensions between landlords and tenants. Land raids and rent strikes continued well into the 1920s (Cameron, 1996). It also did little to stem the outward flow of people. Depopulation became a major social problem. In 1831, the population of the Highlands constituted 8.5% of the total Scottish population; 100 years later, it was only 2.6%. Education proved a far more effective way of clearing people than eviction.

The memory of the Highland Clearances still has the power to evoke strong emotions among the descendants of those cleared. They are interpreted as an act of greed on the part of the ruling class – it acted to protect its wealth and power at the expense of the people. While not all landlords were as rapacious as, say, the Sutherlands, the Clearances are the nearest thing to ethnic cleansing in modern Britain.

WILLIAM W. KNOX

See also: **Lethal Violence (in Scotland); Policing 18th- and 19th-century Scotland; Prisons and Punishment in Scotland; Scottish Criminal Courts, The (c.1747–1850)**

Readings

Cameron, E.A. (1996) *Land for the people? The British government and the Scottish Highlands, c. 1880–1925*. East Linton: Tuckwell Press.

Devine, T.M. (1994) *Clanship to crofters' war: The social transformation of the Scottish Highlands*. Manchester: Manchester University Press.

Hunter, J. (1976) *The making of a crofting community*. Manchester: Manchester University Press.

Richards, E. (2008) *The Highland clearances: People, landlords and rural turmoil*. Dublin: Birlinn.

I

IMPERIALISM

As was the case in Britain, criminal law in the British Empire was primarily concerned with the protection of property, the security of persons and the maintenance of public order. Most scholars agree that race played a crucial factor in the differential prosecution of violent offences, murder most especially (Kolsky, 2010). The intertwined issues of race, violence, law and imperialism were particularly visible in instances of social disorder, which were more likely to be defined and prosecuted as riot or rebellion when Asian or African subjects were involved. Among the most famous of such instances was the 1865 Morant Bay Rebellion in Jamaica. The episode was triggered by the prosecution of a black Jamaican for trespassing on an abandoned plantation. When a group of protesters led by the Baptist preacher Paul Bogle attempted to disrupt the courtroom proceedings and failed to disperse on being read the Riot Act, a violent altercation ensued. Seven black Jamaicans were killed by the militia, and the protesters, in turn, killed 17 white colonists, including the presiding magistrate. The colonial governor, John Eyre, then deployed government troops to pursue and arrest Bogle and his supporters. In the days that followed, soldiers killed 439 Jamaicans and arrested many hundreds more. Of the latter, 354 would eventually be executed (including Paul Bogle), in several cases after highly questionable trials, and over 600 men and women would be flogged (Heuman, 1994). Eyre also ordered the arrest and execution, under martial law, of George William Gordon, a Jamaican politician and businessman who had vehemently criticised British colonial rule. Gordon's treatment prompted some in Britain to question the constitutionality of Eyre's actions, raising the issue of whether crown colonies were ultimately to be ruled by law or by military authority (Kostal, 2005).

Such extreme instances, however, were hardly the only moments in which issues of race and imperialism shaped the character and conduct of British law and legal discourse. Immigration law and the attempts by 'white-settler colonies' (eg Canada, Australia, South Africa) to restrict the entry and mobility of Indian and Chinese migrants offered another. Fierce popular opposition to such immigration in the latter half of the 19th century forced politicians, judicial officials and legal scholars to question the balance between British constitutional principles, political and economic expediency, and the need to accommodate an increasingly vocal and influential electorate of working-class, white colonial residents (Lake and Reynolds, 2008). In the final decades of the 19th century, various means were employed to restrict immigration without violating the constitutional preclusion against explicitly race-based legislation. Among the more common were a 'head tax' demanded of Chinese immigrants on entry or versions of the so-called 'natal test', which required prospective entrants to pass an English-language exam. Australia led the way in immigration control, though the legal constraints on immigration followed an upwards trajectory in Britain as well via the Aliens Act (Dummet and Nichol, 1990).

The balance of authority between Britain and the colonies in matters of law, in immigration as in other realms, varied over time. Throughout most of the 19th century, although colonial judiciaries and legislatures enjoyed considerable independence, they remained under the suzerainty of the metropolitan government and its various offices. As such, the ultimate arbiter of serious cases, and the final destination of appeals, was the Judicial Committee of the Privy Council (JCPC), which operated as the 'high court of Empire'. The JCPC's authority was abrogated as colonies moved towards self-governance. Such was the case with Canada, which established its own Supreme Court in 1875, and with Australia under the terms of the 1901 Constitution. One of the first laws passed by the newly established Australian Federated Parliament, it is worth noting, was the Immigration Restriction Act 1901. This, the culmination of the 'White Australia' policy, was targeted specifically at Asian immigrants and was part of the campaign to garner support for federation from the Australian working class and radical leaders (Auerbach, 2009).

SASCHA AUERBACH

See also: **Australia, Crime, Law and Punishment; British Empire, The**

Readings

Auerbach, S. (2009) *Race, law and 'the Chinese puzzle' in imperial Britain.* New York, NY: Palgrave Macmillan.

Dummet, A. and Nichol, A. (1990) *Subjects, citizens, aliens, and others: Nationality and immigration law.* London: Weidenfeld & Nicolson.

Heuman, G. (1994) *Killing time: Morant Bay Rebellion Jamaica.* Knoxville, TN: University of Tennessee Press.

Kolsky, E. (2010) *Colonial justice in British India: White violence and the rule of law.* Cambridge and New York, NY: Cambridge University Press.

Kostal, R.W. (2005) *A jurisprudence of power: Victorian empire and the rule of law.* Oxford and New York, NY: Oxford University Press.

Lake, M. and Reynolds, H. (2008) *Drawing the global colour line: White men's countries and the international challenge of racial equality.* Cambridge and New York, NY: Cambridge University Press.

INDENTURED LABOUR

Indentured servitude first became common in British North America in the 17th century (Galenson, 1984). This system, in which those seeking passage to the Americas signed long-term labour contracts and were required to work off the debt of their passage, was populated mainly by Europeans. By the late 17th century, it had largely been phased out as the roles of indentured servants were filled by enslaved Africans. The widespread revival of indentured labour in the Caribbean and South America followed hard on the heels of slave emancipation in the British Empire (1834). The new cohort of labourers was recruited primarily via British-controlled territories in India and through the 'treaty ports' of south-eastern China. The first territory to receive a contingent of Indian labourers was Mauritius (in 1829), followed by Demerara (British Guiana), Trinidad and Jamaica in the late 1830s. Chinese labourers began to arrive in Cuba, a Spanish-controlled territory, in 1847, and the following decade saw further Chinese immigration to British Guiana, Trinidad and Peru (Northrup, 1995). By mid-century, indentured labour had become a global phenomenon in both colonial agriculture and industry. Chinese and Indian workers could be found from the railroad projects of the US and Canada to the tea plantations of Ceylon and the sugar plantations of Fiji.

Although the system has been compared to slavery, it bore closer resemblance to a milder form of penal servitude, and it is the latter (in the form of indentured servitude) as much as the former that set the precedent for 19th-century indentured labour. The harsh disciplining of workers through legal restrictions on movement and activity was central to its operation. Similar to the slaves they had replaced, indentured workers were confined to the plantations or work sites to which they had been assigned, were required to carry a pass whenever they ventured beyond such confines, and were subject to severe penalties for a wide range of labour-related offences. Punishments for these offences ranged from the docking of pay to imprisonment, beatings and floggings. At the behest of employers, local magistrates and police employed vagrancy laws to prevent workers who had completed their term of indenture from remaining free of plantation employment for extended periods, thus guaranteeing a steady labour supply regardless of contract turnover. The indentured labour system included a grievance process by which labourers could seek redress for unfair prosecutions, violations of contract terms or harsh treatment. The local magistracy, however, which operated in close alliance with the employers and landowners, offered little respite.

One of the most extraordinary aspects of indentured labour, from a legal standpoint, was the empowerment of ordinary European colonists to act against Indian and Chinese labourers with a level of legal authority ordinarily reserved for police or military forces. The Assam labour code authorised planters to stop and arrest any indentured worker found outside a plantation. In the Transvaal (South Africa), where harsh conditions, strict mobility limitations and segregated compounds prompted frequent absenteeism, the government went to the extreme measure of issuing military rifles to local householders as protection from the gangs of absconding Chinese indentured miners who were allegedly resorting to banditry (Auerbach, 2009).

The application of penal labour laws continued to be severe and widespread even into the early 20th century. In the 1890s, upwards of 20% of the entire indentured labour force faced conviction for one violation or another in any given year (Tinker, 1974). The harshness of this labour regime prompted strong protest from the British Foreign and Anti-Slavery Society and the Aborigines Protection Society (Grant, 2004; Heartfield, 2011). This did not prevent Allied forces from recruiting 150,000 Chinese labourers for European service between 1914 and 1918. Mohandas Gandhi and other Indian nationalists, as well as Indian government officials, also objected to the methods of both recruitment and employment of Indian labourers. In the midst of the First World War, the Indian government, under pressure from multiple fronts, acted to halt all further emigration under the indenture scheme as of 1916.

SASCHA AUERBACH

See also: **Slave Trade, The; Slavery in the Americas**

Readings

Auerbach, S. (2009) *Race, law, and 'the Chinese puzzle' in imperial Britain*. New York, NY: Palgrave-Macmillan.

Galenson, D.W. (1984) 'The rise and fall of indentured servitude in the Americas: An economic analysis', *Journal of Economic History*, 44(1): 1-26.

Grant, K. (2004) *A civilized savagery: Britain and the new slaveries in Africa, 1884–1926*. London and New York, NY: Routledge.

Heartfield, J. (2011) *The Aborigines' Protection Society: Humanitarian imperialism in Australia, New Zealand, Fiji, Canada, South Africa, and the Congo, 1836–1909*. Oxford and New York, NY: Oxford University Press.

Northrup, D. (1995) *Indentured labour in the age of imperialism, 1834–1922*. Cambridge: Cambridge University Press.

Tinker, H. (1974) *A new system of slavery: The export of Indian labour overseas, 1830–1920*. London and New York, NY: Oxford University Press (for the Institute of Race Relations).

INDUSTRIAL SCHOOLS

Industrial schools were institutions for young offenders in England and Wales, those at risk of offending and those in need of care and protection. Their mission was to reform delinquent and neglected children by removing them from their families and surroundings and providing them with structure, discipline, basic education and employment training. At a time when children could still be sent to adult prisons, they were intended as an alternative to traditional penal measures. In this sense, together with reformatory schools, they can be seen as part of what Garland (1990) has termed 'the new penality', referring to the rise of a modern penal system that treated different categories of offenders in distinct ways.

First set up in Britain in 1857 by the Industrial Schools Act, they were inspired by earlier models, including Aberdeen's Industrial Feeding Schools, the Philanthropic Society's farm school and continental juvenile agricultural colonies in France and Germany (Cox and Shore, 2002). Over time, industrial schools were set up in many parts of the (former) British Empire, where some still exist under this name (eg in some parts of the Caribbean).

Industrial schools admitted those up to the age of 14 found guilty of committing an offence or found to be in need of protection. Reformatories admitted offenders up to the age of 16. Although certified by the state, almost all these institutions were run by charities. Children as young as seven could be admitted to an industrial school and would typically remain there until they were released into work on licence – usually at the age of 13 or 14. Boys' schools offered training in agricultural work and, later, in trades such as tailoring. A number of boys' schools had direct links with the army and navy, and many of their young inmates were discharged directly into one or the other, notably, into army bands (Bailey, 1987; Stack, 1994). Girls were trained – almost without exception – to become domestic servants and almost all were found work upon release in private houses or commercial laundries. Difficult, disruptive or 'untrainable' inmates could be discharged to asylums, the workhouse, back to their families or to the streets (Cox, 2012 [2003]).

Industrial schools were certified and part-funded by the state, notably, over a decade before the establishment of state elementary schools for the mass population in 1870. However, almost all were managed and part-funded by Church charities. This meant that the schools were divided along religious denominational lines, with separate institutions for Catholic, Protestant and Jewish children. Most admissions came via the summary courts or, from 1908 onwards, from the new juvenile courts. However, industrial schools also accepted voluntary admissions, for example, from parents who could no longer cope with, or afford to maintain, their children. In most cases, parents were expected to contribute to school costs.

After a period of initial and rapid expansion, the number of industrial schools declined in the early 20th century. This was mainly due to the increasing use of non-custodial measures such as fines and probation, introduced in 1907. The combined number of industrial and reformatory schools fell from 185 in 1915 to 135 in 1923. The Children and Young Persons Act 1933 amalgamated the two types of school into 'approved schools' and brought them under tighter state control.

Industrial schools were part of a diversified British penal estate. They played a part in the later development of today's young offender institutions and homes for 'looked-after children'. Victorian state investments in the schools can be seen as part of a wider early public investment in efforts to reduce crime and break cycles of destitution and delinquency. Their combination of a relatively long period of detention followed by a structured, if often poorly paid, work placement seems to have contributed to a low rate of reoffending on release. However, the emotional impacts of separation from family and often harsh school regimes are much harder to assess. A new study by Godfrey, Alker, Cox and Shore (forthcoming) traces the life courses and life chances of 400 children (mostly boys) sent to industrial and reformatory schools in the late 19th and early 20th centuries. One of its findings is that the schools, although often extremely harsh, helped to reduce the likelihood of post-release reoffending over the life course, largely because they placed young people directly into employment. (For photos and locations of industrial schools, see: http://www.childrenshomes.org.uk/)

PAMELA COX

See also: **Borstals; Juvenile Crime and Justice in Scotland; Juvenile Crime in Britain; Reformatory Schools**

Readings

Bailey, V. (1987) *Delinquency and citizenship: Reclaiming the young offender, 1914–48.* Oxford: Clarendon.

Cox, P. (2012 [2003]) *Bad girls in Britain: Gender, justice and welfare, 1900–1950.* Basingstoke: Palgrave Macmillan

Cox, P. and Shore, H. (eds) (2002) *Becoming delinquent: European youth, 1650–1950.* Aldershot: Ashgate.

Garland, D. (1990) *Punishment and modern society: A study in social theory.* Oxford: Clarendon.

Godfrey, B., Alker, Z., Cox, P. and Shore, H. (forthcoming) *Young criminal lives: Life courses and life chances in England from 1850.* Oxford: Clarendon.

Stack, J. (1994) 'Reformatory and industrial schools and the decline of child imprisonment in mid-Victorian England and Wales', *History of Education*, 23: 59–79.

INEBRIATE INSTITUTIONS

Inebriate institutions emerged in England over the last two decades of the 19th century in response to growing concerns about habitual drunkenness. By the second half of the century, drunkenness was the single largest category of crime in England and Wales, accounting for up to a quarter of all crime. By 1860, it was estimated that there were up to 600,000 habitual drunkards in Britain (Morrison, 2008). Traditional criminal justice responses, consisting of small fines and short terms of imprisonment, were increasingly viewed as inadequate, albeit for two divergent reasons. On the one hand, medical reformers and humanitarian philanthropists claimed that the traditional system was unduly punitive, punishing what were, in effect, diseased persons. On the other hand, it was argued that the standard response failed to control or stem the burgeoning population of habitual drunkards. Proponents of this view argued that short terms of imprisonment unwittingly lengthened the life of habitual drunkards, enabled them freedom to commit further offences between sentences and represented an administrative and fiscal burden on the state.

Responding to these concerns, the first inebriate institutions were introduced through the Habitual Drunkards Act 1879, and the Inebriates Act 1898. Both Acts only permitted the voluntary admission of drunkards to privately managed government-licensed 'retreats'. Those who entered retreats were expected to pay for their 'treatment' and were therefore predominantly drawn from the middle and upper classes. The early Acts therefore failed to address the problems of the recidivist drunkard constantly cycling through the police court for drunk and disorderly offences, or those who committed more serious offences either under the influence of alcohol or where alcohol was considered a contributory factor to offending. To address these gaps, the Inebriates Act 1898 introduced two new types of inebriate institutions: state inebriate reformatories to house the more serious criminal drunkard; and certified inebriate reformatories to cater for the police court recidivist drunkard. The 1898 Act, for the first time, allowed for the compulsory committal of habitual drunkards to inebriate institutions for a period of between one and three years.

While the Inebriates Acts 1879–98, were not explicitly gendered, women were vastly over-represented within inebriate institutions. By 1904, despite accounting for only 20% of drunkenness convictions, women comprised 91% of those in inebriate retreats, and of the 3,636 compulsory committals to inebriate reformatories between 1899 and 1910, 84% were female. By 1906, nine of the 11 inebriate reformatories in England were licensed to receive women only, while the remaining two received both sexes. Inebriate institutions were thus always destined to be gendered institutions (Morrison, 2008).

A number of authors have claimed that the introduction of inebriate institutions represented a key shift in British penology: from individual responsibility to assumed irresponsibility; from moral to medical treatment models; and from punitive containment to constructive rehabilitation (Garland, 1985; Zedner, 1991; Radzinowicz and Hood, 1990; Wiener, 1994). Such claims, however, are not borne out by the weight of historical evidence. For police court recidivists, who had hitherto received up to a month's imprisonment, inebriate institutions represented a significant extension of control. Rurally located, inhabitants were isolated from family, friends and children for up to three years. The deterrent function of reformatories was routinely noted, and they typically had longer and harder labour requirements and more restricted diets than local prisons. Finally, despite rhetorical claims, there is little evidence that reformatories ever offered any medical treatment, with moral and religious persuasion the main mechanism of reform.

Within two years of their introduction, compulsory detention within inebriate institutions was deemed a failure, with up to two thirds of inebriates reoffending. A 1912 Bill to extend the powers of Inebriates Acts was superseded by the Mental Deficiency Act of 1913, which reclassified habitual drunkards as 'defectives' and allowed for their indeterminate containment. The last inebriate institutions 'closed' in 1920, though many were simply reclassified and continued to operate as institutions for the 'mentally defective' (see Morrison, 2008).

BRONWYN MORRISON

See also: **Deviant Women; Drunken Women; Semi-penal Institutions for Women**

Readings

Garland, D. (1985) *Punishment and welfare: A history of penal strategies.* London: Gower.

Morrison, B. (2008) 'Controlling the "hopeless": re-visioning the history of female inebriate institutions c. 1870–1920', in H. Johnston (ed) *Punishment and control in historical perspective.* Basingstoke: Palgrave MacMillan, pp 135–57.

Radzinowicz, L. and Hood, R. (1990) *A history of English criminal law and its administration from 1750: Volume 5.* Oxford: Clarendon Press.

Wiener, M.J. (1994) *Reconstructing the criminal: Cultural, law and policy in England, 1830–1914.* Cambridge: Cambridge University Press.

Zedner, L. (1991) *Women, crime and custody in Victorian England.* Oxford: Oxford University Press.

INFORMAL JUSTICE

Historically, the term 'informal justice' refers to punitive responses to wrongdoing made not by the state, but rather by communities or groups acting outside the legal system. In broad terms, what distinguished informal justice from mere criminality was that the actors claimed to be legitimised by the fact that they were sanctioning behaviour that had transgressed a generally accepted moral code; they claimed to be acting in a broader community interest rather than simply their own. Often, the punishments inflicted were structurally similar to those imposed by the official justice system.

In both urban and rural British communities long into the 19th century, crowds often reacted spontaneously to the discovery of thieves, fraudsters, sexual offenders and so on by dragging them to the nearest river, pond or trough to be ducked. However, ducking was also a possible legal sanction until at least 1809, when an alleged scold was ducked at Leominster by order of the magistrates. Similarly, as the impromptu pelting of offenders was common, so, too, was exposure to the wrath of the crowd at the pillory a feature of the formal criminal justice system until 1837.

More distinctive were the shaming processions, replete with their own symbols and rituals that combined to form a distinct rhetoric of popular customary justice. Common throughout European culture, and known by such terms as Charivari in France, Katzenmusik in Germany and Shivaree in America, these are generally referred to in Britain as examples of 'rough music'. Broadly speaking, these processions were of three types: in the first, the offender was dragged out from his or her home and paraded through the community; in the second, a substitute would impersonate the wrongdoer and cry out the name and offence that occasioned the event; and in the third, an effigy was employed that was burnt at the end of the proceedings (Banks, 2014). The central figure might be mounted on a long pole or 'stang' (in the North, such events were commonly called 'stangings'), carried in a basket, tied to a ladder or forced to ride backwards on a donkey – this last being an understood form of humiliation since classical times. The resulting procession was accompanied by beating upon household utensils, tools, horns, drums and so on to create as much discordant noise as possible in order to draw attention to the event.

Rough music was often staged to reflect offences that were not recognised or that were inadequately penalised by the formal justice system. 'Blacklegs' who worked while their colleagues were on strike might be 'rough musicked', as well as vendors who raised prices and tried to profiteer in times of food crisis, or those who sold short measures (Storch, 1998). Rough music was also employed against those who tried to interfere with the customary gathering and gleaning privileges of the poor. However, the practice was regarded as particularly appropriate for the penalisation of inappropriate sexual or gender behaviour. Offenders who committed marital infidelity, bigamy or incest might be targeted. In addition, medieval and early modern society was concerned to penalise men who had allowed themselves to be dominated by their wives. Hogarth's *Hudibras encounters the Skimmington* illustrates such an event. A husband is forced to ride backwards on an ass, while a man mounted next to him and dressed in women's clothes, beats him with a ladle (a 'skimmington'). Leading the procession are horns raised on a pole, a traditional sign of a cuckold, and a display of women's garments intended to mock the husband's masculinity. The whole is accompanied by the beating of pots and pans.

By the second half of the 19th century, it was becoming rather rare for the offender to be actually seized; effigies were more commonly employed. In some districts, processions became refocused upon, in particular, the punishment of wife-beaters (Banks, 2014). Into the early 20th century, practices similar to rough music, so-called 'white-shirtings', can be seen in labour disputes in mining areas (John, 1984, p 78). As late as the 1950s in some villages, those who offended against sexual mores might still be rough musicked. Increased mobility, expanding economic opportunity, changing morality and declining community cohesion served, however, to undermine the practice.

STEVE BANKS

See also: **Corporal Punishment; Duelling; Lynching**

Readings

Banks, S. (2014) *Informal justice in England and Wales, 1760–1914: The courts of popular opinion.* Woodbridge: Boydell and Brewer.

John, A.V. (1984) 'A miner struggle? Women's protests in Welsh mining history', *Llafur,* 4(1): 72–90.

Storch, D. (1998) 'Popular festivity and consumer protest: food price disturbance in the Southwest and Oxfordshire in 1867', *Albion,* 14(3): 209–34.

JURIES

The jury system is probably one of the oldest elements of the contemporary criminal justice system, though it has not survived unchanged or unchallenged. It is debatable how old it is, but it is clear that juries were used in English criminal trials by the 12th century and a man's right to be judged by his peers featured in Magna Carta (1215). Juries have also sometimes been used to decide the facts in matters of civil law (eg defamation) and to determine the cause of death in coroners' courts in cases of sudden and unexplained death.

For hundreds of years, there were grand juries as well as trial juries. Grand juries originally informed the authorities about crimes that had been committed in their area. Later, they were tasked with examining evidence that a crime had been committed before a case was sent for trial. The role of the grand jury in England and Wales eventually became downgraded as a result of the increased role of magistrates in pre-trial proceedings and was ended in the early 20th century. However, the grand jury system still exists in some of the states of the US and its use remains controversial.

For centuries, trial juries were made up of 12 'good men and true'. Their job was to decide on the facts of a case and the guilt – or otherwise – of the accused. 'Good' not only inferred their personal integrity and probity, but also social standing, as only men of property were allowed to be jurors. John Beattie (cited in Green, 1988) established that in late 17th-century London, jurors came from the 'broad middling ranks' of society. Trials during the next 100 years were very swift affairs, only lasting 30 minutes or so each, with verdicts quickly decided and juries hearing several cases in succession. Moreover, although defendants had the theoretical right to challenge individual jurors, it is probable that this right (called peremptory challenge) was used only occasionally (Brown, 2000). While, even in the late 18th century, juries were sometimes sympathetic towards the people they tried, especially in cases that could theoretically result in a capital sentence, their decision-making arguably became increasingly shaped by judicial guidance (Langbein, 2005). In the 19th century, the use of juries was reduced when defendants on certain charges were given the option of trials in magistrates' courts instead.

The jurors' property qualification was codified by 1825 legislation that confined jury service mainly to holders of property assessed at not less than £30 in London, and £20 elsewhere in England and Wales. This law remained in place until 1974, though inflation reduced the real value of the property qualification. Yet, people became increasingly reluctant to serve on juries and there were complex rules under which certain categories of individuals (including Members of Parliament, clergymen, lawyers, the police and even veterinary surgeons) could claim an exemption. In 1964, it was claimed that only 22.5% of people on the electoral register were actually eligible for jury service (Logan, 2013).

Women were permitted to be jurors in 1919; yet, very few women actually served since those who were married were not regarded as householders in their own right. Feminist organisations campaigned for a change in the law, arguing that jury service was both a right and a duty of citizens. In addition to the discriminatory impact of the property qualification, women jurors who were impanelled were subjected to discrimination from lawyers, who advised their clients to use peremptory challenge to exclude women, and even occasionally from judges, who had powers to order all-male juries. For example, the infamous Moors Murders case of 1966 was heard only by male jurors due to peremptory challenge. In 1974, eligibility for jury service became linked to the electoral register (Logan, 2013).

The right to trial by jury still exists, though peremptory challenge is no longer allowed. However, juries can now be dispensed with if there is a 'real and present danger' of jury tampering. Occasionally, the competence of jurors is questioned, as in the 2013 trial of a former cabinet minister's ex-wife, when a jury asked the judge as to the meaning of the term 'reasonable doubt'.

ANNE LOGAN

See also: **Advocacy in Criminal Trials; Assizes; Legal Representation**

Readings

Brown, B.R. (2000) 'Peremptory challenges in the 19th century', *Osgoode Hall Law Journal*, 38(3): 453–94.

Green, T.A. (1988) *Twelve good men and true.* Princeton, NJ: Princeton University Press.

Langbein, J. (2005) *The origins of adversary criminal trial.* Oxford: Oxford University Press.

Logan, A. (2013) 'Women and jury service in England and Wales, c. 1920–70', *Women's History Review*, 22(5): 701–16.

JUVENILE CRIME AND JUSTICE IN SCOTLAND

The impetus for juvenile justice reform in the 19th and early 20th centuries should be seen in the context of a growing recognition of the special position of children within the criminal justice system. It also occurred against the backdrop of an increasing body of child welfare legislation intended to offer children more protection, whether from exploitation in the workplace or from abuse in the home. In the criminal justice sphere, this was reflected in Scotland, as elsewhere in Britain, in the extension of summary procedure, which saw children's cases processed more quickly, avoiding the contaminating impact of long periods in prison awaiting trial. Inspired by philanthropic reform movements, new diversionary approaches were created: the day industrial school system in Scotland and the reformatory movement in England. Despite underlying differences in attitude towards young offenders, reformers in both countries campaigned for legislative support for these institutions, resulting in a statutory UK framework of residential reformatory and industrial schools catering for thousands of criminal and destitute children. The penal character of these institutions marked a significant departure from the welfarist ideals of the original Scottish day industrial schools (Kelly, 2016). As more progressive approaches, such as probation, were adopted in the early 20th century, these institutions fell out of favour.

The turn of the century saw new ideas gaining ground, such as individualised justice and scientific approaches. Special courts for children were established in other jurisdictions and the American model, with its focus on new medical therapeutic ideas, proved especially influential. Under the Children Act 1908, juvenile courts were introduced in Britain. The Act also effectively abolished child imprisonment. While this was undoubtedly a very significant measure conceptually, in practice, it was less of a watershed than might be supposed. In Scotland, the early juvenile courts continued to proceed much as before, with the main difference being that children were separated from adults appearing in court. The Morton Report (1928), in its review of juvenile justice in Scotland in

1928 was critical of the continuing lack of specialist magistrates and the failure to establish a genuinely specialist court for children's cases. It therefore recommended the setting up of a system of specially constituted justice-of-the-peace juvenile courts composed of people specially qualified to deal with children's cases. This was given legislative effect in the Children and Young Persons (Scotland) Act 1932, which allowed for such courts to be set up under the authority of the secretary of state. However, only four areas took the opportunity to set up the new type of specialist courts: Aberdeen, Ayrshire, Fife and Renfrewshire. The majority of juvenile cases in Scotland continued to be heard before sheriff courts, burgh courts or regular justice-of-the-peace courts rather than specialist panels. This contrasted with England, where specialist juvenile courts were established across the country under the Children and Young Persons Act 1933. From the early 1930s, a clear divergence emerged in the development of juvenile courts in Scotland and England, with Scotland adopting the idea of specialist juvenile courts in a limited way compared to England, where it was fully implemented.

The idea of formulating a completely fresh approach to reform was not seriously addressed again until the Report of the Kilbrandon Committee in 1964. Following the Report, juvenile justice in Scotland was transformed with the creation of the children's hearings system under the Social Work (Scotland) Act 1968. The system was founded on the Kilbrandon philosophy: a welfare-based response to children in trouble aimed at avoiding the criminalisation and stigmatisation of children. In recent years, this underpinning philosophy has faced challenges stemming partly from issues related to the politicisation of juvenile justice and the impact of a range of competing rationales in contemporary youth justice (McDiarmid, 2011).

CHRISTINE KELLY

See also: **Juvenile Crime in Britain**

Note

This work was supported by the British Academy.

Readings

Barrie, D. and Broomhall, S. (2014) *Police courts in nineteenth century Scotland, volume 2: Boundaries, behaviours and bodies.* Farnham: Ashgate.

Kelly, C. (2016) 'Continuity and change in the history of Scottish juvenile justice', *Law, Crime and History,* 1: 59–82.

McDiarmid, C. (2011) 'Juvenile offending: welfare or toughness', in E. Sutherland, K. Goodall, G. Little and F. Davidson (eds) *Law making and the Scottish Parliament: The early years.* Edinburgh: Edinburgh University Press, pp 225–49.

Morton Report (1928) *Report of the Committee on Protection and Training*. Edinburgh: HMSO.

Ralston, A. (1988) 'The development of reformatory and industrial schools in Scotland, 1832–1872', *Scottish Economic and Social History*, 8: 40–55.

JUVENILE CRIME IN BRITAIN

A large proportion of crime prosecuted in the past was committed by young people. This statement implies two things: that young people (and boys in particular) committed more crime of a kind likely to be reported; and that younger offenders have, at different points in time, been particular targets for intervention. That said, it is important to remember that societies with high youth crime rates are often those in which young people account for a high proportion of the overall population.

Definitions of childhood and youth have changed over time. However, it remains possible to document the consistent involvement of boys, and, to a lesser extent, girls, in youth crime and disorder from at least the early modern period onwards. Historians have captured this in their accounts of riotous street cultures, subcultures and gangs, property crime of many kinds, and violent crime, from assault and vandalism to manslaughter and murder (Pearson, 1983; Griffiths, 1996; King, 1998; Shore, 1999; Davies, 2009; Ellis, 2014). To explain shifts in youth crime rates, historians look to broad demographic factors as well as to socio-economic trends, such as shifts in the youth labour market. They also consider changes in the state's ability and willingness to intervene to prevent and punish youth crime.

The view that juvenile delinquency is far from 'new' was set out by Geoffrey Pearson (1983) in his now classic text *Hooligan*. The book charts a series of 'moral panics' around disorderly young people, starting with those sparked by Thatcherism in Britain in the 1980s and going back to the late 19th century. Pearson (1983) argued that these panics tell us more about the 'history of respectable fears' about young people than they do about the history of youth crime itself. Other studies bear this out. There is often a sharp distinction between public and media concern around (and fascination with) spectacular youth subcultures and the less spectacular, more mundane, world of the youth justice system. That youth justice system itself has a long history. It was established in Britain in various stages and involved the introduction of new reform institutions, legislative categories and judicial processes. From the early 19th century on, efforts were made to remove children from adult prisons and to create separate reform institutions for them (eg industrial schools, reformatory schools and borstals).

Until the mid-19th century, children facing criminal charges in Britain went through the same judicial process as adults, though those between the ages of seven and 14 were presumed, through the principle of *doli incapax*, to be incapable of criminal intent. Where children were accused of a minor (non-indictable) offence, they would appear before a summary court presided over by a magistrate. Where they were accused of a more serious (indictable) offence, they would initially appear in a summary court but could then be committed for full trial before a judge and jury. Starting in the 1840s, reforms were introduced which meant that the majority of accused children would only appear in the summary courts. The Juvenile Offenders Act 1847 allowed all those under the age of 14 to be tried in a summary court, while the Summary Jurisdiction Act 1879 extended this to all those under 12 charged with any indictable offence except murder or manslaughter and all those under 16 consenting to be thus tried (Shore, 1999; Cox, 2012 [2003]).

This was an important development because it marked a further separation in the legal treatment of children, but, notably, and unlike many other European legal systems, it preserved the possibility of continuing to treat some child offenders in a similar way to adults in certain extreme circumstances. This remained the case even after the introduction of the juvenile court (essentially a special kind of summary court) in England under the Children Act 1908. This helps to explain why two pre-teen boys, John Venables and Robert Thompson, faced a full trial for the murder of two-year-old James Bulger in 1993.

Since the early 19th century, children have been brought into the criminal justice system for their own protection, both as victims of crime themselves (including neglect and physical or sexual abuse) and in attempts to stop them becoming adult offenders. This kind of 'welfare policing' has been most commonly studied through the experiences of girls (Jackson, 2000; Gelsthorpe and Worrall, 2009; Cox, 2012 [2003]) but was, and is, also extended to large numbers of boys. For example, the state greatly expanded the admissions criteria for industrial schools in the 1870s and 1880s to include not just those under 14 formally charged with an offence, but destitute orphans, destitute children of a serving prisoner, children judged by a parent or step-parent to be beyond their control, refractory child paupers, and children whose families were linked to the sex trade. The result was a dramatic rise in the number of children, the majority of them boys, sent to industrial schools. According to Radzinowicz and Hood (1990, pp 181–2), annual admissions increased from 5,700 in the late 1860s to over 20,000 in the mid-1880s. These figures declined in the early 20th century, along with youth prosecutions. This is likely to have been a product of the combined effects of rising living standards, falling inequality, decreasing family size and the consolidation of the early welfare state, which enacted many measures 'in the name of the child' (Cooter, 1992; Hendrick, 2003).

After the Second World War, however, both recorded youth crime and levels of custodial sentencing increased again (Bradley, 2014; Goldson and Muncie, 2015). Over the course of the 20th century, state responses to youth crime veered between an emphasis on welfare (meeting needs) and justice (punishing deeds). Many debates around youth crime focused on questions of race (Solomos, 1991) and social exclusion (Macdonald, 2006). Today, recorded total crime is falling and, with it, recorded youth crime. Recent work in this field has focused increasingly on children as victims, rather than perpetrators, of crime. As Gal (2011) argues, children are the group most likely to be victimised yet least likely to report the crimes against them.

PAMELA COX

See also: **Borstals; Industrial Schools; Juvenile Crime and Justice in Scotland; Reformatory Schools**

Readings

Bradley, K. (2014) 'Becoming delinquent in the post-war welfare state: England and Wales, 1945–1970', in H. Ellis (ed) *Juvenile delinquency, 1850–2000: East–West perspectives*. Basingstoke: Palgrave, pp 227–47.

Cooter, R. (ed) (1992) *In the name of the child: Health and welfare, 1880–1940*. London: Routledge.

Cox, P. (2012 [2003]) *Bad girls in Britain: Gender, justice and welfare, 1900–1950*. Basingstoke: Palgrave Macmillan.

Cox, P. and Shore, H. (eds) (2002) *Becoming delinquent: European youth, 1650–1950*. Aldershot: Ashgate.

Davies, A. (2009) *The gangs of Manchester*. Preston: Milo Books.

Ellis, H. (ed) (2014) *Juvenile delinquency, 1850–2000: East–West perspectives*. Basingstoke: Palgrave.

Gal, T. (2011) *Child victims and restorative justice: A needs–rights model*. Oxford: Oxford University Press.

Gelsthorpe, L. and Worrall, A. (2009) 'Looking for trouble: a recent history of girls, young women and youth justice', *Youth Justice*, 9(3): 209–23.

Godfrey, B., Alker, Z., Cox, P. and Shore, H. (forthcoming) *Young criminal lives: Life courses and life chances in England from 1850*. Oxford: Clarendon.

Goldson, B. and Muncie, J. (ed) (2015) *Youth crime and justice: Critical issues* (2nd edn). London: Sage.

Griffiths, P. (1996) *Youth and authority: Formative experiences in England, 1560–1640*. Oxford: Oxford University Press.

Hendrick, H. (2003) *Child welfare: Historical dimensions, contemporary debates*. Bristol: Policy Press.

Jackson, L. (2000) *Child sexual abuse in Victorian England*. London: Routledge.

King, P. (1998) 'The rise of juvenile delinquency in England, 1780–1840: changing patterns of perception and prosecution', *Past and Present*, 160: 116–66.

Macdonald, R. (2006) *Youth, the 'underclass' and social exclusion*. London: Routledge.

Pearson, G. (1983) *Hooligan: A history of respectable fears*. London: Macmillan.

Radzinowicz, L. and Hood, R. (1990) *A history of English criminal law and its administration from 1750, volume 5: The emergence of penal policy in Victorian and Edwardian England*. Oxford: Clarendon Press.

Shore, H. (1999) *Artful dodgers: Youth and crime in early nineteenth-century England*. Woodbridge: Royal Historical Society.

Solomos, J. (1991) *Black youth, racism and the state: The politics of ideology and policy*. Cambridge: Cambridge University Press.

LEGAL REPRESENTATION

Prior to the introduction of the police courts, and eventually the introduction of a Director of Public Prosecutions in 1879, criminal trials were private affairs in that the victim, or a person with an interest in the alleged crime, had to personally bring a prosecution for a crime to court. This would involve a number of responsibilities, including gathering evidence, attending the pre-trial hearing such as at the magistrates' courts, ensuring witness attendance and the eventual arguing of their case in front of a jury. All of these responsibilities could be of great expense to the lay prosecutor.

However, in this system of private prosecution, parties to a criminal trial had the option to seek legal advice and representation. This advice could be sought from a range of legal actors, most notably, solicitors, attorneys and barristers. The development of establishing legal representation from the Assize of Clarendon in 1166 to the present day was a long and slow process, but certainly from the 14th century, attorneys, solicitors and barristers were appearing in civil and, to a lesser extent, criminal trials (Holdsworth, 1903).

Doctrines of legal representation such as legal privilege and legal representatives having an overruling duty to the court developed in the 16th century. It was the development of such professional ethics and regulation that led, from the 16th century, to the increasing divergence in the roles of attorneys and barristers (Cocks, 1983). The main contributors to this divergence were the rise of the Inns of Court and regulations surrounding the judiciary. There continued to be similarities between barristers and attorneys, but these increasingly diverged as attorneys generally came from a lower, less wealthy class, and, subsequently, this was increasingly reflected in the types of cases with which they were involved. More significantly, attorneys could only appear in the specific court to which they had been called and could not move between different courts or areas of law as other types of lawyers were permitted (Pue and Sugarman, 2003).

Solicitors were more commonly used in matters that were non-litigious, which did not require court attendance; matters included the drafting of wills or the compliance with property requirements. Where solicitors were involved in litigation, they had far more freedom than attorneys in that they could move freely between courts. During the 18th and 19th centuries, solicitors were most commonly found in the Court of Chancery (Langbein et al, 2009). Solicitors were sometimes consulted in criminal matters, mostly by wealthier people accused of committing a criminal offence. However, due to a dearth of historical records, it is unclear how frequently solicitors were employed for pre-trial criminal matters. The role of solicitors in criminal trials has, until very recently, been limited by their lack of rights of audience and thus their forbiddance to speak in criminal courts.

In the 18th century, the prevalence of solicitors was greatly increased by the growing use of state-employed solicitors. Such officials were employed to represent the interests of the state, including the Mint, the Post Office and the Bank of England. The Bank of England, in particular, retained a number of solicitors to investigate and conduct prosecutions in their fight against the forging of bank notes and financial instruments (McGowen, 2007).

Barristers became increasingly prevalent in criminal courts throughout the 18th and 19th centuries, fulfilling a number of representative roles, including speaking for the accuser or the accused in court hearings, but also providing legal advice pre-trial. The role of the attorney has been subsumed into other roles but the distinction between solicitor and barrister continues today, though in an increasing diminished form.

CERIAN CHARLOTTE GRIFFITHS

See also: **Advocacy in Criminal Trials; Assizes; Quarter Sessions**

Readings

Cocks, R. (1983) *Foundations of the modern Bar*. London: Sweet and Maxwell.
Holdsworth, W. (1903) *A history of English law*, vols 1–17. London: Methuen & Co.
Langbein, J., Lerner, R.L. and Smith, B.P. (2009) *History of the common law. The development of Anglo-American legal institutions*. Wolters: Kluwer Aspen Publishers

McGowen, R. (2007) 'Managing the gallows: the Bank of England and the death penalty, 1797–1821', *Law and History Review*, 25(2): 241–82.

Pue, E.W. and Sugarman, D. (2003) *Lawyers and vampires. Cultural histories of legal professions*. Oxford and Portland, OR: Hart Publishing.

LETHAL VIOLENCE (IN SCOTLAND)

Generally, historians of modern Scotland have tended to disregard areas of historical inquiry that explore the darker side of humanity. Focus has mainly been concentrated on questions of national identity and how it has changed over the course of the last 300 years or so. However, while there has been a mushrooming growth of published work on homicide in other countries, Scotland still seems to be largely, as Crowther remarked in 1992, 'a country without a criminal past' (Crowther, 1992, p 82). What work that has been carried out by Scottish historians has mainly focused on: the 18th century, by Knox (2015) and Kilday (2007); the 19th century, generally by Donnachie (1995) and, specifically on the geography of homicide, by King (2011); and later in the 19th century, by Conley (2007) – as well as a comparative piece by Connolly (1999). There exists no historical study of lethal violence in 20th-century Scotland, though data can be retrieved from the various annual publications of the Scottish Office on crime and prisons.

Historians of violence have tended to be dazzled by Elias's (2000 [1939]) theory concerning the growth and development of civilising behaviour. This theory emphasises the centralisation of power in the state and the expansion of the economy, which created chains of dependency as crucial to the decline in violence. As new ideas concerning appropriate behaviour spread from the elite downwards, individuals became less likely to resort to violence to resolve conflicts. Whereas in medieval society, a man's honour was upheld by the sword, in the more civilised world of the 18th and 19th centuries, it was maintained through the law courts. Longitudinal studies of homicide rates (see Eisner, 2001) have, it is argued, borne out Elias's thesis as they have fallen continuously since the late medieval period to the present day.

The problem with this dominant narrative is that the longitudinal studies that have been carried out to support the theoretical position of Elias fail to account for the rises and falls in homicide rates. Indeed, data for Scotland show, in the 18th century, two spikes (1710–29 and 1790–99), both linked to political tensions – associated with the Union and the Jacobite cause in the first period and political radicalism in the second – and a long plateau (1730–89). This is a more accurate reflection of homicidal activity than a linear fall. The murder rate in Scotland for most of the 18th century was a fraction of what it was in other Western

European countries; a phenomenon reflected in the small number of executions in the period 1767–97, which averaged six per year. The most common cause of homicide tended to be arguments in the workplace, at home or in a public place, sometimes, but not as common as has been supposed, with drink as a compounding factor. Men, usually of lower social status, rather than women were overwhelmingly both the perpetrators and victims of murder.

If King (2011) is correct, then homicide rates mushroomed under the impact of widespread economic and social dislocation associated with urban and industrial growth in the first half of the 19th century. From 1805 to 1856, recorded rates increased by 250%. Homicide travelled in a direct route from east to west, reflecting the massive shifts in population distribution. Then, in line with the rest of mainland Britain, they began to decline after 1860 (Conley, 2007); at 40%, this was a much steeper fall than other parts of the UK. Unfortunately, there are no published studies for the first half of the 20th century but it seems as if rates began to rise again quite steeply in the 1980s. Soothill et al (1999) show that average yearly homicide rates were 19.15 per million compared to 11.28 for England and Wales, a phenomenon connected with the rise of gang cultures and the ubiquity of knife carrying among young working-class males in the west of Scotland. This has serious implications for those historians who have been deeply influenced by the civilising theories of Elias. One would have expected the homicide rate to decline even further given the progress in medical science but the truth remains that a Glaswegian had a statistically greater chance of being murdered in the 1980s than in the 1780s.

WILLIAM W. KNOX

See also: Highland Clearances, The; Protest and Policing in Scotland

Readings
Conley, C.A. (2007) *Homicide, gender and national identity in late nineteenth century England, Ireland, Scotland and Wales*. Columbus, OH: Ohio State University Press.

Connolly, S.J. (1999) 'Unnatural deaths in four nations: contrasts and comparisons', in S.J. Connolly (ed) *Kingdoms united? Great Britain and Ireland since 1500: Integration and diversity*. Dublin: Four Courts Press, pp 200–14.

Crowther, M.A. (1992) 'Scotland: a country with no criminal record', *Scottish Economic and Social History*, 12: 82–6.

Donnachie, I. (1995) 'The dark side: a speculative survey of Scottish crime during the first half of the nineteenth century', *Scottish Economic and Social History*, 15: 5–24.

Eisner, M. (2001) 'Modernization, self-control and lethal violence: the long-term dynamics of European homicide rates in theoretical perspective', *British Journal of Criminology*, 41: 618–38.

Elias, N. (2000 [1939]) *The civilizing process* (two vols). Oxford: Blackwell Publishers.

Kilday, A.-M. (2007) *Women and violent crime in Enlightenment Scotland.* Woodbridge: The Boydell Press.

King, P. (2011) 'Urbanization, rising homicide rates and the geography of lethal violence in Scotland, 1800–1860', *History*, 96: 231–59.

Knox, W.W.J. (2015) 'Homicide in eighteenth-century Scotland: numbers and theories, *Scottish Historical Review*, XCIV: 48–73.

Soothill, K., Francis, B.J., Ackerley, E. and Collett, S. (1999) *Homicide in Britain: A comparative study of rates in Scotland, England and Wales.* Edinburgh: Scottish Executive Central Research Unit.

LICENSING

Licensing has developed as a means for authorities to regulate the trade and consumption of alcoholic drinks. Although there had been a variety of (mainly local) controls on the alcohol trade prior to this, the origin of modern licensing in England and Wales is usually located in the Alehouse Act 1552. This Act stipulated that sellers of beer and ale must possess a licence granted by local magistrates. This requirement later came to encompass the selling of wine and spirits too, and, although being abandoned for beer-selling from 1830 to 1880, the licensing of alcohol sellers has become a historically entrenched form of regulation. It has also expanded to incorporate requirements beyond the simple possession of a licence. For example, a 1753 statute insisted that licence applicants must provide character references and, from the mid-1860s, a succession of Acts of Parliament established statutory limits on opening hours for public houses.

The objective of much licensing legislation has been to reduce or manage public disorder (see Valverde, 2003), which occurs within licensed premises or is attributed to persons drinking within licensed premises. The preamble to the Alehouse Act 1552 justified the legislation with reference to the 'abuses and disorders' that occur in 'common alehouses and tippling houses' (Hunter, 2002, p 66). Later developments, such as the creation of new offences of permitting drunkenness on licensed premises in 1872 or the prohibition on selling alcohol to under-18s in 1961, can similarly be linked to concerns about public disorder. More recently, the Licensing Act 2003 echoed this rationale by listing 'the prevention of crime and disorder' as the first objective of licensing.

However, licensing is not purely about public order. The early development of licensing was also connected to the association of drunkenness with poverty and a fear that social mixing in drinking establishments might foster religious dissent or political subversion (Jennings, 2010; Hailwood, 2014). It is further apparent that some licensing reforms in the 18th, 19th and 20th centuries were linked to the idea that drinking was a moral problem (Yeomans, 2014). Moreover, under the Police Reform and Social Responsibility Act 2011, authorities with a remit for public health now have a greater role in licensing.

Licensing thus entails multiple objectives and can involve multiple parties too. It is also important to stress that licensing practices 'on the ground' have varied considerably. For centuries, licensing laws allowed magistrates considerable discretion to decide who could trade alcoholic drinks in their jurisdictions. Some were permissive in this regard, as shown by the 'free licensing' policy of Liverpool magistrates in the 1860s, but some magistrates actively worked to reduce the number of licensed premises in their areas in the late 19th century (Jennings, 2011). The licensing system has thus produced significant local variations since its introduction in the 16th century.

Since the Licensing Act 2003, the authority to grant licences has rested with local councils, not magistrates. Statutory limits on opening hours have also been removed, leaving licensing authorities with the discretion to decide on the hours in which alcoholic drinks can be bought or sold in local areas. However, the essence of licensing remains the same: sellers of alcohol must obtain the permission of the relevant local authority. As such, licensing has proven to be a remarkably enduring means for regulating the sale and consumption of alcohol.

HENRY YEOMANS

See also: **Temperance Movements**

Readings

Hailwood, M. (2014) *Alehouses and good fellowship in early modern England*. Suffolk: Boydell and Brewer.

Hunter, J. (2002) 'English inns, taverns, alehouses and brandy shops: the legislative framework, 1495–1797', in B. Kümin and T.A. Tlusty (eds) *The world of the tavern*. Aldershot: Ashgate, pp 65–82.

Jennings, P. (2010) 'Liquor licensing and the local historian: inns and alehouses 1753–1828', *The Local Historian*, 40(2): 136–50.

Jennings, P. (2011) *The local: A history of English pub*. Stroud: History Press.

Valverde, M. (2003) 'Police science, British style: pub licensing and knowledges of urban disorder', *Economy and Society*, 32(2): 234–52.

Yeomans, H. (2014) *Alcohol and moral regulation: Public attitudes, spirited measures and Victorian hangovers*. Bristol: Policy Press.

LIFE-COURSE ANALYSIS

Largely building on sociological and criminological underpinnings and the historical method of prosopography, the life-course methodology has increased in popularity among crime historians. Criminologists emphasised the link between criminal behaviour and individual background, and historians have consequently increasingly applied life-course perspectives in their analysis. 'Life course' refers to a sequence of socially defined events and roles that individuals enact over time (Giele and Elder, 1998). This longitudinal approach is a trajectory from cradle to grave, aiming to uncover a line of development that includes: getting a job, having children, being imprisoned, marrying or migration. It is not possible to uncover internal decision-making, but the paths that individuals forged for themselves can still be uncovered – through an investigation of potential turning points (eg marriage or criminal punishment). As such, this approach forces a perspective in which offending is seen as it was: unusual and secondary in the lives of most offenders. Notwithstanding the importance of structural factors and historical context (eg changing criminal legislation), it is important to explore offenders' lives before they became officially labelled 'criminal' (Giele and Elder, 1998). Also important, based on the work of Sampson and Laub (2005), is the continued focus on the individual offender in their life after crime, which enables questions of desistance to be explored.

Along with this growing life-course approach has been a development in collective biography (Giele and Elder, 1998). The need to form a collective portrait of offenders based on their socio-demographic characteristics and backgrounds has been recognised. These details help to reveal the underlying reasons for crime, which control mechanisms and structural changes fail to explain. Thus, it is important to examine groups of individuals who were 'born at roughly the same time and experienced approximately the same historical events' (Giele and Elder, 1998, pp 19–20). This kind of collective approach has already long been practised in the discipline of history – known as prosopography. Prosopography essentially involves the statistical analysis of common factors and experiences of a specific cohort, allowing both individual and group-level analysis of elite and *non*-elite subjects (Beck, 2003). Making this approach so valuable is the solution it provides for fragmentary sources. Detailed information can be used in group analysis to supplement individuals who have gaps in their histories. This, along with detailed biographies, avoids masking human agency as far as possible.

The recent upsurge in the digitisation of historical documents is instrumental to historical research and particularly to the method of nominal record-linkage. It allows the study of non-elite criminal lives on a relatively large scale. Criminals, especially, have been well documented. Most criminal justice-generated documents consist of information on the crime and criminal in question, and when combined with detailed historical newspapers, thorough narratives can emerge. In research that depends largely upon documents generated by and for the state, each additional piece of information is important for historical interpretation. This is where record-linkage becomes invaluable. Record-linkage is the bringing together of information concerning a historical individual derived from independent sources – this allows greater information about an individual to be collected and corroborated (Godfrey, 2011).

Now becoming mainstream and more refined, nominal data-linkage can be used to link together criminal records, newspaper reports and census and parish records, enabling a life-event map of each offender to be formed and enabling cradle-to-grave analysis. These grids sequentially order the life events of the individuals, allowing an understanding of the progress of a person's life. It allows the layering of data and the linking of a range of events in a person's life with their criminal convictions (Godfrey, 2011). While significant interactions, events and decision-making will remain hidden in history, interpretation based on available evidence and knowledge of relevant social and economic histories will aid the construction of life-grids. This method was largely pioneered by Godfrey et al (2007). A demonstration of this interdisciplinary method in action can be seen in their study of low-level persistent criminality in Crewe – where they incorporate biographical data into life-course analysis.

EMMA DEBORAH WATKINS

See also: **Digital History**

Readings

Beck, W. (2003) 'The Prosopographia Imperii Rani and prosopographical method', in A. Cameron (ed) *Fifty years of prosopography – the later Roan Empire, Byzantium and beyond.* Oxford: Oxford University Press, pp 11–22.

Giele, J.Z. and Elder, G.H., Jr (1998) 'The life course and the development of the field', in J.Z. Giele and G.H. Elder Jr (eds) *Methods of life course research: Qualitative and quantitative approaches.* London: Sage, pp 5–28.

Godfrey, B. (2011) 'Historical and archival', in D. Gadd, S. Karstedt and S.F. Messnerp (eds) *The Sage handbook of criminological research methods.* London: Sage, pp 158–74.

Godfrey, B., Cox, D. and Farrall, S. (2007) *Criminal lives: Family, employment and offending.* Oxford: Oxford University Press.

Sampson, R.J. and Laub, J.H. (2005) 'A life-course view of the development of crime', in R.J. Sampson and J.H. Laub (eds) *Developmental criminology and its discontents: Trajectories of crime from childhood to old age.* London: Sage, pp 12–45.

LOCAL PRISONS

The term 'local prison' was originally given to refer to gaols, houses of correction and Bridewells that were administered by local authorities. The term was first used in the Prison Act 1865 and aided in distinguishing between the two prisons systems, long-term (convict prisons) and short-term, operating at the time. Local prisons served the local courts, holding those people who were remanded in custody awaiting trial, awaiting sentence or waiting to be transported overseas or executed. In addition, local prisons held those sentenced to periods of imprisonment of up to two years and those imprisoned for debt (until 1869).

Although it was not until 1865 that legislation first used the term 'local prisons', local prisons had existed since at least the Middle Ages and had largely fulfilled the aforementioned role since that time. Local prisons were the gaols, houses of correction and Bridewells that served their local community, existing at both the county and the town level. Historically, there was a legal distinction between gaols and houses of correction or Bridewells, but the Gaols Act 1823 allowed existing buildings to be legally designated as either gaols or houses of correction, putting into law practice that appears to have been operating in a number of areas. It was often difficult to distinguish between the prisons; some towns and districts had a gaol and house of correction on the same site, others had a number of places of confinement, but before the 19th century, these were often quite small, sometimes only a gatehouse or lock-up.

Houses of correction had their origins in the 16th century and the term 'Bridewell' was adopted in some places after King Edward VI gave over Bridewell Palace in 1553 for use to house and teach habits of industry to the vagrant and the poor. The origins of the house of correction were to reform prisoners through discipline and industry, though it is claimed that these goals fell by the wayside during the late 17th and into the 18th century. Similar institutions emerged across Europe at the time, for example, Spinhuis in Germany and Rasphuis in the Netherlands.

At the end of the 18th century, the prison reformer John Howard's survey, *The state of the prisons*, estimated that there were 244 local prisons. James Neild, another prison reformer, put the figure at 317 by the early 19th century. From the Gaols Act 1823, and the appointment of prison inspectors in 1835, the government put increased pressure on local authorities to ensure uniformity across prison regimes up and down the country. The government took control of the local prison system in April 1878 under the Prisons Act 1877; this meant that the administration of the system was taken over by the Prison Commission. The government immediately rationalised the system, closing down some small prisons and amalgamating others, reducing the number from 112 to 69 local prisons (McConville, 1995).

The role of local prisons has continued largely unchanged. Local prisons came to the fore again in the early 1990s when a large-scale disturbance broke out at Strangeways prison in Manchester in April 1990. Previous disturbances in prisons had been in long-term institutions, and were often put down to serious offenders with 'nothing to lose'. The subsequent inquiry into the disturbance, the Woolf Report (Woolf and Tumin, 1991), was hugely influential on the prison system. Local prisons have a long history but they remain central to the prison system today, holding the overwhelming majority of people who are sent to prison at some point in the process. Local prisons are categorised as 'closed', usually with a Category B security classification. Since the early 1990s, the prison population in England and Wales has continued to increase, and the pressure on local prisons – as overcrowded, poorly resourced and having dilapidated buildings, where constructive activity is limited, and where prisoners can be locked up for 23 hours per day – has continued; indeed, they are 'generally thought of as the prison institutions least fit for their purpose' (Jewkes, 2008, p 156).

HELEN JOHNSTON

See also: **Convict Prisons; Prison Reform; Prison Riots**

Readings

Jewkes, Y. (2008) 'Local prisons', in Y. Jewkes and J. Bennett (eds) *Dictionary of prisons and punishment*. Cullompton: Willan Publishing, pp 156–7.

McConville, S. (1995) *English local prisons: Next only to death, 1860–1900*. London: Routledge.

McConville, S. (1998) 'Local justice: the jail', in N. Morris and D.J. Rothman (eds) *The Oxford history of the prison*. New York, NY: Oxford University Press, pp 266–94.

Woolf, Lord Justice and Tumin, Judge (1991) *Report of an inquiry into prison disturbances in England and Wales in April 1990*. London: HMSO.

LYNCHING

'Lynching' is a broad and historically contested term that most commonly refers to informal acts of normally lethal group violence and is particularly associated with the US. In the first half of the 19th century, lynching was prevalent in the American Midwest, South and West, where it was fuelled by: fears of lawlessness and ineffective judicial institutions; popular scepticism of state authority; a commitment to local, communal notions of justice; violent vigilante traditions; and opposition to legal reforms that promoted due process and the rights of the accused. Lynching also served to uphold established hierarchies of race, class, ethnicity and gender, and mob victims were drawn from diverse groups that were considered a threat to social and political order, including white gamblers, horse stealers and abolitionists, Native Americans, Hispanics, and African-American slaves (Pfeiffer, 2011).

By the late 19th century, the main targets of lynch mobs were African-Americans, who comprised 73% of the more than 4,700 men and women known to have been lynched in the US between the early 1880s and the Second World War. Lynching was also increasingly concentrated in the South, where it was underpinned by a distinctive regional culture of law and violence and a virulent and pervasive racial ideology that denied the humanity and constitutional rights of black citizens. Southern advocates of lynching argued that the practice was essential to protect white women from the bestial sexual urges of African-American men that had been unleashed by the abolition of slavery and could not be reined in by formal court proceedings in which victims could be publicly shamed if called to testify and defendants were liable to evade 'justice' on account of legal technicalities. Records show that, in practice, allegations of rape were behind fewer than one in four cases of lynching. Supposed murderers were the most common targets of mob violence, but victims also included men and women accused of non-capital offences and some whose only 'crime' was to violate racial mores in ways that challenged white supremacy (Brundage, 1993).

Lynching peaked in the 1890s and early 1900s at an average of more than 100 cases per year. It served in this period to reinforce white supremacy at a time of both heightened class tensions among white people and intense interracial conflicts that stemmed from economic depression in the rural South, the success of the Populist movement and increased African-American involvement in politics, manufacturing and farm tenancy. Reflecting the seriousness of the threat to white power, new forms of lynching emerged at this time that involved the torture and post-mortem mutilation of victims, which were carried out before crowds of thousands. The impact of these dramatic and macabre events resonated in black communities far beyond the immediate localities in which they occurred (Wood, 2009).

Through the first half of the 20th century, there was a gradual decline in the frequency of lynching, but this was an inconsistent process, with notable surges in lynching activity in the years immediately after the First World War and during the Great Depression in the early 1930s. Lynching's decline, in part, reflected the entrenchment of alternative systems of racial control in the South, including segregation, disfranchisement laws and peonage (debt slavery), but it also resulted from a concerted anti-lynching movement that had its roots among African-American activists in the late 19th century, notably, Ida B. Wells, whose pioneering publications in the 1890s unveiled the racist myths behind the claims of lynching's proponents. The anti-lynching cause was taken up in the 1910s by the National Association for the Advancement of Colored People (NAACP), which concentrated its efforts on securing the passage of federal anti-lynching legislation that would allow for the prosecution in federal courts of mob participants and state officials who aided them. Anti-lynching Bills were passed by the House of Representatives on three occasions between 1922 and 1938, but all were blocked by Southern Democrats in the Senate. The NAACP's campaign nonetheless played an important role in publicising the horrors of lynching and building popular opposition to the practice across the nation (Waldrep, 2008). By the 1920s, even middle-class white people in the South increasingly considered lynching a blight on the reputation of their region and a barrier to economic development. Anti-lynching activism also pushed the Justice Department to begin serious investigation of lynching cases in the 1940s. Despite the fall in recorded lynchings, however, the practice persisted in more secretive forms for several more decades and the American criminal justice system continued to ignore white-on-black murders. So-called 'legal lynchings' also remained commonplace in which black defendants were executed following swift, discriminatory and barely regulated court proceedings that blurred the line between the rule of the mob and the rule of law (Klarman, 2006).

JAMES CAMPBELL

See also: Indentured Labour; Informal Justice; Slavery in the Americas

Readings

Brundage, W.F. (1993) *Lynching in the New South: Georgia and Virginia, 1880–1930.* Urbana, IL: University of Illinois Press.

Klarman, M.J. (2006) *From Jim Crow to civil rights: The Supreme Court and the struggle for racial equality.* Oxford: Oxford University Press.

Pfeifer, M. (2011) *The roots of rough justice: Origins of American lynching.* Urbana, IL: University of Illinois Press.

Waldrep, C. (2008) *African Americans confront lynching: Strategies of resistance from the Civil War to the civil rights era.* New York, NY: Rowman & Littlefield.

Wood, A.L. (2009) *Lynching and spectacle: Witnessing racial violence in America, 1890–1940.* Chapel Hill, NC: University of North Carolina Press.

M

MACMILLAN AND WOLFENDEN COMMITTEES, THE

During the early to mid-20th century, social purists, feminists, politicians and police called for the government to establish inquiries into the effectiveness of the solicitation laws used to control prostitution in England and Wales. Although it was not illegal to be a prostitute, the solicitation laws criminalised soliciting to the annoyance of members of the public, making it difficult to work as a prostitute without falling foul of the law. Controversially, women who solicited were defined in law as 'common prostitutes', a specific category of offender, and they could be convicted on the evidence of just one police officer, who was left to infer at their own discretion whether the solicitation had, in fact, caused any 'annoyance'.

By the 1920s, concern about the way in which the solicitation laws were being implemented led to national debate. For social purists in the National Vigilance Association, who considered prostitution a threat to social order, the law needed to do more to discourage prostitution (Weeks, 2012). However, others argued that laws against prostitution should be abolished, with prostitution instead approached as a moral, rather than a criminal, matter. One of the groups who took the latter view, the Association for Moral and Social Hygiene, were also critical of the gendered double standard that arose from criminalising the women who sold sex but not the men who bought it. In 1922, the double standard in policing women but not men for soliciting was brought into sharp relief when Sir Almeric Fitzroy was arrested for 'annoying' women in Hyde Park only to have his conviction overturned when one of the annoyed women turned out to be a prostitute (Slater, 2012). As a high-profile case that attracted criticism of both the police and the law, officers became increasingly wary of the negative publicity that they might attract when trying to implement the solicitation laws.

As such, the Home Office established the Street Offences Committee, chaired by Hugh Macmillan, in October 1927. The Macmillan Committee was asked to review 'the law and practice ... in connection with prostitution and solicitation for immoral purposes in streets ... and to report what changes, if any, are in their opinion desirable' (Home Office Notice, National Archives: HO45/12663). The Committee was intended to be politically neutral, representing no one particular set of party-political interests, and it included both legal professionals and religious leaders. When the Macmillan Committee published its report in November 1928, it recommended removing the term 'common prostitute' from law and making it an offence for anyone, man or woman, to importune for sexual services. However, as Helen Self (2003) notes, the Committee's report made repeated references to morality, indicating that the legal debate about prostitution continued to be informed by wider anxieties about sexual promiscuity as a threat to social order. The Macmillan Committee's report also appeared indecisive and compromised, with various members making it known that there were aspects of the report about which they were not entirely convinced. Consequently, the Macmillan Committee's recommendations were not implemented and the solicitation laws continued to lack clarity and provoke debate.

In 1954, the Home Office set up another committee charged with examining the law's role in maintaining moral decency on the streets. The Committee on Homosexual Offences and Prostitution was chaired by John Wolfenden, who thought that while homosexuality could be addressed as a matter for moral, rather than legal, debate, prostitution needed to be considered in law as a practical matter pertaining to conduct on the streets (Mort, 2010). The Wolfenden Committee published its report in 1957; it recommended increasing penalties for solicitation, retaining the use of the term 'common prostitute' in law and removing the need for any proof that a citizen had been annoyed by the solicitation. These proposals were enacted in the Street Offences Act 1959, and they set the benchmark for the relationship between prostitution and the law thereafter, with subsequent legal reviews, including those as recently as 2014's 'Shifting the burden' (All-Party Parliamentary Group on Prostitution and the Global Sex Trade, 2014) continuing to frame prostitution as a form of transgression inimical to order on the streets.

SAMANTHA CASLIN

See also: **Prostitution (19th century); Prostitution (early 20th century)**

Readings

All-Party Parliamentary Group on Prostitution and the Global Sex Trade (2014) *Shifting the Burden Inquiry to assess the operation of the current legal settlement on prostitution in England and Wales.* Retrieved from: https://appgprostitution.files. wordpress.com/2014/04/shifting-the-burden.pdf

Mort, F. (2010) *Capital affairs: London and the making of the permissive society.* London: Yale University Press.

Self, H. (2003) *Prostitution, women and misuse of the law: The fallen daughters of Eve.* London: Frank Cass.

Slater, S. (2012) 'Lady Astor and the ladies of the night: The Home Office, the Metropolitan Police and the politics of the Street Offences Committee, 1927–28', *Law and History Review*, 30(2): 533–73.

Weeks, J. (2012) *Sex, politics and society: The regulations of sexuality since 1800.* Abingdon: Routledge.

MAGISTRATES

The term 'magistrate' is defined in the Oxford English Dictionary as 'a civil officer charged with the administration of the law'. In England and Wales, the term is used interchangeably with the phrase 'Justice of the Peace' (JP) to denote an unpaid volunteer who deals with minor criminal cases and certain other legal matters, but who lacks formal, legal qualifications. However, as will be seen, there are magistrates who are paid and/or legally qualified.

The office of JP originated in England in the 12th or 13th century, receiving statutory footing in an Act of Parliament of 1327 in which knights and gentry were placed 'a la garde de la pees' in their home districts. Another Act in 1361 made lords and gentlemen in each county responsible for keeping the peace and conferred upon them powers to restrain offenders and to pursue, arrest and punish them. Thereby, the 'keeper's' role became extended into the administration of justice. Moreover, over the following centuries, JPs were given many more administrative duties by Parliament (eg regarding the Poor Laws and the maintenance of roads), becoming effectively the country's system of local government. These arrangements were extended to Wales in 1536 following the Act of Union.

By the 18th century, magistrates' courts (called 'courts of summary jurisdiction') had become more important due to the decline of manorial courts. In rural areas, JPs continued to be men of high social standing, such as members of the gentry. Their courts could be highly informal, with hearings taking place in their own homes. King's (2000) research shows that decision-making was largely a matter of the personal discretion of the JP, with little regard for legal technicalities. In small towns, where courts were more likely to be made up of two or more magistrates, local inns could be used, although permanent courts were sometimes erected. Urban JPs were often drawn from the tradesmen class. In London, such was the volume of criminal cases that men were unwilling to perform the duties unpaid, so a system of 'trading justices' was developed. Unfortunately, the individuals who took on this work were often suspected of only doing it for the money and even accused of corruption. As a result, in 1792, Parliament passed the Middlesex Justices Act, which set up seven new offices in the metropolitan area, each staffed by three salaried judges (London Lives, 2012). This was the beginning of the system of stipendiary magistrates, now known as district judges: trained lawyers who deal with minor criminal cases in urban areas with high volumes of such business.

In the 19th century, JPs lost many of their administrative duties thanks to the growth of new local authorities like Poor Law Guardians, on the one hand, and the centralisation of some services, on the other. For example, in 1877, JPs lost control of the local prisons, which were nationalised under the Prisons Commission, and merely retained rights of visitation. At the same time, the volume of low-level criminal cases brought to courts increased as police forces became better organised. In addition, some offences were re-categorised as suitable for summary jurisdiction, and JPs were also tasked with hearing most of the crimes committed by young people. Magistrates also issued warrants, signed papers and held the initial hearings of serious criminal cases before sending them to higher courts.

A major transformation in the system began in 1906, when the property qualification for magistrates was abolished. For the first time, men from the working classes could become JPs. Thirteen years later, the Sex Disqualification (Removal) Act brought even greater change when women were appointed to the magistracy for the first time. The introduction of women JPs was the catalyst for the creation of the Magistrates' Association and the beginning of proper training for the still amateur and voluntary justices (Logan, 2006). The proportion of JPs who were women rose steadily, reaching nearly a quarter by 1950 and 53% by 2015. However, the first woman stipendiary was not appointed until 1944, and women are still a minority of district judges. Moreover, diversity in the magistracy with regard to age, class and ethnicity remains problematic (Gibbs, 2014).

ANNE LOGAN

See also: **First-wave Feminism; Petty Sessions**

Readings

Gibbs, P. (2014) 'Magistrates – representatives of the people?'. Available at: http://www.transformjustice.org.uk/reports/

King, P. (2000) *Crime, justice and discretion in England 1750–1840*. Oxford: Oxford University Press.

Logan, A. (2006) 'Professionalism and the impact of England's first women justices, 1920–1950', *Historical Journal*, 49(3): 833–50.

London Lives (2012) 'Justices of the Peace'. Available at: http://www.londonlives.org/static/Pretrial.jsp#toc1

MARITAL VIOLENCE

'Marital violence', until the 19th century, was the more common term for what we today refer to as 'domestic violence'. Its name may have changed, but it has a long history, and for much of that history, what constituted marital violence has been a matter for debate. The possibly apocryphal tale of judge Sir Francis Buller, in the 18th century, ruling that a woman could be chastised by her husband as long as he did so with a rule no thicker than a woman's thumb reflected the contemporary debate over the extent to which a husband could 'punish' or chastise his wife. William Blackstone, in the mid-part of the century, emphasised that a wife's relationship to her husband was akin to the servant's or apprentice's, and that, as such, a husband could employ 'reasonable chastisement' when necessary; however, what constituted 'reasonable' was not defined. Ecclesiastical marriage law and the English Church courts similarly failed to define what constituted cruelty, despite it being valid grounds for a marital separation.

How frequent marital violence was in the early modern period has also been debated by historians, but, in reality, the cases that have survived may not be typical, and nor should they be assumed to represent the average woman's experience. The cases that survive tend to be the end result of severe or prolonged instances of violence, rather than expressing a typical experience. Marital violence may not have been as prevalent as some have stated to be the case, judging by the relatively few cases that were heard by magistrates at summary level; the relative informality and low expense of these proceedings would suggest that more wives would seek resolution here than at the Church courts, for example, and yet the percentages are still very small. This is not to say, of course, that marital violence did not occur; however, it does show that many cases may have been resolved informally, and therefore have left no written record of their occurrence. This informal action would have been mediation or intervention within the local community, involving family members, friends or neighbours. During the 18th century, the closeness of neighbours made them the ideal first port of call for wives either escaping violence or trying to avoid further incidences of such violence (Bailey, 2003).

Where this informal action failed, a wife might then seek formal mediation or arbitration before the local Justice of the Peace. A complaint could be brought before him at summary proceedings, the initial stage of the criminal justice system, but wives sought different resolutions. Some may have simply wanted to resolve differences with their husbands, whereas other wives sought recognisances against their spouse, binding them over to good behaviour.

Attitudes towards marital violence shifted over time, though historians have debated when this shift occurred, and to what extent. In the mid-18th century, William Blackstone had stated that marital violence was less tolerated at that point because it was seen as not appropriate behaviour in a 'polite' society. It has therefore been argued that domestic violence became less acceptable publicly, with such incidents increasingly taking place in the private sphere. Although it is likely that there was no straightforward temporal or spatial shift, concepts of politeness and masculinity did lead to violence towards wives being viewed as evidence of an unmasculine lack of control (Foyster, 2005; Bailey and Giese, 2013). Although wife beating continued, its acceptability gradually decreased, and the definitions of what constituted marital violence widened.

Women were increasingly seen as victims, with male aggression continuing to be seen as unacceptable; there were attempts to define wife-beaters as mad rather than rational. The attention shifted to representations of male aggression, set out in opposition to female vulnerability. Domestic violence became, in the eyes of the press, increasingly associated with male self-control – or its lack thereof. Violence towards men by their wives, though written about less and recorded less in court records, similarly existed, but in such cases, husbands were mocked for being unmasculine and failing to 'control' their wives. During the late 18th and 19th centuries, such men were viewed with less sympathy, and seriousness, than their female counterparts.

NELL DARBY

See also: **Sexual Assault**

Readings

Bailey, J. (2003) *Unquiet lives: Marriage and marriage breakdown in England, 1660–1800.* Cambridge: Cambridge University Press.

Bailey, J. and Giese, L. (2013) 'Marital cruelty: reconsidering lay attitudes in England, c. 1580 to 1850', *The History of the Family,* 18(3): 289–305.

Foyster, E. (2005) *Marital violence: An English family history, 1660–1857*. Cambridge: Cambridge University Press.

MARK SYSTEM, THE

Developed and introduced around 1840 in the English penal colony of Norfolk Island just east of Australia, the 'mark system' was a penal system whereby transported convicts, instead of serving fixed sentences, were held until they had earned a number of 'marks' ('marks of condemnation'), or credits, fixed in proportion to the seriousness of their offence (Hirst, 1998; Moore, 2011). Under this system, sentences were served in stages, each increasing in responsibility. Brutal punishments and degrading conditions in the penal colonies were simultaneously reduced. The system was the brainchild of Alexander Maconochie (Barry, 1958). As private secretary to the Lieutenant Governor of Van Diemen's Land, Maconochie was commissioned in 1836 by the (British) Prison Disciplinary Society to undertake an appraisal of the transportation system (Hirst, 1998). His reports were damming but he used the opportunity to set out this innovative alternative penal philosophy. According to Maconochie (1846, 1855), punishment should not be vindictive, nor should the convict be dehumanised – punishment should be about reformation and producing men and women capable of leading a law-abiding life on release. Convicts were informed of the number of marks to be earned at the start of their sentence, and a convict became eligible for release when he or she had obtained the required number. Marks were earned through good behaviour and hard work but lost through idleness or misconduct; thus encouraging reform by placing convicts in control of their own fate.

On leaving Norfolk Island four years later, Maconochie returned to Britain and tried to implement his system in a newly built prison in Birmingham. However, undermined by his staff and the visiting justices, Maconochie's system failed, and he was dismissed two years later (Hirst, 1998). Sir Walter Crofton, chair of the Board of Directors of Convict Prisons for Ireland between 1854 and 1862, took Maconochie's ideas and implemented a modified form of them in Ireland. Known as the Irish system, prisoners progressed through three stages of confinement. During the first stage, the penal stage, prisoners were held in solitary cells for approximately nine months. The second stage involved communal labour in public works prisons. For the third stage, officials promoted prisoners in small numbers to intermediate prisons as a final test of their readiness for an Irish ticket of leave. On moving to England, Crofton brought his ideas with him and Crofton's mark system was implemented in British convict prisons when transportation ceased; simultaneous development led to a similar system operating in the US (Hirst, 1998).

141

Marks were 'the currency of his [Maconochie's] model penal institution' (Moore, 2011, p 41). The exact value varied depended on when and by whom the system was being used. Sometimes, marks were linked to a monetary value, normally a penny, and on other occasions, to an hour's labour. In the system instituted in the British convict station on Gibraltar, for example, the marking scale was '8 marks per diem for steady hard labour, and the full performance of their allotted task, 7 marks per diem for a less degree of industry, 6 marks per diem for a fair but moderate day's work' (Colonial Office, 1866, p 28). Prisoners being held in the prison cells or the infirmary were awarded 6 marks per day. Whilst in the probation class, the first year as a prisoner, a convict had to earn 720 marks on public work. A convict thereafter would have to earn 2,920 marks each year until they reached first class (Colonial Office, 1865, p 29).

Other rewards were linked, and the higher the class, the more liberties the prisoner could expect. During the probation class, the prisoner was not allowed 'gratuity, nor to receive visits, nor to receive nor write letters, except one letter on reception' (Colonial Office, 1865, p 29). In the third class, the prisoner was granted 'a gratuity at the rate of 1s per month for 12 months' and one visit of up to 30 minutes every six months (Colonial Office, 1865, p 30). The prisoner could also receive and write one letter once in six months. The conditions would be similar for prisoners in the second class, but they could now both receive and write a letter every four months as well as 'receive a gratuity of 18s' and 'be allowed 2oz of additional bread' (Colonial Office, 1865, p 30). After the successful completion of these three stages, a prisoner would move into the first class, where he would stay for the rest of his sentence unless upgraded to 'special class' or relegated due to poor conduct. In the first class, conditions were much improved: a prisoner could expect a visit of up to 40 minutes; to receive and write a letter once every three months; to receive a gratuity of 30 shillings; and to receive 2oz of additional bread and baked instead of boiled meat (Colonial Office, 1865, p 30).

Maconochie was one of the first penal reformers to actively endorse a prison policy that prepared prisoners for their return to society by treating them humanely while in captivity. Moore (2011, p 38) maintains that Maconochie's initial ideas can still be seen in the operation of many penal systems in the West and that his legacy extends to 'indeterminate sentences, Borstal, open prisons, reward schemes and stage regimes'.

JO TURNER

See also: Convict Prisons; Penal Servitude; Ticket of Leave; Transportation

Readings

Barry, J.V. (1958) *Alexander Maconochie of Norfolk Island*. Melbourne: Oxford University Press.

Colonial Office (1865) *Annual report on the convict establishment at Gibraltar for 1864*. London: HMSO.

Colonial Office (1866) *Annual report on the convict establishment at Gibraltar for 1865*. London: HMSO.

Hirst, J. (1998) 'The Australian experience: the convict colony', in N. Morris and D.J. Rothman (eds) *The Oxford history of the prison*. New York, NY: Oxford University Press, pp 235–65.

Maconochie, A. (1846) *Crime and punishment: The mark system framed, to mix persuasion with punishment, and make their effect improving, yet their operation severe*. London: Hatchard and Son.

Maconochie, A. (1855) *The mark system of prison discipline*. London: Thomas Harrison.

Moore J. (2011) 'Alexander Maconochie's "mark system"', *The Prison Service Journal*, 198: 38–46.

MEDICAL TESTIMONY IN THE JUDICIAL SPHERE

Medical practitioners have a long history of involvement in the judicial sphere. During ancient Egyptian, Greek and Roman times, for example, medical testimony was drawn upon in both civil and criminal proceedings to help inform the decision-making process. Although rarely mandatory in the legal systems of the ancient world, the testimony of medical witnesses was often perceived as invaluable, especially in cases related to illness, insanity and suspicious death (Watson, 2011). Midwives, in particular, occupied a privileged position among medical witnesses from the ancient to early modern period, being called to give evidence in matters pertaining to impotence, rape, virginity and pregnancy, as well as proof of sexual disease (Ackernecht, 1976). Until well into the 19th century, competence in issues pertaining to the interaction of medicine and law was assumed to be part of the skill set of the everyday medical practitioner. Only with significant transformations in medical knowledge and the medical profession, exemplified by the rise of disciplines such as toxicology and psychiatry in the Victorian era, did forensic medicine begin to develop along the path of a medical speciality.

Broadly speaking, an expert medical witness is one who can give evidence on matters of fact, opinion and causation within the legal sphere, and whose authority is derived largely from their education, training and experience within the medical profession (Watson, 2011). Although all medical witnesses could be 'expert' witnesses (in testifying to matters of fact and opinion), in practice, the courtroom was often a melting pot, wherein medical practitioners of varying levels of skill and experience collectively came to give and hear evidence.

The recognition of medical testimony as 'expert' has no exact date of origin. Medical practitioners long occupied a privileged position within legal proceedings precisely because their knowledge and training were considered to contribute positively to the court decision-making process. This meant that medical witnesses had significant authority within the ancient and early modern courtroom as special jurors or court advisers. The rise of adversarial justice in the 18th century radically changed the manner in which criminal proceedings occurred. Scholarship in the last few decades suggests that medical witnesses no longer occupied the role of adviser or special juror in criminal cases, as they had previously; instead, they were increasingly propelled into a partisan role within the courtroom. The independence of the jury in the decision-making process and the rise of the powers of defence counsel, especially to cross-examine witnesses, reshaped the position and power that medical witnesses could exert within criminal trials (Landsman, 1995). The outcomes of these changes in the criminal justice system arguably helped to undermine the authority and status of medical practitioners within the judicial sphere (Dwyer, 2007).

The increasing judicial and public scrutiny of medical witnesses in the Victorian period did not, however, prohibit their ever-increasing involvement in the public sphere. From the turn of the 19th century, Edinburgh led the rest of Great Britain in the teaching of progressive continental ideas on forensic medicine to students of both medicine and law. In Scotland in 1839, Professors Traill, Christison and Syme collectively authored *Suggestions for the medico-legal examination of dead bodies*, which set out guidelines by which medical men should conduct investigations into suspicious deaths. The guidelines stipulated that at least two medical practitioners should be entrusted with a post-mortem, and that these medical *men* needed to be professionally respected and distinguished. By 1868, *Suggestions* had been revised and incorporated into the Crown Office's *Regulations to be observed in criminal and other investigations*, an act that signified the already broad general acceptance of medical practitioners as integral to the investigation of crime and pursuit of justice. Culturally, the rise of the newspaper and the increasing devotion of column inches to sensational criminal trials created a platform for the elite practitioners of forensic medicine to showcase their scientific skill to a wide audience. Toxicologists like Alfred Swaine Taylor and Robert Christison were the 19th-century forerunners to the celebrity pathologists of the 20th century, whose skills as scientists, medical professionals and courtroom witnesses were to make them household names.

KELLY-ANN COUZENS

See also: **Criminal Corpse, The; Legal Representation**

Readings

Ackernecht, E.H. (1976) 'Midwives as experts in court', *Bulletin of the New York Academy of Medicine*, 52(10): 1224–8.

Christison, R., Syme, J. and Maclagan A.D. (1868) 'Appendix I: medico-legal suggestions', in *Regulations to be observed in criminal and other investigations*. Edinburgh: Crown Office, pp 1–14.

Dwyer, D.M. (2007) 'Expert evidence in the English civil courts, 1550–1800', *The Journal of Legal History*, 28(1): 93–118.

Landsman, S. (1995) 'Of witches, madmen, and products liability: an historical survey of the use of expert testimony', *Behavioural Sciences and the Law*, 13: 131–57.

Watson, K.D. (2011) *Forensic medicine in Western society: A history*. London and New York, NY: Routledge.

MERCY

'Mercy' is an ancient concept, rooted in religion and connected to kingship. In both respects, it expresses sovereign power and overrides the rules that dictate punishment for crime. Mercy has been granted historically through: reprieves, which suspend the infliction of punishment; commutations, which reduce prescribed punishment; and pardons, which relieve criminal offenders from serving penalties prescribed by law. In England and other monarchies, kings and queens have historically granted pardons on acceding to the throne, on royal birthdays and on the anniversary of their coronations. Pregnant women and insane persons facing the death penalty have also customarily received reprieves. In times of revolt, monarchs have frequently turned to mercy to quell rebelliousness and to attempt to restore peace (King, 2000). English rulers manipulated mercy in the early years of the American Revolution by offering pardons to rebels willing to swear loyalty to the crown, but their defeat demonstrated that mercy provides no guarantee of rule (Strange, 2016).

Jurist William Blackstone, the most significant English legal authority of the late 18th century, wrote that pardons were both necessary and just. As the number of capital statutes piled up over the 18th century, totalling over 200 by the time his *Commentaries on the laws of England* appeared (1765–69), the use of judicial and royal pardons provided a critical counterbalance to severity. Conditions could be attached to pardons, commuting the original sentence, but still subjecting offenders to punishment and banishment (King, 2000). From the early 18th to the late 19th century, over 200,000 criminals convicted in British courts were pardoned on condition that they be transported elsewhere in the Empire. In Australia, the prime destination after 1787, convicts were treated harshly, but many managed to qualify for pardons, particularly those with valued skills. In this outpost, mercy began to merge with the concept of earned release in the form of 'tickets-of-leave', or the supervised release system later known as parole (Finnane, 1997).

For legal modernisers, mercy's idiosyncratic and personal nature was objectionable, even if cloaked in beneficence. Enlightenment figures Cesare Beccaria and the Baron de Montesquieu condemned the intermixing of severe and cruel penalties with capricious pardons, which typically favoured the wealthy. Contradicting Blackstone, they predicted the demise of mercy in an ideal system of penal laws, based on mild but certain punishment. Their ideals bore fruit over the mid- to late 19th century as penitentiaries offered an alternative to the old reliance on corporal and capital punishment. Although incarceration became the dominant mode of punishment, involving the deprivation of liberty for specified periods of time, mercy remained a factor in crime and justice. Prisoners, their families or their friends could still petition for clemency, particularly offenders sentenced to death.

In the 20th century, mercy's association with capital punishment resurfaced as the death penalty's scope narrowed. In the public mind, reprieves and pardons for murder – one of the few remaining capital crimes – were the most visible expressions of sovereign mercy in action. Yet, behind the scenes, bureaucrats and politicians worked through capital cases. In England, the Home Secretary's office began during Victoria's reign to advise the monarch on cases that might or might not merit mercy (Strange, 1996). The formalisation of protocol reached its zenith by mid-century. In Canada, the head of the Remissions Branch produced a 'Capital case procedure manual' in 1941, which spelled out rules for case processing, covering requests for transcripts and judges' reports, and the preparation of summaries for cabinet members, with the Governor General, representing the monarch, the official dispenser of mercy (Strange, 1996).

No pardon can restore life, but posthumous pardons express mercy's symbolic role in expunging guilt and restoring the reputation of unjustly or unfairly convicted individuals. In 2006, Queen Elizabeth II exercised the royal prerogative when she pardoned 306 British servicemen executed in the Great War for desertion and cowardice (Novak, 2016). In contrast, calls to pardon the last man executed in Canada for treason in 1885, Métis leader Louis Riel, have split the public, with many urging that the stain of colonial oppression remain (Strange, 1996). However, for most wrongfully convicted individuals, and ex-prisoners burdened with criminal records, petitioning for pardons has become a routine route for the restoration of rights in the early 21st century.

CAROLYN STRANGE

See also: '**Bloody Code', The; Ticket of Leave; Transportation**

Readings

Finnane, M. (1997) *Punishment in Australian society*. Melbourne: Oxford University Press.

King, P. (2000) *Crime, justice, and discretion in England, 1740–1820*. Oxford: Oxford University Press.

Novak, A. (2016) *Comparative executive clemency: The constitutional pardon power and the prerogative of mercy in global perspective*. New York, NY: Routledge.

Strange, C. (ed) (1996) *Qualities of mercy: Justice, punishment and discretion*. Vancouver: University of British Columbia Press.

Strange, C. (2016) *Discretionary justice: Pardon and parole in New York from the Revolution to the Depression*. New York, NY: New York Press.

NATIONAL SOCIETY FOR THE PREVENTION OF CRUELTY TO CHILDREN

The 19th century was characterised by class divisions, social deprivation, high levels of poverty and great hardship, and child labour. Additionally, child abuse, cruelty and neglect were endemic among the poorer sections of society. During the 19th century, child cruelty and neglect were considered tragic consequences of life among the poor. Child labour exploitation was tolerated as it was cheap; children were also able to carry out many tasks that adults could not, for example, crawling into confined spaces. Furthermore, much child cruelty was deemed necessary to discipline the child. Much of this cruelty took place within families, schools and factories. The well-known principle of 'spare the rod and spoil the child' indicated that the corporal punishment of children was considered an appropriate measure in child rearing. Parental rights were paramount, including the right of parents to punish their children. The family was deemed to be a private and sacred enclave into which the law had no place to venture (Bilston, 2006).

In 1883, Thomas Agnew, a banker from Liverpool in the UK, visited New York in the US; during this trip, he was invited to see the work being undertaken by the New York Society for the Prevention of Cruelty to Children. On his return to the UK, he was determined to provide support to the children of Liverpool and set up the Liverpool Society for the Prevention of Cruelty to Children. A year later, in 1884, the London Society for the Prevention of Cruelty to Children (LSPCC) was founded. Through the tireless campaigning of the LSPCC in 1889, the British Parliament passed the Prevention of Cruelty to Children Act to protect children from abuse and neglect. Following the passing of this legislation and an increase in the number of branches across the country (32 branches across England, Wales and Scotland), the LSPCC was renamed the National Society for the Prevention of Cruelty to Children (NSPCC). The NSPCC was granted a Royal Charter in 1895; Queen Victoria became Patron and Reverend Benjamin Waugh was appointed as Director. Despite the good intentions of the charity, it has been argued that these 'philanthropic societies became the agents of Victorian middle-class intervention in the family life of the poorer classes, for mistreatment of children was more readily attributed to the poor' (Wolff, 2008).

Since its founding, the NSPCC has been the UK's leading children's charity. The purpose of the society, as set out in its Royal Charter, Article 3, is to 'prevent the public and private wrongs of children, and the corruption of their morals' (NSPCC, 2002, p 14). More recently, it specialises in child protection, with a number of statutory powers granted through the Children Act 1989 that enable it to take legal action to safeguard children at risk. This includes the power to apply for a court order to remove a child from danger. At the time of writing, the NSPCC has more than 180 teams and projects throughout England, Wales and Northern Ireland. The society's role is to:

- prevent children from suffering significant harm as a result of cruelty;
- help children who are at risk of such harm;
- help children who have suffered cruelty to overcome its effects; and
- work to protect children from further harm.

Despite these laudable aims, a number of criticisms have been made of the NSPCC, including the claim that it has been instrumental in redefining the concept of 'abuse'. The definition of abuse includes not only acts of physical and sexual violence and abuse, but also damaging a child's self-esteem and shouting at a child. When the definition of abuse is extended to include these acts, the rise in allegations of abuse should come as no surprise. Thus, Searing (2014) claims that the 'NSPCC has become a self-promoting organisation whose own existence is more important to it than its stated function'. Indeed, she argues that in 'recent years it has moved away from direct work' with children (Searing, 2014). She further contends that the government made 'the mistake of allowing the NSPCC to be too closely involved in the Serious Case Review system' (Searing, 2014). Rather, they should be addressing the failings of some children's services in protecting children at risk of abuse and harm.

As an independent charity, the NSPCC relies on public donations to fund its work. Over the years, this fund-raising has been called into question, with some arguing that the society has ramped up public fear over child neglect and cruelty in order to increase donations, and that the NSPCC has a vested interest in fostering this fear, thus attracting attention and funds. It also raises the public and professional profiles of its executives; this may also then have an impact on salaries of such executives (Black, 2015). New Philanthropy Capital (Goodall and Lumley, 2007, p 84) highlighted that while campaigns such as the NSPCC's 'Full Stop' campaign have 'achieved some success in keeping child abuse in the public eye, there is no evidence that it leads to fewer cases of abuse'. Furthermore, Black (2015) argues that the desire to ramp up fear and 'reorganise society around child protection' results in suspicion of adults, especially those working with or around children. This, Black (2015) argues, 'seems to be exactly what ... the NSPCC want'.

The numerous criticisms of the NSPCC should not distract from the work undertaken in raising awareness of and supporting children and young people who are at risk of abuse. Rather, as previously indicated, the NSPCC should continue to focus on supporting children and young people, and address the failings of children's services.

SHARON MORLEY

See also: **Marital Violence; Sexual Assault**

Readings

Bilston, B. (2006) 'A history of child protection', The Open University, Open Learning. Available at: http://www.open.edu/openlearning/body-mind/childhood-youth/working-youngpeople/history-child-protection

Black, T. (2015) 'The NSPCC: still fostering fear and suspicion', *Spiked*. Available at: http://www.spiked-online.com/newsite/article/the-nspcc-still-fostering-fear-and-suspicion/17087#.WFKXcYXXLIU

Goodall, E. and Lumley, T. (2007) *Not seen and not heard: Child abuse – a guide for donors and funders*. London: New Philanthropy Capital.

NSPCC (National Society for the Prevention of Cruelty to Children) (2002) 'Royal Charter of Incorporation'. Available at: http://www.nspcc.org.uk/globalassests/documents/about-us/nspcc-royal-charter-bylaws-council-regulations.pdf

Searing, H. (2014) 'The NSPCC has lost its way'. Available at: http://www.radical.org.uk/barefoot/nspcc.html

Wolff, L. (2008) 'Child abuse', in *The Encyclopaedia of children and childhood in history and society*. Available at: http://www.faqs.org.childhood/Bo-Ch/Child-Abuse.html

'NEW' POLICE, THE

Over the course of the 19th century, publically funded police forces were introduced across England and Wales, and these are generally referred to as the 'new police'. Other areas of the UK also reformed policing within a similar time period but the course of development differed, particularly in Ireland. Before this, policing had been performed by a variety of public and private figures, such as parish constables, nightwatchmen and the Bow Street Runners. The general trend of reform was a shift from policing as a widely dispersed social function to a position where it was performed primarily by specialised organisations of trained, professional officers, who were controlled by a mixture of central and local government.

There is debate about exactly what novel features marked these forces out from their predecessors but common characteristics attributed to them are that they wore uniforms, were subject to military-style discipline and were organised hierarchically (see Emsley, 1991). The first 'new' police force is generally recognised as being the Metropolitan Police, who began patrolling the streets of London in 1829. Forms of paid policing had been developing from the late 18th century but the provision of a police force became compulsory in towns after 1835. Four years later, legislation enabled the introduction of county-wide constabularies in areas that chose to do so, and in 1856, police forces became compulsory across England and Wales.

One key characteristic of the 'new' police was that the prevention of crime was to be their main focus rather than reactive detection and punishment. Prevention relied on the visible surveillance of public spaces through regular and regimented beat patrols by uniformed officers. Historians have questioned the degree to which prevention was entirely novel, as well as the extent to which it actually dominated the remit of the 'new' police. Such patrols had previously been carried out by nightwatchmen, and while a good technique for controlling the streets and dealing with public disorder, the need to detect crime persisted. Bow Street officers continued to operate after the introduction of the Metropolitan Police and forces increasingly incorporated plain-clothes departments from the 1840s. The 'new' police also became heavily involved in the surveillance of particular problematic groups, such as habitual offenders and prostitutes, and, from the 1870s, began to amass an extensive network of bureaucratic records on offenders and offences (Godfrey, 2014). One of the less frequently mentioned roles that the 'new' police adopted was the prosecution of crime, previously the responsibility of victims, and this was a defining feature of the English model, which gave considerable power to the police through their ability to define the limits of criminality.

Various interpretations have been offered for the emergence of new forms of policing at this historical point, which can broadly be classified as orthodox, revisionist and counter-revisionist (see Reiner, 2010). Orthodox histories present an essentially teleological account of unproblematic and inevitable progression from old communal self-policing systems to the new professional forces. Revisionist discussions draw on a quasi-Marxist perspective, challenging the conservative assumptions of orthodox work, and instead emphasising class conflict in a newly emerging industrial world as the impetus for reform. This represents the police as domestic missionaries tasked with instilling new middle-class notions of discipline upon workers. Revisionists emphasise the order-maintenance role of the 'new' police and see reform as problematic and deeply, sometimes violently, contested. Their emphasis on the undeniable connection between policing and changes to wider relations of power provided a more critical lens through which to examine reform, but this work has been criticised for overemphasising hostility to the 'new' police and such analyses remain essentially teleological. Counter-revisionist work merges elements of orthodoxy and revisionism to highlight the diverse and complex experience of reform across the country. Greater attention is paid to the heterogeneity of class relations and the compromise and debate involved in the reform process at both a national and a local level (see Philips and Storch, 1999). Such accounts are detailed and sophisticated but offer more tentative interpretations that sometimes lack a framework for understanding the interrelation between local diversity and general patterns of reform.

MARYSE TENNANT

See also: **Bow Street Runners, The; English Detectives; Nightwatchmen; Parish Constables**

Readings

Emsley, C. (1991) *The English police: A political and social history*. London: Routledge.

Godfrey, B.S. (2014) *Crime in England, 1880–1945*. London: Routledge.

Philips, D. and Storch, R.D. (1999) *Policing provincial England, 1829–1856*. Leicester: Leicester University Press.

Reiner, R. (2010) *The politics of the police*. Oxford: Oxford University Press.

NEWSPAPERS AND CRIME

From the 18th century, newspapers have been one of the pre-eminent means of disseminating stories about crime. Reading the news was a popular pastime, and by the beginning of the 19th century, there were 52 metropolitan and over 100 provincial newspapers available (Black, 2010 [1987]). Early newspapers featured a wide range of topics, of which crime and justice formed a significant part (Ward, 2014). James Abree, printer of *The Kentish Post* or *Canterbury Newsletter*, devoted approximately one third of his reportage annually to stories of offending, indicating how newsworthy he considered this subject (Snell, 2007). Reports, advertisements and information on crime presented a picture of the actions of offenders, the consequences of their misdeeds and the reactions of society towards them. Accounts of serious offences such as murder, sexual assault, smuggling and violent robbery were frequently reported in the 18th century. However, the early newspapers' depiction of offenders was quite different to that offered in other printed genres, such as the pamphlets. Newspapers presented a wider and more diverse range of offending that included petty criminality. Reports of people playing football on the Sabbath, neglect of duty, fraud, drunkenness and trespass presented a more realistic depiction of offenders' activities that located their actions in the relatable arena of the everyday.

Rarely, however, did the newspapers explore offenders' motivations. Only the most infamous criminals, such as the murderers Mary Blandy (in 1751) and Gill Smith (in 1737), received more substantial coverage and these reports were appropriated from the pamphlets. As serial publications that valued diversity of content and reported cases as the details emerged, newspapers had insufficient space to provide in-depth detail or to focus on crimes that offered a neat, predefined narrative. Eighteenth-century reports were short and succinct and the resulting portrayal of criminality was that it was chaotic, unpredictable and occurred without context. Tales of unpremeditated crime resulting from sudden and unexpected circumstances outnumbered premeditated acts. More culprits were shown to be men than women, and threats within the community were emphasised over those within the home. The offenders were, more often than not, ordinary people caught up in the pressures of ordinary life and their offending was sparked by mundane disagreements over, for example, a pot of beer or payment of a game of skittles. During the 19th century, however, crime reports became ever-more sensational, focusing on the most dramatic offences and scandalous offenders, as editors sought to increase circulation by provoking stronger emotions in their readers.

Many offenders were shown receiving punishment for their crimes. Reports featuring corporal punishment such as whipping and branding outnumbered those of execution. However, newspapers were the first printed source that featured a large number of crimes for which the offender was never identified, tried or punished. Moreover, newspapers featured many reports of offenders successfully evading justice. The newspapers, therefore, gave the impression that criminals had a good chance of getting away with their crimes and this was certainly a less reassuring depiction of justice than that presented in other literary genres.

It was not unusual for newspaper advertisements to feature crime. In working to trace criminals, they revealed something of the nature of offending and sometimes who the suspects were, as well as placing the offender and his/her crime within a specific community. Many advertisements revealed local concern about anticipated crime and sought to deter potential offending through warnings of prosecution. Often, the anticipated offences involved activities with contended legal status, such as poaching, gleaning, smuggling and rioting. Other advertisements revealed insights into fractured personal relationships by warning the readers against helping runaway apprentices or servants, trusting known deviants, or getting involved in specific disputes. Sometimes, advertisements featured apologies from lawbreakers with their promises not to offend again. Such action often formed part of a mediated settlement with the victim. All this reveals something of the communal context in which offenders lived and operated and the impact of their behaviour. While early newspapers often conveyed transgressions dispassionately, occasional items revealed the abhorrence felt towards offenders. Dugal Paterson was 'severely pelted by the populace' during his time in the pillory for attempted rape and constables had to protect him from the crowd's 'fury'. Other reports suggest fear towards, for example, criminal gangs. In publishing lists of trials and verdicts, and the location and time of upcoming punishments, newspapers facilitated the readers' potential participation in the justice process, if only as observers. Never before had a literary source gathered such a large and diverse range of stories about criminals and offered such a nuanced and complex picture of their actions and place in society.

ESTHER SNELL

See also: **Broadsides; Crime Pamphlets**

Readings

Black, J. (2010 [1987]) *The English press in the eighteenth century*. London: Routledge Revivals.

Snell, E. (2007) 'Discourses of criminality in the eighteenth-century press: the presentation of crime in *The Kentish Post*, 1717–1768', *Continuity and Change*, 22(1): 13–47.

Ward, R.M. (2014) *Print culture, crime and justice in eighteenth century London*. London: Bloomsbury.

NIGHTWATCHMEN

Nightwatchmen were one of the main law enforcement officers in the traditional system of policing that preceded the introduction of the 'new' police. The first legal obligation to provide some form of watch at night was introduced in 1285 by the Statute of Winchester, though many towns are likely to have carried out such an activity prior to this. Boroughs were to provide 12 men each night to watch the streets, usually from sunset until sunrise, and smaller towns between four and six. Traditionally, this watch was performed as a civic duty, with householders serving in turn, though women and the infirm were permitted to pay a substitute to act on their behalf. However, by the late 1500s in the City of London and Westminster, paid substitutes had become common, and eventually the obligation to serve was replaced with the requirement to pay local taxes to fund the watch (Beattie, 2001). This also happened increasingly in other towns across England and Wales throughout the 17th and 18th centuries, often through the introduction of local Acts. These generally enabled the appointment of improvement commissioners to oversee and pay a nightly watch, often combining this with the provision of street lighting in certain areas. Large towns, such as Manchester and Chester, adopted this approach from the 1760s, with smaller towns following suit in the first quarter of the 19th century. In the 1830s, permissive legislation enabled any town to levy a rate for lighting or watching, provided that there was sufficient support from the local ratepayers, and this seems to have been adopted fairly widely (Philips and Storch, 1999).

When night watches were introduced, it was common for towns to be surrounded by walls, and use of the streets after dark was tightly controlled through a curfew, after which the gates were closed and the streets cleared. The night watch were responsible for enforcing this control by apprehending any strangers or suspicious 'night walkers' found within the town's boundaries during the curfew. They had the power to arrest such people, though their authority was less than that of parish constables, to whom they had to deliver their suspects to be taken before a magistrate. Constables also played a role in supervising and regulating the watchmen. Over time, the imposition of these curfews declined and watchmen began to function more to provide a generalised surveillance of the streets after dark. This coincided with the introduction of greater levels of regulation and supervision over the watch, partly prompted by more secure public funding, as well as increased powers for watchmen and the development of more mobile patrols. Better provisions were also made available, such as clothing and weapons, along with infrastructure, including watch houses in which to secure suspects overnight.

Traditional or orthodox histories of the police tended to highlight how inefficient and corrupt the old system of policing was, often portraying watchmen as old, infirm or lazy. More recent work has highlighted the significant developments that took place from the 16th century onwards and this has offered a powerful challenge to such accounts (see Reynolds, 1998; Beattie, 2001). The available evidence is often scant, and the lack of uniform control over the system encouraged variability, but the night watches in many towns by the 19th century are unlikely to have been as inadequate as orthodox histories imply. Reforms to the watch also anticipated many of the features that have been attributed to the 'new' police, including the classic preventive device of the regular patrol of defined beats, leading Beattie (2001, p 85) to argue that 'the mandate of the new Metropolitan force – to defeat crime by intensive and perpetual surveillance – was in fact the ancient duty of the old watch'.

MARYSE TENNANT

See also: **Magistrates; 'New' Police, The; Parish Constables; Watch Committees**

Readings
Beattie, J.M. (2001) *Policing and punishment in London, 1660–1750.* Oxford: Oxford University Press.

Philips, D. and Storch, R.D. (1999) *Policing provincial England, 1829–1856.* Leicester: Leicester University Press.

Reynolds, E.A. (1998) *Before the bobbies: The night watch and police reform in metropolitan London, 1720–1830.* London: Macmillan.

ORGANISED CRIME

Historically, organised crime has tended to be understood as a modern phenomenon, constructed in a 20th-century context. From that century, local criminal gangs developed their structures, economies and networks in ways that had a more 'professional' and increasingly transnational reach. Moreover, law enforcement organisations, such as the Flying Squad in London from 1916 and the Federal Bureau of Investigation (FBI) in the US from 1908, were formed with the specialised function of investigating serious and organised crime. Forms of criminal organisation had existed long before the 'invention' of organised crime in the 20th century. However, as Clive Emsley (2011, p 87) has noted, in England, '"Organised crime" was a term not much used in the first two-thirds of the twentieth century. But from the close of the nineteen century policemen and others were beginning to speak and to write of the professional criminal'.

In other countries, such as Italy and the US, organised crime was an earlier concern for governments and states. In the Italian region of Sicily, from where the Cosa Nostra or Mafiosi originated, the term 'Mafia' was first used in an official document in 1865, in a letter about an arrest near Palermo (Gambetta, 1996, p 136). In America, organised crime has been specifically linked to the arrival of immigrant groups in the later 19th and early 20th centuries. The US was home to many groups of immigrants, who would be linked to racketeering, protection and other illegal activities in its major cities (Wright, 2006). Many criminologists have drawn on the 'alien conspiracy thesis' to explain the rise of organised crime in American society. This thesis is particularly associated with the work of criminologist Dwight Smith (1976), who argues that American society has been historically preoccupied with placing the blame for crime on immigrant groups. A significant literature about organised crime appeared from the 1960s. One of the most important texts, and arguably the most contested, was Donald R. Cressey's (2008 [1969]) *The theft of the nation*. Cressey had been a consultant on organised crime for the President's Commission on Law Enforcement and Administration of Justice, convened by Lyndon Johnson, to address the threat of organised crime in America. The model put forward by Cressey established the syndicate model, claiming that organised crime in North America was comprised of an alliance of 24 Mafia families. This was a view of organised crime as highly structured, tight-knit and hierarchical. It has been popularised in popular culture, particularly through Mario Puzo's (1969) novel, *The Godfather*, and the films of the 1970s. According to Cressey (2008 [1969], p 111), the highest Mafia authority was the 'Commission', which was made up of the rulers of the most powerful 'families'. Cressey's detailed reconstruction of the structures and management of the 'Commission', 'families' and geographically based 'councils' is nothing less than a bureaucracy.

While this work remained important in shaping definitions of organised crime, other sociologists argued that crime networks were far from organised in the rigid, bureaucratic way described by Cressey (Wright, 2006). In Britain, particularly in the post-war period, the involvement of organised crime groups in gambling, prostitution and protection rackets resulted in increasing attention from law enforcers. For example, from the late 1930s through to the 1950s, the Sicilian/Maltese Messina brothers ran prostitution rackets in London until they were exposed by the crime reporter Duncan Webb. Billy Hill, the self-styled 'Boss of Britain's Underworld', was also active in this period, operating protection rackets and the black market during the war. After the war, he was involved in project crimes. These ambitious organised armed robberies often employed significant violence. The Great Train Robbery of 1963 was typical of this form of organised crime event (McIntosh, 1975). The 1960s were also dominated by the rise of the family firms, the most well-known included the Kray Twins of East London and their rivals, the Richardsons, from South London. In the later 20th century, British organised crime became more global, less local and arguably more diverse. Indeed, late modern organised crime has increasingly been characterised by border crossings. The international traffic in drugs and people for sex and work since the 1990s, as well as the emergence of the Internet, has shaped and continues to shape organised crime in new, more wide-reaching and more dangerous forms.

HEATHER SHORE

See also: **Organised Crime (United States of America); Underworld, The Criminal; Youth Gangs**

Readings

Cressey, D.R. (2008 [1969]) *Theft of the nation: The structure and operations of organised crime in America*. New York, NY: Harper Row.

Emsley, C. (2011) *Crime and society in twentieth-century England*. Harlow: Pearson Education.

Gambetta, D. (1996) *The Sicilian mafia: The business of private protection*. Cambridge: Harvard University Press.

McIntosh, M. (1975) *The organisation of crime*. London: Macmillan Press.

Smith, D.C. (1976) 'Mafia: the prototypical alien conspiracy', *The Annals of the American Academy of Political and Social Science*, 423: 75–88.

Wright, A. (2006) *Organized crime*. Cullompton: Willan Publishing.

ORGANISED CRIME (UNITED STATES OF AMERICA)

In the popular imagination, 'organised crime' in the US is synonymous with the Mafia, the Mob or La Cosa Nostra, a secretive criminal organisation, usually composed of White ethnics, particularly Italian-Americans, bound by codes of silence, intimidation and violence, which profits from the manufacture, sale, distribution or trafficking of banned substances, as well as labour racketeering, construction and municipal services such as garbage collection. There is no single definition of organised crime, and in the early 21st century, the term covers: street, motorcycle and prison gangs; local, state and regional crime syndicates; domestic and international cartels; and transnational crime–terrorism alliances. To ensure longevity, groups are highly adaptive as they take advantage of changing economic opportunities, or respond to new external political, crime control and national security initiatives.

No single ethnic group has monopolised criminal activity, though gangs with strong ethnic ties were common in the 19th and early 20th centuries. There were frequent confrontations between the Irish Dead Rabbits and Five Point Gangs, the native-born Bowery Boys, and the New York Police in the 1840s and 1850s, as post-famine immigration swelled the ranks of Irish youth gangs and heightened nativist violence. They were also linked to the rise of urban political machines and city bosses, where local ward bosses and saloon keepers used these gangs as political muscle to ensure voting on election days (Ashbury, 1928).

Italian 'Black Hand' and Jewish extortion gangs plagued local business in Chicago and New York in the 1900s and 1910s, while African-Americans dominated the policy and bolita rackets in many parts of the US. The advent of national prohibition – the outlawing of the saloon and liquor trades between 1918 and 1933 – enabled local gangs and formerly small-time gangsters from different backgrounds to reap huge financial rewards from Americans' continuing thirst for liquor. Detroit's Jewish Purple Gang controlled the wholesale liquor supply from Canada in the Great Lakes region, which generated enormous profits, but they remained a smaller outfit. Other figures such as Johnny Torrio and his protégé Al Capone in Chicago built powerful criminal syndicates that enabled them to climb the social ladder from seedy vice lord to celebrity bootlegger, and to swiftly neutralise rival challengers. Seven members of a rival Irish-dominated North Side Gang were gunned down at the behest of the Torrio/Capone organisation on St Valentine's Day 1929 (Nelli, 1976; Repetto, 2004).

The term 'Mafia' surfaced in early 1890s' New Orleans following the killing of the police chief and the lynching of 11 of the Italians who had been indicted for the murder. In the 1920s, the Mafia was one of many Italian or Italian-American gangs supplying liquor and narcotics, but its dominance of New York City by the early 1930s is also linked to a series of turf wars and the cementing of the five-family structure. The end of Prohibition led many syndicates to diversify into racketeering and the control of labour unions, including longshoremen and teamsters, particularly of membership dues and kickbacks for the awarding of contracts, and later pension funds. The links between organised crime and police corruption also continued through the 20th century, as exposures involving the New York Police Department and other police departments demonstrated (Repetto, 2004; Critchley, 2009).

By the 1940s, the Mafia had established a heavy presence in the burgeoning gambling resort of Las Vegas, and seemed to be a formidable and largely untouchable 'organisation'. This, and the revelation of a Mafia summit meeting in Appalachin, upstate New York, in 1957, brought increased media attention and political manoeuvring. Senate investigations (Kefauver in the early 1950s and McClellan in the 1950s and early 1960s) were the precursors to a concerted law enforcement and legislative effort to eliminate organised crime – generally understood in narrow 'Mafia' terms – in the late 1960s and 1970s. Authorities, including the Federal Bureau of Investigation, used wiretapping and informants to gather intelligence, and the Racketeer Influenced and Corrupt Organizations Act 1970 to target 'kingpins', with noted successes in the 1980s and 1990s, including the conviction and imprisonment of 'Teflon Don' John Gotti Jr in 1992 (Repetto, 2004).

Despite there being gangs organised according to a particular ethnicity, profiting from illegal booze, narcotics, gambling, fraud and legal commodities has generally always been a multi-ethnic and multi-racial enterprise, in which native-born white Americans have been just as active as others. Nevertheless, the association with particular ethnic or racial groups continues: the 1980s were dominated by popular and political anxiety over Columbian drug cartels, the cocaine trade and the blight of US cities such as Miami; then, African–Americans and crack cocaine became prominent in the 1990s; and, more recently, the rise of Mexican cartels supplying drugs (such as cocaine and methamphetamines), guns and humans (including sex trafficking) are now important targets for Mexican and US law enforcement agencies (Woodiwiss, 2005).

In the early 21st century, there are Russian, Asian and Italian 'Mafias' profiting from traditional commodities, as well as from technological innovations, thus counterfeiting, credit card and identity fraud, money laundering, automobile insurance fraud, and various forms of cybercrime, as well as alliances between terrorist organisations and organised crime groups to promote narco-terrorism, orviolent terrorist-style attacks on national or regional anti-narcotics policymakers and police. Organised crime therefore covers a host of different organisations and alliances, from the local marijuana grower and street-level drug gang to sophisticated and transnational networks.

VIVIEN MILLER

See also: **Organised Crime; Underworld, The Criminal; Youth Gangs**

Readings

Ashbury, H. (1928) *The gangs of New York: An informal history of the underworld.* New York, NY: A.A. Knopf.

Critchley, D. (2009) *The origin of organized crime in America: The New York City Mafia, 1891–1931.* New York, NY: Routledge.

Nelli, H. (1976) *The business of crime: Italians and syndicate crime in the United States.* New York, NY: Oxford University Press.

Repetto, T. (2004) *American Mafia: A history of its rise to power.* New York, NY: Henry Holt and Company.

Woodiwiss, M. (2005) *Gangster capitalism: The United States and the globalization of organized crime.* New York, NY: Carroll & Graf Publishers, Inc.

PARISH CONSTABLES

The office of parish constable was familiar to Shakespeare's audiences. Dogberry, the constable in *Much ado about nothing*, is ridiculed for the evasions he uses to avoid carrying out his duties. Although the same criticism was levelled at parish constables until their end, it is misleading and exaggerated.

In representing parish constables as the precursors of the 'new' police, some histories have emphasised their failings and thereby reinforced a narrative of progress in the creation of police forces in the 19th century, but this Whig interpretation is simplistic. The office, status and duties of the parish constable were fundamentally different from those of the police constable, for he was a functionary whose primary role was to carry out the orders of the local magistrates and to bring problems to their notice. He was not a 'crime fighter'; although he was expected to detain offenders and bring them before the justices, he relied in law and in fact upon his neighbours' physical assistance, as well as their reporting and prosecution of offences. Additionally, his duties extended beyond the policing of law and order to include the regulation of labour, commerce and industry (Nutt et al, 1996 [1734]). Dogberry would have needed heroic powers to discharge all his duties properly.

The parish constable wore no uniform but carried a staff of office. He was chosen by his neighbours and held office for a year, though after 1850, the constable was selected by the local magistrates. Some were reappointed for several years and made something of a career of the office, for, although it was not salaried, the holder could expect to generate income from fees and expenses. The constable received a fee for serving a summons, for bringing vagrants, drunks and felons before the magistrates, and for bringing prisoners to gaol. He could claim expenses from a prosecutor (usually the victim of a crime) for his efforts in apprehending an offender and could expect rewards from a grateful public.

The parish constable was an agent, using his judgement and discretion on behalf of the state to ensure the functioning of the criminal justice system and to provide a service to the victims of crime (Williams, 2014). He was thus quite different from the system of police forces that started in London in 1829. The shortcomings of the parish constable became more apparent with the industrialisation and urbanisation of Britain, but there were serious attempts to adapt the system for the new industrial age. Whereas the Municipal Corporations Act 1835 and the Rural Constabulary Act 1839 allowed the formation of police forces in towns and counties, the Parish Constables Act 1842 offered counties an alternative in which a superintending constable could be appointed to organise and oversee the parish constables of a county.

The evidence given to the Select Committee on Police in 1852 was very critical of the parish constable and superintending constable system, and this evidence has supported the teleological view of Critchley (1972) and others, who regarded the police force system as a necessary and inevitable reform. Many of the witnesses who spoke in 1852 were police 'professionals' like John Dunne, later the Chief Constable of Cumberland and Westmorland. There was, however, nothing inevitable about the demise of the parish constable, and this system could be seen as a precursor of the community policing that has been advocated in recent years (Tilley, 2008).

The forces set up following the County and Borough Police Act 1856 took over many of the parish constable's duties and reduced his earning power. A number of parish constables became police constables, but the system limped on. The demise of the office was piecemeal, with parish constables becoming redundant in, for example, Lancashire and Manchester by the 1850s, whereas in Cumbria, with police stations far apart, they continued to be appointed, with some continuing to act with vigour and determination even into the 1870s. This is hardly surprising, for, as Emsley (2009, p 143) has observed, parish constables were individuals whereas the police force was a system.

GUY WOOLNOUGH

See also: **Bow Street Runners, The; 'New' Police, The; Nightwatchmen**

Readings

Critchley, T.A. (1972) *A history of police in England and Wales*. Montclair, NJ: Patterson Smith.

Emsley, C. (2009) *The great British bobby: A history of British policing from the 18th century to the present*. London: Quercus.

Nutt, E., Nutt, R. and Gosling, R. (1996 [1734]) *The compleat parish officer*. Devizes: Wiltshire Family History Society.

Tilley, N. (2008) 'Modern approaches to policing: community, problem-orientated and intelligence-led', in T. Newburn (ed) *The handbook of policing*. Collumpton: Willan Publishing, pp 373–403.

Williams, C. (2014) *Police control systems in Britain, 1775–1975: From parish constable to national computer*. Manchester: Manchester University Press.

PARRICIDE

Parricide refers to the unlawful killing of one's parent, though the literature may also refer to *matricide* (the killing of one's mother) and *patricide* (the killing of one's father). Parricide did not always have such a specific definition: the term initially referred to the killing of any close relative, and this broader definition is still used in many parts of the world (eg South Korea). Compared to other forms of family homicide, *parricide* is a relatively rare homicide dynamic, and constitutes between 2% (in the US) and 5% (in South Korea) of all homicides.

The killing of one's parents has always fascinated the public imagination. It is a staple of Greek tragedy (see Sophocles' *Oedipus Rex*, c. 429BC) and is used as a powerful metaphor to conceptualise psychosexual conflict in psychoanalytic theory (see 'The Oedipus complex' in Freud's [1910] *The interpretation of dreams*). 'Honour thy Father and thy Mother' is listed as one of the Ten Commandments in the Hebrew Bible (Exodus 20: 1–21) and this religious doctrine underlines the seriousness with which parricide was traditionally held. Indeed, parricide was often considered to be a form of *regicide* (the killing of one's King) because parents had civil sovereignty over their offspring, and debates as to whether parricide constituted *petty treason* continued well into the 19th century (Walker, 2016). Due to this, parricide used to be seen as an aggravating murder and the most severe punishments were meted out in response. Documents such as murder pamphlets, execution ballads and trial transcripts from early modern Europe found frequent references to both the 'unnaturalness' and the 'heinousness' of parricide, and most were unsympathetic towards the protagonist, regardless of the context (see, eg, *The wofull lamentation of William Purcas*, 1624). Famous historical cases of parricide include the case of Mary Blandy in 18th-century England, who poisoned her father with arsenic and was sentenced to death in 1752, and the case of Lizzie Borden in 19th-century Massachusetts, US, who was acquitted of bludgeoning her father and step-mother in 1892. Despite Borden's acquittal, her case has spawned numerous books, films, plays, songs and even a well-known children's playground rhyme ('Lizzie Borden took an axe and gave her mother forty whacks; When she saw what she had done, she gave her father forty-one'). Perhaps the most well-known parricide in the UK concerns the case of 25-year-old Jeremy Bamber, who was convicted in 1986 for the murder of his adoptive mother, father, sister and two nephews. Bamber is serving a life sentence for this *familicide*, a crime for which he maintains his innocence.

Despite some of the most notorious cases involving female perpetrators, parricide is largely a male practice: approximately 90% of perpetrators of parricide are male, though mothers and fathers are equally likely to be victims. Modern-day media and academic discourses tend to focus on adolescent offenders and parricides that involve multiple victims and/or perpetrators. This is despite the fact that: (1) very few cases involve offenders who are under the age of 18; and (2) most parricidal incidents involve one-on-one encounters. Most parricides take place in the family home and – at least in England and Wales – most methods involve the use of sharp or blunt objects. Approximately 80% of parricide offenders are detained following conviction, whether in prison or in a secure hospital (Holt, forthcoming). Dominant explanations for parricide are extremely limited and have tended to draw on Heide's adolescent parricide offender typology, which comprises: (1) the severely mentally ill child; (2) the severely abused child; and (3) the dangerously antisocial child (Heide, 2013). However, such individualistic approaches tend to obscure the cultural, developmental and gendered contexts that shape everyday conflict between parents and offspring, which, in rare cases, produce fatal outcomes. In contrast, historical analyses of 19th-century case files have been useful in pointing the way towards a more contextualised approach to parricide in its identification of different *sources of conflict* across the lifecycle that might produce parricidal encounters (eg Shon, 2009). Sometimes, approaches to disinterring a violent past can be theoretically illuminating for criminologists who are attempting to understand a violent present.

AMANDA HOLT

See also: **Lethal Violence (in Scotland); Violence; Women and Violent Crime**

Readings
Heide, K.M. (2013) *Understanding parricide: When sons and daughters kill parents.* Oxford: Oxford University Press.

Holt, A. (forthcoming) 'Parricide in England and Wales (1977–2012): an exploration of offenders, victims, incidents and outcomes', *Criminology and Criminal Justice*.

Shon, P.C. (2009) 'Sources of conflict between parents and their offspring in nineteenth-century American parricides: an archival exploration', *Journal of Forensic Psychology Practice*, 9(4): 1–31.

Walker, G. (2016) 'Imagining the unimaginable: parricide in early modern England and Wales, c. 1600–c. 1760', *Journal of Family History*, 41(3): 271–93.

PATRICK COLQUHOUN

Patrick Colquhoun was a merchant, magistrate, statistician and pioneering police reformer who is famous for helping to shape a wider discourse on law enforcement and crime prevention. Born in the Scottish town of Dumbarton in 1745, Colquhoun served as the chief magistrate of Glasgow and as a local Justice of the Peace in the 1780s. Like others in his native Scotland, Colquhoun was concerned with safeguarding the interests of property and commerce and was very much a product of Scottish Enlightenment discourse. In 1783, he founded the world's first chamber of commerce in Glasgow and wrote extensively on how to promote the progress of manufacturing and business. He helped to pioneer policing initiatives in Glasgow in the late 18th century (Barrie, 2008).

In 1792, Colquhoun was appointed as one of London's first stipendiary police magistrates. A few years later, he published his seminal study, *Treatise on the police of the metropolis* (Colquhoun, 1796), which provided the most detailed analysis of crime and police in London hitherto carried out. Colquhoun viewed crime both as a structural consequence of commercial expansion and a change in the habits, manners and immorality of the lower orders (Dodsworth, 2007). He called for the creation of a centralised police force to prevent and detect crime, as well as the establishment of a public prosecutor to relieve victims of the expense of prosecuting criminals. His ideas drew and built upon those of others, from Sir John Fielding's criminal information network, to the 18th-century French model of policing, which Colquhoun believed had reached 'the greatest degree of perfection' (Colquhoun, 1796). Colquhoun's growing reputation as an authority figure on policing was illustrated in 1797, when he was invited by a group of leading London West India merchants to establish a private river police funded by dock owners. Three years later, he helped to convert this organisation into the publicly funded Thames River Police – one of the earliest statutory preventive police forces in England. He died in 1820.

Historians do not agree on whether Colquhoun's reputation as an influential police reformer is deserved. Older, institutional police histories portray him as a pioneer of the concept of crime prevention and the architect of the Metropolitan Police Act 1829 (Avery, 1988). Moreover, he has been described as 'the first major writer on public order and the machinery of justice to use "police" in a strict sense closely akin to modern usage' (Radzinowicz, 1956, p 247). Others, though, paint Colquhoun as a marginal figure of little importance, whose ideas had little bearing on the construction of the Metropolitan Police Act 1829. Far from being groundbreaking, his concept of prevention reflected a broader, European, notion of police that was concerned with the regulation, order and governance of communities in the name of the common good (Neocleous, 2000). According to Reynolds (1998, p 84), he was, at best, 'a transitional figure between older, broader views of policing and the narrower, more modern definitions'.

However, although Colquhoun's recommendations for policing the metropolis of London were not put into practice, his *Treatise* and the Thames River Police helped to politicise the issue of policing and to stimulate a new level of interest in it. His *Treatise* went through seven editions between 1796 and 1806. Colquhoun is also likely to have continued to exert influence over policing beyond London: civic leaders in Edinburgh consulted with him over the framing of the Edinburgh Police Act 1805 and his *Treatise* was cited by police reformers throughout the world (Barrie, 2008). His contribution to the emergence of police transcended institutional influence and the concept of crime prevention. His *Treatise* helped to shape a wider intellectual discourse on the need to control more effectively the condition of labour and society's 'underclass', which was a function that the 'new' police would undertake in the 19th century (Dodsworth, 2007). Indeed, with its concern about how best to supervise the working classes and manage poverty, his *Treatise* has been viewed as a forerunner for the emergence of preventive social policy as much as preventive policing (Neocleous, 2000). In locating the causes of crime in the overall structure of the economy and society, Colquhoun's work was important to the development of classical criminology and provides an outstanding resource for exploring the historical relationship between poverty, social policy and state power.

DAVID G. BARRIE

See also: **'New' Police, The; Policing 18th- and 19th-century Scotland**

Readings
Avery, M.E. (1988) 'Patrick Colquhoun (1745–1820): "A being clothed with divinity"', *Journal of Police History Society*, 3: 24–34.

Barrie, D.G. (2008) 'Patrick Colquhoun, the Scottish Enlightenment and police reform in Glasgow in the late eighteenth century', *Crime, Histoire & Sociétés/ Crime, History & Societies*, 12(2): 59–79.

Colquhoun, P (1796) *A Treatise on the Police of the Metropolis: Explaining the various crimes and misdemeanors which at present are felt as a pressure upon the community; and suggesting remedies for their prevention*. London, UK; Printed by H. Fry, for C . Dilly.

Dodsworth, F. (2007) 'Police and the prevention of crime: commerce, temptation and the corruption of the body politic, from Fielding to Colquhoun', *The British Journal of Criminology*, 47(3): 439–54.

Neocleous, M. (2000) 'Social police and the mechanisms of prevention: Patrick Colquhoun and the condition of poverty', *British Journal of Criminology*, 40(4): 710–26.

Radzinowicz, L. (1956) *A history of English criminal law and its administration from 1750, volume 3: Cross-currents in the movement for the reform of the police*. London: Steven and Sons.

Reynolds, E.A. (1998) *Before the bobbies: The night watch and police reform in metropolitan London, 1720–1830*. Stanford, CA: Stanford University Press.

Yeats, G.D. (1818) *A bibliographical sketch of the life and writings of Patrick Colquhoun by Iatros*. London: G. Smeeton.

PENAL REFORM PRESSURE GROUPS

Pressure groups with an interest in the reform of the penal system of England and Wales date back to the early 19th century. A pressure group is a formal organisation that seeks to alter public policy (often by securing legal changes) from outside Parliament. Although the group may have supporters within the legislature, it is mainly organised from without. Some of the earliest pressure groups in UK politics were the anti-slavery and anti-Corn Law movements. The first penal reform groups were contemporaries of these better-known campaigns, with which they also shared some supporters.

The earliest-known group to lobby for penal reform was the Society for the Diffusion of Knowledge upon the Punishment of Death and the Improvement of Prison Discipline (active c. 1808–28). This body, backed mainly by members of the Religious Society of Friends (Quakers) and some Anglican clergymen, initially supported Sir Samuel Romilly's parliamentary Bill to abolish capital punishment for pickpocketing. It later produced a series of publications recommending the use of new, penitentiary-style prisons as punishment and opposing the use of the death penalty for all but the most serious crimes (Gregory, 2012).

The question of the death penalty remained a focal point for penal reform pressure groups into the early Victorian period. In 1846, the Society for the Abolition of Capital Punishment (SACP) became the first body to campaign for the total abolition of the death penalty (Gregory, 2012). Once again, Quakers took a prominent role, and there was noticeable overlap between SACP supporters and those of peace and temperance causes. In addition, the SACP initially received the backing of Unitarians and Anglicans, and even of the prominent journalist and novelist Charles Dickens, though he split from it in 1849 because he did not support total abolition. Like its predecessors, the SACP waxed and waned depending upon the strength of its financial and human resources, but, ultimately, it failed to abolish the death sentence, despite the ending of public executions in 1868 (Gregory, 2012).

Meanwhile, the SACP's secretary, the Quaker William Tallack, had formed another group in 1866, named the Howard Association, after John Howard (1726–90), who had first drawn public attention to the issue of prison conditions in 1777. Tallack thereafter played down the death penalty issue, concentrating instead on the promotion of new ideas for dealing with offenders, such as probation, and on critiquing the prison system. Association members were not duty-bound to oppose capital punishment (Rose, 1961).

Soon after Tallack's retirement in 1901, new questions arose regarding the prison system, prompted by the treatment of women imprisoned for their activities as suffragettes. This gave rise to the establishment of a new group, the Penal Reform League (PRL), in 1907. In 1919, the PRL was taken over by Margery Fry, a gifted social activist and administrator from a Quaker background, who had been a committed campaigner for women's rights in the law-abiding wing of the women's suffrage movement. Fry was determined to make something of the 'small, sleepy concern' that she had agreed to run (Logan, 2016). She immediately began to arrange the merger of the PRL with its older, wealthier counterpart, the Howard Association, to form the Howard League for Penal Reform (HLPR). She gave members of the new body a vote on whether opposition to the death penalty should be part of the new society's programme, but even though the vote went in favour, she decided that there should be a separate campaign on capital punishment. This led to the formation of the National Campaign for the Abolition of the Death Penalty (NCADP) in 1923 (Ryan, 1978).

Under Fry and her immediate successors, the HLPR became the archetype of an 'insider' pressure group, with well-cultivated contacts within government and the co-option of leading members onto official advisory committees (Ryan, 1978). Inevitably, it was challenged from outside by groups with seemingly more radical agendas, such as the Prison Medical Reform Council (c. 1942–46) and, later, Radical Alternatives to Prison (Ryan, 1978). The latter group, established in 1970, was a product of the New Left of the 1960s and took penal reform activism into a new era of social movements. A myriad of groups have been set up in the last 40 years, but the HLPR (now a registered charity) remains the country's premier penal reform pressure group, combining lobbying Parliament with public information campaigns.

ANNE LOGAN

See also: **Capital Punishment (England and Wales); First-wave Feminism; Gladstone Report, The; Prison Reform; Temperance Movements**

Readings
Gregory, J. (2012) *Victorians against the gallows.* London: IB Tauris.
Logan, A. (2016) 'The Penal Reform League and its feminist roots', *Howard League for Penal Reform ECAN Bulletin,* 28: 6–11. Available at: http://howardleague.org/wp-content/uploads/2016/03/ECAN-Bulletin-Issue-28-February-2016.pdf
Rose, G. (1961) *The struggle for penal reform.* London: Stevens.
Ryan, M. (1978) *The acceptable pressure group.* Farnborough: Saxon House.

PENAL SERVITUDE

Penal servitude was a method of imprisonment that rose to prominence in England and Wales during the second half of the 19th century. First introduced as an alternative to convict transportation to Australia, sentences of penal servitude became the dominant form of punishment for serious offenders for almost a century. Penal servitude was finally abolished in 1948 when the law removed legal distinctions for different kinds of imprisonment and strove to ensure a uniformity of treatment and experience among prisoners in England and Wales.

Penal servitude was first legally recognised as a form of punishment by the Transportation Bill of 1853. With opportunities to transport lawbreakers abroad rapidly reducing, an alternative punishment had to be secured for Britain's serious and habitual offenders. Subtitled 'An Act to substitute, in certain cases, other punishments in lieu of transportation', the Bill discontinued the practice of transporting convicts to Australia for all but those sentenced to 14 years to life. Men and women who would have served lesser sentences in the colonies were now required to serve time in England's convict prisons. Institutions such as Millbank and Pentonville were already in operation and more convict prisons were opened as the century progressed (in the early years of penal servitude, male convicts could also spend their sentences on the prison hulks). The Act set equivalent terms of imprisonment to substitute for terms of transportation to Australia and was also responsible for introducing the first long-term imprisonment sentences as primary punishment in the UK (Godfrey et al, 2010). In addition, the Act repatriated the 'ticket-of-leave' parole system, which had been developed in Australia, for those in England serving terms of penal servitude. There were subsequent amendments to the Act in 1857, 1864 and 1891 that further modified the terms of penal servitude, establishing, for example, a minimum tariff of five years on a first offence and a minimum tariff of seven years for subsequent offences resulting in penal servitude.

The institutions designated to receive prisoners undergoing penal servitude operated differently to those housing prisoners on summary convictions and shorter sentences. The penal servitude regime sought to punish prisoners but also, importantly, to morally reform them. Prisoners undergoing penal servitude were confined in separate cells for large portions of each day so that they might have time to reflect on their transgressions. For a long period, particularly in male institutions, the silent system forbade prisoners to talk and some were even required to wear uniforms that obscured their identities so that associations between inmates could not be formed. Under such a system, prisoners were plunged into a world of isolation and silent contemplation. While women might be put to productive or menial labour, such as sewing shirts, laundry or cleaning, male inmates might find themselves required to carry out similar tasks or hard labour during their incarceration. The hope of such regimes was to exhaust the body and reshape the minds of criminals.

Penal servitude was eventually abolished almost a century later by the first clause of the Criminal Justice Act 1948, which argued that the treatment in prison under modern conditions of persons sentenced to penal servitude did not materially differ from the treatment of persons sentenced to imprisonment, and commanded that 'the legal distinction between imprisonment and penal Servitude should be abolished'. Both sentences of penal servitude and hard labour were replaced with equivalent terms of imprisonment so that, no matter the sentence, the experience within prison walls would be uniform.

The Criminal Justice Act not only abolished the legal difference between sentences of penal servitude and other kinds of imprisonment, but also ended the distinction between 'convict' and other prisons so that all institutions became equal under the new law. The third and final result of the end of penal servitude was the abolition of the ticket-of-leave parole system, which required prisoners released from convict institutions on licence to keep police informed of their place of residence until their sentence had expired.

LUCY WILLIAMS

See also: **Convict Prisons; Ticket of Leave; Transportation**

Readings

Godfrey, B., Cox, D. and Farrall, S. (2010) *Serious offenders: A historical study of habitual criminals.* Oxford: Oxford University Press.

Tomlinson, M.H. (1981) 'Penal servitude 1846–1865: a system in evolution', in V. Bailey (ed) *Policing and punishment in nineteenth century Britain.* London: Croom Helm, pp 126–49.

PETTY SESSIONS

Petty sessions were the lowest rung of the criminal justice system until replaced by magistrates' courts. They were courts that primarily heard cases without a jury – summary courts – or cases that could be heard by summary jurisdiction. This meant that justice was pronounced summarily by a magistrate, rather than a decision being made by a jury.

They emerged out of summary proceedings carried out by magistrates, with the name being first recorded in the Statute of Artificers of 1562 (5 Eliz I c.4, §40). By the start of the 17th century, a three-tier system of petty, quarter and general sessions was being referred to in England and Wales. However, in Scotland, the role of magistrates remained less important than that of the sheriff, and although a similar type of summary proceedings existed, they were limited in power and less important than their English equivalent (NRS, 2015).

Summary proceedings did not operate formally in terms of location or time, but depended more on the individual magistrate's availability and willingness to conduct proceedings. Therefore, there were considerable differences between locales. This informality extended to how sessions were recorded – although magistrates were advised to make notes of proceedings, not all did, and those who did, did so in an, again, individualistic way, which means that surviving records can vary in terms of style and what they record.

Summary proceedings were presided over by a magistrate, or Justice of the Peace (JP), working either alone or with one or more other local magistrates. A clerk of the peace was also present, acting either as recorder of cases or as a provider of legal information to the magistrates (Cunningham, 1884). The latter did not have to have any legal training as a property qualification was the primary means of enabling a commission of the peace until the latter 18th century. Gradually, the clerical magistrate and others from a lesser background than the gentry became able to gain a commission as the workload of magistrates put pressure on existing justices and meant that it became a less attractive position.

The cases heard by magistrates at summary level were varied, including minor offences such as petty larceny, assault and employment disputes. Social regulation was also dealt with here, with magistrates adjudicating on issues such as the keeping of bawdy houses, drunkenness and swearing in public. They also dealt with administrative cases, involving the Poor Laws, the licensing of inns, excise, rates and taxes (Baker, 2007). They heard bastardy examinations, and were also where more serious cases – felonious thefts and other criminal offences – would be first heard, before indicted onto the higher courts.

By the end of the 18th century, summary proceedings were gradually becoming more regularised and organised, and this became formalised as petty sessions at the start of the 19th century, though, again, this formalisation did not occur wholesale across the country at the same time. In Ireland, the Petty Sessions (Ireland) Act 1827 (7 & 8 Geo IV c.67) had the stated aim of 'securing a uniform and effectual mode of procedure'. In England and Wales, the Summary Jurisdiction Act 1848 (11 & 12 Vict c.42) homogenised the process, with petty session records being passed onto quarter sessions. In 1879, a further Summary Jurisdiction Act (42 & 43 Vict c.49) standardised record-keeping (Cunningham, 1884).

The introduction of formal petty sessions was, in part, a response to the growing powers of magistrates and the increase in offences that were coming before the court. Petty sessions took on part of the work previously carried out at quarter sessions, and JPs became stipendiary – paid – magistrates, with a greater degree of training. The geographical area that came under the jurisdiction of each petty session was based on Hundreds, the old administrative units, with groups of Hundreds banded together as a division.

The administrative function of petty sessions, and their divisions, were gradually changed and transferred to magistrates' courts under a succession of Acts and orders in the post-Second World War period. From the early 1970s, the three-tier criminal justice system became a two-tier system of crown courts and magistrates' courts. However, magistrates' courts still continue to deal with less serious offences, without a jury, and magistrates can still only issue certain punishments, just like their predecessors at petty sessions.

NELL DARBY

See also: **Assizes; Magistrates; Quarter Sessions; Scottish Criminal Courts, The (c.1747–1850)**

Readings

Baker, J.H. (2007) *An introduction to English legal history* (4th edn). Oxford: Oxford University Press.

Cunningham, G.W. (1884) *The Summary Jurisdiction Acts, 1848–1884*. London: Shaw & Sons.

NRS (National Records of Scotland) (2015) 'Justices of the Peace records'. Available at: http://www.nrscotland.gov.uk/research/guides/justices-of-the-peace-records

PHILANTHROPIC INSTITUTIONS

Referring to the late 18th century, Sim (1990, p 131) describes the emergence of 'A network of institutions and practices designed specifically to deal with deviant women who were classified into different social groups: the prostitute, the criminal, the lunatic and the undeserving poor'. The inception of one of these new institutions – the philanthropic institution – was opened in Whitechapel, London in 1758 (Bartley, 2000). Its success, in conjunction with developments in social welfare policies, led to the formation of other philanthropic institutions for women, particularly in the first two decades of the 19th century. Examples include Bristol Female Penitentiary, London Female Penitentiary and Leeds House of Rescue (Bartley, 2000). Philanthropic institutions operated as an environment in which women's spiritual and moral welfare was guaranteed to be reclaimed. The institutions became 'less a site of temporary refuge and more a refuge of last resort', providing for women and girls who had been or were at risk of becoming 'utterly abandoned by society' (Smith, 2007, p 34).

The process of reforming deviant women was unequivocally about the working class being 'saved' by their middle-class 'superiors' since it was predominantly working-class women who were targeted by individuals who 'possessed the time, money, social connections and the local social conscience' to achieve this (Bartley, 2000, p 25). Many wealthy individuals – some famous and some otherwise – set up their own private philanthropic institutions for prostitutes and deviant women:

> Josephine Butler brought ailing prostitutes back to her home; Angela Burdett-Courts provided the money for Charles Dickens to supervise Urania Cottage; Adeline, Duchess of Bedford founded and helped manage her own institution. Even the Prime Minister, William Gladstone, was a fervent rescuer of prostitutes. (Bartley, 2000, p 26)

Philanthropic institutions were considered 'part of a Christian "archipelago" of reform' that stretched across the UK, with most cities having at least one institution dedicated to the reformation of deviant women (Bartley, 2000, p 25). In the north-west of England, for example, Liverpool Female Penitentiary, Liverpool Rescue Society and House of Help, and the Bolton Committee for the Reclamation of Unfortunate Women were all erected in attempt to exert some form of official control over unruly working-class women.

The principal role of the female philanthropic institution was moral regeneration, moral treatment and the restoration of feminine values of domesticity, docility, honesty and motherhood. Middle-class philanthropists, in direct contrast to radical feminists who asked questions regarding the sexual division of labour and the justice of existing social structures, held faith in the existence of separate spheres for men and women and the 'efficacy of the social institutions that they sought to reform' (Rafter, 1985, p 45). Philanthropists therefore did not seek to alter or dismantle the existing social order; they essentially reinforced and strengthened the status of the patriarchal state (Rafter, 1985). They were described by Rafter (1985, p 46) as social feminists whose 'faith in the intrinsically moral, nurturing and domestic nature of women' prompted a feminisation of the institutional architecture and routines under their control; female philanthropists could then act as feminine role models to facilitate moral reformation. It was largely believed by all philanthropists that for female delinquents to be reformed, they had to be isolated from men and placed under the supervision of women. Although the existence of social feminism enabled the establishment of philanthropic institutions for women, the penological shift authorised the application of double standards of femininity and respectability.

Armed with belief in inherent differences between the sexes, they naturally sought to establish all-female institutions, prisons uncontaminated by male influence, in which criminal women would receive sympathetic care from members of their own sex (Rafter, 1985, p 46).

Such sympathetic care by other women, however, came at a price. The gendered management legitimised female administrators to be locked into 'narrow, sexually stereotyped roles' that reflected the public sphere (Rafter, 1985, p 46). Ultimately, philanthropic institutions worked at maintaining and promoting social harmony among working-class members of society. Institutional members saw themselves as 'civilising agents' and mediated between the rich and the poor, with their acts of charity expected to 'bind society together and create and maintain social order' (Luddy, 1998, p 157). It was believed that this would produce significant societal benefits by promoting morality among the lower classes.

KIRSTY GREENWOOD

See also: **Inebriate Institutions; Semi-penal Institutions for Women**

Readings

Bartley, P. (2000) *Prostitution: Prevention and reform in England, 1860–1914*. London: Routledge.

Luddy, M. (1998) 'Religion, philanthropy and the state in late eighteenth and early nineteenth-century Ireland', in H. Cunningham and J. Innes (eds) *Charity, philanthropy and reform from the 1690s to 1850*. Basingstoke: Macmillan, pp 148–67.

Rafter, N. (1985) *Partial justice: Women, prison and social control*. New Jersey, NJ: Transaction Publishers.

Sim, J. (1990) *Medical power in prisons: Prison medical service in England, 1774–1988*. Milton Keynes: Open University Press.

Smith, J.M. (2007) *Ireland's Magdalen laundries and the nation's architecture of containment*. Manchester: Manchester University Press.

PICKPOCKETING

Larceny from the person became a capital offence in England in 1565. In this early statute, the Act had to be effected 'privily, without his [the victim's] knowledge, in any place whatsoever'. Until 1808, when the Act was reformed by Sir Samuel Romilly, it remained a crime punishable by death. In early 'rogue literature', which circulated in the 16th and 17th centuries, larceny from the person was more colloquially referred to as pickpocketing. While the death penalty was certainly available as a means of punishing this crime, in practice, by the 18th century, pickpockets were more likely to be transported to America, or from 1788, to Australia. Pickpocketing tended to be perceived as an urban crime. Moreover, for much of its 18th-century history, it was frequently associated with female criminality and deviance, in particular, with prostitution. Along with the highway robber, the pickpocket featured significantly in the criminal typologies that were constructed by 18th-century writers. During the 18th century, as many as 50% of pickpockets tried at the Old Bailey sessions were women, and there is evidence to suggest that the female involvement in this crime increased dramatically during wartime. Thus, pickpocketing was essentially a crime of economic need, and during wartime, with many less men being prosecuted, women were far more likely to appear in the court.

However, the nature of pickpocketing as an offence shifted in the early 19th century, with the rising concern about juvenile offenders. From 1815, with the end of the French Wars, there were increasing anxieties about the number of children who committed crime. Juvenile delinquency was arguably discovered as a subject in this period (though, of course, these concerns were not without precedent), and, consequently, legislative developments attempted to define and separate the juvenile offender from the adult criminal population (Shore, 1999). Given the opportunistic and petty nature of much juvenile crime, pickpocketing was unsurprisingly one of the offences at which children and young people were thought to excel. Stereotypes developed that strongly associated the nimbleness, fleet-footedness and dexterity of youth with the crime. These stereotypes would be perpetually linked in the mind of the public with the serialisation (during 1837–39) of Charles Dickens' (1838) *Oliver Twist, or, the parish boy's progress*. The Artful Dodger was a clever and charismatic caricature of the youthful pickpocket. Moreover, the Dodger's progress through the criminal justice system and transportation to the colonies was mirrored by the prosecution strategies of the court.

While, after the early 19th century, pickpocketing was no longer a capital crime, it was still a crime that attracted considerable attention in urban contexts. Throughout the 19th century, concerns persisted about forms of pickpocketing like hustling (groups of youths 'hustled' their victim in order to pick his pocket), and from the 1830s, many newspapers reported on the activities of the swell mob, a group of sophisticated and urbane pickpockets who 'infested' urban social spaces and places of entertainment such as theatres and pleasure gardens (*Gentleman's Magazine*, 1837).

The pickpocket was not only a feature of British urban life. Thus, Louis-Sébastian Mercier wrote about the pickpocket in early 19th-century Paris, and former detectives turned authors, such as Philip Farley (1876) and Thomas Byrnes (1886), included the pickpocket in their galleries of American rogues and professional criminals. Moreover, the stereotype of the pickpocket continued to thrive in modern society and remained a common criminal type in the genre literature that proliferated in the 20th century. For example, Georges Simenon (1967) wrote about *Maigret's pickpocket*, and Raymond Chandler kept a list of 'pickpocket lingo' in his notebooks (Chandler, 1976). Moreover, with the advent of the hippy trail and the opening of tourist markets in India, warnings about the Delhi pickpocket became and remain a common theme in guidebooks. In the criminal justice system of England and Wales, larceny from the person has been subsumed into the broader category of theft, under the Theft Act 1968. It remains nearer its original form in American law, though its definition varies from state to state.

HEATHER SHORE

See also: **Female Thieves; Juvenile Crime; Juvenile Crime and Justice in Scotland; Juvenile Crime in Britain**

Readings
Byrnes, T.F. (1886) *Professional criminals of America*. New York, NY: Cassell.

Chandler, R. (1976) *The notebooks of Raymond Chandler*. New York, NY: Ecco Press.

Dickens, C. (1838) *Oliver Twist, or, the parish boy's progress*. London: Richard Bentley.

Farley, P. (1876) *Criminals of America*. New York, NY: Phillip Farley.

Gentleman's Magazine (1837) 1, July–December.

Gilfoyle, T. (2006) *A pickpocket's tale: The underworld of nineteenth-century New York*. New York, NY: W.W. Norton & Company.

Mercier, L.S. (1802) *Paris delineated*. London: H.D. Symonds.

Palk, D. (2006) *Gender, crime and judicial discretion, 1780–1830*. Woodbridge: Boydell Press.

Shore, H. (1999) *Artful dodgers: Youth and crime in early nineteenth-century London*. Woodbridge: Boydell Press.

Shore, H. (2015) *London's criminal underworlds, c. 1720–c. 1930*. Basingstoke: Palgrave Macmillan.

Simenon, G. (1967) *Le Voleur de Maigret*. Paris: Presses de la Cité.

PLEADING THE BELLY

Throughout the 18th and 19th centuries, a process established under both Roman and English law saw the impanelling of special 'juries of matrons' to examine female defendants who pleaded pregnancy. More specifically, these juries – comprised of midwives in Scotland (Louthian, 1752, p 57) but possibly just married women drawn *de circumstantibus* from within the courtroom in England (Oldham, 1985, p 16) – were charged with ascertaining whether defendants were 'with quick child'. Quickening was the detection of foetal movement and the point in a pregnancy at which life was believed to commence. Pleas of pregnancy were submitted in both civil and criminal cases, for different purposes. Pleas entered in civil cases most often pertained to inheritance, whereby female defendants sought to prove that they were pregnant by their deceased husbands to protect the inheritance of their unborn children from rival claims. In criminal cases, capitally convicted women 'pleaded the belly' after sentencing in an attempt to stay their execution. To execute a pregnant woman, Archibald Alison asserted in his early 19th-century tome on the practice of Scottish Law, 'would be an unseemly or barbarous step' (Alison, 1833, p 657). In both Scotland and England, therefore, pregnancy constituted grounds for the temporary respite of a death sentence – and also occasionally of lesser punishments inflicted on the body, such as flogging – '*in favorem prolis*' (in favour of the child). In theory, a successful plea only granted a reprieve until the birth of the child or the pregnancy proved to be false. In his magisterial *Commentaries on the laws of England*, William Blackstone (1769, p 388, emphases in original) explained the process thus:

In case this plea be made in stay of execution, the judge must direct a jury of twelve matrons or discreet women to enquire the fact: and if they bring in their verdict *quick with child* (for barely, *with child*, unless it be alive in the womb, is not sufficient) execution shall be staid generally till the next session; and so from session to session, till either she is delivered, or proves by the course of nature not to have been with child at all.

In practice, John Beattie (2001, p 297) has suggested that a significant number of the women who were reprieved on the grounds of pregnancy were likely pardoned, especially after 1718, when pardons could be made conditional upon transportation.

The earliest documented submission of a pregnancy plea in an English criminal case was 1228 (Forbes, 1988, p 26), though 18th- and 19th-century legal commentators dated its origins back to ancient Roman Law. James Cockburn has suggested that 'pleading the belly' was a relatively common practice in the 16th and 17th centuries (though the numbers varied widely from session to session). Based on an exhaustive search of the *Proceedings of the Old Bailey* between 1677 and 1800, James Oldham (1985, p 34) has suggested that pregnancy pleas were likewise a frequent occurrence in London until the mid-18th century, especially between 1714 and 1720. From the 1760s, however, the practice declined and juries of matrons were sworn far more sporadically, though the process was not legally superseded until the introduction of the Sentence of Death (Expectant Mothers) Act in 1931.

Historians have proposed a number of theories to explain this decline in the late 18th and 19th centuries. Thomas Forbes (1988) has drawn attention to repeated concerns about the incompetence of the juries printed in British medical journals from the 1830s to suggest that the authority of 'matrons' on matters concerning the female body had been superseded by the rise of the medical man long before the law recognised this shift. Changes in patterns of prosecution and punishment, especially the availability of transportation and imprisonment as alternatives to hanging in the 18th century and growing concerns about the death penalty in the 19th century, also explain why fewer women were in a position to need this last-ditch plea. We need to be cautious about reading too much into 18th-century views that women were flippant about the legal process because they could enter a pregnancy plea and that they used it to abuse the system (eg by stacking the courtroom with their friends or endeavouring to become pregnant while in gaol). While many women probably did enter the plea because they had 'nothing to lose', there was no guarantee that the jury would find in their favour. Repeatedly low success rates suggest that this was not an easy way to cheat the system.

JOANNE McEWAN

See also: **Benefit of Clergy; 'Bloody Code', The**

Readings

Alison, A. (1833) *Practice of the criminal law of Scotland.* Edinburgh: William Blackwood.

Beattie, J.M. (2001) *Policing and punishment in London, 1660–1750: Urban crime and the limits of terror.* Oxford: Oxford University Press.

Blackstone, W. (1769) *Commentaries on the laws of England. Volume 4.* Oxford: Oxford University Press.

Forbes, T.R. (1988) 'A jury of matrons', *Medical History*, 32: 23–33.

Louthian, J. (1752) *The form of process before the Court of Justiciary in Scotland* (2nd edn). Edinburgh: Printed by Hamilton, Balfour and Neill.

Oldham, J.C. (1985) 'On pleading the belly: a history of the jury of the jury of matrons', *Criminal Justice History*, 6: 1–64.

POLICE COURT MISSIONARIES

The London Police Courts Mission (LPCM), the first of its kind, was established in 1876 as a means of 'rescuing drunkards found in London courts' (Blocker et al, 2003, p 158). Missionaries from the LPCM worked with magistrates to develop a system of releasing offenders on the condition that they kept in touch with the missionary and accepted guidance in order to try and reduce reoffending. By 1886, the Probation of First Time Offenders Act allowed courts in the UK to follow the London example of appointing missionaries. The Probation of First Offenders Act 1887, however, was the first time in which probation appeared in English law and officially enabled magistrates to refer offenders to a supervisor – most commonly, a police court missionary attached to a charitable agency. The largest of these agencies was the Church of England Temperance Society (CETS). CETS was founded in 1862 as the Church of England Total Abstinence Society, with its initial aim being to convert individuals to engage with teetotal activities (Vanstone, 2004). By 1872, CETS widened its focus from promoting temperance to attempting to both remove the causes of intemperance and promote the welfare of prisoners, appointing its first police court missionary in 1876 (Carey and Walker, 2002; Vanstone, 2004).

Although many rural regions were reluctant to appoint police court missionaries, the busy port city of Liverpool held CETS, the Catholic Aid Society, the Liverpool Ladies Temperance Association and the Wesleyan Mission, which all supplied missionaries in order to cope with the demand of drunken and deviant behaviour placed upon the criminal justice system (Carey and Walker, 2002). The official role of police court missionaries was to provide moral support to defendants appearing before magistrates, including their immediate family. They 'encouraged defendants to sign the temperance pledge to stop drinking' and provided practical support ranging from obtaining paid work to finding care institutions for children who had been abandoned by their parents (Alker and Godfrey, 2015, p 85). Their objective was to 'Imprint a moral framework upon young offenders, drunks, would-be-suicides, habitual low-level offenders and the poor of the inner cities. They offered valuable service to the magistrate and practical aid to those whom the magistrate delivered into their hands' (Alker and Godfrey, 2015, p 85).

Their operative aim was a distinctive moral enterprise: providing an alternative to both punishment and imprisonment by offering advice, assistance, friendship, mercy and practical help via a deeply Christian ethos and intolerance to alcohol. Canton (2013, p 20) states that many missionaries were prompted to carry out their moral work due to a 'dismay at the futility, if not cruelty, of successive punishments' handed out to individuals, with little to no attempt to help or assist them in deflecting from crime. By the late 19th century, police court missionaries broadened their knowledge of intemperance and criminal behaviour by approaching drunken women, prostitutes and other female criminals, and distributing bibles, CETS journals and tracts to over 415 courts in the UK (Blocker et al, 2003):

> In one year James Mercer the Police Court missionary for the diocese of Liverpool made 1097 daily visits to the police courts and saw a hundred prisoners who were given a free breakfast, a few earnest words ... and invited to sign the 'pledge'. (Ayscough, 1923, cited in Vanstone, 2004, p 8)

In 1907, the Probation of Offenders Act gave the LPCM missionaries official status as probation officers while maintaining their missionary tradition. The Act allowed courts to suspend punishment and discharge offenders if they entered into a recognisance of between one and three years; one condition of which was supervision by an individual named in the probation order. By 1907, there were 146 police court missionaries operating in courts in the UK, and with the implementation of the Probation of Offenders Act 1907, missionaries were employed as paid state agents, forming the 'transition from voluntary to statutory provision' (Carey and Walker, 2002, p 60). Although it would be a gross oversimplification to claim that the current probation service formed from such missionary work, CETS's police court mission visibly demonstrates the transition in Britain from voluntary reform to state social welfare (Carey and Walker, 2002).

KIRSTY GREENWOOD

See also: **Probation; Temperance Movements**

Readings

Alker, Z. and Godfrey, B. (2015) 'War as an opportunity for divergence and desistance from crime, 1750–1945', in S. Walklate and R. McGarry (eds) *Criminology and war: Transgressing the borders.* London: Routledge, pp 77–93.

Blocker, J.S., Tyrell, I.R. and Fahey, D.M. (2003) *Alcohol and temperance in modern history.* Oxford: ABC-CLIO.

Canton, R. (2013) *Probation: Working with offenders.* London: Routledge.

Carey, M. and Walker, R. (2002) 'The penal voluntary sector', in S. Bryans and C. Martin (eds) *Prisons and the voluntary sector: A bridge into the community.* Winchester: Waterside Press, pp 50–62.

Vanstone, M. (2004) *Supervising offenders in the community: A history of probation theory and practice.* Aldershot: Ashgate.

POLICING 18TH- AND 19TH-CENTURY SCOTLAND

In the 18th century, Scottish towns and counties relied upon a variety of local officials, representatives and institutions to enforce law and order. Authority was vested in local justices and (in counties) landowners, who were responsible for appointing a number of lesser local officials, constables, town officers and watchmen. Some positions, such as that of town officer, were salaried and full-time. Most, though, were unpaid, amateur and voluntary, most notably, the office of constable. Edinburgh employed a town guard to patrol the streets at night, but other towns obliged local householders to 'watch and ward' on a rotational basis as part of their unpaid, personal service to the community. Much of the day-to-day supervision and control of local communities was carried out by Church elders, who were responsible for policing sexual and public morality.

Full-time, professional policing in Scottish towns emerged in the late 18th and early 19th centuries from a series of Local Police Acts, the most significant of which were introduced in Glasgow in 1800 and Edinburgh in 1805. These initiatives evolved out of an emerging consensus among men of property that new statutory tax-raising police powers were necessary to meet the needs, challenges and expectations brought by rapid urban expansion and growing concerns with crime and disorder. National Burgh Police Acts in 1833, 1850 and 1862 permitted, but did not compel, the extension of police provisions to less populous urban centres, which meant that there was an uneven pattern of adoption throughout the country. The 'police' concept in urban Scotland at this time was, as in many parts of Europe, broadly conceived: it was concerned with the regulation and administration of the local community for well-being, security and the common good. Police commissioners, who were typically elected from among qualified local male householders, were responsible for overseeing a range of municipal services, including lighting, paving, cleansing and law and order. Police legislation was integral to municipal governance and was closely aligned with the development of the local state and middle-class demands for a greater say in the administration of civic affairs.

While some scholars have championed Scottish municipal policing initiatives as heralding the birth of modern policing in Britain (Dinsmor and Goldsmith, 2005), others have belittled them as little more than glorified 18th-century improvement measures (Hart, 1951). The Scottish municipal police model certainly had links with the past, but it also established important connections with modern policing practices. Full-time watch and police forces, operating under a bureaucratic hierarchical command structure, were set up to prevent crime. Moreover, provision was often made in police legislation for the establishment of police courts in order to expand judicial capacity, facilitate the prosecution of a larger volume of criminal cases and provide for a speedier, more efficient system of summary justice. The Scottish urban police model that was established in the early 1800s did not represent the coming of 'new' police, nor the triumph of a new model, but it did form an important bridge between the 'old' and the 'new' police idea from which modern policing would evolve (Barrie, 2008; Carson and Idzikowska, 1989).

Landowners in Scottish counties since 1747 had the power to levy a compulsory tax on landed property for defraying the cost of apprehending and prosecuting criminals. National legislation in 1839 extended this power and provided a new structure of law enforcement for counties to adopt. Like the burgh national statutes, the 1839 Act was permissive. The financial consequences of vagrancy were often central in determining whether landowners adopted it, with many doing so primarily to prevent the wandering poor from becoming a burden on local Poor Law and charitable funds (Carson and Idzikowska, 1989). Also important, though, was the influence of the 'moral entrepreneur' John List, Superintendent of the Midlothian Police, who campaigned long and hard for county police reform in the face of a perceived rise in rural crime and unrest (Smale, 2013). The County and Burgh Police Act 1857 completed the transition to a policed society by compelling county authorities to establish police forces and assume responsibility for policing towns that had not yet embraced reform. Central government extended greater influence over the shape and nature of

Scottish policing over the course of the century through government directives and grants, but it was, for the most part, willing to let Scottish civic and rural elites determine law enforcement arrangements in line with the country's separate legal and administrative traditions and local circumstances.

DAVID G. BARRIE

See also: **'New' Police, The; Patrick Colquhoun; Protest and Policing in Scotland**

Readings

Barrie, D.G. (2008) *Police in the age of improvement: Police development and the civic tradition in Scotland, 1775–1865.* Cullompton: Willan Publishing.

Carson, K. and Idzikowska, H. (1989) 'The social production of Scottish policing, 1795–1900', in D. Hay and F. Snyder (eds) *Policing and prosecution in Britain, 1750–1850.* Oxford: Clarendon Press, pp 267–300.

Dinsmor, A. and Goldsmith, A. (2005) 'Scottish policing – a historical perspective', in D. Donnelly and K. Scott (eds) *Policing Scotland.* Cullompton: Willan Publishing, pp 40–61.

Hart, J.M. (1951) *The British police.* London: Allen & Unwin.

Smale, D. (2013) 'Alfred John List and the development of policing in the counties of Scotland, c. 1832–77', *Journal of Scottish Historical Studies*, 33(1): 52–80.

POLICING (20TH CENTURY)

The 'new' police forces of the 19th century were well established across England and Wales by 1900. Their presence, initially resented by many working-class communities, was, by the turn of the century, widely accepted. A slow process of professionalisation contributed to the forging of a national police identity, despite the existence of more than 200 separate forces, and agitation for better pay and conditions leading to a number of strikes in the early part of the century. The dislocation of two world wars placed huge pressures on the police, with severe reductions in the numbers of men available to serve, exacerbated by the addition of a number of extra wartime duties (Emsley, 2010). By the 1950s, sometimes portrayed as a golden age for the police, the tensions and strains of the first half of the century had abated and the distinctively English local bobby was considered a source of national pride. The general trend in relation to the organisation of the police over the century, however, was one in which power was increasingly concentrated 'in the hands of police officers and central government at the expense of local government' (Godfrey et al, 2008, p 56). Movement towards a more centralised approach was evident after the First World War but the most dramatic shift came with the Police Act 1964. This reduced the number of forces in England and Wales to just 49 (later 43) and was accompanied by a less formal process of centralisation in which local mechanisms of control, such as watch committees, were weakened, while central government took an increasingly directive role.

Technological advances across the century also had an impact on police practices in several ways (Williams, 2014). The increasing use of motor cars from the 1930s, in particular, generated challenges for the police. Middle-class road users, who had rarely been subject to police attention, were increasingly at the sharp end of traffic regulation, but a more mobile population also raised demands with which traditional policing methods struggled. During the 1960s, the unit beat system of policing, which replaced foot and cycle patrols with motorised mobile units responding to directives from a central control room, became increasingly common. The traditional bobby on the beat, which had been the mainstay of policing since the inception of the 'new' police, was on the decline, leading to suggestions that the police had become a 'fire brigade' emergency service increasingly distanced from their local communities.

Police–community relations were also strained by the wider socio-economic changes of the 20th century as crime became progressively more politicised in an increasingly divided society (Reiner, 2010). Political demonstrations and industrial unrest, combined with a more paramilitary approach to policing public order, brought the police into conflict with a number of social groups. Relations with minority ethnic communities were particularly fraught, with allegations of over-policing contributing to rioting in several large cities in the 1980s. In the following decade, the Stephen Lawrence case raised further concerns, prompting the Macpherson Report, which labelled the police as institutionally racist (Reiner, 2010). Growing awareness of diversity also impacted internally upon the police, with the slow incorporation of women officers, which had begun in response to the pressures of war, and greater representation of minority ethnic groups. Added to this, allegations of corruption, miscarriages of justice and abuses of police power, increasingly prevalent, at least in the media, from the 1960s onwards, generated a repeated cycle of scandal and reform, raising some concerning and intractable questions about police accountability. A number of reforms were introduced from the 1980s to try and address this decreasing legitimacy, including the greater codification and regulation of police powers, as well as the development of (varyingly) 'independent' complaints procedures. The final decade of the century saw a shift towards less prominent questioning of both legitimacy and accountability prompted by the growing political consensus over law and order between the Left and Right of British politics.

MARYSE TENNANT

See also: 'New' Police, The; Watch Committees

Readings

Emsley, C. (2010) *The great British bobby: A history of British policing from 1829 to the present*. London: Quercus.

Godfrey, B.S., Lawrence, P. and Williams, C.A. (2008) *History and crime*. London: Sage.

Reiner, R. (2010) *The politics of the police*. Oxford: Oxford University Press.

Williams, C.A. (2014) *Police control systems in Britain, 1775–1975*. Manchester: Manchester University Press.

PRISON REFORM

The period of 'prison reform' is located at the end of the 18th and beginning of the 19th centuries; it is also referred to as the period during which the 'birth' of the modern prison occurred. This period was marked by the activity of a small number of men and women who campaigned for changes in prisons. Most notable in spearheading this campaign were John Howard, whose interest in prisons was ignited by his appointment as High Sheriff of Bedfordshire in 1773, and Elizabeth Fry, who began visiting female prisoners at Newgate prison in London in 1813. Howard was a non-conformist and Fry was a Quaker; they both moved in particular social circles and, through family and religious connections, were connected not only with other philanthropic endeavours of the period, but also with the emerging industrialists and entrepreneurs of the early 19th century (Ignatieff, 1978).

Howard's initial interest led to a large survey of all of the prisons in England and Wales, and subsequently across Europe. Publication of the first survey, *The state of the prisons*, in 1777 drew considerable attention to the unregulated, diseased and squalid conditions in many gaols and houses of correction across the country. Most importantly, Howard's criticisms did draw the attention of the magistrates and county gentlemen, who oversaw the administration of the counties under their jurisdiction, and encouraged their interest in prisons. This provoked a large number to try to do something about the prison conditions within their locality and it is estimated that around 45 prisons were rebuilt during the latter decades of the 18th century (Evans, 1982).

At the national level, the government passed the Penitentiary Act 1779, which allowed for the construction of two penitentiaries to hold offenders before they were transported overseas. While these penitentiaries never came to fruition, those involved in the proposal (Howard, William Blackstone and William Eden) had begun to think that prisons not only should be healthier and more regulated, but might also have the potential to change a person's behaviour; that prisoners could 'do penance' for their crimes.

Howard was most successful in the abolition of gaol fees and garnish; he had discovered that fees were paid by prisoners for all aspects of living (bedding/straw, water, food and so forth) as well as for entry to (garnish) and release from prison. During his visits, he found a number of prisoners who remained in prison having served their sentence but who were unable to pay the discharge fee and be released. The Gaol Fees Abolition Act 1815 abolished all fees and instructed that the prisons be run by paid gaolers and staff, as well as be financed and maintained by the local authorities rather than as profit-making enterprises. Further recommendations from both Howard and Fry were written into the Gaols Act 1823, which instructed that all prisoners should be divided into classes according to their gender and their (alleged) offence. This Act was a particular success for Fry, who had been campaigning for female prisoners to be supervised only by female staff and for female staff to be present when male officers were in female sections of prisons.

It is certainly the case that the 'reformed' prisons of the 19th century were improved in terms of health, sanitation and orderliness from those of the 18th century. From the 1820s onwards, there was a shift in the new prison towards establishing the best mode or system through which to change or alter prisoners' behaviour. Whether this new 'well-ordered' prison bought a new and different type of discomfort to the prisoner in the form of physical and mental isolation, long hours of hard labour, discipline, and monotony is a point of debate, as is the possibility that the creation of the modern prison opened up new systems of surveillance, discipline and regulation across wider society (Foucault, 1991; McGowen, 1998; Johnston, 2015).

HELEN JOHNSTON

See also: **Convict Prisons; Local Prisons; Penal Reform Pressure Groups**

Readings

Evans, R. (1982) *The fabrication of virtue: English prison architecture, 1750–1840.* Cambridge: Cambridge University Press.

Foucault, M. (1991) *Discipline and punish: The birth of the prison* (trans A. Sheridan). Harmondsworth: Penguin.

Ignatieff, M. (1978) *A just measure of pain: The penitentiary in the Industrial Revolution.* London: Macmillan.

Johnston, H. (2015) *Crime in England, 1815–1880.* Abingdon: Routledge.

McGowen, R. (1998) 'The well-ordered prison', in N. Morris and D.J. Rothman (eds) *The Oxford history of the prison*. New York, NY: Oxford University Press, pp 71–99.

PRISON RIOTS

The history of the prison in Britain has not been frequently scarred with major riots. Therefore, what justifies concentration on such events? There are two key rationales: the first has been highlighted by Sykes (1958) in his early sociological analysis of the prison, who states that power 'unexercised is seldom as visible as power that is challenged'; and the second is the problem of maintaining discipline and order on a daily basis, which is never far removed from the problem of disorder (Sparks et al, 1996). Riots have historically attracted public and political attention, creating significant increases in the amount of evidence available about the institution in which they occur and generating short-lived but sharp increases in political discussion about penal policy. New journalism, or, as it was later framed, the tabloid press, has fed avidly and often speculatively on prison riots, exploiting the readiness of the public to accept vivid but not always factual descriptions of the worst excesses of prisoner behaviour. Post-riot official investigations have, within the constraints of legal process, generated accessible, after a time, evidence from inmates and prison officers, giving a voice to those who have often been silent in prison histories.

These forms of evidence highlight the extent to that an institution that has been referred to as 'total' because of the way it segregates inmates from the outside world has actually been affected profoundly by external as well as internal pressures. Inmate aggression, staff morale, power relations, institutional diversity and administrative difficulties exist within broader circumstances of prison authorities and hierarchies, policymaking, and economic constraints. These are what have been called 'the structural circumstances of confinement' (Carrabine, 2005, p 896). Any consideration of the causality, process and/or impact of prison riots must locate wider relevant contexts. One key way in which the balance between internal and external influencing factors has been framed is within the concept of legitimacy. This necessitates an examination of the moral basis upon which prisons have been operated and an acceptance that some regimes can be more legitimate than others. According to Beetham (1993), legitimacy takes the form of three criteria: conformity to rules, justifiability of rules in terms of shared beliefs and, finally, legitimation through expressed consent. However, deciphering consensual behaviour by prisoners is problematic as they live within a highly restricted environment.

Examination of prison riots over time reveals continuities. In the aftermath of significant outbreaks, specific groups of male prisoners (usually those perceived to be the most recidivist and least likely to reform) have been identified and received most of the blame for disorder. With the possible exception of the Woolf Report following the Manchester Strangeways riot of 1990, official investigations in the aftermath of prison riots tend not to delve into issues of policy that may have played a contextual role, but to follow a narrower remit of who did what, when and to whom during the disturbance. In the aftermath of major riots, prisoners have tended to assert that their actions, at least initially, were legitimate demonstrations of grievances.

Specific prison riots tend to take on a representative form until overtaken, often after some time, by riots that are vivid enough and reported on sufficiently to replace the power of the previous riot in public memory. Prominent examples of these in Britain are: the Chatham Prison riot in 1861; the Dartmoor Prison riot in 1932; the Hull Prison riot in 1976; and the riot in Manchester Strangeways Prison in 1990. Although these riots attained prominence in penal history, they were not isolated instances, but only the most significant of multiple disturbances happening at a similar time. Riots reveal not only aggression and antagonism between prisoners and prison officers, but also a level of cooperation and mutual regard. In most cases, prison riots have been suppressed within a short time, though a rooftop action by a small number of prisoners did not end until 25 days after the riot in Strangeways Prison began. Discipline is restored, thereby ultimately reaffirming the regimes and methods of prison authorities.

ALYSON BROWN

See also: Convict Prisons

Readings
Beetham, D. (1993) *The legitimation of power*. London: Macmillan.
Brown, A. (2013) *Inter-war penal policy and crime in England*. Basingstoke: Macmillan.
Carrabine, E. (2005) 'Prison riots, social order and the problem of legitimacy', *British Journal of Criminology*, 45(6): 896–913.
Sparks, R., Bottoms, A. and Hay, W. (1996) *Prisons and the problem of order*. Oxford: Clarendon Press.
Sykes, G.M. (1958) *Society of captives*. New Jersey, NJ: Princeton University Press.

PRISON TOURISM

Prison tourism is part of the concept of 'dark tourism'. Dark tourism refers to public travel to locations associated with suffering, disaster and/or death, or the 'curious connection between the sad, the bad and their touristic representations' (Strange and Kempa, 2003, p 387). In recent years, decommissioned and operational prisons have become increasingly popular as tourist destinations, serving to enmesh the concept of punishment with the leisure experience. The imposition of punishment has historically kindled the public imagination. In Britain, during the 18th and early 19th centuries, many forms of punishment were performed publicly. This spectacle of judicial terror was fundamental in presenting the certainty of harsh punishment to wrongdoers, but for the public, it often constituted a means of prurient entertainment. In Western states, the development of imprisonment as the primary penalty for offenders did not lead to a decrease in public curiosity about the treatment of offenders. On the contrary, the shift arguably enhanced public interest. In the 20th century, prison tourism has become an increasingly popular means through which the 'private' world of the prison could be subject to the public gaze.

It is difficult to identify the origins of prison tourism but prisons have been visited for a variety of reasons for centuries. During the 18th century, the public visited debtors' prisons like the Marshalsea and King's Bench Prison, sometimes out of fascination with the institution and its inmates but often to supply and support those imprisoned. Later, visitors were drawn to prisons such as Pentonville and Dartmoor in order to appreciate the (real and symbolic) power of the external architecture. There was interest among people 'of substance' in gaining access to prisons in order to evaluate the new monuments of progressive penal philosophies and civic pride. Whatever the motive, the increase in visits to prisons over this time suggests that they became a source of interest for educational reasons but also due to a perverse glamour.

One of the earliest dedicated and commercially oriented prison tourist ventures was the prison ship *Success*. Used to incarcerate convicts, and then as a reformatory, it was purchased as an entrepreneurial enterprise and opened as an exhibition in 1890. Touring in Australia, the UK and America, *Success* remained in operation for 55 years. Notably, the *Success* exhibition relied upon some sensational and stereotypical features evident in later prison museums. In addition, it crystallised a duality within prison museums between their educational and entertainment value. The acclaimed advance in penal reform since transportation ended lent this exhibition a licence to exaggerate and even fabricate experience (artefacts were included that had no direct relation to the ship). Penal policy was depicted as a linear, reformative process from a less civilised past, and the ship as an educative and entertaining memorial to that shameful but simplified past.

What became clear in the 20th century was that the cultural importance and economic utility of prisons as tourist attractions depended on the individual prison and its physical structure. Prisons were increasingly designed with anonymity, not visibility, in mind. However, these new designs, through stark contrast, accentuated the 'see and beware' architectural power of 19th-century institutions (Jewkes, 2012, p 33). The tourist 'gaze' is shaped not just by what the tourist sees, but also by what s/he expects to see (Buddhabhumbhitak, 2010). Hence, prisons that now have a second life as tourist attractions in the UK largely fit with an expected 19th-century architectural form as physical icons of disciplinary systems of segregation and isolation.

In conclusion, prison museums can be valuable to test or challenge dominant, popular stereotypes and ideologies. They have an occasion to present the visitor with the personal, emotional and psychological aspects of imprisonment, as well as the broader historical and structural contexts within which it has developed and exists. However, tensions between educational and entertainment objectives remain, as does a tendency to concentrate upon more sensational aspects of imprisonment and prison experience.

ALYSON BROWN and ALANA BARTON

See also: **Crime Heritage**

Readings

Anon (no date) 'The history of the convict ship "Success"'. Available at: https://archive.org/details/cu31924030386290

Barton, A. and Brown, A. (forthcoming) 'Show me the prison! The development of prison tourism in the UK', *Crime, Media, Culture*.

Buddhabhumbhitak, K. (2010) 'Tourism immersion or tourist gaze', in P. Burns, C. Palmer and J. Lester (eds) *Tourism and visual culture: Theories and concepts*. Wallingford: CAB International.

Jewkes, Y. (2012) 'Aesthetics and an-aesthetics: the architecture of incarceration', in L. Cheliotis (ed) *The arts of imprisonment: Control, resistance, empowerment*. Farnham: Ashgate, pp 25–44.

Strange, C. and Kempa, M. (2003) 'Shades of dark tourism: Alcatraz and Robben Island', *Annals of Tourism Research*, 30(2): 386–405.

PRISONS AND PUNISHMENT IN SCOTLAND

The French philosopher Michel Foucault has hugely influenced the way historians and social scientists think about the issues of discipline and punishment. In his seminal work, he drew a distinction between punishment in an absolute monarchy and that taking place in a bourgeois democratic polity. In the former state, punishment, which was to demonstrate the majesty of power, was inflicted on the body; in the latter, concerned that the punishment should fit the crime and that individuals could and should be rehabilitated, it was visited on the mind or soul (Foucault, 1975). Foucault's distinction between the two forms of regime is somewhat arbitrary as practices such as torture can be found to have continuity regardless of the nature of the polity. Moreover, he makes little distinction between different states, or their levels of development.

Taking Scotland as an example, punishment by hanging for crime in the 18th and 19th centuries was on a much reduced level when compared to neighbouring England. The main reason for this was that England had many more statutes, known as the 'Bloody Code', covering a bewildering range of crimes for which hanging was prescribed. In Scotland, there were fewer than 50 crimes that carried a capital tariff and this persisted into the 19th century. Between 1805 and 1832, there was one execution in Scotland for every 298,000 people, while in England, it was one for every 155,000 (McKinlay and Smyth, 2005). Criminals north of the border could be executed for crimes against property (horse stealing, forgery), as well as crimes against the person (rape, serious assault) and even animals (bestiality). The punishments varied in their severity, for example, a farmer was sentenced to be strangled and burnt at Aberdeen for the 'detestable crime of bestiality' (*Caledonian Mercury*, 1729); a homicide considered as heinous might lead to the perpetrator's right hand being cut off before hanging. For other serious crimes, the punishment might be banishment for life or transportation to the colonies for seven years to life. Capital punishment was brought into line with England under the terms of the 25 Geo. 11. C.37 statute passed around the middle of the 18th century. However, the indignity of public hanging could be multiplied by allowing the body to hang in chains, that is, to rot, or offer it up for public dissection. For lesser crimes, fines, whipping, the pillory, banishment and transportation were the most common methods of punishment. There were no custom-built prisons in Scotland in the 18th century and the makeshift Tolbooths or Bridewells were used to hold prisoners for a maximum of three months.

These public displays of brutality became increasingly offensive to middle-class sensibilities and were gradually replaced by a system of incarceration, which placed emphasis on the reform of character. Executions were brought indoors in 1868, and the number of crimes against property carrying a capital tariff was reduced; the last man to be hanged for a property-related crime in Scotland was in 1834, after that, hanging was only used in murder cases. Transportation effectively came to an end in 1857 when judges under the Penal Servitude Act were given the power to sentence prisoners destined for transportation to penal servitude for less than 14 years. The system was becoming more humane but, in spite of this, there was no end to the use of physical force, for instance, the whipping of children under 15 years of age continued, being limited to a maximum of 12 strokes of the birch rod. This practice was only abolished in 1962.

For younger criminals, useful toil was seen as the best preventive method and, as such, they were sent not to prison, but to industrial schools or reformatories, where they learnt to labour. The adults were imprisoned in separate institutions divided on the basis of gender. The system was increasingly centralised over the course of the 19th century; from 178 places of incarceration in 1839, the number was reduced to just 14 by 1900, all under the control of the Scottish Office. Life in prison was hard as sentences could often be accompanied by recommendations for solitary confinement and/or limitation of a prisoner's diet to bread and water for periods of time. In the course of the 19th century, hard labour was increasingly used by judges for certain offences. The treadmill, the hand crank and picking oakum were all used in Scottish prisons. The 20th century has witnessed the abolition of physical punishment, but it remains the case that Scotland still locks up more of its citizens than any other country in the European Union.

WILLIAM W. KNOX

See also: 'Bloody Code', The; Protest and Policing in Scotland; Scottish Criminal Courts, The (c.1747–1850)

Readings
Caledonian Mercury (1729) 19 May.
Foucault, M. (1975) *Discipline and punish: The birth of the prison.* New York, NY: Random House.
McKinlay, A. and Smyth, J. (2005) '"Un spectacle de plus mortifiants": Foucault, le pouvoir et l'échafaud', in A. Hatcheul, K. Starkey and E. Pezet (eds) *Gouvernement, organisation et enterprise: l'heritage de Michel Foucault.* Québec: Presses de l'Université Laval, pp 147–68.

PROBATION

Largely hidden in a myriad of unrecorded, undocumented conversations and transactions between probation workers and the people they supervised, the history of probation is partial (in both senses of the word). Its history varies according to often competing ideologies and personal motivations, and is invariably described too neatly in terms of linear time periods of moral and religious influence, ideology, and methodology. It is, at once, obscure and clear.

Nevertheless, it is known that it is an international story of imagination and innovation juxtaposed with unremarkable daily routine, full of contradictions, tensions and differences. Less well known is the fact that its entrenchment in the legal systems of the world invariably resulted from the sponsorship and commitment of national champions such as Edouard Julhiet, an engineer in France, and Howard Vincent, a Member of Parliament in the UK. Within a period of approximately 40 years, it spread in various forms across the world, for example, 1873 in Massachusetts, 1893 in France and 1916 in Uruguay. Those forms encompassed substitution for imprisonment coupled with supervision, conditional suspension of either proceedings or conviction after a finding or admission of guilt, or imposition of sentence, or of a sentence already imposed, each with or without some form of supervision (Vanstone, 2008).

In England and Wales, probation emerged from social philanthropy, which was driven not only by religious and humanitarian conviction, but also middle-class and political anxiety about the perceived threat posed by the degenerate and inebriate poor (McWilliams, 1983). It was transformed from an ideal to reality by the Probation of First Offenders Act 1887, though it did not involve formal supervision; that element was introduced in the Probation of Offenders Act 1907, which extended its provision to people with previous convictions and allowed for the appointment of probation officers (Gard, 2014).

By 1912, probation officers had their own organisation (the National Association of Probation Officers) and professional aspirations, which would subsequently be associated closely with the nascent sciences of psychology and psychiatry, and fleetingly with eugenics and the Mental Hygiene movement (Vanstone, 2004). Probation officers would soon be drawn into processes of assessment, categorisation, selectivity and control, and, in this sense, were implicit in the incarceration of those deemed undeserving, as well as the supervision and control of those they embraced. So, although the probation project has a reasonable claim to have been a humanising factor in the processes of the criminal justice system, it has also been an active partner in judgements about desert and the imposition of punishment and social control.

Further legislation, namely, the Criminal Justice Acts of 1925 and 1948, established probation officers in probation areas, which were overseen by probation committees, and endorsed probation's place in the courtroom. For a substantial part of the 20th century (at least until the mid-1980s), it remained a morally justified, well-respected, autonomous, innovative and idiosyncratic organisation focused, largely but not entirely, on the necessity of individual change for reform and rehabilitation, and on practice based on acts of faith and belief more than the lessons of research. However, the more recent history is one of increased levels of accountability, greater focus on research evidence, acceptance of the need for effectiveness, concern with the management of risk and, significantly, political governance (Mair and Burke, 2012). Clearly, government concern with the purposes, practices, organisation and outcomes of public service agencies is necessary, and it is arguable that an increase in such concern was rather overdue by the mid-1980s. Furthermore, it is equally valid to suggest that the subsequent setting of national objectives and priorities in 1984, the setting down of national standards, and government prescribed three-year plans led to improvements in policy and practice. On the other hand, it can be argued that the increasingly punitive culture and the ideological drift of that political governance has run counter to the development of an open, reflective, evidence-based service (Vanstone and Priestley, 2016).

For some, the concept of probation ended in England and Wales, first, when it was made a sentence in its own right by the Criminal Justice Act 1991 and, second, when the consent requirement was removed (except for drug- or mental health-related conditions) by the Crime (Sentences) Act 1997. That obituary seemed premature because in the first decade of the 21st century, despite (or perhaps because of) the integration of the service into the National Offender Management Service, there remained a lingering hope that probation might survive political interference and retain its focus on applying its considerable experience of helping people who offend to find constructive ways of living their lives. However, the introduction of contestability, whereby outside agencies (eg community rehabilitation companies) can take over aspects of probation work, and the privatisation of large sections of probation work through the current UK government's Transforming Rehabilitation Strategy, with a reduced probation service to supervise 'high-risk offenders', has made the future of probation precarious at the very least.

MAURICE VANSTONE

See also: Police Court Missionaries; Temperance Movements

Readings

Gard, R. (2014) *Rehabilitation and probation in England and Wales, 1876–1962.* London: Bloomsbury.

Mair, G. and Burke, L. (2012) *Redemption, rehabilitation and risk management.* Abingdon: Routledge.

McWilliams, W. (1983) 'The mission to the English police courts 1876–1936', *The Howard Journal of Crime and Justice,* 23(3): 129–47.

Vanstone, M. (2004) *Supervising offenders in the community: A history of probation theory and practice*. Aldershot: Ashgate.

Vanstone, M. (2008) 'The international origins and initial development of probation: an early example of policy transfer', *British Journal of Criminology*, 48(6): 735–55.

Vanstone, M. and Priestley, P. (2016) *Probation and politics. Academic reflections from former practitioners*. London: Palgrave Macmillan.

PROHIBITION

The 13-year 'experiment' with prohibition officially began at midnight on 17 January 1920, though the majority of states in the US had already outlawed alcohol. The manufacture, sale and transportation of any 'intoxicating liquor', defined as any beverage that contained more than 0.5% of alcohol, were all illegal under the Volstead Act, but the production and distribution of alcohol for industrial and scientific use continued under a detailed permit system. Medicinal and sacramental exemptions meant that doctors, priests, rabbis and pharmacists, for example, could apply for permits to purchase liquor. It was also still possible to possess and consume alcohol within an individual's private home.

Advocates of prohibition such as the Anti-Saloon League and the Women's Christian Temperance Union envisaged the disappearance of social and economic problems associated with drinking, such as alcoholism, domestic violence, poverty, unemployment and low work productivity. Often characterised as rural, native-born, white, middle-class Protestants, the Drys were particularly hostile to the working-class ethnic or immigrant saloon. Crime rates were frequently linked to lower-class intemperance, and in the southern states, the 'liquor question' was bound up with black disfranchisement, racial segregation and the maintenance of white supremacy. However, prohibition reforms did receive significant support from different ethnic, religious and racial groups in the early 20th century (Okrent, 2010).

National prohibition was to be enforced by the Treasury Department and the Justice Department; revenue agents would make the arrests and district attorneys would prosecute, but they were soon overwhelmed by the number of Volstead violators. Initially, the Prohibition Bureau employed 1,550 agents in 18 administrative districts, with support from another 3,000 customs agents and special officers in other government departments, as well as state police forces, highway patrols and local sheriffs' officers, but all had other law enforcement priorities. The 48 states were also expected to actively enforce both state and national prohibition (Kobler, 1993; Okrent, 2010). Most state legislatures passed supplementary liquor laws, as in New York in 1921, but New York was also to repeal its state enforcement legislation in 1923, leaving enforcement to federal officers (Lerner, 2007). By 1927, only a third of the states were still prepared to fund state enforcement.

There were simply never enough agents to effectively police the massive territory of the US, and the Prohibition Bureau never received enough money to pay decent salaries or properly train its agents. Many took bribes to supplement their low incomes and to look the other way. Liquor flowed into the US by railroad, truck, speedboat and airplane, often with the assistance of customs officials and shipping clerks. A coastal 'Rum Row' stretched from Newfoundland down the eastern seaboard to the Florida Keys and the Bahamas as schooners packed with branded liquor waited in international waters for customers in speedboats to ferry the contraband ashore (Kobler, 1993).

Domestic producers also flourished but their noxious liquor frequently led to gut rot and alcohol poisoning. In the popular image of the prohibition years, bathtub gin and exotic cocktails were consumed in the illegal but fashionable speakeasies, with concealed entrances and passwords, collapsible shelves, and hidden cellars to thwart raids. Every speakeasy, nightclub or buffet flat operator had to pay protection money to local police to stay in business (Lerner, 2007). Liquor consumption did decrease in the early 1920s, probably by up to 40%, as a result of rising costs rather than effective enforcement, but gradually rose throughout the rest of the decade.

Almost as soon as prohibition came into effect, government-bonded liquor warehouses were raided and trucks carrying medicinal and industrial liquor were hijacked by criminal gangs. By the early 1920s, national prohibition had facilitated the expansion of the illegal liquor market and its monopolisation by urban crime syndicates such as Torrio/Capone in Chicago and smaller outfits such as the Purple Gang in Detroit (Kavieff, 2000). Torrio and Capone built a large, disciplined, ethnically diverse criminal organisation that established control over Chicago through the brutal elimination of rival gangs – as exemplified in the St Valentine's Day Massacre of 1929 – intimidation, political manipulation and corruption. The Chicago Crime Commission estimated the Capone syndicate's profits at about US$60 million per year by the late 1920s (Ruth, 1996; Okrent, 2010).

From 1929, the stock market crash and resulting economic misery, the emergence of a powerful repeal campaign, and a 1931 report by a national crime commission on the failings of enforcement and rise of organised bootlegging all helped to turn popular and political opinion. Prohibition opponents argued that reopening distilleries and breweries would create jobs and divert money from gangsters' pockets to the Treasury. Repeal was a speedy affair and Americans could again purchase alcoholic drinks legally by the end of 1933 (Kobler, 1993; Okrent, 2010).

VIVIEN MILLER

See also: **Licensing; Organised Crime (United States of America); Temperance Movements**

Readings

Kavieff, P. (2000) *The purple gang: Organized crime in Detroit 1910–1945*. Fort Lee, NJ: Barricade Books.

Kobler, J. (1993) *Ardent spirits: The rise and fall of prohibition*. New York, NY: Da Capo Press.

Lerner, M. (2007) *Dry Manhattan: Prohibition in New York*. Cambridge, MA: Harvard University Press.

Okrent, D. (2010) *Last call: The rise and fall of prohibition*. New York, NY: Simon & Schuster.

Ruth, D. (1996) *Inventing the public enemy: The gangster in American culture, 1918–1934*. Chicago, IL: University of Chicago Press.

PROSTITUTION (19TH CENTURY)

Women defined as prostitutes were visible and familiar sights on the streets of Victorian Britain. Predominantly working-class, their public presence generated anxiety, pity and fascination among middle-class commentators about this 'Great Social Evil'. The Victorian 'prostitute' was an identification fraught with instability. In his contemporary investigations, Henry Mayhew pointed to six main groups: kept mistresses; *demi-mondains*; low lodging house women; soldiers' and sailors' women; and park and thieves' women (Bartley, 2000). Mayhew stratified women by the class of men they serviced, which also reflects more complicated arrangements than straightforward payment for sex. Unmarried mothers or women who cohabited with partners could also be defined as prostitutes, and many women sold sex occasionally in times of want. Thus, the reliability of statistics for the extent of prostitution is questionable as the definition of a prostitute changed depending on what criteria was used to collect the information.

Some sources in the 1860s argued for half-a-million prostitutes in England, though police statistics estimated 30,000, but prosecutions for prostitution were much lower than this (Bartley, 2000). The Vagrancy Act 1824 had created the legal category of 'common prostitute', who could be imprisoned for a minimum of a month if found to have behaved riotously or indecently in public. The Metropolitan Police Act 1839 and the Towns Police Clauses Act 1847 enabled the arrest of common prostitutes, and fines for being 'public nuisances' (Walkowitz, 1980, p 14).

Women who sold sex were the subject of persistent campaigns of rescue, regulation and suppression. At the end of the 18th century, readings of female sexuality that had been brimming with barely controlled lust were replaced by passivity and lack of sexual appetite. The imagery of a powerless, and therefore forgivable, character justified interventions of reform and inspired the establishment in 1758 of the first 'rescue' home, the Magdalen Hospital for Penitent Prostitutes in London. By the middle of the 19th century, societies concerned with the rescue and reclamation of 'fallen' women had proliferated (Bartley, 2000).

In 1864, Parliament passed An Act for the Prevention of Contagious Diseases at Certain Naval and Military Stations. This, together with an 1866 statute and an 1869 amendment, were known as the Contagious Diseases Act (Women). Under the Acts, special policemen were responsible for the identification of common prostitutes in order to compel them to submit to a registration scheme. If a woman did not consent, she was brought before a magistrate to prove that she was neither a prostitute nor engaged in 'immoral' sex with men. Once registered, she underwent a fortnightly speculum examination, and if found to have venereal disease (VD), was admitted to a lock hospital for up to nine months. The penalty for infringement of the Acts was two months' imprisonment. Both male and female pressure groups were established to oppose the extension of the Acts to more areas of Britain. The charismatic Josephine Butler led the Ladies' National Association and generated support from newly politicised women who were appalled that the Acts regulated prostitution and protected male customers from contracting VD. Rallies across England and Wales accusing the authorities of 'instrumental rape' often ended in disarray and violence towards Butler and her supporters (Walkowitz, 1980). When the Acts were repealed in 1886, a 'social purity' movement grew from the campaigns, which endeavoured to suppress prostitution. The National Vigilance Association was formed to remove women from houses of alleged 'ill repute' and close down theatres where prostitutes openly sought customers.

Changes to the law concerning child prostitution were accelerated by revelations in the *Pall Mall Gazette* in 1885, when editor W.T. Stead exposed how he had procured a 13-year-old virgin for £5. The resultant demonstrations and uproar led to the passing of the Criminal Law Amendment Act 1885, which had hitherto been generating little interest among Members of Parliament. The Act raised the age of consent to 16 and made 'soliciting of prostitution' in the street an offence. Landlords could also be prosecuted for letting rooms for 'immoral purposes'. Walkowitz (1980) argues that this led to the rise of the male pimp as women could no longer cohabit for protection, and the diminution of what had previously been a woman-led profession.

LESLEY HULONCE

See also: **Macmillan and Wolfenden Committees, The; Prostitution (early 20th century)**

Readings

Bartley, L. (2000) *Prostitution, prevention and reform in England, 1860–1914.* London: Routledge.

Hulonce, L. (forthcoming) *Prostitution and women's work in England and Wales.*

Laite, J. (2011) *Common prostitutes and ordinary citizens: Commercial sex in London, 1885–1960.* Basingstoke: Palgrave Macmillan.

Mahood, L. (1990) *The Magdalenes, prostitution in the nineteenth century.* London: Routledge.

Mayhew, H. (1861) 'London labour and the London poor'. Available at: https://archive.org/details/londonlabourand01mayhgoog

Walkowitz, J. (1980) *Prostitution and Victorian society, women, class and the state.* Cambridge: Cambridge University Press.

PROSTITUTION (EARLY 20TH CENTURY)

Prostitution was a huge source of moral and legal debate in 20th-century Britain. Just as Victorian social commentators and welfare workers placed a great deal of emphasis on the categorisation of prostitution as a social problem, the early part of the 20th century saw considerable attention directed towards efforts to define and discourage the sale of sex in exchange for money or gifts. The laws used to control prostitution had not changed since the 19th century, but changes in women's behaviour, dress and their increased social freedom made it harder for the police to identify and single out potential prostitutes while on patrol. At the same time, anxieties about an increase in promiscuity led to debate about whether more should be done to control prostitution. The press and social purists in organisations like the National Vigilance Association fuelled concern about prostitution by linking it to fears that significant numbers of British women were acting indecently and increasingly putting themselves at moral and physical risk. They shared doubtful and sensationalised stories about young women being drugged, kidnapped and sold into a 'white slave trade'. In the moral panic that ensued, the Criminal Law Amendment (White Slave Trade) Bill was passed in 1912. It targeted men and women who lived off the earnings of prostitution and made the 'controlling or directing' of prostitutes' movements a criminal offence (Laite, 2011).

However, this new law did not ease concerns about prostitution, nor did prostitution become considerably reduced. The start of the First World War saw potential new markets for prostitution open up with the stationing of soldiers in camps across the country. As a result, the behaviour of young, working-class women was increasingly scrutinised. Fears that young women were experiencing 'khaki fever' – that they were keen to seduce soldiers – meant that distinctions between prostitution and promiscuity were questioned (Woollacott, 1994). Alongside the category of the professional prostitute, the 'amateur prostitute' grew in cultural prominence. Young women willing to engage in pre-marital sex with soldiers and other men who gave them gifts and paid for nights out were said to be engaged in a form of prostitution. In 1918, in a bid to deter women from behaving promiscuously, the government introduced Defence of the Realm Act regulation 40d, which made it an offence for a woman to have sex with a soldier if she had a venereal disease. As Julia Laite (2011) notes, it was a controversial measure that the police tended to use in limited fashion against women known to work as prostitutes.

While police statistics for the interwar years suggest that arrests for prostitution went into decline in cities like Liverpool and London following the return to peacetime, it must be noted that these statistics reflect the propensity of individual police forces to prosecute women for solicitation rather than actual prostitution. In fact, prostitution continued to provoke considerable public debate and cultural anxiety, but the way prostitution was conducted and some high-profile scandals made the issue more difficult for the police to control (Caslin, 2010). The years between the wars increasingly saw prostitution conducted away from the streets. Although the Criminal Law Amendment Act 1885 had made brothel-keeping a target in law, the proliferation of nightclubs in the 1920s provided alternative venues where prostitutes could work covertly. In 1928, Sergeant George Goddard inadvertently brought the relationship between prostitution and nightclubs to national attention when it emerged that he had been bribed by some London nightclubs to allow prostitutes to work from there without facing prosecution (Shore, 2013). Indeed, prostitution continued to be practised in diverse and hidden ways during the first half of the 20th century. During and after the Second World War, attention turned to the use of taxi cabs for prostitution, and by the 1950s, a clampdown on prostitution in public places encouraged the creation of an indoor 'call-girl' network (Weeks, 2012).

SAMANTHA CASLIN

See also: **Macmillan and Wolfenden Committees, The; Prostitution (19th century)**

Readings

Caslin, S. (2010) 'Flappers, amateurs and professionals: the spectrum of promiscuity in 1920s' Britain', in K. Hardy, S. Kingston and T. Sanders (eds) *New sociologies of sex work.* Farnham: Ashgate Publishing, pp 11–22.

Laite, J. (2011) *Common prostitutes and ordinary citizens: Commercial sex in London, 1885–1960.* Basingstoke: Palgrave Macmillan.

Shore, H. (2013) '"Constable dances with instructress": the police and the queen of nightclubs in interwar London', *Social History*, 38(2): 183–202.

Weeks, J. (2012) *Sex, politics and society: The regulations of sexuality since 1800.* Abingdon: Routledge.

Woollacott, A. (1994) '"Khaki fever" and its control: gender, class, age and sexual morality on the British home front in the First World War', *Journal of Contemporary History*, 29(2): 325–47.

PROTEST AND POLICING IN SCOTLAND

Wherever there are inequalities in the distribution of power and wealth, those who occupy subordinate positions in society will from time to time protest. These protests can take various forms depending on whether a society is largely rural and agricultural or urban and industrial. The form of protest will also dictate the response by those in authority. In pre-industrial society, the most common form of protest or riot was the food riot, a challenge easily met by the deployment of soldiers. As these disorders were highly infrequent, there was no need for a regular coercive body. In an industrial society, protest might take various forms – economic, social and political. Given the large concentrations of people in cities and towns, there was a perceived need for the authorities to have continuous monitoring of the population, hence the setting up of a paid body of men to assume this task.

Riots were principally engaged in by working people who were driven by hunger or other pressures from the growing commercial and industrial economy into defending their 'rights': the moral economy of the poor in confrontation with the new market values and the ascendancy of property (Thompson, 1963). In rural society, the most common form of riot was over food, but due to improvements in transport and the growth of the economy, this form of protest gradually disappeared. The last recorded event took place in North-East Scotland in 1847 (Richards, 1982). Protests of this nature were easily contained by the landlords and the law through the deployments of troops. They rarely threatened the political status quo and there is little evidence that the participants were highly politicised.

The cities were a different prospect. Their rapid growth and the anonymity they afforded the denizens meant that the old paternalistic methods of social control long practised in rural society were ineffective in controlling the population. Working-class city dwellers flouted the emerging bourgeois morality. Drunkenness, promiscuity and violence were decried by the Church and middle-class reformers, and made the demand from the middle classes to establish 'regiments' for the protection of 'the lives and property of the community' a pressing one (Devine, 1994). Glasgow established the first professional police force in Britain in 1800. Other burghs were slow to follow and it was only the threats posed by working-class movements such as trade unionism and Chartism that prompted their introduction. Outside the main centres of population, only 12 out of 183 burghs empowered to do so had set up a police force by 1847. However, with the last throes of Chartist activity in 1848, there was a rush to join the club. By 1852, 67 burghs were maintaining a police force in Scotland. It was clear that the police were there largely to impose order rather than prevent crime.

After 1850, protest underwent a transition, giving way to issues connected to everyday identities based on class, gender, religion and territory. These were complex, contradictory and competitive forms of protest. Sectarian riots, in the main, took the form of intra-class skirmishes between rival immigrant Irish Catholic and Protestant communities. However, while the participants were working-class, unlike the 18th and early 19th centuries, these disturbances were less obviously to do with class relations, as witnessed in the food riots, and more to do with issues concerning identity. These clashes continued through the 19th century and could be very violent, for example, an Irish Home Rule demonstration of 3,000 Irish Catholics in Coatbridge was attacked by a mob of Orangemen that led to rioting over two days in August 1883. Even when the Home Rule crisis was over and Ireland was partitioned in 1921, tension between the two communities continued, reaching a climax in the 1930s when Protestant extremist groups led attacks on the Catholic communities of Edinburgh and Glasgow. Working-class protests were, in some ways, rather tame when it came to violence. The middle-class female Suffragettes carried out arson attacks on property and intimidated politicians. However, like their protesting ancestors, none of these groups' actions led to many fatalities. The state, operating through coercive groups such as the police and soldiers, was less discriminating: figures for the period show that of the 20 major disturbances that occurred in Britain between the Porteous Riot of 1736 in Edinburgh and the Chartist demonstrations in 1848, only 12 people were killed by the crowd, whereas the courts ordered 118 people to be hanged and soldiers shot a further 630 (Logue, 1979). Violence was and is the monopoly of the state.

WILLIAM W. KNOX

See also: **Highland Clearances, The; Public Order Law; Riot Act, The**

Readings

Devine, T.M. (1994) 'Urbanisation and the civic response: Glasgow 1800–1830', in A.J.G. Cummings and T.M. Devine (eds) *Industry, business and society in Scotland since 1700: Essays presented to John Butt*. Edinburgh: John Donald, pp 183–96.

Logue, K. (1979) *Popular disturbances in Scotland, 1780–1815*. Edinburgh: Longuet.

Richards, E. (1982) 'The last Scottish food riots', *Past and Present*, Supplement 6: 1–59.

Thompson, E.P. (1963) *The making of the English working class*. London: Victor Gollancz Ltd.

PUBLIC ORDER LAW

Public order law traverses a range of crimes, which can include relatively minor offences such as the shouting of obscenities in the street, to serious offences such as riot and violent disorder. Throughout British history, the law has developed and adapted in response to specific threats and concerns, such as insurrection and provocative or disorderly political activism and public protest. Yet, the development of such laws regulating public order has also sought to balance 'the competing demands of freedom of speech and assembly on the one hand and the preservation of the Queen's Peace on the other' (Williams, 1967, p 9).

Following a series of civil disorders in the early 19th century that culminated with the Peterloo massacre in 1819, the state passed a series of Acts to counter the fear of revolutionary movements. These Acts added to the existing law, such as the Riot Act 1714 and common-law powers under breach of the peace. Most significant were the Unlawful Drilling Act 1819 and the Seditious Meetings Act 1819, which represented the government's fear of rebellion. Although they were largely preventive as they aimed to restrict the meetings and training that could have potentially led to a revolutionary threat, they also gave the state power to restrict the liberty of political radicals who may not have threatened disorder or engaged in unlawful activity.

For example, the suffragettes were arguably unjustly targeted by police when they heckled political speakers, despite heckling being part of the contemporary political culture in the early 20th century (Lawrence, 2003). The Liberal government introduced the hastily passed Public Meeting Act 1908, which created an offence of disorderly conduct at a meeting with the purpose of preventing the transaction of business. The ineffectiveness of the Act was highlighted during a series of disorders involving fascist and anti-fascist movements in the 1930s. Although the Public Order Bill was rushed through Parliament in the wake of the Battle of Cable Street in 1936, where the police were confronted by anti-fascists determined to prevent the fascist march through East London, the provisions within it also reflected concerns about the radical Left. The resulting Public Order Act 1936 proscribed the wearing of political uniforms and paramilitary organisations, revised and nationalised existing local provisions related to threatening, abusive and insulting words and behaviour, and provided the police with the power to prohibit processions in advance.

Fifty years later, the Public Order Act 1986 amended much of the 1936 Act. The disorder that preceded this Act included the Miners' Strike (1984–85), disorder involving the National Front and anti-fascists (including Southall in 1979), football hooliganism, and the inner-city riots in Bristol, Brixton, Manchester and Liverpool (1980–81). The diversity of these disorders is reflected in the scope of the 1986 Act, which extends the police power to regulate public assemblies, processions, threatening words or behaviour and racial hatred.

The Human Rights Act 1998 (HRA), which has incorporated the European Convention on Human Rights (ECHR) into UK law, has provided positive legal rights of freedom of assembly and freedom of expression under Articles 10 and 11, respectively. Yet, although these rights are not absolute, the shift from the system of residual freedom has placed a larger onus on the police to impose the least restrictive measures available. Lawyer David Mead (2010, p 204) emphasises the impact of the HRA by stating that the move from a 'residual, liberty based system to one based on positive rights brings a shift in the burden of proof'. This means that public authorities must provide an objective basis for any ban or condition that they impose on public assemblies and all restrictions must be justified in Article 11(2) terms. Effectively, chief constables are required to enforce the least restrictive measures open to them in relation to the potential for disorder when imposing conditions on public assemblies.

IAIN CHANNING

See also: **Breach of the Peace; Riot Act, The; Unlawful Assembly**

Readings

Card, R. (2000) *Public order law.* Bristol: Jordans Ltd.

Channing, I. (2015) *The police and the expansion of public order law in Britain, 1829–2014.* Abingdon: Routledge.

Lawrence, J. (2003) 'Fascist violence and the politics of public order in inter-war Britain: the Olympia debate revisited', *Historical Research*, 76(192): 238–67.

Mead, D. (2010) *The new law of peaceful protest: Rights and regulation in the Human Rights Act era*. Oxford: Hart Publishing Ltd.

Williams, D. (1967) *Keeping the peace: The police and public order*. London: Hutchinson & Co Ltd.

QUARTER SESSIONS

Quarter sessions were a court session originating in 13th-century England and Wales. They were formally instituted in the early 14th century, when, under Edward III, a general commission of oyer and terminer, an Anglo-French phrase meaning 'to hear and determine', was given to two or more Justices of the Peace (JPs) to collectively hold a session of the peace. In 1388, JPs were ordered to sit four times a year in their counties – hence the term 'quarter'. Although the role of JP was a more marginal one in Scotland, quarter sessions had been formally established in Scotland by 1612 (Findlay, 2000).

Quarter sessions were the second tier of the criminal justice system – above petty sessions, later known as magistrates' courts, but below the assizes. They were local county and borough courts, usually held four times a year, and were generally held in each county seat, such as in Oxford or Gloucester. Each quarter session was named after the traditional time of year when they were held – they traditionally sat at Epiphany (January to March), Easter (April to June), Midsummer (July to September) and Michaelmas (October to December). However, by the late 18th century, Middlesex, which heard a larger number of cases than many other places, had become something of an anomaly within the court system, with the Middlesex quarter sessions taking place eight times a year rather than the normal four (Burn, 1837; Hitchcock et al, 2012).

Each session was, fundamentally, a meeting involving two or more JPs, one of whom acted as chair, sitting with or without a jury. This is where criminal charges and civil and criminal appeals were heard, with the magistrates having a clerk of the peace present for legal advice. The system was slightly different in county boroughs, which were allowed their own quarter sessions but with a recorder instead of a bench of justices.

In medieval England, the quarter sessions would comprise justices, juries, officials, clerks and prisoners. Therefore, quarter sessions in major towns were held in places such as the local castle, as was the case at York, for example. However, some sessions were held in smaller towns, in a variety of buildings from inns to rented rooms, and could last over several days. Magistrates traditionally decided the date and place that the quarter sessions would be held at their previous meeting, and in many counties, they moved round a series of market towns rather than holding the court in the same place each time. However, this led to some JPs only attending sessions in places that were easily accessible to them, meaning that attendance varied. Again, the Middlesex sessions were slightly different, as, from 1612, they were held at a purpose-built sessions house in Clerkenwell (Hitchcock et al, 2012).

A quarter sessions court could sit with or without a jury. Where a jury was involved, it had a wide jurisdiction and could hear both civil and criminal cases. It could hear murder cases, assaults, thefts and poaching – the most common type of offences committed in a predominantly rural society. It did not have the jurisdiction to hear cases involving treason or forgery, though it could refer the most serious crimes to the assize courts.

However, the quarter sessions also had an important part to play in local administration, dealing with taxes, the appointment of local officers and licensing issues, as well as setting the county rates. Quarter sessions also heard many offences relating to vagrancy or to disorderly conduct, with the system clearly being used to monitor and repress anti-social behaviour, or behaviour perceived as being immoral. Poor Law administration could also come before the quarter sessions, and the increasingly wide remit of the Vagrancy Acts in the 18th and early 19th centuries also brought vagrants, gypsies, fortune-tellers and deserting husbands before the courts.

The courts of quarter sessions continued to exist until the Courts Act (1971 c.23) replaced both them and the assize courts with one entity, the Crown Court. This Act came into effect in 1972. In Scotland, the equivalent was the district court, created in 1975 under the District Courts (Scotland) Act (1975 c.20). In Ireland, after the Municipal Corporations (Ireland) Act of 1840 (3 & 4 Vict c.108), only three quarter sessions survived, with the remaining ones abolished. Under the

Irish Free State, the Courts of Justice Act 1924 abolished quarter sessions and transferred their business to the Circuit Court.

NELL DARBY

See also: **Assizes; Juries; Magistrates; Petty Sessions**

Readings

Burn, R. (1837) *The Justice of the Peace and parish officer, volume 5* (28th edn). London: T. Cadell.

Findlay, J. (2000) *All manner of people: The history of the Justices of the Peace in Scotland.* Edinburgh: The Saltire Society.

Hitchcock, T., Shoemaker, R., Howard, S., McLaughlin, J. et al (2012) 'London lives, 1690–1800'. Available at: http://www.londonlives.org

Landau, N. (1984) *The Justices of the Peace, 1679–1760.* Berkeley, CA: University of California Press.

Shoemaker, R. (2001) *Prosecution and punishment in London and Middlesex.* Cambridge: Cambridge University Press.

REFORMATORY SCHOOLS

The Youthful Offenders Act of 1854, along with an early Act establishing Industrial Schools (1857), set up the first formally state-sanctioned institutions for delinquent and semi-delinquent children under 16 years of age. Previous to this, there had been more informal prototypes, deriving from the philanthropic or voluntary sphere. For example, the Philanthropic Society set up its first institution for homeless and criminal children, as well as children of convicted felons, in 1788 at St. George's Field in Southwark. Moreover, a later initiative by the Refuge for the Destitute in Hackney received some central government funding (King, 2006). In other countries, similar institutions evolved through state and private voluntary collaborations around the same period. Most notable was the Mettray Penal Colony in France, outside the city of Tours, which was a private reformatory housing male juvenile delinquents and young people aged up to 21.

The establishment of the reformatory school in England and Wales is strongly associated with the work of the reformer Mary Carpenter (Horn, 2009). She campaigned for the removal of children from adult prisons and the establishment of reformatory institutions. While the 1854 Act can be seen as a realisation of Carpenter's campaigning, it is important to note that a provision of two weeks' imprisonment in an adult prison remained part of the Act until it was finally abolished under an Act of 1899. In theory, the reformatory school only took those children who had been convicted of a felony. In contrast, the industrial school accepted children who committed petty thefts and misdemeanours or were in a position of neglect and/or vulnerability. In practice, there was overlap between the two forms of institution. The majority of reformatory school inmates were male, though there were some mixed schools and some schools that specifically held girls, the first of which was opened in Bristol by Mary Carpenter. After the publication of her book in 1851, Carpenter called the first conference on reformatory and industrial schools in Birmingham. From this period, it is clear that an extensive network of reformers who focused on juvenile crime developed. As a result, the reformatory school model was a transnational phenomenon, with institutions established in many countries, including Ireland, America, Australia, India and South Africa.

From their establishment in 1854, reformatory schools received some central government funding. While they also drew limited support from charity, earnings of the inmates and parental contributions, funding from government was essential to the success of the regime. This meant that the reformatories were subject to a Home Office inspection regime from the early days. Nevertheless, within two decades of the establishment of the reformatory, serious problems started to emerge. Accusations of the mistreatment of boys and poor conditions in the schools periodically appeared; however, it would be from the Training Ship establishment that accusations turned into 'scandals' that needed to be investigated (Radzinowicz and Hood, 1986). Three of the naval training ships were certified as reformatories: the Clarence (for Catholic boys) and Akbar on the Mersey, and the Cornwall on the Thames. The ships were subject to a number of outbreaks of mutiny and incidents of arson in the later 19th century. Most notable was the Akbar Scandal of 1910, when the *John Bull* magazine ran an exposé about allegations of violence and serious ill-treatment on the land-based incarnation of the ship (which had been closed by this time), the Heswall Nautical Training School. While investigations into the Akbar Scandal ended with the staff of the institution largely being exonerated, it did lead to the establishment of a Departmental Committee on Reformatory and Industrial Schools in 1913, which recommended increased Home Office control and more involvement from local authorities in the management of the schools, among other reforms. After the First World War, committals to the schools were to sharply decline. The pre-war Children Act 1908 had introduced a new sensibility into the debate about children and crime, and the reformatory and industrial school establishment represented an outdated form of institutionalisation. In 1932 and 1933, Children and Young Persons Acts finally amalgamated the two institutions into the Approved School for children 'in need of care and protection' (Hendrick, 1997, p 51).

HEATHER SHORE

See also: **Borstals; Industrial Schools; Juvenile Crime and Justice in Scotland; Juvenile Crime in Britain**

Readings

Carpenter, M. (1851) *Reformatory schools for the children of the perishing and dangerous classes, and for juvenile offenders*. London: C. Gilpin.

Hendrick, H. (1997) *Children, childhood and English society, 1880–1990*. Cambridge: Cambridge University Press.

Horn, P. (2009) *Young offenders: Juvenile delinquency, 1700–2000*. Stroud: Amberley Publishing.

King, P. (2006) *Crime and law in England, 1750–1840: Remaking justice from the margins*. Cambridge: Cambridge University Press.

Radzinowicz, L. and Hood, R. (1986) *A history of criminal law and its administration, vol. 5, the emergence of penal policy*. Oxford: Oxford University Press.

RESPECTABLE CRIMINAL, THE

The respectable criminal is largely missing from the history of crime literature; at best, this offender type warrants a few lines of passing comment, more often nothing at all. This is for two main reasons: first, it is a reflection of the 'inherent conservatism' (Jenkins, 1987, p 97) of the subject field in replicating the class-biased nature of contemporary understandings of crime and criminality, and of the activities of the justice system and its agents; and, second, it is a pragmatic response to the hidden nature of much 'respectable' offending, and the difficulty of tracing it through the historical record (Robb, 1992; Locker, 2005). Despite this neglect, the respectable criminal has a critical place in crime history.

Historically, the term 'respectable criminal' is something of an oxymoron. Throughout history, crime has been viewed almost exclusively as an activity carried out by the unrespectable, while respectability was characterised by honesty, and therefore conferred a non-criminal status. Although not exclusively so, respectability had an obvious class skew, as did criminality. Thus, while differentiations between the 'respectable' and 'unrespectable' lower classes confirmed that a lower status did not preclude the possibility of propriety, the respectable were perceived mainly to be drawn from the higher social classes. Equally, while a higher-class standing did not entirely exclude the possibility of criminality, the 'criminal classes' were believed to reside within society's lower echelons.

Of course, as the historical record attests, some respectable offenders were brought to justice, and such scenes were symbolically important. As Hay et al (1988, p 33) note, the sight of a person of respectability on the gallows served an important function in propagating the myth that the law was impartial. Conversely, while highlighting equality, the relative rarity of respectable criminals reinforced the class-skewed nature of criminality. The association between class and criminality was further cemented in the 19th century, including through the work of social anthropologists like Henry Mayhew, who ventured into London's rookeries in search of the 'criminal classes', and documented their lives and traits. However, paradoxically, as the 19th century unfolded, changes within the business environment gave rise to new forms of criminality that were inherently associated with respectable people and respectable activities. The white-collar workplace became a site of vulnerability to crime, rather than its panacea; as such, this period witnessed the widespread emergence of the respectable criminal.

In practical terms, the respectable criminal was problematic. The growth of business arrangements generated unprecedented amounts of capital, brought with it new armies of white-collar workers and necessitated a considerable expansion of trust arrangements. Coupled with the sluggishness of the legislative and business arenas in keeping pace with such developments, there came a plethora of opportunities for criminal enterprise.

In ideological terms, given the significance of respectability as a measure of honesty, the widespread emergence of the respectable criminal was deeply unsettling for Victorian society. For the first time, contemporaries were not able to clearly separate criminal from non-criminal. Appearance, social class or employment position were no longer a bar to crime, or a guarantee of honesty. In addition, if criminals could not be easily observed, they could not be easily avoided, detected or prevented.

The paradox of the respectable criminal required a resolution, and one of the main strategies used by Victorian contemporaries was to reconstruct this offender type as either a 'RESPECTABLE criminal' (and therefore not really criminal) or a 'respectable CRIMINAL' (and therefore not really respectable). Such debates were regularly played out in the courtrooms of Victorian England, as well as in popular commentaries on crime. Through this strategy, the notion of the respectable criminal as an oxymoron remained in place, traditional aetiologies of why people were criminal, and equally why they were respectable, remained largely intact (even in the face of a growing respectable criminal presence), and the focus of concern remained firmly centred upon the criminal (ie lower) classes (Locker, 2008).

JOHN LOCKER

See also: Criminal Class, The; Financial Crime; White-collar Crime

Readings

Hay, D., Linebaugh, P., Rule, J., Thompson, E.P. and Winslow, C. (1988) *Albion's fatal tree: Crime and society in eighteenth-century England*. London: Peregrine.

Jenkins, P. (1987) 'Into the upperworld? Law, crime and punishment in English society', *Social History*, 12(1): 93–102.

Locker, J.P. (2005) 'Quiet thieves, quiet punishment: private responses to the respectable offender, c. 1850–1930', *Crime, History & Societies*, 9(1): 9–31.

Locker, J.P. (2008) 'The paradox of the "respectable offender": responding to the problem of white-collar crime in Victorian and Edwardian England', in H. Johnston (ed) *Punishment and control in historical perspective*. Basingstoke: Palgrave Macmillan, pp 115–34.

Robb, G. (1992) *White-collar crime in modern England: Financial fraud and business morality, 1845–1929*. Cambridge: Cambridge University Press.

RIOT ACT, THE

The Riot Act 1714 was enacted during a period of considerable disorder across England, which was highlighted by the Sacheverell Riots in 1710 and the Coronation Riots in 1714. It was repealed with the passing of the Criminal Law Act 1967. Under the Riot Act, if 12 or more persons were 'unlawfully, riotously, and tumultuously assembled together, to the disturbance of the publick peace', the justices were required to read the Riot Act, which ordered all persons to disperse and depart to their habitation or lawful business. It represented the ultimate power of the state as it created a felony punishable by death to any person who had not dispersed within an hour of its reading. Most significantly, mere presence at the scene was enough to warrant the death penalty and no specific act or intention was necessary to prove guilt. Moreover, the justices were empowered to command all citizens 'of age and ability' to assist them to seize or apprehend 'such persons so unlawfully, riotously and tumultuously continuing together after proclamation made', and if any of the rioters were 'killed, maimed or hurt', then the justices, and those assisting them, 'shall be free, discharged and indemnified' of any crime. The words to the proclamation were as follows:

> Our sovereign Lord the King chargeth and commandeth all persons, being assembled, immediately to disperse themselves, and peaceably to depart to their habitations, or to their lawful business, upon the pains contained in the act made in the first year of King George, for preventing tumults and riotous assemblies. God save the King.

Vogler (1991) highlights that the statutory offence of riot differed from the common law offence as it was not necessary to prove a specific act or intention (common purpose) of those assembled, and presence was merely enough to hang the accused.

In the 19th century, the suppression of a riot necessitated the cooperation of the magistrates, the police and the army. A good example of how these relationships intertwined was with the Featherstone Riot of 1893. During the national miners' strike, the chief constable of West Riding sent a telegram to the barracks at York requesting cavalry and infantry. With the police and the army unable to quieten the rioters who engaged in stone throwing and setting fire to buildings in the colliery, the magistrate read the Riot Act. The effect of the army who had fixed bayonets may have only provoked the crowd further, who continued to throw stones. Within the hour of the reading of the Riot Act, the troops were given permission by the magistrate to fire shots, and after the second round of firing, it was realised that two men had been shot. In the following Featherstone Inquiry, it was established that although an hour had not passed, the authorities or the army were not held accountable for the two deaths as they still had a common law duty to restore order and it was considered that they had no alternative left but to fire.

Although the Riot Act was still utilised after the creation of the modern police force, this use diminished and its last recorded use was in 1919 during the police strikes. In the Liverpool area, there were a significant number of police officers that supported the strike and widespread looting occurred. The Riot Act was read in Birkenhead, where 96 police officers, from the total force strength of 225, were on strike. Despite there being 700 military with machine guns present in the town, extreme measures were not utilised. With the repeal of the Riot Act, the magistrates also lost their influence in times of serious disorder. Writing in the same year that the Criminal Law Act was passed, Williams (1967) highlighted how the chief constable was now more likely to cooperate with the military authorities during severe disorder, which had been a traditional role of the magistrates. Vogler (1991, p 3) notes that its legacy was still considered in 1981 during the inner-city riots, when the Metropolitan Police commissioner 'argued vigorously for its re-enactment'.

IAIN CHANNING

See also: Breach of the Peace; Public Order Law; Unlawful Assembly

Readings

Channing, I. (2015) *The police and the expansion of public order law in Britain, 1829–2014*. Abingdon: Routledge.

Vogler, R. (1991) *Reading the Riot Act: The magistracy, the police and the army in civil disorder*. Milton Keynes: Open University Press.

Williams, D. (1967) *Keeping the peace: The police and public order*. London: Hutchinson & Co Ltd.

SCOTTISH CRIMINAL COURTS, THE (c.1747–1850)

In the early 18th century, the Scottish criminal justice system was characterised by multiple jurisdictions and a lack of centralised control. The High Court of Justiciary, and its accompanying three circuit courts, were the most senior criminal courts in the country and were staffed by judges and advocates appointed by government representatives. The majority of courts, though, were run by individuals unconnected with the central state. There existed an elaborate and extensive system of private, local courts – royal, seigneurial and ecclesiastical – and there were wide-ranging variations between them in terms of judicial authority, day-to-day business and legal procedure (Davies, 1980). In the Scottish Highlands and counties, judicial power was either purchased or inherited and was firmly under the authority of landowners and clan chiefs in seigneurial, sheriff courts and, to a lesser extent, Justice of the Peace courts (Kilday, 2007; Findlay, 2000). In towns and cities, it was predominantly in the hands of magistrates in burgh and guildry courts. Scots Law functioned largely as a collection of local practices, usages and conventions. There was little consistency in decision-making or sentencing, and little regulation of procedure in a system established on custom and tradition rather than precise statutory codification (Davies, 1980). Justice was often administered informally to suit private and religious interests, and criminal prosecutions – especially in the inferior courts – were relatively rare. Indeed, Scots were more likely to be brought before a Church court than a criminal court in the first half of the 18th century (Leneman and Mitchison, 1998). Church courts were a vital mechanism for policing sexual morality and for maintaining social stability, and they often worked with legal authorities to curb bad behaviour. Although Church courts had no authority to deal with serious crimes, they were responsible for prosecuting and punishing a wide array of misdemeanours and minor offences.

The Heritable Jurisdiction Act 1747 streamlined the Scottish court structure. The Act extended central control over the Scottish judicial system by weakening, and in many instances breaking, the feudal structure of authority that tied local courts to landowners and clan chiefs (Farmer, 1997). It also established regulations regarding court sittings, duties and justice qualifications, and extended the influence and jurisdiction of the High Court of Justiciary. Widely regarded as laying the foundations for the modern Scottish criminal justice system, the abolition of heritable jurisdiction heralded the downfall of a complex legal system in favour of a more structured, centralised and uniform system (Davies, 1980).

By the late 18th century, the number of Scottish criminal courts had been significantly reduced and their roles and powers clarified. More serious criminal cases – which included treason, fraud, serious assault, rape, grand larceny and murder – were tried before juries in the High Court in Edinburgh (or in one of its circuit courts) or in sheriff courts. The overwhelming majority of criminal prosecutions were undertaken by the public prosecutor – the procurator fiscal – under the authority of the Lord Advocate in the Crown Office in Edinburgh (usually for indictable crimes tried before the High Court and circuit courts) and under the authority of magistrates and sheriffs in the respective local courts. However, financial considerations and constraints often deterred procurators and justices from pursuing formal, legal action. Criminal trials before the High Court of Justiciary averaged approximately a dozen or so per year in the second half of the 18th century before rising significantly in the first half of the 19th century in line with a broader rise in recorded indictable crime (Donnachie, 1995; Crowther, 1999). The most common cases that were tried were theft, housebreaking, mobbing and rioting, robbery, serious assault, and murder. In local courts, justice was often administered informally and consisted of non–custodial punishments that were cheap to carry out and did not incur legal or aliment costs. To pursue a criminal prosecution was expensive, convoluted and time-consuming; it consisted of a whole raft of written pleadings, including libels, summonses, warrants, declarations and proofs, and many local courts simply did not have the judicial capacity to dispose of a high number of cases. It was common for those in custody suspected of less serious crimes not to be prosecuted so long as they agreed to leave the town or county, which ensured that the level of recorded crime and offences was much lower than the level committed. Even though heritable jurisdiction had been abolished, Scots in many rural and Highland communities continued to have a mindset that was geared towards informal, local, 'rough' justice (Cameron, 1983).

In the justiciary courts, men were between seven and 10 times more likely than women to be prosecuted for a criminal offence (Kilday, 2007). The number of men prosecuted for violent crimes was twice that for women, but the latter were much more likely to be indicted for crimes against the person relative to their total number prosecuted (Kilday, 2007). The justiciary courts showed little leniency towards criminal women, who were perceived to have rebelled against gender expectations as well as the law, and so violent women were particularly likely to be convicted and to receive stricter sentences (Kilday, 2007).

Conviction rates were high and it was rare for the accused to be acquitted. Scottish courts were more likely than those in England to convict and punish those on trial as the public prosecutor weeded out weak cases. Indeed, trials only proceeded when the charges were perceived to be incontrovertible. Although proceedings were conducted under the governing principle of the presumption of innocence, in practice, there was often a strong presumption of guilt (Crowther,1999). Reprieves and pardons were rare: sentences were normally carried out in full (Kilday, 2012).

The justiciary courts had a wide range of punishments at their disposal, from the death penalty or transportation for the most serious crimes, to corporal punishment and imprisonment for less serious ones. Banishment and transportation were the most common, not least because they were relatively cheap. That said, the overall percentage of Scots transported was lower relative to the population than in England, Wales and Ireland, which, in all likelihood, was due to the lower number of criminal prosecutions (Prentis, 2004). The Scottish justiciary courts were also less likely to resort to the death penalty for property crimes than courts in England, with the annual rate of executions for property offences relative to the population nine times lower in Scotland than in England in the third quarter of the 18th century (Young, 1998; King, 2015). According to the clerk of the High Court, the number of executions for all of Scotland between 1767 and 1797 did not average more than six per year (Cameron, 1983). There was, though, much geographical variation. Capital sentences were more likely to be passed in the High Court in Edinburgh, and much less likely to be passed in the Scottish western and northern periphery (King, 2015). As in England, the closer a court was to the centre of legal and political power, the more likely a judge was to utilise the state's ultimate sanction. The relatively low number of hangings was partly due to the fact that Scotland had a separate legal system and did not embrace the expansion in capital crimes that came to characterise the infamous 18th-century English 'Bloody Code'. However, it also reflected a general reluctance to execute for all but the most serious of crimes. Indeed, public prosecutors were reluctant to prosecute under capital charges for fear that juries would be unwilling to convict (Crowther, 1999; Knox, 2015). As Scotland had a public prosecutor, the Scottish legal profession and ruling elites responded to periods of heightened tension by increasing the number of non-capital prosecutions, which made the courts less reliant upon severe, exemplary punishment and mercy to impose judicial authority and protect private property (Crowther, 1999). Those who opposed attempts to bring Scottish legal practice more into line with English practice in the early 19th century contended that the lower execution rate in Scotland was proof that Scots Law was morally superior (Smyth and McKinlay, 2011), but this should not disguise the fact that the Scottish justiciary was willing to impose the ultimate sanction, especially to thwart those deemed guilty of sedition or who threatened the interests of the state (Davis, 2005). Fewer capital crimes and conviction rates did not necessarily mean that the Scottish system was always more merciful and lenient than its English counterpart (Crowther, 1999).

In response to a perceived rise in property crime and middle-class demands for better protection of private property, the statutory powers of local summary courts were greatly expanded in the early 19th century. In the larger urban centres, police legislation made provision for the establishment of new police courts to deal with lesser offences, less serious crimes and infringements of local by-laws. Often referred to as magistrate courts, these centres of civic and criminal justice soon replaced burgh courts as the main local courts in Scottish towns. They were integral to the growth in municipal administration, the expansion in summary procedure and the development of the modern Scottish criminal justice system (Barrie and Broomhall, 2014). Police courts, in most towns, met daily and were not constrained by the procedural rules that made trials in burgh courts expensive and time-consuming. As the principal place of summary jurisdiction in many towns, police courts allowed for a speedy form of criminal justice, facilitated the prosecution of a large volume of crimes and offences, and were symbolic of a greater willingness on the part of local officials and the general public to bring forward prosecutions for the common good (Farmer, 1997; Barrie, 2008). By the mid-1830s, these courts were dealing with over 37,000 cases each year (Barrie and Broomhall, 2014). Most police courts could imprison for between 30 and 60 days, depending on the terms of the local Police Act, and were staffed exclusively by lay magistrates (except in Edinburgh, where the local sheriff-substitute also served on the bench).

Police courts were an integral part of the rise of the policeman-state and were the places where people were most likely to experience the law (Gatrell, 1992). The police, under the authority of the procurator fiscal, were charged with bringing forward prosecutions for offences and contraventions in the public interest – the expense of which was to be defrayed by a new police tax levied on all property rated above a certain level. A prime function of these courts was to control and more effectively regulate the behaviour and morality of the urban populace, especially in public spaces; day-to-day business was dominated by assaults, drunk and disorderly conduct, and petty thefts. These courts were also important forums for resolving interpersonal and community disputes and were accessible to large sections of the urban populace.

Summary justice expanded significantly in rural areas, too, in the 19th century. The powers of sheriff courts to try offenders in a summary manner – and to punish them – increased significantly from mid-century. Sheriff courts also tried fairly serious crimes under solemn procedure (before a jury) and could impose fines of up to £50 and imprison for up to two years (Farmer, 1997). They therefore served as an important bridge in handling cases deemed not serious enough to warrant a judicial trial, but too serious to be dispensed with summarily. By the late 19th century, they were, along with police courts, the primary local centres of criminal justice in Scotland.

DAVID G. BARRIE and JOANNE McEWAN

See also: **Assizes; 'Bloody Code', The; Petty Sessions; Quarter Sessions**

Readings

Barrie, D.G. (2008) *Police in the age of improvement: Police development and the civic tradition in Scotland, 1775–1865.* Cullompton: Willan Publishing.

Barrie, D.G. and Broomhall, S. (2014) *Police courts in nineteenth-century Scotland. Volume 1: Magistrates, media and the masses; volume 2: Boundaries, behaviours and bodies.* Farnham: Ashgate Publishing.

Cameron, J. (1983) *Prisons and punishment in Scotland: From the Middle Ages to the present.* Edinburgh: Canongate.

Crowther, M.A. (1999) 'Crime, prosecution and mercy: English influence and Scottish practice in the early nineteenth century', in S.J. Connolly (ed) *Kingdoms united? Great Britain and Ireland since 1500: Integration and diversity.* Dublin: Four Courts Press Ltd, pp 225–38.

Davies, S.J. (1980) 'The courts and the Scottish legal system, 1600–1747: the case of Stirlingshire', in V.A.C. Gatrell, B. Lenham and G. Parker (eds) *Crime and the law: The social history of crime in Western Europe since 1500.* London: Europa Publishers, pp 120–54.

Davis, M.T. (2005) 'Prosecution and radical discourse during the 1790s: the case of the Scottish sedition trials', *International Journal of the Sociology of Law,* 33(3): 148–58.

Donnachie, I. (1995) '"The darker side": a speculative survey of Scottish crime during the first half of the nineteenth century', *Scottish Economic and Social History,* 15(1): 5–24.

Farmer, L. (1997) *Criminal law, tradition and legal order: Crime and the genius of Scots Law, 1747 to the present.* Cambridge: Cambridge University Press.

Findlay, J. (2000) *All manner of people: The history of the Justices of the Peace in Scotland.* Edinburgh: Saltire Society.

Gatrell, V.A.C. (1992) 'Crime, authority and the policeman-state', in F.M.L. Thompson (ed) *Cambridge social history of Britain, 1750–1950*. Cambridge: Cambridge University Press, pp 243–310.

Kilday, A.-M. (2007) *Women and violent crime in Enlightenment Scotland*. Woodbridge: The Boydell Press.

Kilday, A.-M. (2012) 'Contemplating the evil within: examining attitudes to criminality in Scotland, 1700–1840', in D. Lemmings (ed) *Crime, courtrooms and the public sphere in Britain, 1700–1850*. Farnham: Ashgate Publishing, pp 147–66.

King, P. (2015) 'Rethinking the Bloody Code in eighteenth-century Britain: capital punishment at the centre and on the periphery', *Past and Present*, 228(1): 159–205.

Knox, W.W.J., with Thomas, L. (2015) 'Homicide in eighteenth-century Scotland: numbers and theories', *The Scottish Historical Review*, XCIV, 1(238): 48–73.

Leneman, L. and Mitchison, R. (1998) *Sin in the city: Sexuality and social control in urban Scotland 1660–1780*. Edinburgh: Scottish Cultural Press.

Prentis, M.D. (2004) 'What do we know about the Scottish convicts?', *Journal of the Royal Australian Historical Society*, 90(1): 36–52.

Smyth, J. and McKinlay, A. (2011) 'Whigs, Tories and Scottish legal reform, c. 1785–1832', *Crime, Histoire et Societes/Crime, History and Societies*, 15(1): 111–32.

Young, A.F. (1998) *The encyclopaedia of Scottish executions, 1750–1963*. Orpington: Eric Dobby.

SECURITY INDUSTRY, THE

There is no universally accepted definition of 'the security industry'. Scholars of private security (mostly criminologists) tend to adopt the definition that best suits their purposes. However, in pursuit of a history of the security industry, one might define it as a discrete group of firms that compete to provide products and/or services, through the market, in response to consumer demand either for protection against loss or harm (eg transit guarding, burglary insurance), or for other policing functions (eg private investigation, policing labour disputes). However, if one regards the security industry as a social (rather than simply a commercial) phenomenon, then the changing social role and status of these firms as providers of security are also central to its history.

The British security industry – in the sense of a publically recognised body of private firms providing protection against crime – emerged between the late 18th and mid-19th centuries (Churchill, 2015). At this time, the industry was composed largely of the leading lock and safe firms, which, in contrast to the long-established small lock-making workshops, exploited large-scale factory production. These firms developed the first security brand identities, and some makers' names (notably, Bramah and Chubb) became closely associated with the promise of 'perfect' protection against crime. Furthermore, these companies pioneered innovation in security technologies, and thereby established a link between brand-name security and cutting-edge design.

Since the late 19th century, the security industry has progressively diversified into new products and services. In some areas, Britain took the lead, notably, in burglary insurance, which was first marketed in 1889 (Moss, 2011). However, more commonly, British security enterprise followed developments forged in America, for example, in the construction of purpose-built safe deposits (which first arrived in Britain in the 1870s) and in the expansion of burglar alarm production (also towards the close of the century). Above all, America led the way in the development of private policing companies, which provided diverse services, including private investigation, industrial guarding and strike breaking (Miller, 2013). By contrast, formal private police organisations in 19th-century Britain were mostly employers' associations, which exercised monopolistic surveillance over particular industries or territories (Godfrey and Cox, 2013); not until the interwar years were there signs that a genuine *market* in private policing was emerging in Britain. It is the growth of this market – rather than the growth of private policing as such – which perhaps constitutes the greatest departure from the established structure of security enterprise since the Second World War (see also Jones and Newburn, 1998).

More broadly, the contemporary era has witnessed further diversification in security enterprise, and substantial consolidation within the security industry itself. Electronic security has assumed an ever-greater share of security enterprise, particularly with the expansion of surveillance technologies (closed-circuit television, tracking devices, etc) and computer security software and systems management. The latter half of the 20th century also saw the progressive consolidation of major national security firms by merger and acquisition; many once-famous brand names are now subsumed within various international security conglomerates.

Further research on this neglected field is required, yet one can nonetheless venture a few general claims regarding the history of the security industry. First, the formation and subsequent growth of the security industry has paralleled the rise of public policing; hence, historically, there is no conflict between the public and private supply of security. Second, while markets in policing developed prodigiously in America, the development of the security industry more broadly was as much a feature of modern British as it was of American history (cf Miller, 2013). Finally, innovation in private security provision has been driven primarily by the needs of private companies; while they have since extended to public and domestic settings, most major forms of private security provision owe their origins to demand for the protection of commercial and industrial property.

DAVID CHURCHILL

Readings

Churchill, D. (2015) 'The spectacle of security: lock-picking competitions and the security industry in mid-Victorian Britain', *History Workshop Journal*, 80: 52–74.

Churchill, D. (2016) 'Security and visions of the criminal: technology, professional criminality and social change in Victorian and Edwardian Britain', *The British Journal of Criminology*, 56(5): 857–76.

Godfrey, B. and Cox, D.J. (2013) *Policing the factory: Theft, private policing and the law in modern England.* London: Bloomsbury.

Jones, T. and Newburn, T. (1998) *Private security and public policing.* Oxford: Clarendon Press.

Miller, W.R. (2013) 'A state within "the States": private policing and the delegation of power in America', *Crime, Histoire et Sociétés/Crime, History and Societies*, 17(2): 125–35.

Moss, E. (2011) 'Burglary insurance and the culture of fear in Britain, c.1889–1939', *The Historical Journal*, 54(4): 1039–64.

SEMI-PENAL INSTITUTIONS FOR WOMEN

'Semi-penal' institutions were originally developed during the 18th and 19th centuries to accommodate the increasing number of 'exceptional cases' within the prison system (Weiner, 1990). Exceptional cases included juveniles, drunkards, 'imbeciles', 'lunatics', vagrants and women, but it was predominantly the latter who became the target of this form of intervention. Perceived, at once, as fragile *and* dangerous, 'deviant' women were considered unsuitable for the prison environment but still needful of regulation. Consequently, a plethora of institutions, such as asylums, homes, refuges and reformatories, was established, their primary purpose being the containment, supervision, control and, importantly, feminisation of a range of 'deviant' females, including prostitutes, criminals, 'wayward' girls, inebriates, the 'feeble-minded' and unmarried mothers (Barton, 2005).

As *semi*-penal institutions, they could not be described as 'official' organisations of containment and control, like custodial institutions. However, being semi-*penal*, neither did they offer the wholly 'informal' forms of management found within the domestic landscape. Instead, they represented a hybridisation of the regulatory methods and disciplinary techniques employed in both arenas. Thus, custodial features such as set periods of confinement, rigid timetables and compulsory labour were combined with familial attributes of domestic training, religious instruction and moral guidance in a network of institutions that provided seclusion and separation (from the wider world) *and* constant surveillance.

Semi-penal institutions represented an important element of the 'penal–welfare' complex. On occasions, the state clearly played a role in their creation and management. The Inebriates Act 1898, for example, provided for the creation of certified and state reformatories to supplement the voluntary institutions already in existence, and during the 19th century, there existed government-appointed Her Majesty's Inspectors of Reformatories. Notwithstanding these interventions, for the most part, they were private organisations, housed in privately owned buildings, run and managed by non-statutory bodies (eg the Temperance Society or one of the various gentlemen's and ladies' charitable organisations), and therefore almost completely beyond the reach of state regulation.

Like many of those involved in early Victorian philanthropic movements, the members of the managerial committees were generally the wealthy and influential 'urban elite'. The middle-class 'gentlemen' of the committee would take care of business arrangements and provide a form of paternalistic authority (setting rules, managing finance, appointing staff), while the 'ladies' would oversee the domestic arrangements of the institution. Like many parents in Victorian middle-class families who were not generally closely involved in the everyday lives of their children, neither the 'gentlemen' nor the 'ladies' of the committees were active in the daily custody of the inmate population. Instead, the day-to-day supervision and reform of inmates was undertaken by a group of women, usually known as matrons, who symbolised a very particular form of gender-class power (Barton, 2011). Unlike the 'elite' women on the management committees, matrons were generally (respectable) working-class and responsible for imposing maternal discipline that would mirror the 'normal' parent–child relationships found in (respectable) families (for a discussion of the role of matron's in women's prisons, see Hannah-Moffatt, 2001). Considered to have natural maternal abilities *and* moral authority (even if they did not have children of their own), these women were considered ideally placed to oversee the religious and domestic salvation of their charges.

By their own rhetoric, semi-penal institutions aimed to 'protect' and rescue women from, or impede their progress towards, the brutality of prison. However, in reality, they served to extend those disciplinary measures normally confined to the prison to, what Weiner (1990) terms, cases of 'less-than-full criminality'. Fitting in securely with 18th- and 19th-century notions of unacceptable female behaviour, these institutions targeted a whole range of women who had failed to adhere to, or achieve, required standards of femininity. For example, young women deemed to be 'at risk' or 'wayward' by their husbands and families constituted a significant proportion of residents.

The ascendancy and consolidation of the semi-penal project had the effect of expanding what was already a fairly encompassing system of social control and regulation for working-class females in the 18th, 19th and early 20th centuries. While the first half of the 20th century saw the demise of these traditional reformist institutions, many of the fundamental concepts that underpinned the reformatory movement persisted and were apparent in the rise of other non-custodial institutions for women, such as halfway houses and probation hostels (Barton, 2005).

ALANA BARTON

See also: **Industrial Schools; Inebriate Institutions; Philanthropic Institutions; Reformatory Schools**

Readings
Barton, A. (2005) *Fragile moralities and dangerous sexualities: Two centuries of semi-penal institutionalisation for women.* Aldershot: Ashgate.
Barton, A. (2011) 'A woman's place? Uncovering maternalistic forms of governance in a 19th century reformatory', *Family and Community History*, 14(2): 89–104.
Hannah-Moffatt, K. (2001) *Punishment in disguise: Penal governance and Canadian women's imprisonment.* Toronto: University of Toronto Press.
Weiner, M.J. (1990) *Reconstructing the criminal: Culture, law and policy in England 1830–1914.* Cambridge: Cambridge University Press.

SEXUAL ASSAULT

'Sexual assault' is a generic term used in common law systems, including England and Wales, which covers a range of non-consensual sexual acts perpetrated against adults and children including penile and non-penile penetration, and physical touching of parts of the body in a sexual context. Historically, the criminalisation of such acts operated with a gender bias because of the masculine domination of the law and criminal justice process. Until the late 20th century, women were denied a say in the very crimes most likely to affect their personal intimacy. Consequently, the law regulated and protected hetero-normative male-on-female sexual assaults but failed to extend criminal liability to female offenders and protection to young boys or those abused in same-sex relationships. This reflects the Christian theology that viewed sexual intercourse as a natural means of procreation. Homosexual activities (even where consensual), incest and child sexual abuse and exploitation were regarded as 'unnatural' offences, and in early modern times, were dealt with under ecclesiastical law.

Criminal prosecutions against those alleged to have committed a sexual assault have always been problematic because of the difficulty of establishing the truth of what occurred (Foucault, 1990 [1978]) and proving that the complainant did not consent. Rarely are independent witnesses present. Typically, the accused would claim that the complainant had consented or that he believed any refusal was part of her 'seductive play' (Clark, 1987, pp 21–3.). Until the state's establishment of a director of public prosecutions in 1879, complainants or their families were expected to initiate and sponsor criminal proceedings themselves. Judges and juries expected to receive testimony from the prosecutrix which proved that any sexual assault was committed against her will. Any suggestion that she had 'permitted' intercourse or sexual contact needed to be unequivocally refuted by evidence that she had no choice due to fear, force or fraud. Young children were further compromised. Lacking comprehension of the nature or seriousness of any sexual violation, they would be more likely to 'acquiesce' to the demands of the accused, who would then claim that the child had impliedly 'consented' to the assault.

Accessing primary sources to examine the historiography of sexual assaults is problematic. Rape was 'barely visible' in court records, with just 203 indictments at the Old Bailey from the mid–16th century to the end of the 18th century, when the courts started to suppress official publications of transcripts of sexual crimes (Wiener, 2004). By the 19th century, the discourse became heavily censured and desexualised. Consequently, in both the formal legal context and official public discourse, sexual assaults were generally referred to as 'offences against the person', 'crimes of violence' or 'crimes of morals', and specifically as 'carnal knowledge', 'felonious assault', 'gross indecency', 'criminal assault', 'attempt to ravish' and so forth. The use of 'ravish' to describe sexual assaults promoted female passivity and reinforced masculinity, blurring the distinction between seduction and violation, and between violation and violence. Despite the lack of official court sources, Victorian newspapers provide a useful and authentic alternative for reference material as lawyer-reporters, employed by the press as court reporters, filed significant detail about criminal trials that were published on the crime news pages (Stevenson, 2014).

The most serious sexual assault, rape, comes from the Latin *raptere*, meaning to take or seize. Initially, it was perceived as a crime against property rather than a crime against the person so proof of abduction was as important as proving the *violentis concubis* of sexual violation. In medieval times, rape was punishable by death but it was also an 'emendable' offence, reflecting the notion of property ownership. As chastity was highly prized, a woman or young girl's male protector could recover financial compensation from her assailant for the loss of his daughter's virginity or his wife's reputation. A woman could also redeem her defiler by agreeing to marry him. Rape could only be committed by penile intercourse *per vaginum*, making it a gender-specific crime; to this day, women cannot be charged with rape. Forced anal intercourse involving male or female victims was unnatural and charged as sodomy. In the late 18th century, a more systematic form of criminal law emerged to manage crime, shifting the emphasis from rape as a property crime to one of a crime of violence.

The Offences Against the Person Act 1828 confirmed that it was a felony for a man to have unlawful carnal knowledge of a woman without her consent and removed the requirement of 'emission of seed' to prove penetration. The death penalty was repealed in 1841 and replaced with penal servitude for life or not less than three years (Offences Against the Person Act 1861, section 48). It was left to the judiciary to develop rules about the extent to which circumstances including the use of threats, violence, coercion, deception and intoxication could legally negate consent (Stevenson, 1999). The respectability imperative was paramount in all cases of sexual assault: in court, deference to male respectability would often outweigh a woman's stereotypical conformity to the respectability tropes of the day which included the avoidance of compromising situations and absolute moral behaviour. Likewise, a woman forfeited her respectability by the fact of having been raped; a man only lost his respectability if convicted.

Unlawful carnal knowledge referred to sexual intercourse outside the bonds of marriage. In 1736, the jurist Sir Matthew Hale, underlining the patriarchal concept of marriage, asserted that husbands enjoyed an 'irrevocable privilege' granted by virtue of the marriage contract, which gave them immunity from any charge of marital rape. This was only opinion, not law, but in the case of *R v Clarence* (1888), nine of the 13 judges of the Queen's Bench Division effectively rewrote the law, accepting Hale's proposition that a wife was her husband's 'legal property' and so could not refuse him even if the sexual intercourse would cause her harm, in this case, infecting her with gonorrhoea. It was not until *R v R* (1991) that the House of Lords would overturn this decision, holding it to be a common law fiction.

The homosexual voice was also silenced. Male rape was not expressly acknowledged until the enactment of section 142 of the Criminal Justice and Public Order Act 1994, which also formalised the crime of marital rape. Buggery, consensual or otherwise, against a man or woman was made a capital crime in an Act of 1533, which was later extended to include bestiality. It was incorporated into the 1828 Offences Against the Person Act and the capital element removed by the 1861 Act, the last execution for buggery was in 1835. Together with buggery, bestiality and incest, homosexual acts of gross indecency and importuning ('dirty actions') were all occasionally prosecuted under the generic term 'unnatural offences', making it impossible to distinguish one from the other. Typically, these are very briefly referred to by the judge in his opening remarks at the start of the assize session but specific details were not reported in the press because such cases were deemed too 'disgusting' or 'abominable' for public consumption. In 1885, because of perceived concerns about homosexual deviancy, the controversial 'Labouchere amendment' was quietly inserted into the Criminal Law Amendment Bill to criminalise consensual homosexual activities conducted in private, essentially making these a sexual assault as the law would not accept factual consent. There was a similar attempt in 1921 to enact an equivalent clause in relation to lesbian activities undertaken in private but this was unsuccessful (Waite, 2005). The criminalisation of private homosexuality continued with sections 12 and 13 of the Sexual Offences Act 1956. After the Wolfenden Report, a concession was made in the Sexual Offences Act 1967 that decriminalised such activity provided that it took place in private, no more than two men were present and both were aged 21 years or over (Weeks, 1989). The age of homosexual consent was therefore much higher than heterosexual consent and clearly discriminatory. The Sexual Offences (Amendment) Act 2000 reduced the age of consent to 18 and the Sexual Offences Act 2003 aligned it with the heterosexual age of consent at 16 years. Consensual homosexual acts in private are lawful except where sado-masochistic practices are involved, as in the highly controversial case of *R v Brown* (1993), or carried out in public toilets (Sexual Offences Act 2003, section 71).

The concept of an age of consent is a 20th-century phenomenon; previously, age bars constituted an age of protection against child sexual assault (Bates, 2016). The first legal provision to protect young girls from sexual exploitation was the Statute of Westminster I 1275, which made it an offence to 'ravish any maiden without age' whether she consented or not, punishable with two years' imprisonment. The age of protection was 12 years, aligned to the age of marriage. Ten years later, the Statute of Westminster II 1285 made the offence a full felony punishable by death, but few, if any, convictions resulted in execution. Elizabeth's Act of 1576 reasserted the death penalty for deflowering a child under the age of 10 years and retained the two-year sentence of imprisonment for those aged between 10 and 12 years.

Judges were ambivalent about accepting the testimony of child witnesses and uncertain about whether it must be received on oath, and, if so, at what age. There are examples in the 18th century of child witnesses as young as five and seven attempting to give unsworn testimony in cases of sexual assault. The issue was settled in the case of *R v Brasier* (1779), when 12 judges unanimously confirmed that such testimony should only be received on oath but that an infant under seven years may be sworn provided that she is sufficiently mature and could answer questions that would test her understanding of religious piety. Even so, juries were reluctant to find guilt as Hale had warned of the dangers of convicting a man singularly on the word of a child, establishing the principle that the testimony of a child must be corroborated by other independent evidence. Children have therefore been regarded as neither reliable nor competent witnesses, and if the victim of sexual exploitation, typically less likely to be believed and trusted. In 2010, Steven Barker was convicted of the anal rape of two-year-old 'child C', who disclosed the abuse to a child psychiatrist when she was three, aged four at the time of the trial, as the youngest ever witness, her unsworn testimony was accepted by the court.

Section 50 of the Offences Against the Person Act 1861 criminalised carnal knowledge with a girl under 10 years (increased to 13 years in 1875) as a felony punishable with a maximum life sentence. Non-penetrative acts or attempted intercourse were typically charged as 'criminal assault' or 'indecent assault'. As Jackson (2000, pp 4–5) confirms, in the 19th century, child sexual abuse was only associated with female children and it was only really 'discovered' from the 1860s onwards as the 'product of a coalition of interests between the social purity societies and the burgeoning child welfare movement'. On 6 July 1885, W.T. Stead's notorious publication of the Maiden Tribute child prostitution scandal in the *Pall Mall Gazette* scandalised Victorian society but helped secure the passage of the Criminal Law Amendment Bill initiated by Josephine Butler's campaign to stop the trafficking of young English girls to the continent. Proponents of the Bill sought to raise the age of protection to 16 years, causing considerable disagreement in the House of Lords. Some peers believed that men needed legal protection from the 'immoral' advances of underage females rather than young girls needing protection from abusive adults. The Criminal Law Amendment Act settled the age of protection at 16 years, but only for girls; a later attempt in 1913 to introduce an equivalent age of consent for boys failed. The Act made carnal knowledge (defilement) of a girl aged between 13 and 16 a misdemeanour punishable with two years' imprisonment, the unlawful carnal knowledge of a girl under 13 (statutory rape) remained a felony punishable with life imprisonment. This distinction endures in the Sexual Offences Act 2003; statutory rape may only be committed against a girl under 13 years but there are other offences of sexual assault that apply equally to girls and boys aged under 13 and under 16, reflecting the different vulnerabilities in age. As with rape, court reports of child sexual offences were censured but case examples can be found in 19th-century newspapers. However, for the first half of the 20th century, there is a dearth of reports of both rape and child sex offences. Research is currently being undertaken by Louise Jackson and Adrian Bingham to explain this. Incestuous acts were prosecuted as rape or indecent assault as incest was not made a secular crime until pressure from the social purity movement forced through the Punishment of Incest Act in 1908. The Act again reflected a gender bias as there was no criminality between a grandmother and grandson. The Sexual Offences Act 2003 replaced incest with gender-neutral offences of familial sexual assault.

KIM STEVENSON

See also: **Marital Violence; Macmillan and Wolfenden Committees, The**

Readings

Bates, V. (2016) *Sexual forensics in Victorian and Edwardian England: Age, crime and consent.* Basingstoke: Palgave Macmillan.

Clark, A. (1987) *Women's silence men's violence: Sexual assault in England 1770–1845.* London: Pandora Press.

Foucault, M. (1990 [1978]) *The history of sexuality I: An introduction* (trans R. Hurley). New York, NY: Vintage.

Jackson, L. (2000) *Child sexual abuse in Victorian England.* London: Routledge.

Stevenson, K. (1999) 'Observations on the law relating to sexual offences: the historic scandal of women's silence', *Web Journal Current Legal Issues,* 4.

Stevenson, K. (2014) 'Outrageous violations: enabling students to interpret nineteenth century newspaper reports of sexual assault and rape', *Law, Crime and History,* 1: 36–61.

Waite, M. (2005) *The age of consent: Young people, sexuality and citizenship.* Houndmills: Palgrave.

Weeks, J. (1989) *Sex, politics and society: The regulation of sexuality since 1800.* London: Longman.

Wiener, M. (2004) *Men of blood, violence, manliness and criminal justice in Victorian England.* Cambridge: Cambridge University Press.

SHERLOCK HOLMES

Sir Arthur Conan Doyle's Sherlock Holmes 'canon' consists of 56 short stories and four novels published between 1887 and 1927. Holmes first appeared in *A study in scarlet* in 1887 in Beeton's Christmas Annual. Doyle killed off the character in *The adventure of the final problem* in December 1893. It is, perhaps, apocryphal that young men wore black armbands of mourning that winter. Doyle returned to Holmes in the serialised (1901–02) *The hound of the Baskervilles,* which was set before the character's death. Lucrative offers from *The Strand Magazine* in the UK and *Collier's Weekly* in the US saw Doyle return once again to the character for a subsequent cycle of stories. The first, *The adventure of the empty house,* revealed that Holmes had not, in fact, died at the Reichenbach Falls, but rather had travelled to Tibet, Mecca and Khartoum during 'the Great Hiatus'. The last Doyle story (*The adventure of Shoscombe Old Place*) was published in *The Strand* in 1927.

Holmes is an iconic figure of crime fiction. Despite his bohemianism, he could move easily through the diverse social worlds of Victorian, Edwardian and interwar London and beyond. He would converse with royalty as insouciantly as he would his network of street urchins and informers, the Baker Street Irregulars. His two most readily identifiable features, a calabash pipe and deerstalker hat, were, in fact, absent from Doyle's original stories. The curiously curved pipe was the addition of the actor William Gillette, who played Holmes on stage between 1899 and 1932, whereas the illustrator Sidney Paget incorporated the deerstalker in illustrations for *The Boscombe Hall mystery* in 1891. Within the fictive world, it is Holmes's faithful companion, Dr John Watson, who documents the pair's cases (save for four of the short stories). Their first meeting is marked by a characteristic Holmesian flourish of 'deduction' ('You have been in Afghanistan, I perceive'). Such displays were modelled on those of Dr Joseph Bell, a teacher that Doyle encountered when studying medicine in Edinburgh. The key recurring characters are rounded out by Inspector Lestrade of Scotland Yard, Holmes's corpulent brother Mycroft (who occupies a position of considerable, if nebulous, power in government) and Professor James Moriarty (described by Holmes as 'the Napoleon of crime'). Curiously, the first collection of stories, in particular, is rather short on crime. Rather, Holmes is largely called upon to ameliorate social embarrassments. In this respect, Holmes often reaffirms a social status quo that he affects to disdain.

Holmes offered a sense of rationality against the roaring chaos of an industrialised world. His application of the scientific method to the study of crime was, of course, not without real-world precedent. For example, we can look back to the work of Alphonse Bertillon (mentioned in *The naval treaty*) and the analysis of 'thumbprints' in the preceding decades, as well as the English-language publication of Cesare Lombroso's work at the turn of the century. Knight (1980, p 79), however, points to 'the aura of science' surrounding the Holmesian method. Indeed, his much-vaunted powers of deduction are, on closer inspection, actually *induction*. He begins with close observation, matches this to his knowledge of the patterns of thousands of earlier cases and then establishes a theory. However, even this occurs with less frequency than might be expected. The appearance of order and science is more important than the reality. What is seen from Holmes is more akin to a heightened common sense. Indeed, as with 'the curious incident of the dog in the night-time': 'the dog did not bark because it knew the murderer' (Knight, 2004, p 57). The reader can grasp Holmes's thought process, but we are mostly positioned alongside Watson, reading in astonishment as the solution is laid out before us. As Holmes admonishes: we see, but we do not observe.

Since the final story in 1927, Sherlock Holmes and the wider supporting cast have continued to feature in original novels, adaptations on stage and screen, museum exhibitions, comics, and games. Holmes' influence can be seen in the socially dysfunctional criminalistics officers of *C.S.I.*, who similarly place a primacy upon the collection and interpretation of physical evidence. One wonders if Holmes would describe *C.S.I.*'s Gil Grissom or Horatio Caine in the same withering terms as his own fictional predecessors Gaboriau's Lecoq ('a miserable bungler') or Poe's Dupin ('a very inferior fellow').

MICHAEL FIDDLER

See also: **Crime Fiction; English Detectives**

Readings

Knight, S. (1980) *Form and ideology in crime fiction*. Bloomington, IN: Indiana University Press.

Knight, S. (2004) *Crime fiction, 1800–2000: Detection, death, diversity*. Basingstoke: Palgrave Macmillan.

SLAVE TRADE, THE

'The slave trade' refers to the trading of millions of people from Africa across the Atlantic to plantations in North and South America, which produced products such as sugar or tobacco meant for consumption back in Europe, between the 16th and 19th centuries. Slavery is the ownership of individuals by other individuals, who control where they live and at what they work. Slavery is one of the oldest institutions; it has existed since ancient times. Most settled countries or cultures at one time or another have used forced labour: the ancient Greeks, the Romans, Incas and Aztecs all had slaves, as did many early modern European countries. Thus, most countries and cultures have experienced servitude, and in the past, it has been considered morally acceptable for some people to own other people. Thus, slavery and a trade in slaves was well established before the Atlantic was opened up and before Britain became involved. However, as Martinez (2014, p 16) claims, this developing transatlantic trade was a 'pernicious' turn in the practice of slavery.

Portugal and Britain were the two most 'successful' slave-trading countries, accounting for about 70% of all Africans transported to the Americas. By the mid-17th century, Britain regarded its colonies in the Americas as sources of raw materials and produce for people at home in Britain. Investors in the colonies needed to organise plantation production to maximise outputs from the abundant land available in the colonies. However, a large labour force was needed for plantation farming. Attempts to employ native peoples failed, and there were insufficient indentured workers and convict labourers, who became free after their term finished and who then had legal rights that precluded their exploitation. Thus, English merchants followed the Spanish, Portuguese, Dutch and French in shipping large numbers of enslaved people from Africa across the Atlantic and putting them to work as a captive labour force on plantations. Britain was the most dominant from around the 1640s to 1807, when the British slave trade was abolished. It has been estimated that, by the 1790s, 480,000 people were enslaved in the British colonies (Thomas, 1997) and that 'an estimated 609,000 slaves arrived in the New World' in the first decade of the 19th century alone (Martinez, 2014, p 12). Overall, it is estimated that Britain transported 3.1 million Africans (of whom 2.7 million arrived) to the British colonies in the Caribbean and North and South America (Thomas, 1997). The slave trade was carried out from many British ports, but the three most important ports were London (1660–1720s), Bristol (1720s–40s) and Liverpool (1740s–1807), which became extremely wealthy. Under the Slave Trade Act 1799, the trade was restricted to these three ports.

By the late 18th century, attitudes towards the trade in slaves began to change. There were those who continued to support it, who argued that it made important contributions to Britain's economy. Others in Britain, who became known as 'abolitionists', began to (successfully) campaign against slavery. The British Abolition of the Slave Trade Act 1807 made trading in slaves illegal. Britain thus became the first major country, followed quickly by the US, to ban its subjects from participation in the slave trade (Martinez, 2014). Subsequent Acts, which provided for the monitoring and suppressing of the trade, as well as international treaties with European and American countries, gave Britain the role of 'international policeman' (Ennals, 2007, p 294). British naval squadrons were set up to patrol the coast of West Africa and the Caribbean, looking out for illegal slavers. The navy also encouraged exploration of the coastal rivers and waterways, bombarded slaving settlements, made treaties with friendly African groups, and encouraged other forms of trade, such as in palm oil. Britain's diplomatic role led to treaties with slave-owning and slave-trading countries (such as Spain, the Netherlands and Portugal) if not to stop the slave trade, then at least to better manage it. Such activities led to the gradual suppression of the slave trade and slavery throughout the Americas. Martinez (2014, p 13) claims that 'the abolition of the transatlantic slave trade remains the most successful episode ever in the history of international human rights law'.

Although the trade in slaves had been abolished in 1807, it took another 26 years to effect the emancipation of the enslaved. Emancipation, though, was replaced with a system of apprenticeship, tying the newly freed men and women into another form of unfree labour for fixed terms, and £20 million in compensation, to be paid by the British taxpayers, to slave owners for lost income from their slaves (Draper, 2009; Hall et al, 2016). The slave trade caused history's largest population migrations; the involuntary movement of over 9.5 million people from Africa to the New World. It assigned them a new habitat in the Americas, transformed them into slave labourers, diluted their local and regional African cultures, and set them aside as people inferior and to forever be discriminated against.

JO TURNER

See also: **British Empire, The; Indentured Labour; Slavery in the Americas**

Readings

Draper, N. (2009) *The price of emancipation: Slave-ownership, compensation and British society at the end of slavery.* Cambridge: Cambridge University Press.

Ennals, R. (2007) *From slavery to citizenship.* Chichester: John Wiley and Sons.

Hall, C., Draper, N., McClelland, K., Lang, R., Dawkins, J. and Young, H. (2016) 'Legacies of British slave-ownership'. Available at: https://www.ucl.ac.uk/lbs/

Martinez, J.S. (2014) *The slave trade and the origins of international human rights law.* New York, NY: Oxford University Press.

Thomas, H. (1997) *The slave trade: The history of the Atlantic slave trade: 1440–1870.* London: Picador.

SLAVERY IN THE AMERICAS

Slaves in the Americas persistently resisted their condition, destabilising the slaveholders' rule through routine defiance of orders, stealing and destroying property, running away, fighting back against their oppressors, and organising large-scale revolts. Both from the slaveholders' perspective and, for the most part, in slave law, these and other forms of resistance were criminal and they met with a fearsome response through extrajudicial punishments and legal proceedings in which the interests of slaveholders were prioritised over the ends of justice.

Slave laws varied across the Americas on account of the distinct legal cultures of European empires and variations among settler societies. In the Spanish Americas, the 13th-century Siete Partidas provided a basis for slavery, but across English, French and Portuguese colonies, slave law was more strongly influenced by local circumstances, including evolving ideas about race and servitude, labour requirements, and acts of resistance by Africans and their descendants. Notwithstanding these differences, judicial institutions in all colonies played a relatively marginal role in everyday matters of slave control as the law allowed slaveholders wide discretion to determine when and how slaves should be punished

(Hadden, 2008). Throughout the Americas, slaveholders could inflict almost unlimited violence on their human property without fear of legal repercussions. Non-fatal abuse attracted almost no judicial concern – though slaveholders sometimes sought compensation in civil proceedings for brutality inflicted on slaves by third parties – and before the 19th century, even the murder of a slave was rarely prosecuted. In most English colonies, the killing of a slave did not even constitute a crime if it occurred in the course of punishment, no matter how trivial the victim's original offence, and with people of African descent widely prohibited from testifying against white people in courts of law, there was little scope for prosecutions even in the most brutal cases (Fede, 1992).

For all the extreme power that slaveholders exercised over their human property, there were circumstances in which the state did assume responsibility for the policing, trial and punishment of slaves. This was the case when slaves were suspected of capital crimes and when they worked or travelled beyond their owners' property. Early in the history of slavery, patrols were formed in rural neighbourhoods to police illegal gatherings of slaves and capture runaways. Armed militia companies took on similar functions, particularly in times of slave unrest and in regions where the white population was heavily outnumbered. In cities, where many slaves were hired out and had an unusual degree of independence, nightwatchmen were routinely involved in arresting slaves for offences ranging from drunkenness and insulting a white person, to curfew violations, running away and theft. All of these officials could inflict summary chastisement, but slaves could also be returned to their owners for punishment or held for a usually cursory examination at a daily court session, where they might be sentenced by the mayor or other city official to be flogged in a public square or jail (Hadden, 2001).

Slaves accused of the most serious crimes were subject in all colonies to distinct laws from free people and they were frequently examined and sentenced in separate and only loosely regulated courts. In the English-speaking Caribbean and North American colonies, slaves charged with capital crimes were normally tried, judged and sentenced by panels of freeholders and magistrates, who convened within days of an arrest, were not bound by common law precedent and sometimes had no legal training, and from whose decisions there was no right of appeal. In the early 19th century, this system was replaced by regular circuit court jury trials in most Anglo-American jurisdictions and the right of enslaved defendants to common law protections was upheld in numerous appellate judgements, yet separate slave trials survived in several states of the US until the mid-19th century. What is more, court proceedings were readily subverted or ignored altogether during slave rebellions, when mass executions and extra-legal killings were carried out with impunity (Morris, 1996).

The reform of slave trial systems was part of a larger transformation in the criminal law of slavery in the 19th century as the state assumed a more central role in policing slaves and new restrictions were imposed on slaveholders. Criminal punishments also underwent significant changes, with the number of crimes for which slaves could be executed reduced, burning at the stake and post-mortem dismemberment largely outlawed, and limits imposed on the number of lashes that slaves might suffer (Morris, 1996). These developments are best understood as an attempt to legitimise slavery in the face of a growing anti-slavery movement. Slaveholders in Jamaica, for example, hoped to delay British intervention to abolish slavery by reforming the institution from within in the 1820s, while in the antebellum South, penal reform was consistent with the claims of paternalism that slaveholders used both to rebut abolitionist attacks and justify slavery to themselves (Paton, 2004). Few of these innovations were of particular benefit to the enslaved, and extreme discrimination and violence survived as central elements of legal culture and law enforcement in slaveholding regions for generations after abolition.

JAMES CAMPBELL

See also: **British Empire, The; Lynching; Slave Trade, The**

Readings
Fede, A. (1992) *People without rights: An interpretation of the law of slavery.* New York, NY: Garland.

Hadden, S.E. (2001) *Slave patrols: Law and violence in Virginia and the Carolinas.* Cambridge: Harvard University Press.

Hadden, S.E. (2008) 'The fragmented laws of slavery in colonial and revolutionary eras', in M. Grossberg and C. Tomlins (eds) *The Cambridge history of law in America volume 1: Early America (1580–1815).* Cambridge: Cambridge University Press, pp 253–87.

Morris, T.D. (1996) *Southern slavery and the law, 1619–1860.* Chapel Hill, NC: University of North Carolina Press.

Paton, D. (2004) *No bond but the law: Punishment, race, and gender in Jamaican state formation, 1780–1870.* Durham: Duke University Press.

SOLITARY CONFINEMENT

Prisons in the late 18th and early 19th centuries were crowded places characterised by noise, squalor, alcohol consumption and largely unfettered intercourse among their inhabitants. Exploitation and extortion were common, and sanitary conditions were poor. Occasional outbreaks of 'gaol fever' (typhus) contributed to a growing level of concern about the need to halt the spread of physical as well as moral degeneration. A key objective of reformers was the design of a system of penal treatment that would prevent the communication of diseases and criminal contacts while simultaneously promoting introspection and reformation. Solitary confinement was seen as a trigger for reflection and a possible catalyst for reform, though it was understood that unalleviated aloneness exacted a considerable psychological toll (see O'Donnell, 2014).

An early experiment with isolation at Walnut Street jail in Philadelphia in 1790 was not a success. In part, this was because of flaws in the institution's design that allowed convicts in adjoining cells to communicate with ease. In addition, the isolation cells were soon deployed as holding pens for refractory prisoners and any notion that they could have had a beneficial impact on the persons within them was jettisoned. A more focused trial took place at Auburn prison in New York in 1821, when solitude without labour was introduced to a newly built cellblock. The cells were tiny, described by Evans (1982, p 318) as 'claustrophobic cubicles' containing 'closeted convicts'. This initiative was a dramatic failure, leading to death and madness among the men who had been so confined. In recognition of the dreadful consequences of solitude unmitigated by labour, and endured in poor conditions, the governor of New York went so far as to pardon a number of prisoners as compensation for the suffering that they had experienced.

The challenge for the reformers was to temper solitude with meaningful work, religious instruction and appropriate visitation, so that the prisoner's conscience could be developed without posing too great a threat to his mental integrity. The issue to be resolved was how, and when, to dilute solitary confinement with company, activity or a combination of both. Two competing philosophies emerged. Auburn developed a system based on silent congregate activity during the day with prisoners kept apart at night. Violations of the rule of silence, which were frequent occurrences, resulted in corporal punishment. What became known as the Pennsylvania system emphasised the separation of prisoners from their peers at all times. They were held in spacious cells where they ate, worked, read their Bibles and reflected on their wrongdoing. They exercised alone in small yards. For the duration of their sentences, they never saw the face of another inmate. They were visited by local worthies and subject to the ministrations of the warden and his staff.

In 1842, Charles Dickens visited Eastern State Penitentiary in Philadelphia and observed the Pennsylvania system in action. The great novelist was horrified by what he saw and unstinting in his criticism. He believed that some of the men he met, who had been held apart for years, had unravelled as a result. He declared that the best of intentions could have dreadfully counterproductive consequences (see

Dickens, 2000 [1842], pp 11–12). Dickens's claims were vigorously rebutted by the Pennsylvania Prison Society in its *Journal of Prison Discipline and Philanthropy.*

The relative merits of the two models excited huge international interest. The Auburn system won out across the US, largely on account of its cost effectiveness and the flexibility of its labour force. The Pennsylvania system held sway outside the US, and Eastern State Penitentiary became the blueprint for prison architects in many countries. Neither involved absolute solitude: the Auburn system allowed prisoners to work and dine together and the Pennsylvania system allowed interaction with visitors and prison staff.

Pentonville prison in London, which incorporated the principle of separation in every aspect of its design and daily operation, became controversial as soon as it opened. *The Times* directed particular attention to the men who were transferred from the 'model prison' to Bethlehem hospital as a result of their inability to cope with uninterrupted aloneness. In November 1843, the newspaper went so far as to describe Pentonville as a 'maniac-making system'.

Solitary confinement remains controversial. It has reached its apotheosis in supermax prisons in the US, where men (and, rarely, women) are denied the possibility of meaningful human engagement, sometimes for decades, and without any pretence that their separation is underpinned by a reformative rationale (for an account of how prisoners cope with such profound aloneness, see O'Donnell, 2016).

IAN O'DONNELL

See also: **Convict Prisons; Local Prisons; Penal Reform Pressure Groups**

Readings
Dickens, C. (2000 [1842]) *American notes for general circulation.* London: Penguin Classics.
Evans, R. (1982) *The fabrication of virtue: English prison architecture 1750–1840.* New York, NY: Cambridge University Press.
O'Donnell, I. (2014) *Prisoners, solitude, and time.* Oxford: Oxford University Press.
O'Donnell, I. (2016) 'The survival secrets of solitaries', *The Psychologist*, 29: 184–7.

SUICIDE

The intentional taking of one's life is defined as suicide. While such a definition appears on the surface as simplistic and cogent, the topic of suicide has attracted scholarly attention for centuries. Violence against the self that is resultant in death is a field of enquiry that incorporates debate from a variety of disciplines, in particular, medicine, the social sciences and philosophy. The study of suicide, first and foremost, is a thematic area of analysis that is bound up in a broader appreciation of cultural values and sentiments towards life and death (Lieberman, 2003; Minois, 2001).

The act of self-murder, later defined as suicide, has prompted a variety of propositions aiming to assess motivations, the rationality of behaviour, what (if any) justifications present as and how the act of suicide fits within the dominant moral reckoning of a given society. Historically, religious doctrine has enacted a powerful influence of condemnation on voluntary death, as has the criminalising of suicide in some legal jurisdictions. Although suicide has been outlawed in some countries, suicide researchers have pointed to the fact that this has had little impact on suicide rates (for an overview, see Kosky et al, 2002).

Self-killing, or suicide, is a reoccurring motif in historical writings, philosophy and art. Classical analyses of voluntary self-killing have largely pointed to its prohibition on moral grounds. However, a willingness to recognise exceptions (as Plato does) to condemnation are offered, such as where madness/ill health presents, or where judicial authority has ordered convicted criminals to ingest poison themselves. The influence of Christianity, Islam and Judaism hardened social attitudes towards violence against the self despite examples where persecuted groups elected to take their own lives for fear of succumbing to the tyranny of political regimes.

Observations of associations between madness and self-killing can be traced to the writings of Ancient Greece and Ancient Rome. With the evolution of medicine and subsequently psychiatry, the medicalisation of attempted and fatal suicide has been pivotal in shaping suicide as an outcome of emotional or psychological abnormality. While suicide may occur in populations who do endure psychosis or mood disorders, it is argued that not all who voluntarily enact violence against themselves are mentally disordered. In essence, if suicide is to be associated with a mental abnormality, then this is contingent on what is defined as mental disorder and the interests at work in constructing suicide as an outcome of mental or emotional aberration. The strength of such narratives is often to be found among those who argue that suicide can be understood as rational free will. In medicalising the act, the medical institution may exert powers to control human behaviour to prohibit suicide (eg compulsion/detention under the law); critics deem this action as interfering with the exercising of free will with no authority. Ethicists and scholars in support of suicide as an act of free will contend that the intervention of the state is only justifiable where harm is inflicted on another person. So long as others are not harmed, there is no legitimacy for intervention (Stevens, no date; Szasz, 1997).

Until suicide was decriminalised in England and Wales by the Suicide Act 1961, attempting suicide was a common law offence and imprisonable. Indeed, it was usual for those convicted of attempting to commit suicide to be imprisoned, though research has shown that magistrates were particularly lenient in such circumstances. For example, Turner (2012) has shown that by the late 19th century, magistrates often dismissed cases of women on such charges, recommending that the woman be returned to her family. The World Health Organization (2014) has reported little impact of legislation in deterring individuals from fatally harming themselves; indeed, prosecutions are likely to worsen any emotional distress already felt.

Assisting suicide remains an offence in England and Wales under the Suicide Act 1961; something that repeatedly attracts criticism from various parties who argue for necessary support to be administered for those who have terminal illnesses or illnesses where their quality of life is severely affected. Opposition by 'pro-life' groups rebuts such criticism, suggesting that any assistance provided to assist in a person voluntarily taking their life may be ill-considered, be a breach of human rights and amounts to practices of euthanasia. Some quarters suggest that in England and Wales, where a conviction under the Suicide Act can carry a sentence of 14 years in custody, this is not a sufficient punishment or deterrent.

The act of suicide as a method of resistance and social protest has attracted much scholarly and public interest. Self-immolation by Buddhist monks in opposition to oppression (eg see the self-immolation in Saigon of Vietnamese Mahayana Buddhist monk Thích Quang Duc in 1963) serves as just one provocative illustration of actions deemed necessary to challenge repressive politics, policies and governance.

The 'suicide bomber' has also emerged as a prominent phenomenon of the contemporary era. As Pape (2003) suggests, it was not until the 1983 attack on the US embassy in Beirut that public consciousness was pricked in the West. It had been some time since the Japanese Kamikaze pilot attacks of the Second World War and the recognition of suicide as an effective act of warfare. Globally, suicide terrorism poses significant challenges in the combating of insurgency. The attacks in 2001 on the World Trade Center in New York City and the bombings of the transport system in London in 2005 are just two examples of what has been conceived as a sharp increase in suicide terrorism from the last decade of the 20th century onwards (Pape, 2003). The 'suicide bomber' has attracted a diversity of inspection, with some experts articulating the sources of radicalisation, and others considering the presence of mental abnormality as a contributing factor (see Lankford, 2011, 2012). Indeed, there is a lack of consensus that suicide terrorism can be accounted for by any single motivating factor.

Studying suicide demands sufficient acknowledgement of the disciplinary contributions, be they from medical domains, political and social science, or philosophical, as well as their intersections. Suicide is deeply entwined with cultural values, and, as such, the voluntary taking of one's own life may challenge, shock or outrage sentiments and public opinion. Understanding suicide as simply a behaviour rooted in individualised pathology may well obscure deeper or more sophisticated phenomena. Indeed, these numerous facets require an intellectual capacity to account for suicide in a multidimensional and multi-causal way (De Souza Minayo et al, 2006).

PAUL TAYLOR and JO TURNER

See also: **Violence**

Readings

De Souza Minayo, M.C., Cavalcante, F.G. and De Souza, E.R. (2006) 'Methodological proposal for studying suicide as a complex phenomenon', *Cad. Saúde Pública*, 22(8): 1587–96.

Kosky, R.J., Eshkevari, H.S., Goldney, R.D. and Hassan, R. (eds) (2002) *Suicide prevention: The global context*. New York, NY: Kluwer Academic Publishers.

Lankford, A. (2011) 'Could suicide terrorists actually be suicidal?', *Studies in Conflict & Terrorism*, 34(4): 337–66.

Lankford, A. (2012) 'A psychological autopsy of 9/11 ringleader Mohamed Atta', *Journal of Police and Criminal Psychology*, 27(2): 150–9.

Lieberman, L. (2003) *Leaving you: The cultural meaning of suicide*. Chicago, IL: Ivan R. Dee.

Minois, G. (2001) *History of suicide: Voluntary death in Western culture*. Maryland, MD: Johns Hopkins University Press.

Pape, R.A. (2003) 'The strategic logic of suicide terrorism', *American Political Science Review*, 97(3): 343–61.

Stevens, L. (no date) 'Suicide: a civil right'. Available at: http://www.antipsychiatry.org/suicide.htm

Szasz, T.S. (1997) *The manufacture of madness: A comparative study of the inquisition and the mental health movement*. Syracuse: Syracuse University Press.

Turner, J. (2012) 'Summary justice for women: Stafford Borough, 1880–1905', *Crime, History and Societies*, 16(2): 55–77.

World Health Organization (2014) 'Preventing suicide: a global imperative'. Available at: http://apps.who.int/iris/bitstream/10665/131056/1/9789241564779_eng.pdf?ua

T

TEMPERANCE MOVEMENTS

Temperance movements were anti-alcohol campaigns that emerged in various countries in the 19th century. Concerns about the role of alcohol consumption in producing violence, public disorder and other social problems had, of course, been expressed in earlier historical periods. However, 19th-century temperance movements were distinct in a number of ways. First, rather than being concerned with the effects that drinking and other factors may have on some wider notion of morals, manners or social order, they were concerned solely with alcohol consumption. Second, temperance movements were highly organised. The largest temperance societies were organised on a local and national level, often employed salaried officials, and pursued a range of coordinated activities. Third, temperance movements occurred on an impressive scale. The first temperance societies were formed in the US in the 1820s and were closely followed by mobilisation in Britain and other countries. Campaigns occurred in many parts of the world, though the movement was strongest in English-speaking and Nordic countries (Levine, 1993; see also Blocker et al, 2003). By 1900, the membership of British temperance societies alone numbered in the millions (Shiman, 1988).

In addition to their target, organisation and scale, temperance movements were further distinguished by certain beliefs and tactics. The first temperance groups tended to endorse abstinence from alcoholic spirits on the grounds that spirits, not beer or wine, were responsible for most drink problems. However, in the 1830s, British and American groups began to promote total abstinence from all forms of alcoholic beverage. Total abstinence was initially to be achieved by encouraging

251

drinkers to take and uphold a teetotal pledge. Especially in Britain, this form of 'moral suasionism' endured until the early 20th century, but from the 1850s, it was increasingly challenged by a prohibitionist strand of temperance in which legislative action was seen as the only way to create a drink-free world. Other branches of temperance also emerged in the second half of the 19th century, including medical temperance and socially ameliorative Anglican temperance. The Church of England Temperance Society became notable for its interest in welfarist-type projects, such as its police court missions. Interestingly, this initiative, which aimed to help offenders control their drinking, is often identified as the beginning of the British probation service.

Discerning the wider influence of the temperance movement is more complex. The campaigning movement declined in the first half of the 20th century. Prohibition had been successfully enacted in some jurisdictions, such as the US and Canada, but did not last long. A form of local control, whereby referenda could be called to decide on the future of the alcohol trade in local areas, also operated in Scotland from the end of the First World War until the mid-1970s. In some places, a subtler impact of the temperance movement was to increase acceptance of the idea that drunkenness was a serious issue (Harrison, 1971) and that beer and wine, as well as spirits, were responsible for it. England did not implement prohibition or local polls, but a gradual hardening of attitudes towards drinking across the 19th century coincided with a tightening of the legal restrictions around drinking and an intensification of moral discourse exhorting people to avoid the 'evils' of drink (Yeomans, 2011). The ongoing regulation of drinking through law, taxation, health promotion and other means illustrates the continued acceptance that all types of alcoholic drink are essentially problematic (Yeomans, 2014). As this idea originated with teetotallers in the 1830s, its ongoing relevance may be the most abiding legacy of the temperance movement.

HENRY YEOMANS

See also: **Police Court Missionaries; Probation; Prohibition**

Readings
Blocker, J.S., Fahey, D.M. and Tyrell, I.R. (2003) *Alcohol and temperance in modern history: An international encyclopaedia.* California, CA: ABC-CLIO.

Harrison, B. (1871) *Drink and the Victorians: The temperance question in England 1815–1872.* London: Faber and Faber.

Levine, H. (1993) 'Temperance cultures: concern about alcohol in Nordic and English-speaking countries', in M. Lader, G. Edwards and D.C. Drummon (eds) *The nature of alcohol and drug-related problems.* Oxford: Oxford University Press, pp 16–36.

Shiman, L.L. (1988) *Crusade against drink in Victorian England*. Basingstoke: Macmillan.

Yeomans, H. (2011) 'What did the British temperance movement accomplish? Attitudes to alcohol, the law and moral regulation', *Sociology*, 45(1): 38–53.

Yeomans, H. (2014) *Alcohol and moral regulation: Public attitudes, spirited measures and Victorian hangovers*. Bristol: Policy Press.

TICKET OF LEAVE

Transportation was virtually abandoned in the early 1850s, and the Penal Servitude Act 1853 introduced tickets of leave for prisoners who could no longer be transported following Australia's refusal to accept more convicts from Britain. A ticket of leave was a document of parole given to convicts who had served around half of their sentence, and allowed them to marry, bring their families from Britain, seek employment and acquire property of their own. However, these liberties were subject to restrictions; 'ticket of leavers' were only permitted to live and work within certain police districts and had to report to the ticket-of-leave muster at least once a year, or their freedoms were revoked.

Tickets of leave consisted of two parts: a ticket was issued to the convict, and it was compulsory that they carry it on their person at all times; and the second part was the 'butt', which was the official copy kept by the government. Unfortunately, many of the tickets have not survived, but the 'butts' have been digitised by Ancestry.co.uk, and are available for researchers to access. The butts contain a wealth of information, including: the convict's name and date of birth; the ship upon which they were transported; their date of arrival; their native place of residence; their trade or calling; the date and place of trial and sentence; a physical description; and the district to which he or she was confined.

The fact that many offenders who were sentenced to transportation were never sent abroad, but released in Britain after a term of imprisonment, required that something be done to deal with convicts both in Britain and the colonies (Bartrip, 1981; Emsley, 1987). In addition, the introduction of tickets of leave for convicts provoked widespread anxieties that the dangerous criminal classes were gaining the upper hand in the weakening authority of the law. Within both the press and Parliament, ticket-of-leave holders were apparently to blame for the spate of garrottings that took place in London in the early 1860s (Davis, 1980; Sindall, 1987). These anxieties led to a hardened response from the government, and a Royal Commission was appointed in 1863 to investigate the legislation related to transportation and imprisonment. Parliament responded harshly. The Garrotters Act, passed in 1863, reintroduced corporal punishment for armed or violent robbery, and the Penal Servitude Act 1864 made mandatory police supervision of ticket-of-leave men and increased the length of penal servitude to five years for a first offence and seven for any further offences.

Thus, the 1850s and 1860s saw a hardening of attitudes towards the reformatory possibilities that imprisonment could provide for serious offenders. The 1840s had signalled the arrival of a modern penal system that rested upon the reformative and deterrent influence of the prison, and the implementation of the Penal Servitude Acts (1857 and 1864) finally abolished transportation and established the modern penal system of long-term imprisonment accompanied by hard labour. Despite the progressive and libertarian principles that had underpinned the ticket-of-leave system, as transportation came to a close and fears sharpened over the reintroduction of criminals to British society, the law responded harshly and revoked the increasingly liberal prison movement. These legislative measures were key movements in the formation of the modern police force, extended legal powers in the surveillance and control over criminals, and reversed the movement towards a reformative prison system.

ZOE ALKER

See also: **Convict Prisons; Garrotting Panics, The; Transportation**

Readings

Bartrip, P. (1981) 'Public opinion and law enforcement: the ticket of leave scares in mid-Victorian Britain', in V. Bailey (ed) *Policing and punishment in nineteenth-century Britain*. New Jersey, NJ: Croom Helm, pp 150–81.

Davis, J. (1980) 'The London garrotting panic of 1862: a moral panic and the creation of a criminal class in mid-Victorian England', in V.A.C. Gatrell, B. Lenman and G. Parker (eds) *Crime and the law: The social history of crime in Western Europe since 1500*. London: Europa Publications, pp 190–213.

Emsley, C. (1987) *Crime and society in England, 1750–1900*. London: Pearson.

Sindall, R. (1987) 'The London garotting panics of 1856 and 1862', *Journal of Social History*, 12(3): 351–9.

TRANSPORTATION

Penal transportation sits at a critical juncture in the history of British punishment. It forms the bridge between a legal code reliant solely on the death penalty for all felonies, and the system of today centred around the modern prison. It emerged alongside incarceration as an effective policy in the early 18th century, when capital punishment reached a limit and alternative, 'secondary' punishments were sought. The Transportation Act 1717 (technically, the 'Piracy Act', 4 Geo. 1. c.11) crafted a new punishment with three capacities: first, as an alternative to the death sentence ('death commuted'); second, as an alternative to whipping and branding (then freedom) for those claiming benefit of clergy; and, third, as a punishment in its own right, notably, with petty larceny (a misdemeanour) reclassified as a transportable offence. It was revolutionary. Unlike death, sentences could be of varied length, opening up the potential of punitive proportionality, and also unlike death, it advanced the prospect of reform of the offender. Yet, it was no soft option. Transportation loomed as a suitably dread alternative to the noose. In the short term, the availability of non-capital punishments may have fuelled the burgeoning Bloody Code. However, over the ensuing 150 years, law reformers would deploy the terrifying option of transportation as a political expedient in retrenching the death penalty. Eventually, its own success at colony building would lead to transportation's demise and the triumph of the prison as the dominant mode of punishment. However, its role was pivotal. Britain could not make the transition from death to incarceration without the intermediate and widely deployed practice of penal transportation to destinations 'beyond the seas'.

Penal transportation became the pre-eminent punishment for felonies. The earliest British statute dates back to 1597, with 'An Act for the punishment of Rogues, Vagabonds and sturdie Beggers' (39 Eliz.1. c.4), and was first practised in 1614, when reprieved convicts were sent to work on plantations in Virginia (Beattie, 2001, Radzinowicz and Hood, 1986). It became an effective policy from 1718 to 1868, its heyday being 1815–52. Around 225,000 people (the majority males) were expelled from Great Britain and Ireland, with perhaps the same number again sentenced but never sent (Shaw, 1966). At first, the destination was America, then Australia, with lesser numbers sent to Bermuda and elsewhere.

Penal transportation equalled exile plus coercion. For the length of the sentence, a convict was required to remain abroad, and to labour. One of the fears of transportation to the American colonies was the implied status as slave, albeit for a fixed duration. In this first phase of transportation, which did not end until the American War of Independence in 1776, the state passed on these property rights over the labour of convicts to shippers, who, in return, bore the cost of passage, knowing that, at the other end, they could sell the convict as an indentured worker. This, of course, had ramifications for who the shippers selected for exile, and how many. Those left languishing in gaols (designed for temporary occupation) could undertake to expel themselves, but the efficacy of 'Do-It-Yourself-Banishment' was muted.

Most convicts were transported to Australia (1788–1868). By this point, the British fiscal-naval state was sufficiently cashed up that it could finance an effective system of transportation, contracting shippers directly. This was essential: here, there was no Chesapeake full of labour-hungry employers. Instead, a colony had to be constructed from scratch. Criminal justice fused with empire, and convicts and their gaolers became shock troops in the British invasion of Australia (Meredith and Oxley, 2007).

British and Australian experiences of transportation were symbiotic. Penal colonies had an inherent tendency to normality: the end of sentence meant emancipation, the birth of children who were free and economic opportunities unavailable in Britain or Ireland, not to mention a more benign and healthier climate and abundant food, as well as, from 1851, gold. Such boons had to be tempered. Horror was an essential ingredient for a government reducing reliance on death but still wedded to exemplary punishment. Each bout of law reform in Britain (1820s, 1840s) was prefigured by an intensification of the penal system in Australia: labour regimes rigidified and freedoms diminished (Meredith and Oxley, 2014). Similarly, each bout of law reform flooded the colonies with more convicts. These became sites of experimentation, especially at locations of secondary punishment like Port Arthur, Norfolk Island and the Female Factories, trialling the separate and silent system, indefinite sentences, the earning of remission, task work and reward, probation, and medical testing. There also followed an interchange of personnel as colonial officials like Alexander Maconochie returned to govern prisons in Britain. Yet, inevitably, the colonies developed, and so, too, did local opposition to convictism. Penal transportation was ended, colony by colony, starting with New South Wales in 1840. Each cessation prompted a prison-building boom in Britain as sentences of transportation were replaced with convict servitude at home ('An Act to substitute, in certain Cases, other Punishment in lieu of Transportation', commonly known as the Penal Servitude Act 1853, 16 & 17 Vict. c.99). When the burgeoning prison estate failed to incarcerate as many as it had transported, the law was changed, returning larceny to summary jurisdiction and the larcenous to houses of correction for short-term detention ('An Act for diminishing Expense and Delay in the Administration of Criminal Justice in certain Cases', commonly known as the Criminal Justice Act 1855, 18 & 19 Vict. c.126).

Could penal transportation have developed without the slave trade? Probably not. The slave trade provided both the mindset that could conceive of the mass movement of people across the oceans, and the technology of ships, shippers and a market in coerced workers. More expensive than death, transportation was cheaper than prison. It provided the empire with colonies (and later wool and wheat), and settlers with labour, consumer demand and a subsidy. It kept the French out. Most significantly, it weaned Britain off the death penalty and it enabled Britain to punish more. It was the single route through which Britain relinquished its unique mix of death and freedom for guilty felons, and reached a new destination in the carceral archipelago.

DEBORAH OXLEY

See also: **Benefit of Clergy; 'Bloody Code', The; Capital Punishment (England and Wales); Slave Trade, The**

Readings

Beattie, J.M. (2001) *Policing and punishment in London 1660–1800.* Oxford: Oxford University Press.

Meredith, D. and Oxley, D. (2007) 'Condemned to the colonies', *Leidschrift,* 22: 19–39.

Meredith, D. and Oxley, D. (2014) 'The convict economy', in S. Ville and G. Withers (eds) *The Cambridge economic history of Australia.* Melbourne: Cambridge University Press, pp 97–121.

Radzinowicz, L. and Hood, R. (1986) *A history of English criminal law and its administration from 1750: Volume 5.* London: Stevens & Sons.

Shaw, A.G.L. (1966) *Convicts and the colonies.* Melbourne: Melbourne University Press.

U

UNDERWORLD, THE CRIMINAL

The concept of a criminal underworld, a subterranean 'other' world inhabited by a 'criminal class', has been a constant in historical discourses. While some historians have referred to medieval and Stuart rogue literature, it is to the explosion of print culture from the 18th century that our modern understanding of the term can be traced. Eighteenth-century print culture did not specifically refer to the underworld; however, the proliferation of criminal biography and increasing crime coverage in the expanding press established a rogue's gallery of criminal types. The highwayman, the thief-whore, the corrupt thief-taker and the criminal gang were familiar staples in this print culture (Shore, 2015). Undoubtedly, urban development, and particularly the growth of London, contributed to the idea of the underworld. Hence, increased urbanisation and migration into cities produced texts that not only entertained, but also provided information and warnings for wary travellers. A thread in this literature can be detected in which the 'world' inhabited by criminals was increasingly portrayed as material and corporeal.

However, it was in the 19th century that the specific terminology of the underworld became common. From this period, in the great urban centres of London, Paris and New York, journalists and other commentators drew on the rhetoric of the criminal underworld in their writing. One of the earliest books to refer to the underworld in its title was the work of the pseudonymic George Ellington, who published *The women of New York; or, the under-world of the great city* in 1869. By the early decades of the 20th century, the use of the term had become fairly common in descriptions and accounts of the urban criminal milieu. In London, one of the first books to extensively describe the underworld in subterranean language was by Thomas Holmes, the secretary of the Howard Association for Penal Reform. In his book, *The London underworld*, published in 1912, there is a clear dichotomy between the upperworld and the underworld. In this text, and others like it, the underworld had become more substantial, a place that existed in the shadows and depths of the city.

Historians have struggled with the concept of the underworld and few have attempted to grapple with it critically (Croll, 2004; Shore, 2015). While there is frequently a consensus that the underworld does not exist in the way described by contemporary commentators and regurgitated by popular historians (Chesney, 1970), the power of the term is difficult to deny. Throughout the 20th century, the impact of the underworld trope moved beyond print culture and into the more formal discourse of politicians and law enforcers. This shift was clearly related to the growth of organised crime in Western Europe and North America. Politicians, police and reformers, concerned about the prevalence of organised crime, exploited the terminology of the underworld in their public prescriptions for fighting crime. For example, in 1928, the reformer Ada Chesterton wrote about the *Women of the underworld*, and between 1928 and 1940, the American journalist Herbert Asbury wrote his histories of the underworld and political corruption in New York, Chicago, San Francisco and New Orleans. The global reporting of gang warfare in American cities, particularly New York and Chicago, and the subsequent explosion of the gangster film genre from the 1930s, fully established the terminology of the underworld into the public vocabulary. Classic 'mob' films, *Little Caesar* (1931), *The public enemy* (1931) and *Scarface* (1932), were hugely influential on popular cultural representations of the underworld. Indeed, the fictionalised representation of Al Capone, played by Paul Muni in *Scarface*, continues to thrill audiences and to shape the mythology of the underworld. The underworld remains a staple paradigm in contemporary discussions about crime. Inevitably, the 'reality' of the overlapping networks that must inform our understandings of the term are difficult to uncover. Thus, press, police and politicians continue to draw on popular cultural representations of the underworld as a means of framing their narrative of serious organised criminality.

HEATHER SHORE

See also: **Criminal Class, The; Organised Crime; Organised Crime (United States of America)**

Readings

Chesney, K. (1970) *The Victorian underworld*. London: Temple Smith.
Chesterton, A. (1928) *Women of the underworld*. London: Stanley Paul.

Croll, A. (2004) 'Who's afraid of the Victorian underworld?', *The Historian*, 84: 30–5.

Ellington, G. (1869) *The women of New York; or, the under-world of the great city*. New York, NY: New York Book Co.

Holmes, T. (1912) *The London underworld*. London: J.M. Dent & Sons.

Shore, H. (2015) *London's criminal underworlds, c. 1720–c. 1930: A social and cultural history*. Basingstoke: Palgrave Macmillan.

UNLAWFUL ASSEMBLY

The common law offences of riot, rout, unlawful assembly and affray were abolished under s 9(1) of the Public Order Act 1986, yet they had been part of English law since the early modern period. In Lambard's *Eirenarcha* of 1591, 'Riot, Route, or other Unlawfull Assemblie, etc.' are described as breaches of the peace that were punishable as misdemeanours (Supperstone, 1981, p 120). In 1840, the Criminal Law Commissioners declared that the division of unlawful assembly, rout and riot, as separate offences was considered 'unnecessary and inconvenient' as the element of unlawful assembly was prevalent in all three. The Commissioners stated that '[I]t seems to be a simpler and more intelligible principle of arrangement to consider the unlawful assembly as the groundwork of the offence and the part execution of the joint design or the motion towards it as aggravations' (Supperstone, 1981, p 121). Therefore, an unlawful assembly was said to consist of:

1. an assembly of three or more persons; and
2. a common purpose (a) to commit a crime of violence or (b) to achieve some other object, whether lawful or not, in such a way as to cause reasonable men to apprehend a breach of the peace (Smith and Hogan, 1973, p 609).

An unlawful assembly then became a rout once members of that assembly *started to move towards* the execution of their 'common purpose' or 'joint design'. Members of the assembly are then guilty of riot when the joint design is either *executed or part executed*.

The offence of unlawful assembly is inescapably linked with the right of freedom of assembly, which affects the liberty of public protest and political activism. Before the Human Rights Act 1998 (HRA) and the incorporation of the European Convention on Human Rights (ECHR), there was no legally defined 'right' of public meeting or freedom of speech. Previously, people were at liberty to exercise freedom of assembly, provided that their actions did not contravene any existing law. Yet, this freedom was subject to the discretion of the judges. For example, in 1936, Lord Hewart CJ emphatically quashed any notion of such rights in *Duncan v Jones*, ruling: 'English Law does not recognize any special right of public meeting for political or other purposes'. Before this, a wide definition of unlawful assembly was provided in *Stephens* (1839) by Justice Patteson, who defined it as 'whenever a body of persons met together in great numbers, in such a manner and under such circumstances as reasonably to excite terror and alarm in the neighbourhood'.

Since the HRA, Article 11 of the ECHR has provided positive legal protection of the right to freedom of assembly in UK law. However, this right is subject to conditions under Article 11(2), which include those that are necessary in the interest of national security or public safety and for the prevention of disorder or crime. Therefore, provisions within the Public Order Act 1986 that permit a chief constable or the Metropolitan Police Commissioner to apply for a ban on public processions do not necessarily conflict with the ECHR. However, they may not prohibit a public assembly (although they can impose conditions relating to duration, number of participants and location). The 1986 Act also created the new statutory offences of riot and violent disorder, which replaced the common law offences relating to unlawful assemblies.

Mead (2010, p 204) emphasises the difference that the HRA had by stating that the move from a 'residual, liberty based system to one based on positive rights brings a shift in the burden of proof'. This means that public authorities must now provide an objective basis for any ban or condition that they impose on public assemblies and all restrictions must be justified in relation to Article 11(2) of the ECHR. Effectively, chief constables are required to enforce the least restrictive measures open to them in relation to the potential for disorder, when imposing conditions on public assemblies.

IAIN CHANNING

See also: **Breach of the Peace; Public Order Law**

Readings

Channing, I. (2015) *The police and the expansion of public order law in Britain, 1829–2014*. Abingdon: Routledge.

Mead, D. (2010) *The new law of peaceful protest: Rights and regulation in the Human Rights Act era*. Oxford: Hart Publishing Ltd.

Smith, J.C. and Hogan, B. (1973) *Criminal law* (3rd edn). London: Butterworths.

Supperstone, M. (1981) *Brownlie's law of public order and national security* (2nd edn). London: Butterworth and Co.

VAGRANCY

Vagrancy is entwined with the criminal law but also with the Poor Law. This is a consequence of the difficulty in defining the vagrant. Tudor legislation made reference to a number of groups that may be considered as vagrants; starting with the Vagabonds and Beggars Act 1494, subsequent legislation referred to Sturdy Beggars, Roaming Beggars and even 'outlandish people calling themselves Egyptians' (Higginbotham, 2016).

There was an additional complication that was crystallised following the 1662 Act for the Better Relief of the Poor. This Act, better known as the Settlement Act, restricted a person's ability to claim poor relief so that such relief was only available in the locality in which they were settled (Humphreys, 1999). Thus, the ability to claim relief when away from that settlement was severely curtailed. Administratively, this posed problems, and following the decision in 1700 to make vagrancy a county charge, policies to deal with vagrancy changed (Eccles, 2012). To deal with this, many counties appointed paid contractors to deal with vagrants or ensure that they were moved onto the next county. There was also an emergent system that saw vagrants tolerated to a greater extent, with Justices of the Peace issuing 'passes' that would allow a vagrant to travel a particular route and maybe even receive some relief through the Poor Law. This clearer link with the Poor Law was one that was to last through to the 20th century.

Vagrancy was still dealt with under the criminal law. An Act of 1744 introduced further measures in an attempt to control 'the number of rogues, vagabonds, and beggars and other disorderly persons [which] daily increases' (Eccles, 2012). Such persons caught under this Act were to be whipped or sent to the house of correction. Importantly, it also made it an offence for a person to return to a parish from which they had been removed as having no settlement. In 1824, further criminal legislation was passed, again seeking to clarify issues surrounding vagrancy and imposing punishments of imprisonment and a month's hard labour. Exceptions were built into the Act so that, for instance, released prisoners could beg their way home. This shows that some connection with poverty and the poor remained. The Poor Law Amendment Act 1834, however, made no mention of vagrancy and so new union workhouses made no provision for the relief of vagrants (Higginbotham, 2016). This, along with a stricter adherence to the Settlement Laws, allowed many unions to avoid relieving vagrants. This was rectified following an order of 1837, which required food and shelter to be provided to any destitute person in 'sudden or urgent necessity'. This was the start of the Poor Law increasing its connection to vagrancy once again.

Workhouses developed 'casual wards' and regulations for dealing with vagrants. The wards were sparse, even for workhouses, and, in theory, a task of work was to be exacted from vagrants. This latter point was enshrined in the Casual Poor Act 1882. Casuals, another name for vagrants, were to be detained for two nights, undertaking a task of work in the full day that they were resident in the workhouse. This was not adhered to by all unions and although attempts were made to enforce a task of work, the vagrant was often released before the second night. Vagrants could also resort to committing petty crime if conditions were found unsuitable – the smashing of workhouse windows, the destruction of workhouse property or being abusive to workhouse staff or Poor Law authorities. These matters would lead to the vagrant going before a magistrate and being sent to gaol (Humphreys, 1999).

The numbers of vagrants fluctuated over the 19th century and it was officially recognised that it was difficult to accurately record numbers as vagrants could be at large, known to the police or in casual wards. Towards the end of the 19th century, there was a general increase in their numbers and so a way-ticket system was reintroduced in some areas allowing vagrants to tramp a designated route over a set period of time. This scheme was administered by the police and also the Poor Law, and was a significant system for dealing with vagrancy by the early 20th century (Higginbotham, 2016).

MATT GARRETT

See also: **Workhouse, The; Workhouse Children**

Readings

Departmental Committee on Vagrancy (1906) *Report of the Departmental Committee on Vagrancy*, Cd. 2852. London: His Majesty's Stationery Office

Eccles, A. (2012) *Vagrancy in law and practice under the old Poor Law*. Farnham: Ashgate Publishing Limited.

Higginbotham, P. (2016) 'The workhouse – tramps & vagrants'. Available at: http://www.workhouses.org.uk/vagrants/index.shtml (accessed 6 December 2016).

Humphreys, R. (1999) *No fixed abode: A history of responses to the roofless and the rootless in Britain*. Basingstoke: Macmillan.

VICTIMOLOGY

While 'victimization is as old as humanity itself' (Fattah, 2000, p 18), the history of victimology is a recent history. Dussich (2006, p 116, emphasis in the original) explains that the term 'victimology' is made up of two elements: 'the Latin word "Victima" which translates into "victim" and the Greek word "logos" which means *a system of knowledge, the direction of something abstract, the direction of teaching, science, and a discipline*'. In a nutshell, if criminology is a discipline concerned with crime and criminality, victimology is a discipline concerned with victims and victimisation. Although victimology as a discipline is relatively recent, criminological discussions about victims can be traced back to the 1700s onwards, wherein victims begin to make an appearance in various works by criminologists (for examples, see Dussich, 2006). Yet, the initial scientific study of victims of crime and the subsequent development of victimology as 'an essential compliment to criminology's well-established research on offenders' did not occur until after the Second World War (Fattah, 2000, p 18).

According to Sebba and Berenblum (2014), the 'veteran writers in the field' of victimology include Van Dijk (1997), Dussich (2006), Fattah (2000, 2010), Kirchoff (2010) and Schneider (2011), while the more contemporary writers of victimological monographs and textbooks comprise Goodey (2001), Spalek (2006) and Walklate (2007) (for more details regarding these writers, see Sebba and Berenblum, 2014).

In all its guises, victimology is concerned with scientifically accumulating, studying and producing quantitative and qualitative data regarding victims and victimisation. This is in order to seek out the precursors to victimisation, including: events, vulnerabilities and the relationship between victims and victimisers; the nature and extent of victimisation; and the experience of victimisation and its aftermath, including public, political and institutional responses to it.

In keeping with criminology, the development of victimology is not mirrored around the world and the extent to which it is established varies (Fattah, 2000). While some 'similarities and commonalities' can be found in some places, 'significant qualitative and even quantitative differences' exist (Fattah, 2000, p 18). However, in more recent times, there has been the establishment of: the World Society of Victimology in 1979 in Munster, Germany; a number of victimological institutes and symposiums in various countries around the world; international journals dedicated to the study of victimology; and various victim assistance programmes and victim services globally.

Indeed, victimology and the landscape of victim campaigns and victim support have been radically transformed since the emergence of the victim within and without academia since the 1940s. Within victimology, concerns have travelled from exploring the role of the victim in order to understand crime, to highlighting forms of victimisation (eg domestic violence), to a critique of criminal justice and service responses to victims, to victims' rights and victim programmes and assistance (including victim therapies), to a more recent focus on resilience, reconciliation and restoration. Central to the latter is the role of the victim in restorative and community justice theories, policies and practices.

According to Fattah (2000), the first systematic approach to *victims of crime* is attributed to Von Hentig's book *The criminal and his victim*. Herein, Von Hentig dedicated his fourth part of the book to the 'provocative title' of 'The victim's contribution to the genesis of the crime' (Fattah, 2000, p 22). Yet, with regard to the discipline of *victimology*, there is no clear agreement on the actual date at which victimology originated. For example, according to Fattah (2000, p 23), 'the need for a science of VICTIMOLOGY' was first stressed by American psychiatrist Wertham in 1949 when he first used the term in his book *The show of violence*. However, Dussich (2006, p 116), in his list of critical dates in victimology, notes that in 1947, 'Mendlesohn coins the term "victimology" in a French journal'. Dussich (2006) designates the establishment of the concept of a 'science to study victims' and of 'the proposed term "victimology"' as located in the early works of Mendlesohn in 1937 and 1940. He contends that these early writings led to the actual proposal of the term 'victimology' in Mendelsohn's seminal article 'A new branch of bio-psycho-social science, victimology' (Dussich, 2006, p 116). It was Mendlesohn who advocated a scientific shift in focus from the study of the criminal to that of the 'victimal' (O'Connell, 2008). Finally, Sebba and Berenblum (2014) consider the origins of victimology to be 1973, the year of the First International Symposium of Victimology.

Both jurists, Mendelsohn and Von Hentig, are deemed by many as 'the founding fathers' of victimology and the 'pioneers of modern victimology' in general, in that they drew academic attention to victims of crime in the 1940s and 1950s (Sebba and Berenblum, 2014, p 10). Mendelsohn and Von Hentig were interested in understanding the relationship between the victim and the offender and they did so by constructing victim typologies (O'Connell, 2008). In so doing, they challenged ideas regarding victim passivity and innocence as they quantitatively classified some victims as 'victim-prone', 'culpable' and 'precipitous'. Thus, initially, the focus was very much rooted in positivistic methods and it concentrated on victims of crime. This was despite Mendelsohn's call for a 'general victimology'.

Domestic and global concern with victims can predominantly be traced to a series of developments that stem from the 1940s onwards. These include: academic interest in the victim, for example, on the part of victimologists and feminists; victim surveys; victim activism (and subsequent initial responses to victimisation in the form of compensation in New Zealand and Great Britain); and other policy responses domestically and internationally. Examples of policy responses include victims' charters in England and Wales (the 2015 Code of Practice for Victims of Crime at the time of writing) and the 1985 United Nations 'Declaration of Basic Principles of Justice for Victims of Crime and Abuse of Power' (United Nations General Assembly, 1985). Victimology was simultaneously influenced by such developments and influential in them.

To date, there are several strands of victimology that have been articulated in different ways, for example: general victimology and penal victimology; positivist, radical and critical victimology; conservative, liberal and radical victimology; victim precipitation theories; lifestyle and routine activities theories; exposure and opportunity theories; social learning and cultural theories and so forth. There has also been a recent interest in the application of a cultural victimology (Walklate et al, 2011) and a visual victimology (Corteen, 2016). O'Connell (2008, p 92) comments that '[d]espite the unresolved scope of victimology', victimological discourse has been dominated by a 'concern for victims of crime'. However, victimology is also associated with emerging disciplines, for example, traumatology and survivorology, and the breadth and depth of victimology, and the concern with victims, victimological and otherwise, is encapsulated in *A companion to crime, harm and victimisation* (Corteen et al, 2016).

The discipline of victimology and the discourses used have prompted many uncertainties, disagreements and disputes to which victimologists have sought to respond and overcome. Sebba and Berenblum (2014) encapsulate the areas of contestation in their overview of the development of the field of victimology. They state that 'questions and controversies' regarding victimology are connected to:

> its historical roots, the extent of its autonomy as a field or discipline, its relationship with criminology, its dual identities as a branch of academic research on the one hand and an ideologically driven social movement on the other, and its ambivalent relationships with

conservative politics, radical criminology and different strands of feminism. (Sebba and Berenblum, 2014, p 8)

To conclude, contemporary victimology prioritises victims and victimisation, including victims of crime and victims of harm. It is concerned with pre-victimisation, victimisation and post-victimisation. While victims of crime still feature highly in the discipline of victimology, the nature of victimological concerns, debates and research is increasingly diverse. Whether it is a sub-discipline of criminology, an extension of criminology or a discipline in its own right remains under discussion. Nevertheless, it is a burgeoning dynamic area of multidisciplinary academic interest, research, policy and practice.

KAREN CORTEEN

See also: **Criminology; Victims**

Readings

Corteen, K. (2016) 'Visual victimology', in K. Corteen, S. Morley, P. Taylor and J. Turner (eds) *A companion to crime, harm and victimisation*. Bristol: Policy Press, pp 266–9.

Corteen, K., Morley, S., Taylor, P. and Turner, J. (2016) (eds) *A companion to crime, harm and victimisation*. Bristol: Policy Press.

Dussich, J.P. (2006) 'Victimology – past, present and future', Resource Material Series no 7. Available at: http://www.unafei.or.jp/english/pdf/RS_No70/No70_00All.pdf

Fattah, E.A. (2000) 'Victimology: past, present and future', *Criminologie*, 33: 17–46. Available at: https://www.erudit.org/revue/crimino/2000/v33/n1/004720ar.pdf

O'Connell, M. (2008) 'Victimology: a social science in waiting?', *International Review of Victimology*, 15: 91–104.

Sebba, L. and Berenblum, T. (2014) 'Victimology and the sociology of new disciplines: a research agenda', *International Review of Victimology*, 20(1): 7–30.

United Nations General Assembly (1985) 'Declaration of Basic Principles of Justice for Victims of Crime and Abuse of Power: resolution/adopted by the General Assembly', A/RES/40/34. Available at: http://www.refworld.org/docid/3b00f2275b.html

Walklate, S., Mythen, G. and McGarry, R. (2011) 'Witnessing Wootton Bassett: an exploration in cultural victimology', *Crime, Media, Culture*, 7(2): 149–65.

VICTIMS

The concept of a 'victim' has a long history; it can be traced back to ancient societies, including Babylonia, Palestine, Greece and Rome. The word is derived from the Latin 'victima', referring to an animal or living sacrifice (Merriam-Webster, 2016). More broadly, it was associated with the notion of suffering, sacrifice and death. In relation to the committing of a crime or harm by an offender or offenders, the victim or victim's family would exact what they perceived to be an appropriate response to the crime committed against them. This idea of retribution is also evident in a number of religious texts with the principle of 'an eye for an eye'. This response to crime posed many problems, for example, inconsistencies in the level of punishments being administered to the offender/s, and blood feuds because of the perceived harshness or brutality of the 'punishment' by the offender or offender's family. It was thought that the punishment should be equal to the crime committed. Prior to this the Code of Hammurabi, dating back to approximately 1754 BC (Prince, 1904), was an attempt to establish a scale of punishments in accordance with the perceived severity of the crime. It is considered to be one of the first known attempts to establish a written code of conduct by the state. However, this was a time when personal retribution was the only resolution for criminal matters.

Since this early attempt to establish a system/set of punishments, there have been a number of developments, including the Magna Carta of England (1215). This charter was issued to grant basic liberties for citizens and rights to victims of abuses of power. This early period was also a time of increasing state control that saw the beginnings of the demise of the victim in resolving criminal matters. Despite this, victims continued to be active in bringing offenders to 'justice'. This situation remained largely unchanged for centuries, with the most significant developments taking place in the 19th century. The 19th century saw the further demise of the victim with the emergence of formal law enforcement, courts and punishment, with the state assuming responsibility for prosecuting offenders (Godfrey and Lawrence, 2005). Alongside developments that marginalised victims in the resolution of crime, more recently, there has been the emergence of the victim rights movement in response to Second World War atrocities. Since the emergence of this movement, there have been a number of codes/charters introduced, particularly within national and international criminal justice systems. These include but are not limited to:

- 1957 in the UK, Margery Fry proposed the introduction of victims' compensation.
- 1963, New Zealand enacted the first Criminal Compensation Act.
- 1965, California was the first state in the US to introduce victim compensation.
- 1966, Japan enacted the Criminal Indemnity Law.

- 1966, the US started to survey victims of crime who did not report it to the police.
- 1967, Canada created a Criminal Compensation Injuries Act (as did Cuba and Switzerland).
- 1985, the United Nations (UN) adopted the 'Declaration of Basic Principles of Justice for Victims of Crime and Abuses of Power'.
- 2005, the UN extended the rights and principles to include victims of international crimes.

Although there has been the introduction of a number of codes, charters and guidance, what is lacking is the legal teeth to enforce them. Without this, the effectiveness of the codes and charters will always be patchy and weak. Victims' rights will only be taken seriously if they are enshrined in law; indeed, 'work continues in the UK and elsewhere to continue to orientate criminal justice policy and practice that is victim-sensitive' (Carver et al, 2016, p 6).

The first systematic analysis within academia of victims of crime was undertaken by Von Hentig (1948) in his work *The criminal and his victims*. He contended that many victims of crime contributed to their own victimisation, either by inciting/provoking the criminal, or creating or fostering a situation likely to lead to the commissioning of a crime. This social construction of a victim has changed over time and is most evident not only in the works of Von Hentig, but also in relation to victim culpability (Mendelsohn, 1956), victim precipitation (Amir, 1971) and the 'ideal victim' (Christie, 1986). It is also evident in more contemporary works, for example: Stanko's (1985) work on feminist victimology; Karmen's (2016) work on survivorology, which focuses on the resilience of victims of crime; and Spencer and Walklate's (2016) work on critical criminology. Historically and contemporarily, the term 'victim' has been inconsistently applied in various arenas of criminal justice, criminal law and academia. This inconsistency impacts on whether a victim is visible or invisible and thus whether they are publically, politically or officially responded to.

SHARON MORLEY

See also: **Victimology**

Readings

Amir, M. (1971) *Patterns of forcible rape*. Chicago, IL: University of Chicago Press.

Carver, L., Morley, S. and Taylor, P. (2016) 'Voices of deficit: mental health, criminal victimisation and epistemic injustice', *Illness, Crisis and Loss*, 25(1): 43–62.

Christie, N. (1986) 'The ideal victim', in E.A. Fattah (ed) *From crime policy to victim policy*. London: Macmillan.

Godfrey, B. and Lawrence, P. (2005) *Crime and justice 1750–1950*. Cullompton: Willan.

Karmen, A. (2016) 'Survivology', in K. Corteen, S. Morley, P. Taylor and J. Turner (eds) *A companion to crime, harm and victimisation*. Bristol: The Policy Press.

Mendlesohn, B. (1956) 'A new branch of bio-psychological science: La Victimology', *Revue International de Criminologie et de Police Technique*, 10: 782–9.

Merriam-Webster (2016) 'Victims', in Merriam-Webster (ed) *Webster's dictionary*. Springfield, MA: G. & C. Merriam Company, Publishers. Available at: https://www.merriam-webster.com/dictionary/victim

Prince, D. (1904) 'The Code of Hammurabi', *The American Journal of Theology*, 8(3): 601–9. Available at: http://www.jstor.org/stable/3153895

Spencer, D.C. and Walklate, S. (eds) (2016) *Reconceptualizing critical victimology: Interventions and possibilities*. Maryland, MD: Lexington Books.

Stanko, E. (1985) *Intimate intrusions: Women's experience of male violence*. London: Routledge & Kegan Paul.

United Nations (1985) 'Declaration of Basic Principles of Justice for Victims of Crime and Abuse of Power', A/RES/40/43, 29 November. Available at: http://www.un.org/documents/ga/res/40/a40r034.htm

Von Hentig, H. (1948) *The criminal and his victim*. New Haven, CT: Yale University Press.

VIOLENCE

In the Middle Ages, lethal interpersonal violence, feuds and murderous grudges were 'a relatively common element in medieval life' (Spierenburg, 2008, p 17). Both the ordinary citizens and the social elites settled their differences with lethal violence. Gradually, however, mechanisms for private reconciliation and recompense were introduced, and by c1600, a significant decline in homicide rates was underway (Eisner, 2001). Indeed, the available indicators suggest that the murder rate fairly steadily declined from the end of the 17th century to the mid-20th century. The 1960s were a historical low for murders, and rates during the 20th century seem to have remained relatively stable, excepting a modest rise at the end of the century. The murder rate has been seen as something of a gold standard in charting levels of violence in society, but murders are relatively infrequent and it may be that the volume crimes of violence, for example, common assaults, are a better index of how violent society was at any given point.

Considering more minor violence, the numbers of assaults, domestic attacks, street fights and drunken pub brawls dwarfed the number of murders committed each year. When criminal statistics were first annually published from 1857, they showed a rise in the number of prosecutions for petty violence, which continued until the 1880s. This confirmed the views of contemporary opinion formers in the newspapers and pamphlets who believed that society was becoming more violent. They asserted that, while the upper and middle classes had learnt more civilised ways of behaving, the working classes (and particularly Irish immigrants) solved their disputes with violence (see Wood, 2004). Gatrell (1980) put it another way, stating that the realities of working-class life in the industrial cities of the UK created social alienation, poverty and competition for space and resources, which created conflict between neighbours and intimates. The figures could just have easily peaked because the police were keen to control the public streets and curb the behaviour of drunken and violent men in public. However, after the highpoints of the 1880s, the statistics on violence began to decline rapidly, falling away to an all-time low by the 1920s. It is possible that the rises in the quality of life for ordinary people had reduced violence-inducing tensions in the cities. If so, then was a fall in the quality of life responsible for the rise in violence between 1920 and the 1990s? This is a difficult question to answer.

It is clear that historians and criminologists are by no means agreed on the extent or meaning of violence and violent crime in history. Changes in public attitudes to violence, police recording procedures and mechanisms, the operation of the criminal justice system, and alterations in actual levels of offending are all likely to be involved in any explanation of the changing nature of violent crime. As Godfrey and Lawrence (2014) noted, deciding whether the violence statistics represent changing levels of public sensitivity to violence, variation in reporting practices or real changes in patterns of offending is hard to establish with any degree of certainty. The sustained attack on patterns of male violence by the courts, the increased capability of the state to survey and control its population, and changing public sensibilities towards inappropriate aggression all have a part to play in explaining changing patterns of violent crime. However, it should always be remembered that violence in domestic houses and children's institutions, which takes place against those in society who do not have access to justice in the courts, often remains unprosecuted and therefore hidden in the criminal statistics.

BARRY GODFREY

See also: **Criminal Statistics; Lethal Violence (in Scotland); Women and Violent Crime**

Readings

Eisner, M. (2001) 'Modernization, self-control and lethal violence – the long-term dynamics of European homicide rates in theoretical perspective', *British Journal of Criminology*, 41: 618–38.

Gatrell, V.A.C. (1980) 'The decline of theft and violence in Victorian and Edwardian England', in V.A.C. Gatrell, B. Lenman and G. Parker (eds) *Crime and the law: The social history of crime in Western Europe since 1500*. London: Europa, pp 238–337.

Godfrey, B. and Lawrence, P. (2014) *Crime and justice since 1750*. London: Routledge.

Spierenburg, P. (2008) *A history of murder: Personal violence in Europe from the Middle Ages to the present*. Cambridge: Polity Press.

Wood, J.C. (2004) *The shadow of our refinement: Violence and crime in nineteenth-century England*. New York, NY: Routledge.

WALES, CRIME AND PUNISHMENT

The history of the regulation of wrongdoing in Wales differs significantly from that in England and the effects of that difference continued to be felt long after the jurisdictions were formally assimilated. Native medieval Welsh Law, the so-called Laws of Hywel Dda, depended heavily on what are usually known as principles of feud and compensation (though neither term is without problem), enforceable by and against kindred groups in the absence of an adequate overarching state machinery of justice. Homicide and the important medieval offence to honour, 'sarhaed', for instance, were both emendable in this way (Jenkins, 1986; Ireland, 2015). While basic principles of English criminal law were introduced into parts of Wales in 1284, the earlier principles of emendation rather than punishment for wrongdoing survived in varying degrees, notably, in the Marcher Lordships outside these areas. Henry VIII's legislation formally imposed English Law on all of Wales, though separate courts administered it, most notably, the superior criminal court of Great Sessions, which existed until 1830 (Watkin, 2012; Ireland, 2015).

The irregular distribution of Justices of the Peace and, much later, of the police, combined with strong traditions of compensation and self-help, the active role of the Church in dispute settlement (later, too, with the rise of Nonconformity, a Church increasingly seen as antithetical to the official religion of the law), strong social bonds, and, in particular perhaps, the prohibition of the use of the Welsh language in court, meant that 'crimes' might often be dealt with by the immediate parties or the community as a whole rather than by submission to the 'English' legal system. The much-remarked absence of serious crime in Wales in the 19th century, which led to its reputation as the 'Land of White Gloves' after the symbolic gift to the judge at an assize with no criminal cases, is partly a result of this tendency, and also of the associated reluctance of Welsh juries (often, like the defendants themselves, unable to follow the evidence presented in English) to convict. There are traces of a reluctance to cooperate with official legal processes and a preference for extra-curial settlements even in cases of homicide as late as the second half of the 19th century, as well as the informal community threat of, or use of, violence in ritualised displays of condemnation of wrongdoers, such as the 'ceffyl pren' ('wooden horse') of South-West Wales, long after the latter practice was in decline in England (Ireland, 2015).

Communal activity and ritual display were also evident in social protests such as the 'Rebecca Riots' and 'Tithe Wars' of the 19th century, with traces as well in the political and industrial protests that marked clashes with authority in that century and beyond. Of these latter, the activities of the 'Scotch Cattle' of the 1820s and 1830s, the Merthyr Rising of 1831 and that at Newport in 1839, and the Tonypandy Riots of 1910 are perhaps the most well known (Jones, 1992, 1996). Protest in support of the Welsh language became significant from the 1960s and a range of social and political motivations lay behind a number of more extreme actions in that decade and beyond, including the use of explosives against a series of targets and, beginning later, a campaign of the burning of holiday homes. Although these activities might proclaim a distinctively 'Welsh' dimension, the mundane reality of crime and the response to it apparently became more similar to that of England within the 20th century. A number of smaller police forces were amalgamated and a number of Welsh prisons were closed. The difference between rural and urban Wales, always significant in charting the rate and extent of the changes outlined earlier, remained, though a decline in the heavy industry that had underwritten the Industrial Revolution brought new problems of criminality in its wake (Ireland, 2015). The prohibition on the use of Welsh in the courts, which dated from 1536, was relaxed by statute in 1942 and its status was further enhanced by legislation of 1967 and 1993 (Watkin, 2012).

RICHARD W. IRELAND

See also: **Australia, Crime, Law and Punishment; Scottish Criminal Courts, The (c.1747–1850)**

Readings

Ireland, R.W. (2015) *Land of white gloves: A history of crime and punishment in Wales.* Abingdon: Routledge.

Jenkins, D. (1986) *Hywel Dda: The law.* Cardiff: University of Wales Press.

Jones, D. (1992) *Crime in nineteenth century Wales.* Cardiff: University of Wales Press.

Jones, D. (1996) *Crime and policing in the twentieth century: The South Wales experience.* Cardiff: University of Wales Press.

Watkin, T.G. (2012) *The legal history of Wales* (2nd edn). Cardiff: University of Wales Press.

WATCH COMMITTEES

Watch committees were in charge of the policing of boroughs (towns or cities) and were responsible for appointing, paying and supervising those who watched the streets and brought offenders to justice. Watch committees were arguably the most democratic form of policing that England and Wales have had.

Watch committees were first set up in London in the 18th century, when Parliament passed a number of watch Acts that allowed inner-city parishes to organise paid night watches (Reynolds, 1998). The Municipal Corporations Act 1835 extended the system to the 178 towns and cities that enjoyed borough status. Each elected borough council was required to form a subcommittee, the watch committee, which was responsible for policing the town. The ex-officio chairman was the mayor, and it was regarded as the most prestigious subcommittee on which to serve (Steedman, 1984). Watch committees continued in their work until 1964 (Critchley, 1972).

The 1835 Act stipulated that the watch committee must 'appoint a sufficient Number of fit Men ... to act as Constables for preserving the Peace by Day and Night and preventing Robberies and other Felonies, and apprehending Offenders against the Peace' (5 & 6 Will. IV, c.76; LXVII). Some watch committees did not trouble to set up a police force at all. When the County and Borough Police Act 1856 set up the system of county policing, it established a system of inspection that was also applied to the borough forces. The Act promised a government grant to watch committees if their force was 'efficient'. Inspections were annual, taking place on just one day, and perfunctory: efficiency was measured by looking at manpower and inspecting the men.

Watch committees could be very active, setting out precisely what they wanted the police in their town to do, often giving them duties such as manning the firefighting equipment and checking on street lighting. Whereas county constabulary chief constables were virtually unassailable once in office, borough chief constables were sometimes sacked summarily by their watch committee. Watch committees met every one or two weeks, and in the minutes, one may find the chief constable called to account for what he is doing about a specific crime, such as a murder or serious robbery, or to explain how he will tackle disorderly behaviour on the street. For example, in Liverpool in 1890, the newly elected watch committee directed Chief Constable Nott-Bower to close the city's brothels (Taylor, 1997). The Chief Constable protested that this would make the problem of prostitution in the city worse; he appealed to the Home Secretary, who refused to intervene on the grounds that he had no power to direct or restrict the decisions of a watch committee. Nott-Bower implemented the policy, though he did have the satisfaction (as he claimed) of being right.

The shortcomings of the absolute power of the watch committee were exposed in 1956 when Captain Athelstan Popkess, Chief Constable of the city of Nottingham, investigated corruption in the city council (Cowley, 2011). His investigations came to nothing but the watch committee then demanded that Popkess report to them the details of his enquiries. He refused on the grounds that they had no right to involve themselves in the enforcement of criminal law, whereupon the watch committee suspended Popkess. The Home Secretary became involved, but while he deplored the committee's actions, he had no power to prevent them.

Watch committees were very jealous of their independence. The Inspectors of Constabulary often urged smaller boroughs to consolidate their police with their surrounding counties, that is, to give up the watch committee's main role, but very few did until forced to do so by the Police Act 1946, which merged 45 borough forces with their neighbouring county force. These watch committees continued to exist, with residual duties such as street lighting, until the Police Act 1964, after which all borough forces were merged and watch committees ceased to exist (Critchley, 1972). The control of all police forces was now in the hands of police authorities and the Home Secretary.

GUY WOOLNOUGH

See also: 'New' Police, The; Nightwatchmen; Parish Constables

Readings

Cowley, R. (2011) *A history of the British police*. Stroud: The History Press.

Critchley, T.A. (1972) *A history of police in England and Wales*. Montclair, NJ: Patterson Smith.

Reynolds, E.A. (1998) *Before the bobbies: The night watch and police reform in metropolitan London, 1720–1830*. Stanford, CA: Stanford University Press.

Steedman, C. (1984) *Policing the Victorian community: The formation of English provincial police forces, 1856–1880*. Abingdon: Routledge, Kegan, Paul.

Taylor, D. (1997) *The new police in nineteenth-century England: Crime, conflict and control*. Manchester: Manchester University Press.

WHITECHAPEL MURDERS OF 1888, THE

In the late summer and autumn of 1888, the east end of London was thrown into panic by a series of brutal murders that claimed the lives of at least five women. The killer was never caught and was soon given the descriptive sobriquet of 'Jack the Ripper'. The victims, all street prostitutes, were murdered and (with one exception – Elizabeth Stride) their bodies were mutilated, with the attacks concentrating on the abdomen of the women. Researchers have generally accepted that there were five 'canonical' victims – Mary 'Polly' Nichols, Annie Chapman, 'Long Liz' Stride, Kate Eddowes and Mary (or Marie-Jane) Kelly – though there is considerable speculation as to the exact number of killings attributable to 'Jack'.

The mystery surrounding the killer's identity has led to over 120 years of research and speculation, and well over 100 possible suspects have been mooted. A whole sub-genre of 'true crime' has arisen, dubbed 'Ripperology', and, every year, dozens of books and television documentaries attempt to solve history's greatest cold case. The lack of any real 'evidence' (in the form of surviving archival or other material) has allowed an entire industry to emerge, fuelled by amateur sleuths (Begg, 2013; Rumbelow, 2004). Until recently, academic historians and criminologists have largely chosen to avoid the subject but new ways of looking at the case, from a cultural and social history perspective, have now tempted a few to give it serious thought (Gray, 2010; Warwick and Willis, 2008).

The murders have been used (by contemporaries and subsequent authors) to highlight the harsh reality of life in Whitechapel in the late 19th century. The poverty and degradation witnessed by journalists and social commentators drawn to the area in the wake of the killings arguably caused as much shock and concern as the murders themselves. Stark contrasts have been drawn between conditions in the east end and those in the more affluent west end of the capital. The murders also coincided with movements for political and social change (such as the rise of trade unions, socialism, slum clearance and temperance), allowing many interested parties to deploy the killings as a metaphor for the parlous moral and economic state of what was contemporaneously termed 'the abyss'.

The role of the press has been highlighted as fundamental to the perpetuation of interest in the case and to the social construction of Whitechapel and its occupants. Newspapers such as *The Star* used sensational reporting of the murders to generate sales, while campaigning editors (like William Stead of the *Pall Mall Gazette*) took advantage of the police's inability to capture the killer to criticise the government or hierarchy of the Metropolitan Police.

The case is also noteworthy for the way in which the public engaged with the murders and the reportage that surrounded them. Hundreds of letters and postcards were sent to the press and police, either offering advice in catching the killer or claiming to be from the murderer himself. The most famous of these are the 'Dear Boss' letter (sent to the central news agency in September 1888) and the 'From Hell' note that was received by the head of the Whitechapel Vigilance Society, Mr Lusk; the latter was accompanied by a piece of human kidney supposedly removed from the body of Catherine Eddowes. It is widely believed that the 'Dear Boss' letter was fabricated by a journalist working for *The Star* and that most, if not all, of the 'Ripper' correspondence was hoax. This tremendous public interaction with the mystery has undoubtedly contributed to its enduring fascination.

The murders were brutal and on a scale not experienced in Britain since the Ratcliffe Highway killings of 1811. All five of the 'canonical' victims had their throats cut and Martha Tabram (not always considered to be a true 'Ripper' victim) was stabbed 49 times. Chapman and Nichols had organs removed and Kelly's body was virtually annihilated. Kelly was the only victim to be murdered indoors and the killer's destruction of her corpse was captured in one of the very first scene-of-crime photographs taken by the police.

The murder of Kelly, in particular, has fuelled speculation as to the identity of the killer, with perhaps the most prevailing myth being the involvement of the Freemasons and the royal family. Most suspects fall into a tripartite typology of 'aristocratic milord', mad doctor or deviant immigrant, and these are most likely derived from a memorandum in the papers of Sir Melville McNaughten who was made Assistant Chief Constable of the Metropolitan Police in 1889. The memo, dated 1894, was revealed in response to a claim by the *Sun* newspaper that a Thomas Cutbush was 'Jack the Ripper'. McNaughten named three men (Montague Druitt, Kosminski and Michael Ostrog) and thereafter most 'Ripper' suspects have fitted one of these 'types'.

It is unlikely that the case will ever be solved to the satisfaction of the army of 'Ripperologists', and in recent years, while theories abound, several writers have turned their attention to researching the lives of the women that were murdered. At last, perhaps, the victims of the 'Ripper' are receiving the recognition they deserve.

DREW GRAY

See also: **Broadsides; Crime Fiction; Crime Pamphlets; Violence**

Readings
Begg, P. (2013) *Jack the Ripper: The definitive history.* Abingdon: Routledge.

Gray, D. (2010) *London's shadows: The dark side of the Victorian city*. London: Continuum.

Rumbelow, D. (2004) *The complete Jack the Ripper*. London: Penguin.

Warwick, A. and Willis, M. (2008) *Jack the Ripper: Media, culture, history*. Manchester: Manchester University Press.

WHITE-COLLAR CRIME

The term 'white-collar crime' was coined by sociologist Edwin Sutherland, and has typically been presented as a modern 20th-century crime type. With few exceptions, criminologists and crime historians have largely ignored the roots of such activities; yet, these roots can be traced back much further than the 20th century. As Robb (1992, p 298) has noted: 'The real origins of white-collar crime lie almost two hundred years in the past in the tremendous financial growth which accompanied the British Industrial Revolution'.

By at least the mid-19th century, a transformation in the nature of commercial enterprise was underway – from one dominated by small-scale capitalism, where individual ownership was typical, to a system of multi-ownership. Beginning with the railway industry, business was increasingly based on the joint-stock model, in which large numbers of shareholders purchased an investment stake in a company. Joint-stock businesses were able to generate unprecedented amounts of capital, and operated at a level beyond that of traditional enterprise. The scale of business heralded various significant changes, which provided new opportunities for criminality among those in respectable, white-collar positions. Joint-stock companies employed new armies of clerks and other white-collar staff, created a more distant working relationship (and therefore weaker personal bonds) between employers and employees, increased the complexity of commercial dealings, and greatly expanded the need for trust within the workplace. Alongside these changes, systems of internal auditing and accounting were often grossly inadequate in detecting dishonesty, leaving businesses vulnerable and enabling some offenders to remain undetected for longer periods of time. Lawmakers were also slow to recognise, and legislate effectively against, the plethora of opportunities for fraudulence that grew out of the new environment.

Collectively, these factors facilitated the proliferation of white-collar crime to such an extent that one contemporary labelled the 19th century 'the era of fraud and embezzlement' (cited in Locker, 2004, p 7). Chiefly vulnerable was the joint-stock company, and such was the scale of its vulnerability to white-collar offending that a number of commentators referred to the issue as the most pressing crime problem of the period. For instance, in 1860, author and social commentator Charles Dickens stated that 'the leading delinquency of the present day, is the robbery of joint stock companies by confidential servants' (cited in Locker, 2004, p 77).

As the 19th century progressed, the white-collar criminal became an increasingly familiar figure within the Victorian psyche, with incidents of fraud and embezzlement passing daily through the courtroom (Locker, 2008, p 117). For example, by the 1870s, the number of embezzlement prosecutions increased fourfold on previous totals, and continued to rise steadily for the remainder of the century. This increase was undoubtedly a product of the expansion of summary jurisdiction for the prosecution of certain embezzlement offences; nevertheless, such changes brought certain varieties of white-collar crime increasingly to the forefront of public awareness (Wiener, 1994; Locker, 2004).

Notwithstanding the fact that a growing amount of white-collar crime was publicly punished, and its public presence increased, scholars have typically signalled that the bulk of such offending remained hidden as employers chose to deal with it through private channels – either owing to concerns about destabilising investor confidence, or in the spirit of benevolence and paternalism towards otherwise respectable employees. However, such claims are overstated. In the case of white-collar offenders, much of the private character of 19th-century justice was, in fact, necessitated by deficiencies in legislative provision, as well as in the difficulties of acquiring sufficient legal proof to determine the precise character of 'financial irregularities' and therefore proceed to the courtroom. Indeed, companies expressed considerable frustration at not having recourse to the law. In its place, private justice could be far from benevolent, and some employers dealt very punitively with suspected or proven fraudsters, including going to considerable lengths to limit their future prospects (Locker, 2005).

JOHN LOCKER

See also: Respectable Criminal, The

Readings

Locker, J.P. (2004) 'This most pernicious species of crime: embezzlement in its public and private dimensions, c. 1850–1930', unpublished PhD, Keele University.

Locker, J.P. (2005) 'Quiet thieves, quiet punishment: private responses to the respectable offender, c. 1850–1930', *Crime, History & Societies*, 9(1): 9–31.

Locker, J.P. (2008) 'The paradox of the "respectable offender": responding to the problem of white-collar crime in Victorian and Edwardian England', in H. Johnston (ed) *Punishment and control in historical perspective*. Basingstoke: Palgrave Macmillan, pp 115–34.

Robb, G. (1992) *White-collar crime in modern England: Financial fraud and business morality, 1845–1929*. Cambridge: Cambridge University Press.

Wiener, M. (1994) *Reconstructing the criminal: Culture, law, and policy in England, 1830–1914*. Cambridge: Cambridge University Press.

WOMEN AND VIOLENT CRIME

Women were only a small proportion of the individuals charged with violent offences in 19th-century England and Wales. Violent crimes also constituted the minority of both indictable and summary convictions received by women in this period.

The majority of violent crime carried out by women was against other adults. While murders committed by women, especially against spouses or lovers, were sensationalised in the Victorian press and have received some of the greatest attention from historians of crime, the majority of violence committed by women was non-fatal. Primarily, the violent crimes that women perpetrated were low-level assaults against other adults. Among all women, prostitutes, and those who heavily used alcohol, were particularly likely to be apprehended and charged with violent crimes of this nature, and especially with violent crimes against the police.

Women committed acts of violence regardless of class or social situation. However, the overwhelming number of women apprehended as violent offenders, and for whom newspaper reports of summary appearances or criminal registers of higher trials exist, were working-class women. In crowded and poorly provisioned houses, women fought over the distribution of resources, over money lent and borrowed, and over perceived slights to social standing. Women fought or assaulted others to prove points or in order to settle scores (Davies, 1999). Much like their male counterparts, women used violence to negotiate issues of property, reputation, status and honour (Archer, 2011). In serious cases of assault and wounding, weapons were used, though this was as likely to be whatever implements came to hand – a glass, a fire poker, a shoe – as a recognised weapon like a knife. More often than not, though, women launched violent attacks or fought with nothing more than their fists and feet. Women were not only the perpetrators of this kind of violent crime, but also often victims. Again, prostitutes were highly vulnerable to becoming victims of violent crime, not only from their customers or the police, but also from other street workers (D'Cruze 1998). Many of the assaults and woundings that saw women brought to court as perpetrators of violent crime were against other women with whom they worked, lived and socialised.

Evidence suggests that women were also not insignificant in number as perpetrators of domestic violence. However, due to the infrequency of prosecutions of this kind brought by men against women and the difficulty of recovering the voices of male victims of female violence, it is difficult to say much with any certainty about the commonality and nature of domestic violence by women.

Women were also those prosecuted most frequently for violent crimes against children. These crimes were not common, but were made highly visible by newspaper coverage when they did occur. In particular, infanticide and neonaticide were violent crimes almost wholly associated with women. While there were several high-profile cases in which women were convicted for the murder or manslaughter of other people's children (best known as the practice of 'baby farming'), most of the harm done to children was by their own parents. Conditions such as puerperal mania (which would now be recognised as post-natal depression or a similar mental health issue), and social and economic difficulties, were overwhelmingly responsible for the violent crimes that women perpetrated against children. Similar to women's violence against other adults, the majority of violent crimes that women perpetrated against children were non-violent. Towards the end of the 19th century, a heightened awareness of child neglect and more specific forms of violent abuse committed against children saw more women brought to court. During the 19th century, women committed, and were convicted of, a range of violent crime. However, though popular fiction cast them as vicious 'femme fatales' or tragic child killers, the reality was somewhat different. Female violence was perpetrated by and against adults, with the majority of convictions for violence falling upon women from the working class. Typically, women's violence was non-fatal and dealt with at a summary level. Police courts handed out fines, admonishments and short custodial sentences to the women that assaulted, or fought with, their friends, relatives, neighbours or the police.

LUCY WILLIAMS

See also: **Marital Violence; National Society for the Prevention of Cruelty to Children; Sexual Assault**

Readings

Archer, J. (2011) *The monster evil: Policing and violence in Victorian Liverpool.* Liverpool: University of Liverpool Press.

Davies, A. (1999) "'These viragoes are no less cruel than the lads'": young women, gangs, and violence in late Victorian Manchester and Salford', *British Journal of Criminology*, 319(1): 72–89.

D'Cruze, S. (1998) *Crimes of outrage: Sex, violence and Victorian working women.* London: University College London Press.

WORKHOUSE, THE

The word 'workhouse' has long been associated with a cruel and discredited Victorian regime. The notorious workhouse system was established by the Poor Law Amendment Act 1834, though 'poor houses' had existed since Elizabethan times. This Act applied to England and Wales; the Irish and Scottish Poor Law Amendment Acts were introduced in 1838 and 1845, respectively. The Scottish 'poorhouse' was not as tactically important as the English and Welsh workhouses (Englander, 1998). However, the Poor Law was much more stringently applied in Ireland, especially during the famine years of the 1840s. The English and Wales Act 1834 generated both censure and support; between 1837 and 1842, *The Times* wrote more than two million words on the new Poor Law and related hundreds of 'horror' stories about workhouses, though many of the more sensationalist pieces proved to be untrue.

The 1834 Act determined that all relief to able-bodied paupers and their dependants should only be given in workhouses, with families separated on arrival. Inmates were segregated according to age, gender and capability in order to provide specialised treatment, as a deterrent and to prevent moral and physical contagion (Driver, 1993). While able-bodied husbands and wives continued to be separated, in 1847, elderly married couples were allowed to share a room. Many workhouse residents were not long-stay inmates, but applied for admission as and when they needed extra help, and left (sometimes without one or more of their children) when their prospects had improved. While no adult was forced to enter a workhouse, in times of great need, it could well have been the only solution available for many poor people.

The principle of 'less eligibility' was also included in the new law, which intended that the standard of living in workhouses was to be lower than that of the poorest independent labourer. In reality, both intentions were unfeasible in practice as a huge number of new workhouses would have had to be built to house all of the recipients of relief, and if workhouse inmates were fed on the diet of the poorest labourers, they would likely starve. Nonetheless, a concrete deterrent remained owing to the widely held punitive and humiliating reputation of the workhouse and its generally forbidding 'Bastille'-type structure.

Guardians of Poor Law Unions across Wales and England were, in theory, answerable to the central Poor Law authorities in London. However, many directives and recommendations issued by them were not always replicated by individual unions and some harsher principles appear to have been mitigated by the 'goodwill' of individual guardians (Henriques, 1968). Conversely, it was never the intention of the Poor Law authorities to starve and mistreat workhouse inmates, but there were abuses of the system at the local level. At Andover workhouse in Kent, the workhouse diet was so meagre that inmates who were employed to crush bones in order to produce crop fertiliser took to eating the gristle and marrow of the mildewed and rotten bones. The subsequent inquiry found dishonesty and fraud by the workhouse master, Colin McDougal, and neglect by the guardians' visiting committee (Crowther, 1981).

One of the foremost charges against conditions in workhouses was that they were overcrowded. This was in some part because several unions refused to build expensive new workhouses, and also because considerable numbers of inmates were sick, disabled or elderly. In the 1860s, workhouse medical officer Dr Joseph Rogers along with *The Lancet* were responsible for exposing the overcrowding, poor hygiene and lack of isolation wards in London workhouses (Hulonce, 2016). By the end of the 19th century, many separate workhouse infirmaries had been built and the majority of workhouse inmates were the elderly and the sick. While many health outcomes relied upon the conduct and characters of individual workhouse medical officers and local Poor Law guardians, workhouse inmates (especially women and children) were nevertheless more likely to receive medical treatment than poor independent labourers.

LESLEY HULONCE

See also: **Vagrancy; Workhouse Children**

Readings
Crowther, M.A. (1981) *The workhouse system 1834–1929*. London: Methuen.
Driver, F. (1993) *Power and pauperism, the workhouse system, 1834–1884.* Cambridge: Cambridge University Press.
Englander, D. (1998) *Poverty and Poor Law reform in nineteenth century Britain, 1834–1914*. London: Longman.
Henriques, U. (1968) 'How cruel was the Victorian Poor Law?', *The Historical Journal*, XI(2): 365–71.
Hulonce, L. (2016) *Pauper children and Poor Law childhoods in England and Wales 1834–1910*. Kindle.

WORKHOUSE CHILDREN

Although the poignant imagery of Oliver Twist continues to symbolise the workhouse child in popular imagination, workhouse children were one of the few groups of paupers who were not held responsible for their destitution under the Poor Law Amendment Act 1834. Poor Law Commissioner James Phillips Kay argued that pauper children maintained in workhouses were dependent 'not as a consequence of their errors, but of their misfortunes' (Poor Law Commission, 1837/38). Although, from the 1850s onwards, the central Poor Law authorities sought to remove children from workhouses, regional boards of guardians often resisted or were unable to implement this policy, and children were both short- and long-term inmates of workhouses throughout the 19th century. Their care and treatment varied from workhouse to workhouse and was largely dependent upon the temperament and integrity of workhouse management and guardians as much as the many directives from the central Poor Law authorities.

Strategies for workhouse children pursued a duality of care and control; they were pitied for their unfortunate start in life but were thought to be in need of education and training to avoid future pauperism or a life of crime. In 1862, the *Poor Law Board report on the education of pauper children* argued that because of their association with adult paupers, children were being 'actually nurtured in vice' (*Poor Law Board report on the education of pauper children by Poor Law inspectors*, 1862), and strategies such as the separation of children from their parents were not done solely to punish, but also to remove children from adults labelled as criminals, prostitutes or idlers. Education was seen as the way to 'lift' children from their indigent circumstances and James Philip Kay argued that education was one of the most important ways of 'eradicating the germs of pauperism from the rising generation' (Poor Law Commission, 1837/38). Children in workhouses were given at least three hours of education daily, and subsequently gained a better education than could be provided by many poor parents.

Children experienced bad treatment and, indeed, cruelty in some workhouses. This, again, was dependent upon who was charged with their day-to-day care, and cruel treatment and harsh beatings were prohibited. Pauper children were beaten for their misdemeanours, but national policy inferred that it should not be a matter of first resort or routine. Schools Inspector Jelinger Symons recorded that he had encountered 'every diversity of schoolteacher from very nearly the best, to decidedly the worst' in workhouse schools, and although Symons did not believe that 'cruelty or severity of discipline' was common in workhouse schools, he felt that they existed in some (Committee of Council on Education, England and Wales (Schools of Parochial Unions), 1847–49).

Contagious diseases, especially skin and eye diseases, were widespread in overcrowded workhouses. Instances of 'the itch' (scabies) especially and 'scald head' (ringworm) were common, as were general eye complaints and the more serious ophthalmia that was a major cause of childhood blindness in the 19th century. However, workhouse medical officers treated children, and the poor conditions in workhouses generally improved following an 1866 inquiry that found many workhouses (especially in London) insanitary and unhealthy.

Contemporary child welfare commentators such as Florence Hill also complained about 'the inevitable consequences' of workhouse life. Hill was convinced that the association between girls and mothers of illegitimate children in workhouses was 'polluting'. Symons had argued that even when the children were in separate rooms from other workhouse inmates, they could hear the 'obscene conversation of the depraved portion of the adults' (Committee of Council on Education, England and Wales (Schools of Parochial Unions), 1847–49). This belief of inherent moral contagion within workhouses continued into the 20th century; although the 1905–09 Poor Laws Royal Commission found little evidence, it was still assumed that workhouses contained many prostitutes. Similarly, in London, with arguably the most overcrowded workhouses, a direct correlation between a workhouse childhood and adult criminality was not borne out. The vast majority of women under 40 years of age who were in London prisons in 1873 had not been educated in workhouse schools.

For those children who had been deserted or neglected by their parents, the workhouse was a refuge of sorts. Children had regular, if monotonous, meals, basic education and health care. Most children moved in and out of workhouses with their parents as part of the mixed economy of welfare in Victorian Britain.

LESLEY HULONCE

See also: **Vagrancy; Workhouse, The**

Readings

Committee of Council on Education, England and Wales (Schools of Parochial Unions), 1847–49, paper no. 1111.

Digby, A. (1978) *Pauper palaces*. London: Routledge.

Driver, F. (1993) *Power and pauperism, the workhouse system, 1834–1884.* Cambridge: Cambridge University Press.

Hulonce, L. (2016) *Pauper children and Poor Law childhoods in England and Wales 1834–1910*. Kindle.

Negrine, A. (2010) 'The treatment of sick children in the workhouse by the Leicester Poor Law Union, 1867–1914', *Family and Community History*, 13(1): 34–44.

Poor Law Board report on the education of pauper children by Poor Law inspectors (1862) c. 510.

Poor Law Commission (1837/38) *Fourth annual report*.

WORKPLACE CRIME

Workers converting to their own use property that they came across as part of their job has a long and contentious history. For long periods of history, the practice was common and tolerated (or even encouraged) by employers, as Styles (1983) and Rule (1992) catalogue. The carpenters who took home oddments of wood for the fire, the hatters who took home odd pieces of felt and the upholsterers who took home stuffing for their own mattresses and cushions were considered by employees and employers alike to be supplementing poor wages with waste products that were of little, if any, use to the employers. However, when the waste subsequently became more valuable, or the scale of the material taken home became excessive, employers grew increasingly intolerant of these workplace customary rights and practices.

Perhaps the most discussed example of 18th-century workplace appropriations was the taking of 'chips' from the Royal Dockyards, when some employees spent the last half hour of the day sawing up good wood to take home for firewood. In 1801, the dockyard employers decided to 'buy out' the workplace custom by increasing wages and banning the taking home of chips (Emsley, 2010). In the 18th century, the wage had been made up of a mixture of cash money and property taken as part of a system of customary perquisites, but from the early 19th century, the employers increasingly sought the use of the criminal law to eradicate practices that were now considered to be 'workplace theft'.

The raft of legislation that was introduced in the 18th century paralleled the criminalisation of customary rights in the countryside (eg the laws that forbade harvesters from gleaning pieces of corn). Nineteenth-century urban and industrial society, however, saw two new approaches to controlling workplace theft. The Worsted Acts (see Godfrey and Cox, 2013) introduced in 1777 a private police force that was responsible for detecting and prosecuting the theft of worsted waste and cloth in West Yorkshire. Although geographically bounded, this agency prosecuted over 4,000 workers between 1840 and 1880, and continued to exist until the Second World War. Many employers across the UK would have looked enviously at the ability of Yorkshire textile manufacturers to call upon this specialised policing agency. The second was the introduction of new forms of workplace organisation – particularly the factory system, with its high walls, gatehouses, watchmen and foremen in every department to ensure that employees both worked hard and left work with nothing that belonged to the employers. If either the factory surveillance system or private police agencies discovered a theft, then the employers could choose to prosecute or to simply dismiss the employee. In times of high unemployment, dismissal without a good reference was perhaps (almost) as harsh a punishment as the courts could impose.

The introduction of the factory system may have reduced the scale of workplace theft, as well as establishing the practice of taking home workplace materials actually as 'theft' in the minds of the employees. However, workplace appropriation continued into the 19th century. Phillips (1977) described large numbers of workplace thefts in the Victorian Black Country, and others have analysed fiddles by bakers, bus conductors, miners, watchmakers and so on in the same period. Similarly, there are several 20th-century studies which show that the practice continues. Although there are relatively few prosecutions for theft by employees in breach of trust (essentially workplace appropriation), it is clear to see that customary rights (or the opportunity to increase one's wages with illegal activity) are still enforced in the workplace today.

BARRY GODFREY

See also: **White-collar Crime**

Readings

Emsley, C. (2010) *Crime and society 1750–1900* (4th edn). Harlow: Pearson Education.

Godfrey, B. and Cox, D. (2013) *Policing the factory: Theft, private policing and the law.* London: Bloomsbury Press.

Phillips, D. (1977) *Crime and authority in Victorian England.* London: Croom Helm.

Rule, J. (1992) *The vital economy. England's developing economy, 1714–1815.* London: Routledge.

Styles, J. (1983) 'Embezzlement, industry and the law in England, 1500–1800', in M. Berg, P. Hudson and M. Sonescher (eds) *Manufacture in town and country before the factory.* Cambridge: Cambridge University press, pp 173–205.

YOUTH GANGS

Gangs are notoriously difficult to define. Researchers from the Eurogang Program offer the following definition: 'a street gang ... is any durable, street-oriented youth group whose involvement in illegal activity is part of its group identity' (Weerman et al, 2009, p 20). However, as historians and sociologists alike have pointed out, the label 'gang' is sometimes randomly and misleadingly applied by those in authority (including police officers), as well as media commentators, to any gathering of young people, especially in the poorer districts of large towns or cities (Shore, 2015). Historical research reveals that youth gangs – as defined by the Eurogang researchers – formed an entrenched, and troubling, presence in Britain's major conurbations during the late 19th century. Historical studies also show that the reporting of gang cases was highly sensationalised, with the effect of stigmatising working-class boys and young men in general.

The earliest reports of sustained gang conflict emerged from Manchester and the adjacent borough of Salford during the early 1870s. Violent territorial feuds were reported throughout the factory districts that ringed Manchester city centre. The participants called themselves 'scuttlers' and the local authorities – along with the press – seized on this new label to justify exemplary punishments for those convicted following outbreaks of gang fighting, or 'scuttling' (Davies, 2008). Remarkably similar reports of clashes between territorial youth gangs surfaced in Birmingham from the mid-1870s – here, the combatants were known as 'sloggers' rather than scuttlers – and in London from the early 1880s.

Common patterns emerged across the three conurbations, both in the nature of gang conflict and in the backgrounds of those involved. In each case, conflict centred on long-standing enmities between territorial fighting gangs. Gang members in all three conurbations routinely fought with weapons, notably, knives and belts. Yet, fatalities were rare. This suggests that late-Victorian gang members abided by a shared fighting code, whereby they set out to scar their opponents, or put them to flight, rather than inflict lethal wounds. Confrontations between rival gangs constituted arenas in which working-class youths could demonstrate toughness and daring. Considerable kudos was derived from participation in these encounters, but reputations came with a cost as leading scuttlers or sloggers were relentlessly targeted by rival gangs, as well as by the police (Davies, 2008).

Gang members in Manchester and Salford, Birmingham, and London shared remarkably similar characteristics. In each case, they tended to be male, aged in their mid- to late teens, and working-class; most lived at home with their parents and siblings. Without exception, they were employed in manual occupations – as labourers, factory operatives, carters or street traders. In Birmingham, iron and brass workers predominated, reflecting the structure of local manufacturing industry; similarly, colliers were conspicuous among scuttling gangs in the mining districts of Manchester and Salford. Few youthful gang members appear to have embarked on criminal 'careers'. Most of their convictions were for crimes of violence or breaches of the peace, rather than offences against property, and the majority of gang members appear to have become more law-abiding during adulthood (Shore, 2015; Davies, 2016).

Press reports systematically misrepresented the dangers posed by scuttlers and their counterparts in Birmingham and London. In reality, most of the victims of gang violence were themselves gang members. However, editorial commentaries in both local and national newspapers tended to depict gang violence as wholly indiscriminate, greatly exaggerating the threat to 'respectable' adults. Gang members relished their notoriety. In Salford, John-Joseph Hillier paraded the streets in a jersey proclaiming his standing as 'King of the Scuttlers'. The label, bestowed upon him by a local newspaper, appears to have bolstered his reputation – at least in his own eyes and those of his peers (Davies, 2008).

Reports of gang activity in late-Victorian Liverpool only partially fit these wider trends. The most notorious of Liverpool's gangs – the 'high rip' of the 1880s – was associated with robbery with violence rather than territorial skirmishing. This raises questions about the structural factors that shaped patterns of gang activity. It is possible that, in Liverpool, territorial affiliation was at least in part eclipsed by the city's deeper sectarian animosities, while the lack of industrial employment in this port city appears to have fostered a more widespread resort to petty theft, street robbery and 'levying' (demanding money with menaces) among underemployed youths, especially in the impoverished North End dockland districts (Sindall, 1990; Davies, 2016).

Across England's major cities, youthful gang members adopted a common uniform adapted from the dress of the London costermonger: peaked caps worn tilted over one eye, 'flashy' scarves, bell-bottomed trousers and belts with heavy brass buckles. Their favoured hairstyle also served to mark them out from their adolescent peers: a close crop, augmented by a long fringe, plastered down on the forehead. The resultant appearance startled middle-class observers (Pearson, 1983). In Birmingham, sloggers were rechristened 'peaky blinders' during the 1890s on account of the fashion of pulling the peak of a cap over one eye (Davies, 2016).

In Manchester and Salford, scuttling persisted for three decades. Police clampdowns and the imposition of exemplary sentences by judges at the city's assize court repeatedly failed to deter the city's warring gangs until they were augmented during the 1890s by the establishment of working lads' clubs. The clubs quickly took root in districts previously renowned as hotbeds of scuttling. They offered new opportunities for participation in sport – including football, gymnastics and athletics – and they found thousands of willing takers. Working lads' clubs did not convert the existing ranks of scuttlers. However, as the clubs grew over the course of the decade, they appear to have reduced the numbers of new recruits into the gangs. By 1900, local commentators were at last confident that scuttling had significantly diminished (Davies, 2008). In Birmingham, too, gang conflicts reportedly diminished around the turn of the century (Gooderson, 2010).

In London, by contrast, reports of gang activity peaked during the late 1890s and persisted into the following decade. As Geoffrey Pearson (1983) showed, 'hooligan' and 'hooliganism' were rapidly adopted as umbrella terms for disorderly youths and their exploits following a spate of disturbances over a Bank Holiday weekend in August 1898. Gang fighting and hooliganism were misleadingly characterised by a sensation-hungry press as both unprecedented and 'un-English' (Pearson, 1983). In fact, as Shore (2015) has shown, Metropolitan gang conflicts first came to the attention of the judges (and the press) following a fatal affray on the Thames Embankment in 1882, while the hooligan panic of 1898 was preceded by reports of a 'pistol plague' among working-class youths the previous year.

Reports of gang activity in England's cities during the 1920s and 1930s were more sporadic and tended to highlight links to organised crime, including extortion and control of illicit gambling. However, the 'racecourse' gangs of these decades cannot be characterised as youth gangs: many of those involved were aged in their 20s, 30s or even 40s. They were more hardened offenders than the hooligans of the 1890s (Shore, 2015).

During the 1920s and 1930s, the British city most commonly associated with gangs was Glasgow. Journalists routinely compared the city's 'gangsters' with those of Prohibition-era Chicago. This was sensationalism at its worst: whereas Chicago witnessed an estimated 500 gang-related slayings during the 1920s, Glasgow's gangsters seldom killed each other or anyone else (Davies, 2013). Nonetheless, while the only meaningful comparison between gang members in the two cities was their shared adherence to a new dress code, modelled on sharp-suited Hollywood gangsters, gangs appear to have been more pervasive, and more entrenched, in Glasgow than elsewhere in urban Britain during the interwar decades. The sheer density of population in the city's tenement districts ensured that young men congregated on the streets in much greater numbers than their counterparts in the major English conurbations. Moreover, religious bigotry – while by no means unique to Glasgow – was more combustible here than in Liverpool, not least due to the 'religious' affiliations of the city's leading football clubs, 'Protestant' Rangers and 'Catholic' Celtic.

In Glasgow during the 1920s, leading sectarian gangs such as the (Protestant) Bridgeton Billy Boys boasted hundreds of members. The 'Billies' and their (Catholic) rivals, such as the San Toy and Kent Star, were run by 'committees', with secretaries and treasurers as well as recognised leaders. The most powerful gangs operated 'senior' and 'junior' sections, mirroring the apprenticeship system in local industries (Davies, 2013). As mass unemployment took hold in the city during the late 1920s, it became increasingly common for men aged in their 20s and 30s to remain active in the gangs. Here, as in London, gang conflicts were increasingly bound up with protection 'rackets', and resort to property crime was widespread.

ANDREW DAVIES

See also: **Organised Crime; Organised Crime (United States of America); Prohibition**

Readings

Davies, A. (2008) *The gangs of Manchester: The story of the scuttlers, Britain's first youth cult.* Preston: Milo Books.

Davies, A. (2013) *City of gangs: Glasgow and the rise of the British gangster.* London: Hodder & Stoughton.

Davies, A. (2016) 'Histories of hooliganism', in D. Hobbs (ed) *Mischief, morality and mobs: Essays in honour of Geoffrey Pearson.* London: Routledge.

Gooderson, P. (2010) *The gangs of Birmingham: From the sloggers to the peaky blinders.* Wrea Green: Milo Books.

Pearson, G. (1983) *Hooligan: A history of respectable fears.* Basingstoke: Macmillan.

Shore, H. (2015) *London's criminal underworlds, c. 1720–c. 1930: A social and cultural history*. Basingstoke: Palgrave Macmillan.

Sindall, R. (1990) *Street violence in the nineteenth century: Media panic or real danger?* Leicester: Leicester University Press.

Weerman, F., Maxson, C., Esbensen, F., Aldridge, J., Medina, J. and Van Gemert, F. (2009) 'Eurogang Program manual: background, development, and use of the Eurogang instruments in multi-site, multi-method comparative research'. Available at: https://www.umsl.edu/ccj/Eurogang/EurogangManual.pdf

Legislation and cases index

Legislation

A

Abolition of the Slave Trade Act 1807 240
Act for the Prevention of Contagious Diseases at Certain Naval and Military Stations 1864 202
Act for the punishment of Rogues, Vagabonds and sturdie Beggars 1597 255
Alehouse Act 1552 127
Anatomy Act 1832 27

B

Bigamy Act 1603 11

C

Capital Punishment Amendment Act 1868 25
Casual Poor Act 1882 264
Children Act 1908 17, 117, 120, 216
Children Act 1989 150
Children and Young Persons Act 1932 216
Children and Young Persons Act 1933 108, 118, 216
Children and Young Persons (Scotland) Act 1932 118
Contagious Diseases Acts (1864, 1866, 1869) 39–41, 202
County and Borough Police Act 1856 166, 277
County and Burgh Police Act 1857 186
Courts Act 1971 4, 212
Courts of Justice Act 1924 213
Crime (Sentences) Act 1997 198
Criminal Justice Act 1855 256
Criminal Justice Act 1925 197
Criminal Justice Act 1948 42, 174, 197

Criminal Justice Act 1982 17
Criminal Justice Act 1991 198
Criminal Justice and Public Order Act 1994 234
Criminal Law Act 1967 219
Criminal Law Amendment Act 1885 202, 204
Criminal Law Amendment (White Slave Trade) Bill 1912 203–4
Criminal Law Consolidation Acts 1861 15–16
Criminal Lunatics Act 1800 56
Criminal Lunatics Act 1860 56

D

Declaration of Basic Principles of Justice for Victims of Crime and Abuse of Power (UN) 1985 267
Defence of the Realm Act 1914 204
Discharged Prisoners' Aid Act 1862 70
District Courts (Scotland) Act 1975 212

E

18 Eliz. 1576 235
European Convention on Human Rights 261–2

G

Gaol Fees Abolition Act 1815 190
Gaols Act 1823 131, 190
Garrotters Act 1863 96, 253

H

Habitual Drunkards Act 1879 110
Heritable Jurisdiction Act 1747 224
Human Rights Act 1998 208, 261–2

Subject index

Page numbers of main subject entries are in bold